CONSTRAINTS AND IMPACTS OF PRIVATIZATION

What are the constraints on privatization? What is the likely impact of privatization? Throughout the 1980s privatization was hailed as a panacea to the problems of the public sector, not only in developed economies but also in the developing world and in the post-Socialist world.

In practice, privatization has often been more difficult to achieve and has produced more uncertain benefits. It has been limited either in relation to the overall size of the public sector, or in relation to the programmes which have been announced. In developing countries and in the post-Socialist world this has often been a consequence of the lack of appropriate resources and this book looks at how these constraints might be overcome. It also considers the impact that privatization, where it has been possible, has had and what effects are likely to materialize.

The book combines a wide cross-section of case studies from the developing world and Eastern Europe, with assessments of developed countries' experience from such notable experts as George Yarrow and Dieter Bos. Contributors include policy makers, professionals and academics.

Professor V.V. Ramanadham is currently co-ordinator of the UNDP Inter-regional Network on Privatization. He has been engaged in research in the field of public enterprise, privatization and industrial economics for over forty-five years, and has numerous publications in the area. Recent books include *Public Enterprise and Income Distribution, The Economics of Public Enterprise, Privatization in the UK* (ed.) and *Privatization: A Global Perspective* (ed.). He is an Associate Fellow of Templeton College, Oxford, and the Founder-Director of the Institute of Public Enterprise, India.

CONSTRAINTS AND IMPACTS OF PRIVATIZATION

V.V. Ramanadham

London and New York

First published 1993
by Routledge
11 New Fetter Lane, London EC4P 4EE

Simultaneously published in the USA and Canada
by Routledge
29 West 35th Street, New York, NY 10001

Typeset in Scantext September by
Solidus (Bristol) Ltd, Bristol
Printed and bound in Great Britain by
Mackays of Chatham PLC, Chatham, Kent.

British Library Cataloguing in Publication Data

A catalogue record for this book is available from the British Library

Library of Congress Cataloging in Publication Data

Constraints and impacts of privatization / [edited by]
V.V. Ramanadham.
       p.   cm.
    "Simultaneously published in the USA and Canada by Routledge"—CIP
t.p. verso.
    Includes bibliographical references and index.
    ISBN 0–415–09826–2
    1. Privatization.   2. Privatization—Developing countries.
3. Privatization—Europe, Eastern.   I. Ramanadham, V.V. (Venkata
Vemuri), 1920–   II. Title: Constraints and impacts of
privatization.
HD3850.C65   1993
338.9—dc20

93–9827
CIP

ISBN 0–415–098262

To my teacher at the London School of Economics
Professor Ronald H. Coase

CONTENTS

CONTENTS

FIGURES

TABLES

TABLES

CONTRIBUTORS

Gusztáv Báger	Director General, Economic Policy, Ministry of Finance, Hungary
Anthony Bennett	Technical Adviser, Department of Economic and Social Development, United Nations, New York
Dieter Bös	Professor of Economics, University of Bonn, Germany
Olivier Bouin	Adviser on Privatization, Czech Republic
Andrew D. Cao	Director of Research and Training, Price Waterhouse, International Privatization Group, Washington DC
Jersy Cieslik	Partner, Ernst & Young, Poland
Carl Greenidge	Minister of Finance, Guyana
John Howell	Partner, Ernst & Young, London
Suresh Kumar	Secretary, Ministry of Industrial Development, and Director General, Bureau of Public Enterprises, India
George Mbowe	Chairman, Parastatal Sector Reform Commission, Tanzania
S.R. Mohnot	Chairman and Executive Director, Centre for Industrial and Economic Research, New Delhi, India
Abulmaal A. Muhith	Retired Public Servant and Senior Consultant, Bangladesh
V.V. Ramanadham	Coordinator, Interregional Network on Privatization, United Nations Development Programme, New York
Alejandro E. Rausch	Consultant, Argentina
Enrique Saravia	Head, Department of Graduate Studies, Escola Brasileira de Administracas Publica, Fundacao Getulia Vargas, Brazil
Alfred H. Saulniers	Adviser, Ministères des Affaires Economiques et de la Privatization, Morocco
Eckstein Shlomo	President, Bar Ilan University, Israel
George Yarrow	Fellow, Hertford College, Oxford

PREFACE

This volume follows the two earlier publications of the United Nations Development Programme (UNDP), resulting from the activities of the Interregional Network on Privatization set up by the Division for Global and Interregional Programmes (DGIP), viz. *Privatization in Developing Countries* (1989) and *Privatization: A Global Perspective* (1993). It focuses on two specific areas: the constraints on the pace and success of privatization, and the impacts of privatization. Both are of utmost relevance to countries which wish to implement privatization as part of economic policy reforms – a point which comes out clearly from the in-depth studies contained in the papers.

The volume commences with my basic working paper which presents an analytical overview of the subject, includes papers from eminent contributors who participated in the Expert Group Meeting held in Geneva in August last, and ends with my concluding review of the papers, keeping in mind the trend of discussions which took place at the Meeting.

I express my appreciation of the spirit of co-operation shown by the contributors with the activities of the Network. I thank Mr Philip Reynolds of the UNDP for his close association with the activities of the Network ever since its inception and his participation in the Geneva Meeting, and Mr Timothy Rothermel, Director, DGIP, for his highly supportive interest in the implementation of the work programme of the Network under his general guidance.

I have pleasure in presenting this volume as an output from the co-operative efforts of the Interregional Network on Privatization.

Professor V.V. Ramanadham
New York
March 1993

1

PRIVATIZATION: CONSTRAINTS AND IMPACTS

V. V. Ramanadham

This chapter addresses two questions: what are the constraints operating on privatization; and what are the impacts of privatization, either experienced or likely to materialize? Incidentally, the interrelationships between the questions are also brought out at relevant places.

One prefatory observation: the focus of this study is analytical, with empirical references occasionally brought in while building up an argument or explaining a point. The country-specific chapters will provide details of actual experiences.

THE CONSTRAINTS

Introduction

There is ample evidence to support the view that privatization has been heavily conditioned by one constraining factor or another in the cross-section of countries in the developing world and in Eastern Europe. Either it has been limited in relation to the aggregate size of the public enterprise sector, or it has been limited when compared with pronouncements of policy and conceived programmes. The following is a selection from authoritative observations in support of this conclusion.

> Apart from a very few countries ... such as Chile and Mexico, the vast majority have not succeeded in substantially reducing the size of the public sector.[1]

> Taken as an indicator of the success or failure of a policy, the extent of privatisation has so far remained fairly limited both as compared with the number of public enterprises in existence and as a percentage of total public sector value added.[2]

A recent Oxford study of seven countries concluded that 'progress ... has been slower than hoped'. 'Actual outcomes had been qualitatively disappointing. Privatisation to date has played only a small role in the reform of the SOE sector.'[3]

It is easy to identify from the growing literature on the subject a large number of countries where privatization has been constrained in some way or other: e.g. Ghana,[4] Kenya,[5] Poland[6] and Hungary.[7]

At the outset we need to annotate the term we use in this analysis, privatization. Basically, it represents marketization of enterprise operations and can be sought through three options – ownership changes, organizational changes and operational changes. These are from the structural or action angle. From the substantive or content angle, the same idea may be re-expressed in terms of privatization of ownership, privatization of management and privatization of enterprise disciplines. Figures 1.1 and 1.2 reflect the details of the options in the two cases.

Each option might be characterized by a different set of constraints (and so might its impacts be different). While there is a general tendency to treat 'privatization' in terms of divestiture, it is analytically useful to address the constraints on (and impacts of) the non-divestiture options distinctly. This is justified, in particular, by the very importance attached to non-divestiture options in many countries. In fact there is none which is totally free from them.

For example, Ghana has a two-phase strategy of privatization: first, rationalization and second, divestiture.[8] Nigeria has a clearly announced four-pronged policy: full privatization, partial privatization, full commercialization and partial commercialization.[9] The last two and the second itself in a sense can be governed by constraints belonging to the category of non-divestiture constraints. In Vietnam a significant segment of the economy is expected to stay in the public sector.[10] Thailand's public enterprises are, in substantial part, not likely to be transformed to private ownership immediately; the 1992–6 plan merely emphasizes 'improved efficiency of state enterprises'.[11] Between 100 and 150 large enterprises are nearly certain to remain in the public sector in Hungary; and new laws are enacted to deal with their stewardship. The Ethiopian proclamation on investment conceives of reserving certain areas for the government, some for its investment in partnership with private investors, and some for future policy determination, while releasing many areas for private investment.[12] China, to cite one more example, has plans, gradually, of appropriate separation between ownership and management; it has applied different forms of 'contract responsibility' in the majority of its public enterprises; it is encouraging a variety of enterprise reorganizations, reform of enterprise employment and wage systems, and the development of new horizontal economic associations and enterprise groups, in an effort to establish a new economic system which approximates to a market economy.[13]

The concept 'constraints' has to be understood not only in terms of the pace and size of privatization but also in terms of the success of privatization. Constraints are not necessarily uniform in the two cases. Both senses apply to divestiture as well as non-divestiture options. This has not been recognized adequately yet. If one may generalize, attention to constraints has, by and large, been limited to divestiture in the former sense, so far.

2

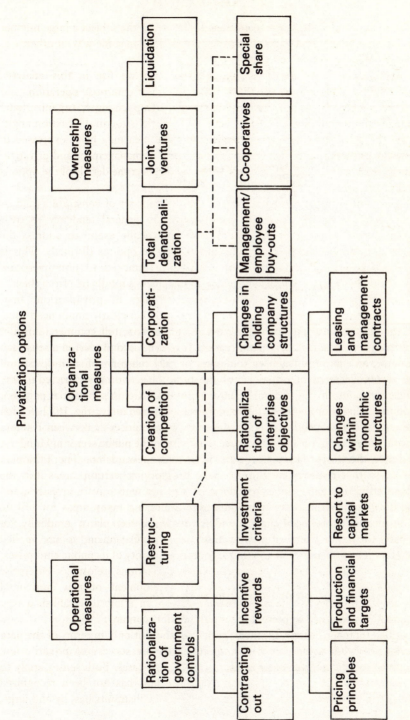

Figure 1.1 Privatization options from the structural angle

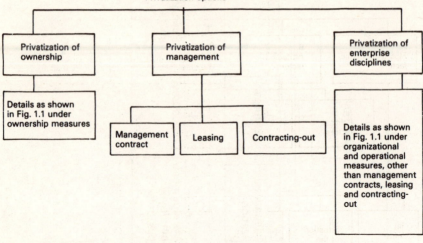

Figure 1.2 Privatization options from the content angle

The idea of constraints on the success of a privatization measure or a series of privatization measures calls for annotation. It goes beyond the mere fact that, for example, an enterprise has been sold away or fully subscribed for. It touches on the accomplishment or otherwise of the basic objective of privatization, viz. efficiency gains in the composite micro-cum-macro sense. (These need some working definition, no doubt.) The more the objective is realized, the higher is the success of privatization in point of results. Where such a success factor is low, it can boomerang on the very pace and size of privatization. It would be desirable, therefore, to keep an eye on the circumstances constraining the success factor, so that remedial measures can be promptly introduced. To illustrate: where efficiency gains are constrained by the emergence of monopoly post-privatization, measures may be introduced to promote competition.

Incidentally, this line of analysis underscores the importance of identifying the impacts (actual or likely) of privatization measures. The second section of this chapter ('The Impacts') will go into this question.

An analytical framework of constraints

Figure 1.3 is designed to present the multitude of constraints in an appropriately classified manner. Many of them apply to the entire range of privatizable enterprises, while some particularly affect specific sectors of activity and a few might be specific to given enterprises.

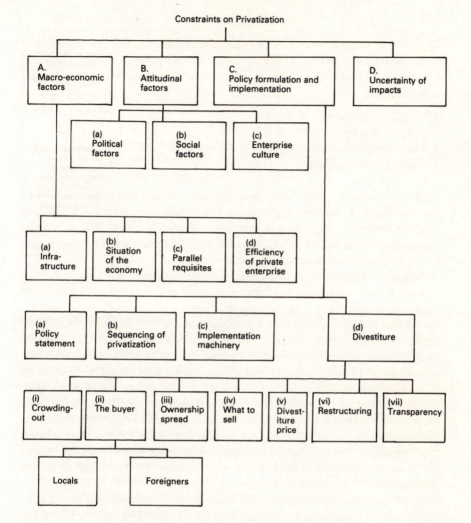

Figure 1.3 Framework of constraints on privatization

Macro-economic factors

These, more or less, reflect the developmental status of the economy. It is fair to say that it is in this respect that the background for privatization varies between being conducive in the developed market economies, and being restrictive – in varying degrees – in developing and centrally planned economies in transition.

Infrastructure

This is an omnibus term and ranges over several factors which individually and jointly provide the setting for the operation of enterprises, including privatized enterprises, and for the very acts of privatization. These may be considered under four headings:

1 legal environment;
2 capital markets;
3 infrastructural services – largely in the nature of public utility facilities; and
4 information facilities.

Legal environment This refers, first, to basic laws and regulations relating to the operations of enterprises, governing and – more importantly – facilitating their establishment, working and exit; laws concerning commercial behaviour, e.g. contracts, and sale of goods; and laws relating to financial institutions, e.g. banks, insurance companies and investment trusts.

Second, it refers to macro-economic laws governing matters such as foreign capital, foreign exchange, taxation, monopoly practices, prices, wages and employment. We shall look at two of these, in illustration. It is common knowledge that many countries have long been rather restrictive on the free influx of foreign capital; the laws had to be amended and/or new laws created permitting its easy inflow deemed vital for the success of privatization. Since this subject is a sensitive one, several governments have faced difficulties in promoting legislation that was sufficiently permissive and yet not provocative of discontent or sense of discrimination among local investors. The more the limits on the entry and privileges accorded to foreign capital, the heavier the constraints on divestiture in countries looking for sizeable foreign capital as a success factor in privatization. Similarly, where legislation to curb monopolies does not exist or is too weak, privatization tends to be constrained under the weight of real or perceived fear of privatized monopolies.

Third, it refers to laws specifically dealing with privatization. There can be several sub-divisions here: e.g. overall laws on privatization; laws on sectoral or specific-enterprise privatization; laws on specific techniques of privatization such as employee buy-outs or voucher distribution; laws on restitution and other issues connected with the claims of past owners; and laws governing the utilization of divestiture proceeds.

It is evident from the literature that many developing countries find themselves constrained in the design and implementation of privatization programmes because important parts of the legal instruments described above are not in place, properly or at all. Experience shows that when they began to promote the necessary legislation delays occurred, clarity was missing, inconsistencies arose, and there remained gaps in legislation. For example, the very conversion of public enterprises into independent economic units endowed with the same status as private companies was facilitated in Albania as late as early 1992, after the passage of the Law on State Enterprises in January that year.[14] 'Great inconsistencies in legislation' are reported in Bulgaria, e.g. in small privatization. Besides there has been a lack of clarity regarding the ownership of businesses which have been on sale, absence of clarity on restitution procedures, and serious errors in the procedural guidelines for auctions. Interestingly enough, illegal privatizations and dishonest appropriations have been possible without violating the letter of the law in many cases.[15] It is said that in China practice differs from the law, e.g. in the area of bankruptcy.[16] In Czechoslovakia, it is reported, there is no valid law for bankruptcy.[17] With reference to Russia, it is said that 'concepts of private property and rule by law had shallow roots even in pre-communist times'.[18]

The issue of restitution has been one of the most knotty bottlenecks in many countries – not only in Eastern Europe but elsewhere too, e.g. in Ghana, Pakistan, Bangladesh and Uganda.[19] Land title is still in the name of the original owners in the case of some 'taken-over' enterprises in Pakistan. The German law on restitution offers itself as an interesting illustration of the legal constraints on privatization. For instance, the sale of a 'claimed asset' makes the seller liable to damages; whereas in the case of the sale of an enterprise the buyer becomes liable in respect of land which is the subject of 'claim' by past owners. An added complication has resulted from the recent legal sanction for the transfer of a restitution claim. The transferee can prove competence as potential owner and manager of an enterprise under divestiture; and his rights have to be duly considered.[20] The Czechoslovak law allows restitution claims to be settled with the new owner – a source of uncertainty for the new owner. The problem is compounded by the desire of certain claimants to buy even parts of the enterprise property which are not strictly the subject of the restitution claim.[21]

Legal constraints have a force *vis-à-vis* non-divestiture options also. The uncorporatized status of a public enterprise can itself operate as a bottleneck in bringing its operations under market disciplines. Statutes of public corporations, unlike companies which operate under the general Companies Act, often contain provisions necessitating certain governmental controls inconsistent with marketized operations. (For instance, such enterprises cannot acquire loans for their business operations without obtaining 'special permission from various organisations' in Ghana.)[22] Statutes that place control in the hands of the workers – e.g. through workers councils – might prove inconsistent with market-oriented decision making. Such legal constraints not only condition the success of a non-divestiture option adopted but limit the interest of the government to adopt it as an effective option and of the management to act on it as a genuine option.

Capital markets The underdeveloped nature of the capital markets operates as a serious constraint on privatization in many ways.

First, divestitures are hard to implement since the local investment potential is too inadequate. There arises a disproportionate interest in wooing foreign capital. (For instance, about 90 per cent of the divestiture incomes in Hungary are reported to have come from abroad, by January 1992.)[23]

The issue of inadequate cash resource potential on the part of the buyers of privatized enterprises warrants deeper analysis. Assuming that there is enough effective demand for a few initial divestitures, the divestiture proceeds can be recycled into the private sector if the government chooses to pay back public debt in corresponding amounts. And this process can be repeated and divestitures for cash consideration can continue to take place. There are, however, several qualifications:

1   The government bond holders who receive cash might not be the ones who are interested in equity subscription.
2   A part of the cash receipts on bond redemptions might find itself diverted to consumption.
3   The government might decide to use the divestiture incomes in other ways than repaying public debt, on consideration of budget balance. This breaks the chain of recycling.

Second, underdeveloped capital markets give a distinctive twist to the techniques of divestiture. They might prompt private sales – through negotiation – as in Ghana up to 1991. (The problems and criticism associated with such sales dampen the government's pace of divestitures.) Divestitures might be undertaken on credit terms, in part, such that the buyers of shares could complete the payment for shares over a period. Or, the government may be induced to divest on the basis of a free distribution of shares (or vouchers), so that ownership privatization occurs without cash figuring as purchase consideration.

Third, capital markets which are unconducive to fast divestitures might interest the government in adopting non-divestiture options, at least as an immediate measure. A major part of East Africa illustrates this.

It is true that sporadic improvizations for the sale of shares can be contemplated, circumventing the disadvantage of unpropitious capital markets. For example, post offices and bank offices can be involved in functioning as places where intending applicants for shares may go, fill in the forms and deposit the application moneys. Jamaica adopted this method, as, of course, did the UK. Some initial success in terms of divestiture may be there; but the lack of market facilities for secondary trading will begin to operate as a dampening factor as time passes and as share owners find it difficult to dispose of their shares or exchange them for different shares. We come back, again, to the primacy of capital markets, especially when the government desires wide-spread ownership of divested shares. Countries such as Ghana have been establishing stock exchanges, almost *de novo*. Their popularity in countries like Pakistan is still limited, as observed in that country's Economic Survey for 1990–1.[24]

In some countries (like Nepal) stock exchanges do exist but the volume of shares quoted is very small. One explanation is that those belonging to the share-owning class are used to holding on to their shares. As divestitures progress and the volume of tradable shares increases, new categories of share owners come in, and the stock exchanges can become active centres for capital mobility.

Infrastructural services   Privatization is under serious constraint in a country whose physical infrastructure, viz. transport, telephone, electricity, water and communications, is weak – e.g. in Mongolia. This constraint is particularly weighty where foreign capital is expected to be the main engine to mobilize divestitures. For, demands being nearly insatiable, it can choose where to go and it prefers to go where the infrastructure is well developed. There is another kind of interrelationship between infrastructure and privatization: the less developed it is, the more likely it is that the government has to take the lead initiative in establishing it. Thus, there will be continuing need for public investments in the infrastructural sectors. To that extent there might be limits to privatization in the sense of market-determined activity.

Two policy measures seem to be necessary. First, the government should formulate proper sequencing of privatization activities to which the development of infrastructural services is effectively geared. Second, the infrastructural activities likely to be in the public sector should, nevertheless, attract energetic non-divestiture options, so that serious mistakes of investment and pricing decisions will not occur on the scale characteristic of such public enterprises for a long time.

Information facilities   This term is employed here to connote more than the availability of information to the potential investors and to the general public concerning privatization policies and programmes. This is, of course, vital for the success of privatization and would be richer, the clearer the policy statement of the government on privatization addressing the implications is. Few countries have issued such a statement yet. Where private sales through negotiation are the major modality of divestiture, the public information gaps can boomerang on the success of privatization in due course.

The more important aspect of the point under discussion refers to the quality of financial information regarding the enterprises. A recent observation from the UN Centre on Transnational Corporations sums up the problem as follows:

> Very often accounting information is so deficient in some enterprises that it is impossible to draw up commercial balance sheets and income statements for interested buyers. More important there is often little relationship among the book value of the assets, the value of the enterprise as a going concern and its sale price.[25]

Broadly, four categories of deficiency in financial information can be highlighted:

1 Accounts are in arrears – e.g. in Uganda; and accounting skills are so poor that the recorded figures might not convey the whole truth of what they are supposed to represent.

2 The revenue and cost figures – or the incomings and outgoings – have been so distorted, especially under the command economies of the East-European type, that the real state of the financial balance of an enterprise cannot be established at once or with ease. This difficulty persists even in a non-centrally planned economy, where the input and output prices concerning an enterprise have been heavily under the impacts of 'administered' pricing. (The impacts could be either favourable or unfavourable on individual, relevant items of cost and revenue, and would be far from uniform among enterprises. And it is not easy to enunciate the net impact on the overall financial position of a given enterprise, without elaborate analysis.)

3 Asset valuations as found in the books often do not represent the true position. The recent revaluations attempted in the case of the first five large enterprises privatized in Poland indicate the varyingly wide deviations of those values from the corresponding book values.[26] In several cases, items such as 'land' are omitted or shown at very low values – e.g. in Hungary. Some revaluations may have occurred quite unsystematically among different enterprises. And financial valuations might be manipulated by 'insiders' interested in a management buy-out.

4 The most crucial part of the information necessary for successful privatization concerns the future earning potential of an enterprise. And this is the most difficult to estimate, especially in a centrally planned economy in transition. It depends on the nature of the market situation which the enterprise encounters under the future economic policies of the government, on the extent of tariff protection it may enjoy, on the nature of technological change that may affect the enterprise, and on the price, wage and employment environment in the transitory stages of shift towards a market economy. Past record is of little help in proceeding with such an estimate; and the processes of establishing a reliable financial base for the divestiture transaction can be tedious and flaw-ridden. Where they arouse suspicion of irregularity or gross inexpertise, there might be serious hurdles in the pace of privatization.

Situation of the economy

One of the powerful hurdles in privatization is the unfavourable state of the economy. Where unemployment is high and rising, where recession persists, where industrial output is on the decline, where inflation remains unabated, where debt servicing proves painful and where standards of living are low and declining, divestitures are not easy to effect. Even certain non-divestiture options might prove difficult to introduce, such as market-oriented price determinations. Eastern Europe and the CIS States amply illustrate the truth of this observation; for in varying degrees they are seriously affected by these macro-economic factors which dampen the investment potential as well as the capacity of tolerance of the public at large.

The statistical data shown in Table 1.1 are illustrative in this context. The

Table 1.1 Changes in the economic situation

	1987–8	1988–9	1989–90	1990–1
GNP (%)				
Bulgaria	0.6	−0.2	−9.5	−5.7
Czechoslovakia	1.0	1.0	−1.3	−1.9
Hungary	1.8	1.0	−1.3	−1.9
Poland	1.9	−1.6	−18.4	−4.3
Romania	1.6	−3.1	−18.46	−3.6
Yugoslavia	0.1	−1.0	−9.16	−5.8
Industrial output (%)				
Bulgaria	5.2	2.1	−6.0	−3.0
Czechoslovakia	2.1	1.0	−3.5	−4.5
Hungary	0.0	−3.4	−9.0	−6.0
Poland	5.1	−3.5	−20.0	−6.0
Romania	3.6	−2.1	−20.0	−9.0
Yugoslavia	−1.0	1.0	−11.0	−4.0
Consumer prices (%)				
Bulgaria	1	9	50	100
Czechoslovakia	2	4	11	35
Hungary	16	18	−30	23
Poland	61	640	220	98
Romania	1	1	5	70
Yugoslavia	118	1256	55	28
Gross debt ($ billion)				
Bulgaria	9	10	11	12
Czechoslovakia	7	8	7	7
Hungary	20	21	20	22
Poland	39	41	42	42
Romania	2	1	4	5
Yugoslavia	19	17	16	17

Source: Plan Econ, Washington DC.

slump in Eastern Europe is described by the UN Economic Commission for Europe as being 'on the scale of the depression of the 1930s'.[27] Due to declines in production in the former Soviet Union more than 15 million workers are likely to lose their jobs this year, 'followed by up to 30 million in later years', in the view of the International Labour Organization.[28]

The constraining impact of recession is not unique to the centrally planned economies in transition. For instance, Jordan's privatization was affected by the depressed state of the economy.[29]

The difficulties have generally been compounded by the fact that many western countries have themselves been undergoing phases of recession. This has affected the prospects of inflow of foreign capital into developing countries and

Eastern Europe both for divestiture and for substantial technological restructuring.

There is another overall problem which several countries like Uganda face. There is an alarming underutilization of industrial capacity, whatever the reason.[30] Rehabilitation of their industrial structures happens to be a top priority; and the most effective means might range over measures other than privatization (or divestiture) – for example, policies conducive to adequate availability of water, electricity, raw materials, major maintenance and improved technology and foreign exchange. Thus, the enthusiasm for divestitures is under check; and the approach to privatization tends to be directed towards non-divestiture options in the immediate context.

Parallel requisites

The success of divestiture is heavily under the influence of a multitude of parallel developments in the national economy. Unless these are in place, divestitures finish up as an end in themselves without necessarily leading to the realization of their basic objectives.

The parallel requisites may be brought under three major headings: overall economic policies, development planning, and budget policies. We can think of various sub-headings under each of these, as indicated in Figure 1.4. All these factors affect the interest and ability of a government to undertake divestitures; they also affect the success of privatization in point of results.

Overall economic policies   Privatization would have limited chance of success unless the overall economic policies of the government were conducive to competition in the input and output markets, unless there were adequate freedom for the entry and exit of foreign capital and for the conversion of the local currency into foreign (hard) currencies, and unless the financial institutions were so designed and regulated as to promote the investment habit on the part of the public and encourage economical financial management on the part of enterprises. Equally fundamental are monetary, interest rate, price and wage policies which determine the extent of inflation and the standard of living.

Development planning   Basic limits to privatization emanate from the kind of development planning that a country adopts; and most developing countries have economic (and social) development plans – usually the five-year plans. The essence of such plans is to inject into the national economy forces of development that would not materialize if left to the market. Privatization, in the sense of marketization, is obviously an opposite concept. If this should succeed, planning which introduces wide-ranging 'administered' interventions in economic development should be given up; or there should be material relaxations in its mandatoriness. It might be designed in an indicative rather than a prescriptive manner, enlarging the area of market-determined decision on the part of

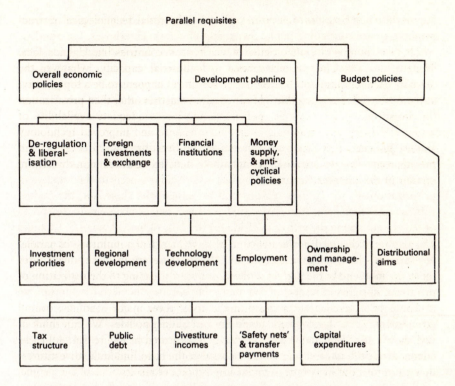

Figure 1.4 Parallel requisites to successful divestiture

enterprises, workers, consumers, investors, etc. There would remain several elements of non-market developments which even a somewhat indicative plan implicitly envisages – e.g. a minimum quantum of investment in basic sectors;[31] a desired size and pattern of investment in underdeveloped regions; a self-sustaining R&D programme; techniques of employment promotion – the more so in a heavily populated country which has high rates of unemployment and a large proportion of people living below the poverty line; some decentralization in property or asset ownership and its impacts on management; and reductions in skewness in the distribution of wealth and income. Few governments in the developing world and centrally planned economies can ignore the imperative of these objectives of national well-being. As observed recently by the President of Uganda, 'if the economy is developed and balanced, you can provide both beer and machines. But if it is a question of choice, either beer or machines, then you find that you need planning.'[32] And it would be necessary to devise techniques of subserving the objectives of planning, despite privatization. These would not be easy but a twofold attempt could be made so as to promote privatization both as an event and by results. For one thing, a genuine beginning may be made with appropriate non-divestiture options, preserving the desired elements of national planning under continuing public ownership of certain enterprises. For another, where divestiture is rational on efficiency criteria, the divested enterprise can be brought into a contractual relationship with the government in respect of the 'socially desired' input and output objectives. In other words, the costs involved in the non-market-oriented but socially desired activities would be met through the budget.

Budget policies   Let us turn to the budget policies that should be in place if privatization were to succeed. To anticipate a major point which the second section of this chapter covers, the budget has to adjust itself to the impacts of privatization. If, for various reasons and at least in the short run, the budget suffers rather than gains from divestitures, changes will be necessary in the spread of the tax net and in the rate of taxation for the sake of budget balance. Changes will also be occasioned in the structure of public finance in terms of the central government, the state governments and the local governments. The establishment of municipalities, e.g. in Poland, along with the transfer to them of privatization rights in respect of the many shops, raises the need for appropriate instruments of revenue and expenditure sharing between them and the central government. Public borrowings should not be such as to 'crowd out' the market; nor should the debt stay high, despite divestiture incomes. There should be adequate effort to create 'safety nets' to assuage the hardship that privatization – divestiture or non-divestiture – might impose on certain sections of the people, workers or consumers, and transfer payments have to be designed in appropriate cases. This sub-heading subsumes expenditures on retraining and redeployment of the work force, including moving it geographically, as might be consistent with the labour requirements of privatized enterprises.

Finally, governments in developing countries and centrally planned economies will find themselves obliged to undertake capital expenditures on improving the infrastructural support for the success of (privatized) enterprises. True, some developments in the direction of private capital injection in 'toll roads' or 'wharf' services are taking place sporadically. But these are likely to remain a fraction of the totality of infrastructural investments necessary. The government budget, therefore, would have a heavy responsibility here.

That several macrorequisites have to be in place for successful privatization is not sufficiently realized in developing countries. Even when it is realized, governments do not seem to have the capacity, technical or resource-wise, to cope with them.

Efficacy of private enterprise

Divestitures tend to be under constraint where the private sector to which enterprises may be transferred exists but nominally or where its efficiency is not demonstrably clear. The former situation refers to the centrally planned economies in transition, where private enterprises have accounted for an insignificantly low share of production, except in agriculture in some cases, for about forty years. Here the primary need is to create private enterprise, simultaneously with the ownership transformation. (Myammar [Burma] and Mongolia are interesting examples.) The efficiency of privatized enterprises will be in the nature of an unknown quantity, barring the enterprises taken over by foreign capital. Apart from inexperience in market-oriented operations, private enterprises begin to operate under unfavourable conditions, which, in Poland, 'combined to distort incentives and produce a serious bias towards unreported, illegal or semi-criminal activities'. Polish managers have been constrained by officials, workers' councils and trade unions – a phenomenon labelled by Ryszard Rapacki and Susan L. Linz as a 'Polish Bermuda Triangle'. They observe, further, that the private sector has engaged in 'dysfunctional entrepreneurial behaviour ... wide spread tax evasion, financial scandals, smuggling, and other activities'.[33]

Turning to the developing countries where private enterprise exists, and on a relatively large scale in some cases, we have a different set of questions to reckon with before wholesale ownership transfer of public enterprises is contemplated. How genuinely private is the private sector? It depends on disproportionately large funding from financial institutions in the public sector. It derives profit more from protected markets than from technical efficiency. Management is not professional, by and large, and ownership is so family oriented that privatization is nicknamed in Nepal 'family-ization'. The role of private enterprises in technology development has been relatively low. Tax evasions are substantial; and considerable sums of foreign exchange earnings are hidden away in foreign accounts. Further, the private sector is confined, by and large, to the categories of trade and secondary or light manufacturing industry, leaving the more basic, less quickly yielding actitivies in the lap of the public sector. For example, the share of public to total investments in industry in Pakistan declined, by intention, from 49 per cent in 1982–3 to 9.5 per cent in 1987–8; and private investments did increase over the period. But most of these were directed towards light industry – e.g. 60 per cent in textiles and agro-based industries; while cement and engineering accounted for 10 per cent each.

The story of the private sector in developing countries would not be complete without a reference to the ubiquitous phenomenon of sick units. These constitute an alarming number, for example in India, which is credited with a thriving, diversified private sector. The debts they owe to the public sector banks, which are in the nature of 'bad or doubtful' debts, are so heavy that the viability of many of the banks themselves is in question, even by conservative official statistics.[34]

The above comments did not refer to the 'social efficiency' aspect of the private sector. If we include that in our analysis, the doubts concerning its efficacy as an immediate alternative to public enterprise in developing countries gain in strength.[35] The consequence for privatization is threefold:

15

1 Enthusiasm for divestiture is dampened, though non-divestiture options can be adopted.
2 Divestitures are followed by limited success in point of efficiency results.
3 The persons gaining ownership transfers might be a front for foreign control.[36]

Attitudinal factors

Political, social and enterprise/managerial attitudes have an important bearing on the pace of privatization and its success.

Political factors

It is difficult to say how important political democracy is as a condition for privatization. There are examples of extensive privatization in political systems not acknowledged as democratic – e.g. Chile under General Pinochet – and too little of it in well-known democracies like India. What is needed is a strong political commitment to privatization. This exists, for example, under military rule in Nigeria,[37] while there is no 'political consensus' in favour of it in India[38] or Trinidad and Tobago.[39]

The political complexities witnessed in the centrally planned economies in their efforts towards transition illustrate how politics can constrain privatization by delaying, first, the laws governing the subject and then the very implementation process. Poland's law, for example, required more than fifteen strides through amendments; and its mass privatization programme has been delayed from time to time and its full range of details are not yet clear to everyone. The relative strengths of the communist party and the reformist parties is of no small importance, either, as the situation in the Czech and Slovak Republics shows.

Social factors

While governments, through internal motivation or external advice, are willing to pursue privatization, social perceptions are not sufficiently enthusiastic yet in countries where the government has long played the central role in economic activity. A recent gallup poll, commissioned by the European Community, on the attitudes to political and economic changes in ten former members of the Eastern bloc found 'high levels of dissatisfaction with post-communist life and gloom', though they believed in a free market economy.[40] Surveys conducted in Poland, Czechoslovakia, Hungary and the former Soviet Union suggested 'a strong resistance to wide salary differences and to performance-related pay'.[41] Such thinking is not limited to centrally planned economies. It applies to some others too – e.g. Ghana,[42] Uganda and Tanzania.

Enterprise culture

In countries long dominated by public enterprise, the enterprise culture that is appropriate to a market economy does not exist. Privatization – whatever the option – is likely to have limited success pending a complete attitudinal change among the major actors – the bureaucrats, the owners, the managers and the workers. There will be continuing needs of an interface between the bureaucrats and the enterprises, but this has to be qualitatively very different from the command-type interventions of the public enterprise and central planning era. 'Owners' as a class have to be born and bred. Managers whose focus was on meeting the commands from above have to learn to behave by market disciplines.[43] And workers who exercised varying degrees of control over the enterprise, to its detriment by and large, and who have generally been characterized by poor work ethics, have to change into partners in enterprise activity, willingly exposing themselves to the risks of the market.[44] The learning curve is, on the whole, a lengthy one. True, the pace of privatization might not be too restrained for this reason, in view of overriding political compulsions. But constraints reveal themselves in two important respects, viz. the techniques of privatization and the success of privatization. Improvements in infrastructural conditions and the parallel requisites, discussed earlier, can soften the constraints. But then they are, by nature, more long term in prospect.

Policy formulation and implementation

Policy statement

A clear statement of policy concerning privatization – its connotation, objectives, options, techniques, implications and sequencing – smooths the process as well as prepares the relevant constituencies for a common understanding of what to expect. This condition, necessary but not sufficient, for successful privatization has not been satisfied in many countries. The comment made with reference to Pakistan, that 'the privatization programme is proceeding on an ad hoc basis and ... the whole process lacks an overall coherent policy framework' holds good in the generality of cases in all regions.[45] Official pronouncements in countries like Nigeria, Nepal and Jamaica are helpful but substantially fall short of the necessary policy enunciations focused on the implications or impacts of privatization. An illustrative list of items to be covered by a comprehensive policy statement is shown in Appendix 1.

Sequencing

Privatization is not a one-day process. It takes years in terms of action and longer in terms of realizing the objectives. Hence, proper sequencing would be necessary. There is hardly a country which is not intent on privatization today.

17

But the pace and content of action varies widely among the countries. A well-conceived sequencing helps privatization as surely as an ill-conceived sequencing or a total lack of a sequencing plan harms it.

Sequencing is not to be understood in the limited sense of which enterprises to divest first and which next. It is much broader in connotation and covers the following aspects.

1 *Privatization options, enterprise-wise, broken down among immediate, short-term and long-term spans.* For instance, is a public enterprise to be put through the ownership, organizational or operational option, with reference to immediate change, change in the short run and eventual change? The Hungarian attempt currently to identify enterprises for temporary or permanent continuance in the public sector illustrates this concept to some extent. It has to go further, specifying the precise technique – e.g. restructuring – in a given case.

2 *Technique of divestiture, enteprise-wise.* Among the available variety – full divestiture, partial divestiture and then public offer, private sale, employee buy-out, free share distribution – appropriate choice has to be articulated, though not too rigidly. This may be done sector-wise where large numbers of enterprises are involved, though the circumstances of certain enterprises in a given sector warrant deviations. The role of foreign capital in different cases has to be spelt out.

3 *Synthesis between privatization and private sector development.* This is of utmost importance in developing countries, including the centrally planned economies in transition, where private enterprise has nearly to be created or nurtured with pediatric care. (The promotion of small businesses in Eastern Europe is a case in point.) The point is really fundamental. What we are aiming at is a rebalancing of the roles of the public and private sectors, which may be achieved in many ways: for example,

(a) the government divests and does not invest any more;
(b) the government divests and also invests but on a smaller scale;
(c) the government does not divest but inducts private capital in public enterprises; and
(d) the government does not divest and does not invest either, but encourages private investments.

The proportion of private ownership improves over time in all these cases, but at different time-oriented rates and in different ways; and there might be an active need for public initiative in promoting private enterprise. This whole area – a relatively neglected one as yet – calls for attention if privatization is to be marked by success.

4 *Co-ordination between privatization and parallel requisites.* Discussed earlier, this aspect should also be considered as an essential part of the sequencing exercise, so that as a pattern of privatization or divestiture occurs, effort can be directed to ensuring that the conditions of success are in place.

Organizational structure

There are several possibilities of top organization in respect of privatization: for example, a ministry for ownership changes, as in Poland and for a time in British Columbia in Canada; a non-ministerial agency such as the State Property Agency in Hungary; a non-ministerial, mammoth holding complex such as Treuhand in Germany; a high-level agency within government like the Technical Committee for Privatization and Commercialization of Nigeria; a composite ministry for public enterprise and privatization like the State Enterprise Commission in Ghana; a public sector financial institution like the National Investment Corporation in the Gambia or the National Bank in Jamaica; major holding companies – not set up for privatization – like CORFO in Chile and IRI in Italy; sectoral ministries and the Treasury as in the UK; sectoral ministries and a Treasury Division as in Sri Lanka; and no specific agency as in India.

It is difficult to argue that any one of these represents the best method. The arrangement is dependent on the country's political circumstances. However, certain organizational desiderata may be enunciated.

First, the organizational structure should be free from 'internal conflicts'. Different ministries have different priorities: for example, the finance ministry needs quick and high divestiture incomes; the sectoral ministry is keen on appropriate restructuring of given enterprises; the labour ministry is interested in minimum lay-offs and prior-devised 'safety nets'; and the privatizing agency itself might feel pressured in favour of quick transactions. Such conflicting interests can lead to confusion and ad hocism; they might delay transactions; and powerful ministries might adopt uncompromising postures. The cleavage between the State Privatization Agency and the Finance Ministry in Hungary is by now well known.[46] Likewise in Czechoslovakia, there is 'absence of agreement or consensus' 'in the governmental bodies between the governments and within the government'.[47] In Bulgaria some of the ministries have turned into 'close systems with numerous conflicts among them'; personal relationships matter; and the reforms are separate and uncoordinated.[48] Laos presents a situation of inadequate co-ordination of powers between the central government and the provincial governments.[49]

Second, the policy-making level should be somewhat distinct from the implementation level. And policy guidelines should be made available to the latter, while implementing privatization in accordance with the relevant laws.

Extensive centralization of implementation in a single agency might lead to slowness and undue standardization of techniques; or it might create a mammoth bureaucracy. The spontaneous privatizations of Hungary and the Malaysian permissiveness in favour of any private party coming forward with a privatizable proposal[50] can help quicken the pace of divestitures. But care should be taken to provide against abuse and ad hocism.

Third, the privatization agencies should be equipped with adequate technical competence. At the policy-making level this refers, in practical terms, to the formulation of the policy statement and the design of measures aimed at coping with the implications of privatization. Visualizing the impacts of divestitures is an important part of the exercise. It is doubtful if the policy levels in a majority of developing countries possess the requisite capability or have obtained from abroad sound advice capable of improving their technical competence in this respect. The latest Report of the UN Economic Commission for Europe[51] as well as a recent article by Louis Emmerij, President of the Development Centre of the Organization for Economic Co-operation and Development,[52] supports this doubt.

At the implementation level, there is a lack in many countries of skills in valuation, flotation, dealing with foreign capital and joint ventures, promoting competition and exercising monopoly controls, restructuring, monitoring privatization as it proceeds and evolving appropriate regulatory structures post-privatization. A proper blending of needed skills from abroad with local skills will be conducive to success in this direction in the long run. Few countries have identified their needs of training specific to privatization; hence there has been no prioritization so as to introduce optimal programmes of training. Sporadic programmes of general management – e.g. in inventory control or accounting – are good in themselves, no doubt, but do not constitute the crucial element in raising privatization capability.

Divestiture

Decisions on divestiture are not easy to take, especially when the scale of divestiture is large and highly diversified. Where it is co-extensive with the whole economy, the decisions have to be good not only in terms of divestiture *per se* but also in being compatible with the transformation of the economy towards the market structure. Where decisions are delayed, because of decisional difficulty, divestiture gets delayed. Where 'inappropriate' decisions are taken, divestitures occur, no doubt, but success in point of results is likely to be constrained.

Let us look at certain major aspects of divestiture decision making.

Crowding out   At the outset the decision has to be good in the sense that it does not 'crowd out' the market, or else, either the divestiture does not succeed, or it succeeds at the cost of investment projects independently conceived by the private sector. And it might prove expensive, too, in terms of costs of flotation, underwriting commissions, and share offer prices.

The buyer   Who is likely to be the buyer? Divestiture decisions are, usually, not taken without some reference to this question. Choice between local and foreign investors is an obviously important issue. Undue emphasis on one or the other might prove incompatible with the success of a flotation or sale. Wrong decisions might lead to unforeseen or unpalatable consequences – e.g. local family groups might improve their economic power, or foreigners might control the ownership and management of enterprises. Due to the complexities inherent in deciding, decisions are sometimes taken casually, or altered or revised too frequently, with the result that the buyers' confidence is dampened. The Himal Cement case in Nepal is an apt example in this connection. The board of the Nepal Industrial Development Corporation decided to sell its shares in that company to an ethnic Japanese resident in Nepal; but the government, reacting to media criticism, stopped the implementation of the decision. This kind of problem is characteristic of several African countries – in particular Kenya, Uganda and Tanzania, where ethnic Asians, though they are nationals, are viewed with emotive disfavour. As a consequence, divestitures that could go ahead, other things being equal, would not succeed because other things are not equal.

Ownership spread   There is a ubiquitous tendency for governments to stress the widest possible spread of shares in the course of divestiture. It is not clear how strictly this is adhered to, for private sales, which have been common, represent the antithesis of this principle. Where a government sticks to the aim of wide ownership, it may have to institute a mechanism for financing the small man who does not have money to acquire shares. Jamaica is contemplating the establishment of an Investment Fund whose purposes include such financing. Short of such measures, the widespread ownership decision might not work and divestitures might accordingly be delayed. We do not consider here the question of whether a very wide spread of shares, even where it succeeds in terms of a divestiture transaction, leads to success from the angle of enterprise efficiency.

What to sell   Which enterprises should the government start selling? If the decision is in favour of loss-making enterprises, few buyers will be interested, and the divestiture programme will not take off, as in Ghana in the early stage. If, on the other hand, the divestitures relate to the profitable enterprises, they will be effected speedily. But questions arise as regards the impacts on the public exchequer and the tax payer and on distributional skewness. If the answers are unfavourable, the quick divestitures cannot be considered as successful in results.

Divestiture price   Fixing the divestiture price is one of the tough aspects of the entire exercise. The lower the price, the easier to sell. But the macro impacts may be quite unfavourable, as the second section of this chapter will show; and the success of divestiture in point of results might be in question.

Restructuring   A question on which fierce debate exists is whether an enterprise should be restructured prior to divestiture or whether the restructuring should be left to be undertaken by the new owner. Restructuring involves a cost, takes time to complete and results in raising the divestiture price. It might be good in many ways; but at the minimum it delays divestiture. In certain cases the turnaround may be so spectacular as to lure the government not to divest, at least for a time. In this way it has a constraining potential against divestiture.

Transparency Divestitures undertaken with limited transparency, as in the case of a negotiated sale or sale to other than the highest tenderer, arouse suspicion and create popular disbelief in the fairness of the transactions. The public digs into the motives of the government or particular groups in positions of power; and the whole programme runs the risk of being questioned, if not objected to. Several cases of spontaneous privatization and sale of assets to hived-off companies in Eastern Europe belong to this category.

This section has been limited to indicating the constraint potential of divestiture. The substantive aspects of the decisions will be considered at some length in the second section of this chapter.

Uncertainty of impacts

One of the constraints on privatization – particularly, but not exclusively, on the divestiture option – is the fear of impacts, of which not all might be favourable. There is, on the whole, far too inadequate an attempt to estimate the multifarious impacts that may be expected of privatization. Apart from the lack of technical skills needed for the exercise, there seems to be some unwillingness on the part of governments to enter into such an exercise, lest it should lead them to doubt, indecision and inaction. Yet the fear is there in the subconscious of policy makers and implementors and it contributes to delays in privatization decisions and actions.

The one area of impacts openly encountered is that of labour lay-offs. A recent one-day strike by bank employees in India protesting the privatization of the public sector banks produced the government's response declaring that banks would not be privatized. And this, at a time when the government is trying to open up the economy, and undertake share divestitures.

Another example: 'in the face of worker opposition' China is tending to slow 'harsh economic reforms needed to shake up state industries'.[53] The ordinary blue-collar workers, who supported market-oriented reforms in the 1980s, are currently agitated against replacing the 'iron rice bowl' with an elegant but far less sturdy 'porcelain' bowl.[54] Herein lies a constraint, not only on divestiture, but on non-divestiture options also.

The higher the rate of unemployment in the country, the weightier the fear of further unemployment as a constraint on privatization. Many economies in the developing and East European countries are featured with serious unemployment – e.g. 20.4 per cent in Trinidad and Tobago in 1991, as stated in the Central Bank's report, 17 per cent in Poland in 1992 and 8.15 per cent in Hungary in January 1992 (as against less than 2 per cent in 1991);[55] and the agreements on redundancy payments are very expensive, termed 'colossal' in Ghana.[56]

The lesson for developing countries is that the likely impacts in the labour sphere and elsewhere should be identified and estimated as far as possible, so that the right sequencing of privatization can be determined; the most advantageous choice between divestiture and non-divestiture operations can be made; and the necessary remedial measures may be initiated to mellow the impacts. Further comments are contained in the second section, whose focus is on the impacts.

Conclusions

First, the constraints on privatization are being realized and are proving effective as privatization programmes have gone into motion. Thus the pace of privatization is delayed in many countries, the first few show pieces apart, and the role of non-divestiture measures is being increasingly realized, though whether those are genuinely and effectively acted upon is another question.

Second, not all countries encounter the same set of constraints, and every constraint is not equally weighty everywhere. Broadly, there can be a classification as follows:

1   Countries where central planning is in transition to a market economy. Here the problem is wider than divestiture; and privatization, whatever the option, has to aim at a wholesale transformation of the society, not only in economic behaviour but in the way of thinking.
2   Countries – other than in 1 – where the size of the public enterprise sector is relatively large. Here two sub-divisions are possible:
    (a) Countries with a semblance of the private sector, including the legal frame-work – e.g. Uganda and Tanzania; and
    (b) Countries with a well-developed and diversified private sector – e.g. India, Brazil and Mexico.
3   Countries where the public enterprise sector is relatively small – e.g. Jordan and South Africa.

Third, the constraints vary in nature, intensity and remediableness, among countries coming under varying levels of development: for example,

1   high-income countries like Germany;
2   middle-income countries, upper and lower, like Mexico and Brazil;
3   low-income countries like India and Sri Lanka; and
4   least developed countries like Bangladesh, Uganda and Haiti.

Fourth, the importance of 'externalities' associated with enterprise operations varies among countries. Constraints on privatization vary correspondingly. The externalities are mainly a function of the stage of development, level of income, size and demography of the country and income and wealth distribution.

Fifth, constraints on divestiture – or even on the non-divestiture option of restructuring – are affected by the recessionary trends in capital-exporting countries and by extreme competition among supplicant countries, especially between the two categories of Eastern Europe and the other developing countries. A majority of African countries seem to be the least attractive for foreign capital.

Sixth, a distinction has to be made between success in the pace of privatizations and their success in point of results. Attention should be paid to the identification and minimization of the factors constraining the latter. The section on impacts goes into further detail.

Seventh, it might not be easy to remove every constraint on privatization. A trade-off approach has to be developed but on the basis of technically sound analysis as between costs and benefits of a given decision; and action should accord, and promptly, to the lessons of the analysis, or else there is danger of waiting for perfection.

Eighth, the risks of private sector behaviour – unpredictable in the case of several countries – should not halt privatization, if this were otherwise justified. But they should be monitored and regulated effectively. Some leakages have to be accepted and efforts should be made to minimize them.

Ninth, privatization calls for suitable changes in the techniques of national development planning. It would be unrealistic to hope for the cessation of development plans in most developing countries. Even as regards the centrally planned economies in transition, where the word 'planning' conjures up past horrors of central planning, there will likely emerge a large bundle of disparate laws and regulations which might be some kind of a surrogate for governmental intervention in the national economy. These ought to be co-ordinated and in such a manner that they do not veer towards the 'command' structures of the former years. By no means an easy task, this needs to be attempted with technical ability. It would be interesting to close this comment with an apparently paradoxical statement made recently by the President of Namibia, that 'private sector growth needs state planning'.[57] The point is that the term 'state planning' calls for a re-interpretation in the privatization era.

THE IMPACTS

Introduction

The impacts of privatization refer to the results directly traceable to the event of privatization. There is, first, the problem of identifying such results as distinct from the results which may have emanated from other economic circumstances. For example, an increase in the profitability discovered in the case of a privatized enterprise might have been the result of a sudden increase in the demand for the product concerned or of the bringing into use of idle capacities; and privatization as such might not have anything to do with these developments. Likewise, improved performance may have resulted from a windfall rise in exports to certain countries – for example, as a sequel to a trade agreement or an inter-government aid; and the fact of privatization may have had little causal relationship here.

There could be an opposite situation in which a macro development might have been induced by the circumstances of a privatized enterprise. An interesting example comes from Guyana, where the privatized telecommunications enterprise – GT&T in which a majority equity (80 per cent) was divested – indulged in irregular practices concerning its foreign exchange transactions on a scale that tilted the exchange rate of the Guyanese dollar downward.[58]

It is not easy to isolate the origins of a recorded result; but this is no reason why an attempt should not be made to establish the degree of responsibility that can be attributed to privatization. A rather obvious situation calling for judicious interpretation is where most enterprises, including privatized enterprises, are found making high profits during a given period.

Second, all impacts are not immediate. Some might be, like a lay-off of labour, if it occurs as soon as privatization takes place. But some might be visible somewhat later, in the short run, for example, where retrenchments are prohibited only for a year (or so) after privatization – as in Pakistan currently – or in the longer term, for example, where a whole segment of production is scrapped and the assets concerned are stripped, or changes in the ownership structure might occur quite differently from the pattern originally hoped for. (Sri Lanka specifies a limit of 5 per cent of total equity on an individual's purchase of shares during divestiture, but does not prohibit the aggregation of one's ownership through acquisition of shares post-divestiture.)[59] The span of time over which the full range of impacts unleashes itself varies from sector to sector, or enterprise to enterprise. One has to identify them appropriately so that one does not mistake the immediate (good or unfavourable) results for the end of the whole story. For, the aim lies in the long-run success of privatization, as distinct from instant results. There is a gradual recognition of the fact that the important implications of privatization are in the long run.[60]

Third, the impacts have to be identified not only in respect of divestitures but in the context of non-divestiture options also. Even among the former, distinction might be worthwhile as between full and partial divestitures, and among the several techniques of sale such as private sales, public flotations, employee buy-outs, and free voucher distribution. In the case of non-divestiture options, the focus may be on establishing how far the objective of marketization has been achieved, as reflected in the results, without recourse to divestiture. An option that calls for particular attention concerns the performance contract which is widely used as a means of rendering the operations of a public enterprise market oriented.

Fourth, certain impacts pertain to individual enterprise, while certain others are related, rather, to the scale and coverage of privatization in the country. Stock exchange effects and fundamental impacts of income distribution are among the latter; while the former may be illustrated by direct lay-offs of labour and changes in the product mix.

Finally, the impacts discovered in certain major instances of privatization or in the context of the cross-section of all privatized enterprises cannot invariably be deduced as representing the full potential of privatization. The impacts might be under the severe constraint of the state of parallel requisites in the economy, as argued in the previous section. If these are not adequately in place, the full potential of privatization impacts would not be in evidence. The analysis of impacts can, therefore, help suggest the adjustments needed in the macro developments or policies.

The impacts

For analytical convenience we may distinguish between micro impacts and macro impacts. The former refer to the input and output results of individual privatized enterprises, the latter to impacts on the rest of the economy in general. These ought not to be overlooked, though they are not easy to establish. The typology of the impacts may be presented as shown in Figure 1.5.

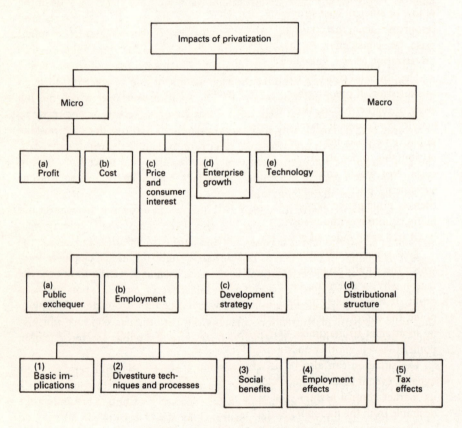

Figure 1.5 Impacts of privatization

Micro impacts

These concern the efficiency expected to be realized in the wake of privatization. The simplest and most publicized result refers to the profit earnings of a privatized enterprise. These are the trump card of a private enterprise. Yet the question remains: how efficient have the operations been? For, profit may have arisen, even without efficiency having been attained in several directions.

The cost may not have been low enough, considering the possibilities of cost economies which could be established as attainable in a given situation. This does not worry the owner if he can nevertheless achieve a desired profit through a combination of other circumstances such as monopoly power and high prices. But it would be desirable for the owner himself, and certainly from the standpoint of national economic performance, for that profit to be raised in a situation of low or efficient cost structures. The latter imply high productivity in the use of resources – men, materials and machines. From this point of view, can the enterprise be considered to have attained improved efficiency over the pre-privatization levels? This should be a main question.

The price and consumer-interest facets of the efficiency concept lend weight to this question. If privatization were to lead to conditions of efficiency through the sway of market forces, there ought to be adequate competition in the sector of activity concerned. If privatization, on the other hand, no more than transferred a public enterprise into a private monopoly (full or significant), the benefits attributable to privatization would not be realized in terms of low prices and low costs. Nor would consumers have the opportunity of being relieved of cross-subsidizing price structures meant for inflating the profits of the enterprise. If there is no effective agency for controlling monopoly practices – and there are many countries without such an agency – the recorded profits cannot *ipso facto* be treated as an index of efficiency gains.

Two other qualifications are necessary. One concerns the rate of growth which the enterprise tends to achieve from year to year. There is, of course, no reason why an enterprise should keep expanding; what matters to it is the rate of profit. If this is likely to be high without further expansion beyond a certain point, the enterprise may decide not to expand. It might even restrict the output in an attempt to maximize its revenue. Whether this is right from the national point of view is another question.

The situation can also be on opposite lines. The enterprise might decide to expand, even if at increasing cost – i.e. even if at declining efficiency – as long as its market control assures it a good profit. Such supra-optimal growth is not desirable from the national point of view.

The criterion, therefore, has to be conceived in terms of growth consistent with the economics of production, rather than of profit potential in a given market situation.

The other qualification to the profit index comes, similarly, from the area of technology. The profit rate might be indifferent to – and might not be the result of – technological progress or R&D efforts on the part of the enterprise. Once again the assumption is that the free market system is not effective enough to drive a technologically static enterprise out of the field with the advent of a technologically dynamic enterprise.

To sum up: the impacts of privatization have to be visualized in terms, not of profit alone, but of cost, productivity, price, consumer interest, growth and technology. Not every one of them is equally important in every case; but they have to be reviewed for the sake of a balanced view on the recorded profit post-privatization.

It is equally important to apply the same analysis to impacts in the context of non-divestiture options. Take management contracts and leases. They can be in particular danger of concentrating on profit in the short run if for no other reason than to prove that the agreements are working well. Further, the contractee is understandably eager to secure an extension of the arrangement, the more favourably to himself the higher the profits he is able to show. Let us turn to the performance-contract option, which in Figure 1.1 comes within the operational options of privatization. In most cases two things seem to attract emphasis and are perhaps realized, viz. price increases and some relief to the government budget. In fact the non-divestiture option termed 'commercialization' in Nigeria has for its operative definition a condition in which a public enterprise does not call for a government subsidy.

In either example mentioned above, profit alone should not be considered as the impact that matters. One has to look at the whole array of criteria shown in Figure 1.5 under the 'micro' heading.

Macro impacts

These are the more important ones for the economy as a whole and are linked with the country's long-term interests. And they take time to evolve themselves as results steady enough for policy analysis and remedial action. Distributional impacts are an apt illustration. Even employment changes – reflected in massive initial lay-offs – may readjust themselves somewhat as time passes. Hence the most practical approach would be to keep in mind the prospects of readjustments in the medium term and estimate the likely trends over the long term.

The public exchequer

The impacts on the public exchequer are among the most important ones calling for identification and estimation. Yet adequate attention has not been paid to this need in most countries. To start with, there has been a popular generalization pertaining to the objectives of privatization, viz. that it improves the situation of the public exchequer. It reduces the budget imbalance, it is argued, and provides the government with resources for its expenditure purposes; and it relieves the government of the need to find resources for investment additions in the public enterprise sector. Unfortunately, these arguments are not conclusively true in every case.

Let us focus on the divestiture option. The fiscal effects of privatization are a function of at least four factors:

1   the financial-flow relationship between the public exchequer and a given public enterprise or all public enterprises taken together;
2   the divestiture price received;
3   the use of the divestiture incomes; and
4   the costs that devolve on the public exchequer, for whatever reason, during and after the divestiture.

It would be helpful to treat the problem in terms of immediate impacts and subsequent impacts.

Government–enterprise financial flows   The primary issue here relates to whether the enterprise is a profit-making or a loss-making unit. Let us consider the latter first. The immediate effect of divestiture will be to relieve the government of the burden of subsidizing the enterprise. This will be a recurring advantage as well, assuming that the enterprise has been a chronic drag on the budget and is likely to stay that way in the foreseeable future. Figure 1.6 illustrates a simplified version of the argument.

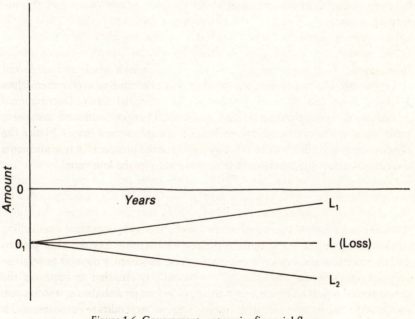

Figure 1.6 Government–enterprise financial flows

29

Assume that O_1L represents the loss of the enterprise, which the public exchequer has to fill in from its other revenues in order to be able to meet the interest charges on the public debt corresponding to its investment in the enterprise. Assume that the line O_1L represents the level of loss likely in the foreseeable future. (The line could be sloping upwards – O_1L_1 – or downwards – O_1L_2 – depending on whether the loss is expected to be narrowing or widening from now onwards.) The area between the X axis and O_1L (O_1L_1 or O_1L_2) represents the relief to the budget from the divestiture, year by year. Whether this will be all the relief, depends on the divestiture price – the second factor mentioned above.

The divestiture price If the divestiture price equals the government's investment in the enterprise, and if it is utilized for repaying a corresponding amount of the public debt, the budget will save the debt-servicing charges and the relief mentioned above is realized.

If the divestiture price is lower than the government's investment and the corresponding figure of public debt attributable to it, a portion of the debt continues after the divestiture, and the budget continues to incur debt-servicing costs on it. The relief that the divestiture offers the budget, therefore, diminishes to that extent. This is the most likely possibility, for a losing enterprise is almost certain to be sold away at a relatively low price.

If, for any reason, the divestiture brings a price which is higher than the investment and the corresponding figure of public debt, the budget gains a little bit from the transaction, over and above the bare discontinuance of the subsidy to finance the losses of the enterprise. Exceptional possibilities of this nature present themselves when the value of the assets of the enterprise divested turns out to be far higher than their book value, as in the case of land, in some cases.

Let us turn to the example of a profit-making enterprise, as shown in Figure 1.7.

Assume that the enterprise makes a profit of OO_2, that the interest costs of the public debt attributable to the government's investment in it are OO_1, and that the two figures are likely to be represented by lines O_2P and O_1I year after year. Divestiture saves the government debt-servicing costs (represented by the area between the X-axis and the line O_1I). But at the same time it foregoes the profits that have been coming in, as represented by line O_2P. On the assumption that the profits have been higher than the debt-servicing costs, year by year, the budget sustains a net disadvantage equal to the area between O_1I and O_2P.

On the lines of earlier analysis, if the divestiture price exceeds the investment and the corresponding quantum of public debt, the direct gain to the budget on grounds of debt-servicing charges saved will be higher; in the opposite circumstance it will be lower. Likewise, if the future profits are expected to take an upward turn (as per O_2P_1), the disadvantage to the budget will increase; in the opposite circumstance, it will decrease.

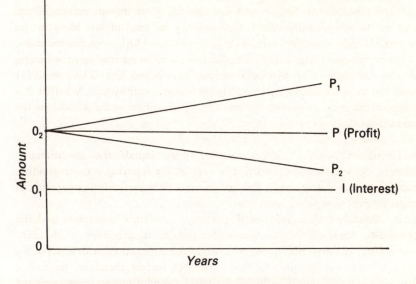

Figure 1.7 Divestiture of a profit-making enterprise

The use of divestiture incomes   The least favourable scenario of fiscal impact would consist of an increasing trend of expected profits and a relatively low divestiture price. Here the divestiture would have a material fiscal consequence. (One might wonder how the assumption of a relatively low divestiture price is compatible with an increasing trend of expected profits. In theory, the wonder is plausible. In the real world the two can go together and often do.) The fiscal impact would be less unfavourable if the profit expectations in the near future are on a declining scale and the divestiture price is relatively high.

   The argument so far has implied that the government uses the divestiture proceeds for repaying the public debt. This may be true in many cases; and in some countries like France it may be statutorily necessary, at least to some extent. Even when the divestiture proceeds are used for other purposes, the situation is analogous to one in which a fresh borrowing for such purposes has been unnecessary, and, therefore, a corresponding addition to interest costs has been obviated. It is also possible, where there is no legal bar, for the government to use the resources (a) for meeting or adding to current expenditures, (b) for financing reductions in certain tax rates, or (c) for capital expenditures. The first direction of use is what generally tempts some to claim that divestitures are a source of fiscal benefit and that the burdens of fiscal deficit are thereby erased. This is true in a limited sense. The divestiture proceeds are capital incomes. They dry up as time goes by. Further, as they are applied to current purposes (a) or (b), the figure of public debt attributable to the divested enterprises remains

31

undiminished, and the debt-servicing costs, unlike under our earlier assumption of debt repayments, will continue to stay in the budget. As time passes and the divestiture proceeds dry up, it will be difficult to maintain the additional commitments of current expenditure and/or the tax reliefs, or even the undiminished debt-servicing costs. If the funds are used for capital expenditures, the costs of the prevailing public debt continue; and whether or not the budget derives any offset through its capital expenditures depends on where these are directed. If they are in the nature of commercial investments, there is just a substitution of one investment for another; and the impact depends on the annual inflow of profit returns from the new capital expenditures. If it exceeds the bare interest costs on the capital involved, the net effect is favourable to the budget – in fact, as if there has been no divestiture in terms of aggregate investment. If, on the other hand, the capital expenditures do not produce significant returns year by year, the net effect is likely to be less favourable or adverse. Where the capital expenditures are triggered by the mere fact that liquid funds are found in the government's hands – e.g. on conspicuous building construction – there will be no real benefit to the exchequer.

There is one claim of fiscal relief which is real, viz. that divestitures relieve the public exchequer of the need to find funds for investment additions. Public borrowing programmes will be lighter for this reason; the interest rates will not be under pressures of increased borrowings; and there will be no 'crowding-out' in the capital markets.

The foregoing analysis has broadly been in terms of divestiture of a single enterprise. As enterprises get divested over time, the profile of fiscal impacts varies correspondingly from year to year. Assuming that, on balance, divestitures touch more of profitable than of losing enterprises, the budgetary legacy would progressively be one of adversity; for the burdens of the losing enterprises disproportionately stay, while the benefits from profitable enterprises are disproportionately lost. This is an important aspect of impact estimation and is closely connected with the concept of sequencing in respect of divestitures. The point gains in significance when we witness that, in many developing countries and planned economies in transition, the lists of enterprises likely to stay long in the lap of the government are expanding and are disproportionately on the side of the low-yielding and losing operations, while the enterprises slated for divestiture are clearly the financially superior ones. (This is not meant to be an argument against the divestitures planned; the emphasis is on the need to be conscious of the overall fiscal effects over time. It is desirable that sequencing decisions are taken in full knowledge of estimated fiscal impacts.)

The above argument may be represented graphically as shown in Figure 1.8.

Assume that as divestitures of profitable enterprises progress, the profit incomes of the public exchequer decline from O_1P to O_1P_1 as years roll by, while the losses from the continuing public enterprises stay at O_2L or, if non-divestiture measures of efficiency improvement prove effective, take the course of O_2L_1. (Both O_2L [or O_2L_1] and O_1P [or O_1P_1] represent the net position after interest

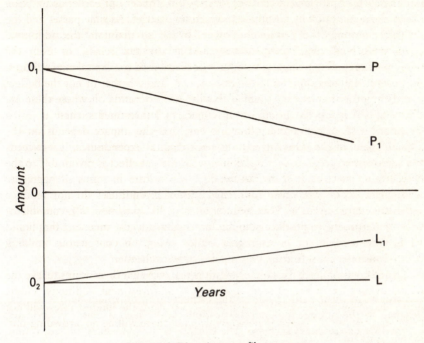

Figure 1.8 Divestiture profile over years

charges on the capital investments or the corresponding public debt figures are taken into account.) Thus the overall initial net budget income of OO_1 minus OO_2 goes on contracting – to OP_1 minus OL or OP_1 minus OL_1 after a few years. This might be slightly higher or lower, depending on whether the divestiture prices generally represent higher than or lower than the corresponding public debt figures.

The costs devolving on the public exchequer

Let us move to other sources of fiscal impacts, apart from the divestiture price and the profit-status of the enterprise(s) concerned. Some of these occur before or during divestiture, and some materialize later. Among the former the most obvious items are:

1 The costs of conducting the transaction: e.g.
   (a) the costs of advisory services;
   (b) the flotation costs; and
   (c) the underwriting commissions.
2 The costs of preparing the enterprise for divestiture: e.g.
   (a) the costs of restructuring; and
   (b) the redundancy costs.

3   The costs of providing incentives for easy divestiture: e.g.
     (a) the assumption by government of certain enterprise debts;
     (b) the writing-off of certain dues owned by the enterprise to the government
         – e.g. borrowings, tax arrears and accrued dividends;
     (c) the upgrading of certain insurance or pension funds through government
         contributions;
     (d) the provision of easy (public) finance for facilitating share purchase by
         'small' or selected groups of subscribers, including workers; and
     (e) the costs of preferences offered to employees for the purchase of shares.
         (These might, alternatively, be reckoned as reductions in divestiture
         incomes.)
4   Certain new costs, post-divestiture; e.g.
     (a) the costs of 'safety nets' for certain affected groups;
     (b) the compensations deemed necessary to persuade the privatized
         enterprise(s) to produce non-commercial but socially necessary outputs;
     (c) commitments of expenditures under several budget heads towards
         consumer subsidization or other directions of transfer payments; and
     (d) the costs of needed regulatory framework consequent on divestiture.

It is true that, on the other side of the estimating arithmetic, one has to give
credence to the argument that privatization causes such a boom in (private)
activity that tax revenues increase. The truth of this argument is limited to that
part of the boom or increased tax base that is traceable to the fact of privatization
only. However, as against this, one has to reckon with two opposite factors, viz.
the prospect of tax evasions and inadequate accounting of foreign exchange
earnings -- on both of which we come across alarming reports from time to time
from several developing countries.

A few comments are necessary on item 2 of the fiscal impacts listed above.
The first of these – the costs of restructuring – can be a considerable figure. Our
discussion is limited to the fiscal effects. We do not go into the wider question of
whether to engage in restructuring or not, though the nature of fiscal effects
might be one determinant of it. Restructuring expenditures can have favourable
eventual impacts on the public exchequer in the following circumstances:

1   Where the enterprise improves in financial performance so as to raise the
     prospects of a high divestiture price more than compensatorily.
2   Where the restructuring exercise makes the selling of the enterprise easy and
     reduces the costs of divestiture – e.g. in finding potential buyers, in
     determining underwriting commissions, in organizing the sales effort (and
     campaign), and in the offer of incentives to likely buyers. In one sense this is
     part of the previous circumstance, in that it helps to improve the net
     divestiture price.
3   Where the restructuring helps consolidate the production base of the
     enterprise in such a way that it minimizes, if not eliminates, the need for
     employee lay-offs and, correspondingly, redundancy payments.

34

4   Where, as a result of restructuring, the enterprise is able to improve its utilization substantially, earn higher profits and help reduce the budget burdens from its operations as long as it stays in the public sector.

5   Where the restructuring provides an occasion for the inflow of foreign capital which ensures the necessary technological changes. If it is assumed that such an inflow is not otherwise likely, there ensues a net addition to the investment quantum in the economy, apart from some convenience from the angle of foreign exchange resources. In both ways the public exchequer derives indirect benefits.

It may be noted that our reference is not to financial restructuring in the main, which – necessary in many cases – ordinarily implies the formalization of a *de facto* equation between the finances of the enterprise and the public exchequer. For example, accumulated losses, erosion of capital, and chronic arrears of debts to the government are a *fait accompli* in so far as the consequences for the public exchequer are concerned. Financial restructuring merely provides a *de jure* framework for establishing them once and for all.

There is an interesting aspect of the restructuring debate, to which we may refer briefly, in conclusion. There is a notion that the costs of restructuring may (or ought to) be met from the proceeds of divestiture. This suggests that they can be met from the divestiture proceeds, that they should be within the quantum of the divestiture proceeds, and that whether a given enterprise attracts restructuring depends on whether some other enterprise provides divestiture proceeds. None of these suggestions is accurate. The Treuhand example (discussed in Chapter 3) shows how high the restructuring costs can be in relation to the divestiture proceeds. The case for restructuring an enterprise is independent of whether another is divested. And the fiscal impacts of its restructuring warrant analysis on the foregoing lines, independently of whether there is a divestiture income to finance it. Divestiture incomes simply ease the exchequer position on restructuring. In fact we may go a step further to suggest that the benefits of restructuring, including (and definitely reflected in) its fiscal effects, are a matter of macro concern to the economy as a whole, considering that resources for such a purpose are scarce. Hence it is necessary for a national ranking of enterprises in the restructuring exercise, so that the cost–benefit picture is the best possible as far as one can estimate. In a way this approach overrides as superficial the debate on whether restructuring in a given case should be undertaken prior to divestiture or left to the new owner.

The other item under point 2 refers to redundancy costs. Whether an enterprise bears them or the government does is a matter of indifference to their fiscal impacts, if it is assumed that the divestiture proceeds will be lower or higher to the extent of such costs. Perhaps, in some cases, the government's decision to undertake the redundancy exercise produces a psychological factor in favour of a divestiture price that more than brings in the costs of redundancy undertaken prior to the transfer of the enterprise to the new owner. This can, therefore, have a favourable fiscal impact.

The issue has a further dimension. The government has two options: either it may deal with each enterprise as an isolated redundancy issue, or it may deal with the generality of enterprises as a common pool. In the latter case there can be a twofold economy. For one thing, a national redundancy insurance fund can be organized, being fed by contributions from all enterprises, public and private. For another, the demands on the use of the fund can be economical, in the sense that interenterprise redeployment possibilities are built into the system. Retraining and geographical movements can also be built in. In this way the public exchequer can cope with the burdens of redundancy in the most ecnomical manner. Ghana illustrates a recent development through the establishment of a national insurance fund to assuage, though not eliminate, the severity of the burdens of redundancy costs.

Employment

The impacts of privatization on employment are undoubtedly the most widely recognized concerns in almost all countries. These may be analysed as follows:

1   Where an enterprise has surplus labour *vis-à-vis* a given production function, privatization aimed at raising its efficiency is likely to lead to some retrenchment. This had happened in the UK even before divestitures took place, as the nationalized industries went through non-divesture exercises, which included effective manpower reductions – e.g. British Airways and British Steel.

2   Privatization might stimulate the new owners to introduce a new production function involving capital-intensive technologies. The average cost might decline, but the wage component – and probably the volume of employment – would decline. There can be one qualification. If the fall in the average cost is so material as to lead to a price reduction and if the demand for the output is highly price-elastic, there might be a strong reason for output expansion requiring some additional labour inputs even under the new technology.

3   The most common motive of profit maximization on the part of a privatized enterprise – within the limits of competition encountered and the goal of long-term prosperity -- induces some restriction in the outputs. This has a corresponding effect on employment.

4   In a sector of activity where entry is free, capital intensity is low, and exit is easy in the physical sense, the producers might grow into such a large number as to create conditions of cut-throat competition. Road transport, restaurant and similar other services, and retail shops are examples. Here the numbers employed – in many cases, owner-workers – would be large indeed. But the enterprise turnover might be considerable; or, the owner-workers and non-owning labour might resign to accepting relatively low levels of wages. Thus while employment might be maintained, the wage incomes are not, as compared with sectors in which entry and exit are not equally easy.

36

Privatization in an underdeveloped region presents this phenomenon in an acute form. Eastern Germany and Slovakia are interesting examples, where, even independently of the entry-and-exit assumption made above, a clear choice of policy presents itself as between a relatively high wage level accompanied by a relatively low volume of employment and a relatively low wage level accompanied by a relatively high volume of employment.

5 Where foreign capital is the prime factor in the success of a divestiture transaction in a developing country, the incentive for it, it must be recognized, is partly a function of the expectation that the advantage of relatively cheap labour will continue. Eastern Europe illustrates this point. For this to prove true in practice, either the prospect of low wages or that of some lay-offs or both should be available. Herein lies one source of impacts in the realm of employment.

In concluding this section, we may note a fundamental aspect of the employment impacts which borders on a micro–macro conflict. For an individual privatized enterprise labour economies, like any other kind of economies, are worth pursuing. But their impact, namely an addition to the volume of unemployment, is what the economy as a whole has to sustain and meet through appropriate policies of transfer payments – an issue which will be considered at some length in a following section.

The micro impact is not without significance even on macro grounds, in another way. Not to economize labour costs at the level of individual enterprises creates a distortion of cost structures among the enterprises. This leads to distorted price structures, leading to distortions in consumption structures, profit structures and eventually investment decisions. There is perhaps no logical reason necessarily favouring all these distortions, once we assume that the basic cause is linked with the desire to preserve excess employment – in varying degrees, in practice, in different enterprises. The benefits associated with this are achievable, alternatively, through appropriate public policies of transfer payments.

This point is so important as to merit some analytical annotation. Assume that there are three enterprises A, B and C operating either in different sectors of activity or in the same activity but located in different regions or serving different consumer groups among which there is limited or no transportability of the product (or service) – e.g. bus transport or cement. Assume, for the sake of simplicity, that their cost structures and demand curves are similar and that they adopt pricing on similar principles. The cost structures are assumed to represent conditions of the most economical labour inputs. The consumers in the three cases are fairly treated *inter se*; and there are no interconsumer inequities. That is, there are no distortions in consumption structures; and the profit conditions and the consequential investment decisions are uniformly determined on that basis.

Let us now introduce the complication of *unequal* deviations from the most economical labour inputs on the part of the three enterprises A, B and C. Clearly, the consumers in the three markets are exposed to varying degrees of inequity caused by various degrees of surplus labour carried by the enterprises. Differences in the financial fortunes of the enterprises and in their investment decisions also follow; and the outputs available for consumption also vary among the three markets. Such results are even more certain if we relax the assumptions of uniform cost/demand structures and of uniform pricing principles in relation to cost structures. The point to note is that, under our assumptions, there is no basis for the distortions except for the varying surplus labour elements in the three cases.

If the surplus elements of labour input are eliminated in every case (that is, if the necessary lay-offs take place), *and* if the aggregate costs of surplus labour are financed through the government budget, the interconsumer inequities are eliminated. And interenterprise distortions in profit and investment decisions are also eliminated. Further, the prices in every case would be the lowest possible, consistent with the most economical labour input.

Possibly the public costs entailed in this process would be recovered partly or wholly through levies of some kind on all enterprises. Their cost structures would correspondingly be higher than they would otherwise be. So would the prices; and so on. But interenterprise inequities among consumers would not be there. The costs of excess labour which built themselves up with some rationale in public enterprises, and which are really in the nature of social costs, would be spread over a broad cross-section of enterprises on criteria of public finance.

If, on the other hand, every enterprise featured by surplus labour wants to deal with the problem through redundancy payments, the cost of financing them would constitute an addition to its own cost structure; and the consumers concerned would be correspondingly under a disadvantage – for no other reason than that the enterprise has been a public enterprise bearing a social cost at a certain level.

The development strategy

The possible impacts on the structure of overall economic development are traceable partly to the context of individual enterprise privatizations and partly to that of a growing series of privatizations.

If a large number of major privatized enterprises succeed in retaining or gaining monopoly control over the market, expectations of efficiency in the performance of the economy are somewhat affected. Where the monopoly power is derived from restrictions on imports in an open or disguised manner, the benefit of international competition is not realized.

If, on the other hand, imports are liberalized, privatized and other enterprises in a given sector might be unable to withstand international competition and tend to decay, unless it is assumed that privatized ownership or management becomes so efficient that it can survive in the face of import competition. It is doubtful that such an assumption proves realistic in many cases, the more so with reference to small-market economies. Here it is even possible that, if foreign owners control privatized enterprises, they would be under the understandable temptation gradually to shift their focus from local production to trading in imported goods. Their brand names, apart from the economies of scale in their global production activities, help in this course of action.

There can be an interesting, perhaps unforeseen, impact. Many economic activities in the private sector – which have been benefiting from non-maximizing price and output policies of certain basic public enterprises like electricity, heavy engineering, and transport – would be in danger of losing the benefits as those enterprises are privatized through divestiture (or even through non-divestiture options of marketization). True, distortions in investment decisions across the board might correct themselves. But certain sectors of activity, in certain regions, might suffer, at least over the short run. Where the benefits lost were in the nature of disguised transfer payments intended for selected industrial activities or for selected regions, privatization would affect the prosperity of the beneficiary activities and regions, unless alternative measures of compensation are devised in their favour. This is a real problem in many developing countries. In a way this takes us to the basic issue of whether certain market failures which some public enterprises were established to counter have in fact ceased to exist. If they persist, the options and techniques of privatization should be so adjusted as to bring about efficiency in operations without annulling the macro elements of desired intersectoral or interregional discriminations. If it is assumed or shown that the latter are unnecessary or wrong, this conclusion does not hold good.

One of the serious concerns that privatization can raise in many developing countries refers to the technological basis of industrial activity. It is well known that technology development, limited as it has been, has so far emerged from the efforts of public enterprise in these countries. They can easily run the risk of a loss of initiative for R&D on the part of many privatized enterprises, whose immediate interest in profit lures them to choose technology options most economical to them in the short run. These can be either simple technologies or minimal turn-key imports of technical know-how. As such practices repeat themselves from year to year, the prospect of technology planning with an eye on the long run and on national technological excellence can suffer. This presents the need for cautious public policy decisions on:

1 whether to insist as a condition of divestiture that the new owners guarantee an agreed schedule of technology development;
2 whether adequate protection through the conferment of monopoly powers should be offered to the enterprises so as to strengthen their incentive to undertake R&D expenditures; and
3 whether the government should set up some national technology fund, built out of general or sectoral levies, so that, without reference to choice on the

part of individual enterprises, desired patterns of R&D expenditures can be made possible in the economy as a whole or in specific sectors.

As the economy gets progressively privatized, it is possible that private investments flow more into light manufacturing than into basic industry. In the absence of such public investments in the latter, the industrial structure of the nation would be too lopsided on the side of light manufacturing; and the development of capital- and intermediate-goods industries might be dwarfed. Likewise there might be a spurt of investment activity in the more lucrative regions of the country, while the relatively backward regions lag behind in attracting private investments. If the privatization policies preclude public investments in such areas, those areas are likely to remain the backwaters of industrial investment.

The distributional structure

The impacts of divestiture on the distributional patterns in the economy may be examined under five headings:

1 basic implications,
2 divestiture techniques and processes,
3 social benefits,
4 employment effects and
5 tax effects.

Basic implications   Where a profitable enterprise is divested, the private sector owners begin to enjoy the benefit of the profit incomes, minus the interest costs of capital, which used to accrue to the public exchequer. Thus there is a shift of benefits from the tax payers to the investors. If the cross-section of investors is richer than the average tax payer, the income redistribution effect is unfavourable.

Additional tax receipts from increased private incomes, no doubt, flow in. But in the pre-privatization era all profit incomes flowed into the public exchequer (or were retained in public enterprises).

It is where the assumption is that a public enterprise is making losses that the conclusion tends to be the opposite. The tax payer, who was bearing the burden of the loss, will be relieved of it. To that extent there is an equitable distributional effect.

The conclusion concerning profitable enterprise rests on two assumptions. The first is that the persons into whose hands the divested shares pass are, on average, far richer than the average tax payer. The other assumption is that the use of the profit incomes at the discretion of the new owners (in the private sector) is, on the whole, likely to be less equitable from the distributional angle than if the same resources were in the hands of the government. Both assumptions are broadly true with reference to most developing countries.

The above conclusion is not in the nature of an argument against divestiture. Strong grounds might exist for divestiture on the criteria of comparative advantage and efficiency of operations in a given case. Moreover, budget measures are possible whereby the inequity of the income shifts indicated here can be mellowed.

Divestiture techniques and processes   Let us go into some detailed aspects of the techniques of divestiture and the processes of implementation, which have a bearing on the distributional impacts. These are taken from the practices adopted in different countries, ranging over:

1   the determination of divestiture pricing;
2   preferential terms to certain allottees of shares;
3   free allotment of shares;
4   the divestiture price mechanism;
5   regional and ethnic aspects;
6   ownership concentration;
7   foreign ownership; and
8   managerial emoluments.

Divestiture pricing   The argument, simply put, is that where the divestiture price is relatively low, the buyer benefits correspondingly at the expense of the seller. In this way there arises a distributional disadvantage of the tax payer. The more the buyer belongs to the higher income brackets, the more severe and obvious the inequity tends to be.

The term 'a relatively low price' calls for annotation. It implies a price lower than the value of the enterprise under divestiture. The latter should be derived from the future earning power of the enterprise. As mentioned in the first part of this chapter, it is not easy to establish this where there exists no proxy for it in continuous stock exchange quotations, where the profit worth of the tangible and intangible assets is not readily discernible from the published balance sheet, and where expert judgements are difficult to make as regards the future environment of markets and technology in which the enterprise will work. These conditions hold good in most developing countries, all the more seriously in the centrally planned economies in transition. It is true that attempts have been made in some countries to improve the valuation process, such as Sri Lanka, where the Valuation Department within the government is entrusted with the responsibility in large part. But its experience is found to be limited to the valuation of assets. Business valuation for establishing future earning power is a different exercise. The UN Centre on Transnational Corporations has recently documented the criticism that some enterprises in eastern Germany have been sold 'at very low prices, based upon the valuation of individual assets and liabilities'.[61]

Circumstantial factors have aggravated the incidence of underpricing. First, several governments have been eager to divest rapidly, whatever the reasons. Filling in current fiscal deficits, even if partially, is an important underlying motivation here. (India is a good example.)[62] It is the finding of the UN Centre on Transnational Corporations from its experience that rapid privatization has usually resulted in 'imprecise and frequently low values'.[63] Second, 'where the goal is complete divestiture as soon as possible, valuation and equity considerations are neglected'.[64] Whether admitted or not, external pressures have been forceful in many cases in favour of quick divestiture transactions. In fact these might even be defended by some as a trade-off for the immediate fiscal benefits likely to be available under overt or implied conditionalities from international agencies. Third, too little of serious thinking has been bestowed on 'prior' restructuring as a justifiable option even in the case of certain enterprises slated for eventual divestiture, left in a run-down condition and reputed to be decrepit. No wonder they attract low price offers. Fourth, there has been an insatiable quest for foreign capital in recent years. Too many countries have been competing for too little of available foreign capital at too fast a pace. While incentives of various kinds are offered by the host countries for the influx of foreign capital, two additional devices seem to have taken hold of the scene: relatively low divestiture prices, and concessions designed to boost the financial advantages of the foreign investor in the course of his operations post privatization. A grotesque example is reported from Guyana:

> British businessman Lord Beaverbrook made £50 million (TT 376 million) in five months from the purchase and resale of the Guyanese national timber company. He bought the company in February 1991 for £9.7 million and five months later sold it for £60 million. In clinching the deal Beaverbrook negotiated a 50-year lease on 440,000 hectares of tropical forest there.[65]

Underpricing, along with writing off of debts, is dubbed in a recent Oxford study an 'endemic feature of the privatisation process in a large number of countries'.[66]

Examples of underpricing – directly or indirectly – are available in both developed and developing countries. Prices quoted in the stock exchange on the first day of trading after divestiture suggested, in a number of cases in the UK, that the nationalized industries were sold too cheap and that there were 'windfall gains for the investor at public expense'.[67] Several reports of the Committee of Public Accounts and the National Audit Office support such a conclusion. Some prices of divested shares rose up to 195 per cent over the public offer price in a few months, in France.[68]

The shares of United Motors Ltd in Sri Lanka rose from Rs11.00 on the date of the first transaction to Rs29.5 in a few months and to Rs63.00 about a year later.[69]

The recent divestitures of shares by the Government of India are widely criticized as a give-away. For example, the SAIL shares divested at Rs11 were selling above Rs100 in the market a few months later.[70] In Pakistan, National

Investment Trust bought shares in Shahtaj Textiles for Rs5.8 million and made a 'windfall' profit of Rs3.335 million in a few days; and in several other cases the value of divested shares 'rose by a factor of 8 to 9 ... soon after the balloting'.[71] Another heavily criticized case of underpricing in Pakistan concerns the divestiture of the Roti plant at Faisalabad at 'a throw-away price' of Rs84 lakhs, while the land itself is worth twice as much in value, apart from the machinery.[72] An interesting example of indirect underpricing through excessively generous terms of sale comes from Guyana in connection with the sale of the Paint Co. Two years' credit on over 80 per cent of the price was allowed at an interest rate of 6.5 per cent, as compared with the government's own rate of 32.5 per cent on borrowings through treasury bills.[73]

Preferential allotments   There has been a tendency in several countries to offer shares to employees on preferential terms. Partly motivated by the government's desire to win labour over to privatization, this technique raises a serious question on grounds of distributional justice. How are the employees of a public enterprise, which is chosen for divestiture, specially merited for the conferment of wealth on preferential terms? If it can be shown that they are not among the lowest income brackets in the country, their justification for receiving beneficial treatment in the acquisition of shares is weakened. In several countries like India, Pakistan and Kenya, public enterprise workers receive wage and related incomes at higher levels than their counterparts in the private sector. (This does not apply to top managers.)[74] Preferential offer of property rights, therefore, has the effect of widening the skewness in income distribution.

 · Some of the well-known examples of preferential allotment of shares to employees come from the UK and France. In the case of BAA each eligible employee was offered 41 ordinary shares 'free'; there was a 'matching offer', under which each eligible employee was offered the right to purchase, at the fixed price, 82 ordinary shares and also two shares, free of charge, for each share so purchased; and there was a 'priority offer' under which each eligible employee could apply for up to 4,082 ordinary shares in priority to public applications.[75] In France employees have benefited from a special allocation (up to 10 per cent of the shares), a special price (up to 20 per cent less), one free share for every 10 shares purchased, and the opportunity of making deferred payments within three years. Moreover, up to 50 per cent of the price could be paid in securities rather than in cash.[76] Poland offers a 50 per cent rebate in the allotment price.[77] Under the Yugoslav law of 1990 employees may acquire 'internal' shares with reductions in price of up to 30 per cent, plus a further 1 per cent reduction for every year of employment.[78]

Free allotment of shares   Going a step further, the government may decide to give away some shares to the employees free of any purchase consideration. The question raised above on macro-distributional grounds repeats itself and gains in weight in this case. Sri Lanka is a typical case in point. In general 10 per cent of the shares of a divested enterprise are given away to the employees. Considering that in most cases the prices quoted in the stock exchange when trading starts are many times higher than the face value of the shares, many of the employees with long service have joined the new rich overnight – a point noted in the press from time to time.[79] In fact, while privatizing bus transport, the government gave 50 per cent of the mobile assets free to the employees.

There is a twofold anomaly common to the two preceding practices of share allotment. While employees in divested enterprises benefit, their brethren working in public enterprises exposed to non-divestiture options do not. In addition, there would be significant disparities in the quantum of benefit that employees in different enterprises receive. Those fortunately placed in the more profitable enterprises enjoy higher wealth and income benefits than those working in less profitable or loss-making enterprises for no reasons connected with their level of efficiency or income status. Many basic, capital-intensive industries, and even electricity in some countries (like India), belong to the latter category.

If we proceed to speculate on the second round of effects, the scenario could take the following shape. The workers might be induced to sell away their shares at a fairly early date; whatever they get in return for no investment on their part could well be an attraction; and the shares could find their way into the hands of persons who are richer and/or smarter as share traders. The latter might be the ones who mop up a disproportionate share of the 'free lunch' in ultimate terms. The assumption is that there is no condition attached to the free shares that the employees who receive them should retain them for at least a stipulated period. There is none such in Sri Lanka; and in some cases, like Ceylon Oxygen Ltd, only about 30 per cent of the free shares still remain with the original recipients, less than two years from the date of the give-away. (The 'loyalty bonus' element in the limited UK give-away is a healthy contrast in this context.)

The free offer of shares to the employees of an enterprise under divestiture has to be distinguished from the general free voucher schemes of countries like Czechoslovakia and Poland, in the context of distributional implications. The latter treat all citizens alike; and, other things being equal, everyone benefits equally to start with. In contrast, free shares to the employees concerned raise problems of distributional disparity, as indicated above.

The divestiture price mechanism   Corruption and technical incompetence apart, there are two sources of genuine error in the mechanism of agreeing the divestiture price, which assume particular significance from the angle of distributional equity. First, there may be some assets whose value-benefit to the new owner might soon far exceed the figure at which, for whatever reason, it was evaluated while agreeing the divestiture price. The easiest example is the site on which the enterprise is located, or the site-cum-building it occupies. In many cases – e.g. the textile mills located in cities like Calcutta and Delhi, or the State Trading Corporation occupying a prime site and building near Connaught Place in New Delhi – the value of such fixed assets would be extremely high if revalued on the criterion of their sale value. It is doubtful, however, if the revalued figure should be entered wholesale in the new balance sheet on the basis of which the enterprise is sold: yes, because so much of potential value is transferred to the new owner; no, because he cannot hope to raise his output prices high enough to meet the finance cost components entailed in the revaluation. It is difficult to arrive at a satisfactory decision. The fear is always there – and this could soon be a fact – that the new owner's main interest is in the site (and the building) rather than in the enterprise as a going concern. He might relocate the operations, or even close them in *de facto* terms, and dispose of the prime property. That is, he might be buying the enterprise not to run it but to strip the assets. He amasses a huge windfall gain – a clear gift from the government to a private party. Many cases of 'repossession' or 'restitution' promised under the new laws of property and privatization in countries like Uganda, Pakistan, Bangladesh and in Eastern Europe run the risk of such distributional inequity. There is no easy solution to this problem. But the government may consider the propriety of introducing a 'claw-in' clause in the mechanism of divestiture price fixing, to the effect that, if within a defined period specified fixed assets – especially land and buildings – are sold away or substantially shifted to other purposes than the type of operations in which the enterprise was engaged at the point of divestiture and in terms of which the divestiture price was agreed, the (new) owner, i.e. the party to which the government divested the enterprise, should offer the government a specified share in the capital gain implicit in the process. Of course, there are several ticklish issues here. The period within which this clause remains operative should be suitably determined, sector by sector and case by case, and with an eye on the nature of potential likelihood of the event of a sale taking place. The modality of the capital gains being amassed needs careful attention and definition; for, there might apparently be not a sale but a merger, which in course of time achieves the capital gain benefit for some non-government party; or there might be a technically unobjectionable shift in the use of the property which, in reality, might constitute a source of, and a cloak for, a big capital gain. The sharing ratio in the capital gains as between the government and the private party should be appropriately designed, and in due recognition of the prevailing capital gains taxes. Above all, there should be an acceptable formula for demonstrating that the high value received by the seller of the property is not the result of his own efficiency in the management and use of the property after his possession of it since the divestiture.

It is not suggested here that the claw-in clause is a simple matter. But the distributional advantage it can deal with, whether it can eliminate it or not, is so real that an attempt is worth making in experimenting with it. The British Government adopted the claw-in technique in the context of the privatization of water.[80]

There are two crucial qualifications. One has to keep in mind the potential of a claw-in clause as a disincentive to the intending buyer of an enterprise under divestiture; and one may legitimately ask: does it work both ways – for example, when an asset is sold at a loss? (Of course, there is an asymmetry between the two ways. Selling at a huge loss can be manipulated to collect an income from the government under the claw-in provision.)

The second error in the mechanism of determining the divestiture price concerns the treatment of development expenditures, especially on technology, which a public enterprise may have been incurring over a number of years. If these were written off every year as a debit to the profit and loss account, there would be no trace of their value as an asset in the balance sheet. If, on the other hand, they stay in the books as deferred expenditures waiting to be written off or capitalized in the future, there is every chance of their being dismissed as a fictitious asset under the bargaining pressures from potential buyers. They will reap the fruits of such developmental expenditures in future years. If their potential contribution to the future earning power of the enterprise is duly recognized and brought into the valuation process, the price determination would be free from this disadvantage. But where it is not, the more so when the development expenditures have not yet reached a state of maturity and the buyers contest their utility, there is every likelihood of their ending up as a burden on the exchequer, whereas their long-term benefits are transferred to the buyers of the enterprise.

This point has great significance in a developing country[81] where public enterprises have systematically incurred huge developmental expenditures, on technology as well as on the very preparation of the civil works and infra-structures in their areas of operation. Some of these may have been infructuous, but then that is part of the game. Divestitures which do not sufficiently provide recognition for such outlays in the course of price determination contain elements of distributional inequity.[82]

Regional and ethnic aspects   One of the impacts, not openly discussed, consists of certain unique distributional trends that divestitures promote in large-sized and multi-ethnic societies. If the private-sector owners of the divested enterprises tend to originate in the more developed regions of the country, the other regions have legitimate reason to point at the regional income disparities which develop in the wake of the divestitures. And income and wealth accumulation might breed itself cumulatively in the regions that dominate in the initial acquisition of divested shares. This is what is feared to be happening in Nigeria, where the Lagos, Ogun, Bendel, Kano and Imo regions have been accounting for very high proportions of share absorption in the many divestitures that have taken place during the last four years, as against regions such as Sokoto and Plateau which have consistently lagged behind.[83]

Likewise a disproportionate segment of the divested shares might land in the lap of certain ethnic groups or tribes, thanks to their 'incumbency' potential for entrepreneurship; and the other sections of the population begin to resent that development. Several African countries – Kenya, Tanzania and Uganda, for example – come within this description. (The 'Asian', though Kenyan, potential for divested ownership as well as that of Kikuyus among the Kenyans themselves excites tensions.) Malaysia provides another example, where the 'Bumiputeras' (sons of the soil, i.e. the Malays) might be unfavourably affected by unfettered acquisitions of divested shares by others. In Guyana there is genuine fear in some quarters that, if ownership of formerly government-owned enterprises passes into the hands of the moneyed private parties, certain corresponding ethnic consequences might ensue in the field of employment, detrimental to the income-earning interests of the African Guyanese people.

The regional and ethnic disparities in income accumulation mentioned above might, no doubt, be inherent in market forces, once these are allowed to operate unrestrainedly. There appears to be a two-fold cause for complaint on the part of the affected sections: first, that it was precisely to offset such a phenomenon that public enterprise had originally been opted for; and second, that divestitures aggravate these distributional inequities, as if on a silver platter.

Ownership concentration   Under this heading we shall begin with an analysis of who owns the divested enterprises and what the distributional implications would be. There is hardly a country which has not announced itself emphatically in favour of a wide distribution of share ownership. One of the finest policy statements in this regard comes from the Gambia: the sale of shares should be such as to 'avoid the concentration of economic power in few Gambian hands thereby resulting in the domination of the economy by a few persons'.[84] Some countries have laid down the limits on share allotment to individual applicants. One of the lowest limits obtains in Nigeria: not more than 1 per cent of the equity of the company concerned.

If all divested shares are 'equally' held by the share holders, the dividends and capital appreciation are equally spread among them. And if the number of shareholders is fairly large, each individual's size of ownership benefit is relatively small. Distributional skewness within the shareholding group in a given enterprise tends to be low, under these two conditions, insofar as the incomes originating in the enterprise are concerned. Unfortunately, neither condition holds good in practice. First, there is an unequal spread of shares among the shareholders in many a case. A large proportion of divestitures – especially of large and medium size – has occurred through trade sales and private negotiations, e.g. in Ghana up to 1991.[85] (In the Philippines, 49 out of 63 reprivatizations were in the nature of negotiated sales.)[86] Such transactions end up by placing almost the total equity of the divested enterprises in the hands of a single entity.

Second, there has been an unmistakable preference for finding a 'core' investor in the hope of managerial efficiency, the more so when foreign investment (accompanied by technology) is eagerly sought. In the case of Sri Lanka this is reflected in a formula which conceives of 60 per cent of equity being allotted in favour of a core investor. Among the techniques of privatization having a similar motive and/or result are the recently initiated 'investor-initiated privatisation method' in Hungary[87] and the opportunity given in Malaysia to a private party to submit a proposal for the privatization of an enterprise he may be interested in.

Third, several divestitures have involved the offer of large blocks of shares to institutional investors. One of the most recent events in this direction occurred in India when the first two rounds of partial divestiture of the central government's shares in public enterprises were deliberately in favour of 'mutual funds'.

There has nevertheless been a ubiquitous slogan in favour of wide share ownership, beginning with the claim in the UK that the number of shareholders in the country rose to 9 million consequent on the privatization transactions. It is true that in the case of divestitures other than trade sales and private negotiations a relatively large number of shareholders enter the picture. But they account for a minor portion of the total share capital. The most telling evidence comes from the UK itself.[88]

From the distributional angle, therefore, the fact remains that the benefits arising from equity ownership are skewed in favour of the large shareholders. A qualification is necessary here. In several cases the large shareholders happen to be financial institutions, insurance companies, pension funds, building societies, etc., and not individuals. However, the benefits eventually reach persons who share in the distributable incomes of the institutions in one way or another. If they are mostly in the higher-income brackets, the ultimate distributional result remains skewed.

Three further questions are of interest in this connection. First, is the ownership concentration (or skewness in favour of the richer brackets in the community) more conspicuous in privatized enterprises than it is in the rest of the private sector? If it is, divestiture should be considered as a factor in aggravating distributional inequalities. While the conclusion needs to be arrived at on an empirical basis and might vary somewhat from country to country, one can speculate on the probable scenario in most developing countries in the following terms. As divestitures have depended largely on trade sales, 'core' buyers and share-block allotments either to domestic or to foreign parties, the likelihood of ownership concentration on the part of divested enterprises might be higher than in the rest of the private sector. A supporting reason is linked with the relatively capital intensive and high-technology features of a major segment of the divestitures.

The second question concerns the degree of effectiveness of allotment practices in favour of the small subscriber. In many cases, as in Sri Lanka, there are no restrictions on share transfers at the stage of secondary trading, so much so that many small holders could part with their shares without any legal hindrance. At least some of these find their way into the hands of bigger equity holders. Thus the initial proportion of 'small' ownership weakens as time passes.[89] Attempts are still exceptional in the direction of monitoring the flows of divested shares. The National Investment Board of the Gambia is one of the few institutions which intend to institute such a monitoring system.[90]

PRIVATIZATION: CONSTRAINTS AND IMPACTS

The third question is related to the government's initiatives aimed at strengthening 'small' share holdings. These can range over a variety of measures. For example, special financing arrangements might be devised for the small subscribers, including the employees; the acquisition of shares on the basis of instalment payments may be made possible, portions of future wages – in the case of employees – being earmarked for such payments; costs of share transfer transactions may be minimized through special arrangements; and certain shares – particularly those gifted or sold preferentially to employees – may be held 'in trust', such that the owners cannot sell them at their discretion within a specified period or that they should sell only into the trust, i.e. to other similarly placed shareholders. All such initiatives call for continued governmental/public involvement and might also entail some elements of public costs. Whether governments would be willing to go that far in stabilizing whatever limited prospect small and wide share ownership has on a long-term basis is doubtful.

It would be fair, in conclusion, to recognize that divestitures can have a positive effect in widely spreading share ownership for one important reason. The stock markets are becoming active (in some countries) mainly because of large volumes of share availability consequent on divestitures, with certain reservations in initial allotment for the small subscribers. And the chronic problem of share owners not being interested in selling their shares on the stock exchange is partly countered in the processes of divestitures. Apart from this, to the extent that employee buy-outs become popular, a new shareholding class emerges, which includes many relatively small holders.

Such developments create new and small shareholders, no doubt. But the lion's share of total equity incomes accrues to a smaller number of richer shareholders.

Foreign ownership   Foreign capital is eagerly coveted in many countries and has been of great significance in some, e.g. Hungary, where by January 1992 nearly 90 per cent of the divestiture incomes have been derived from abroad, and Myanmar where, by 1991, the foreign capital component stood at $ 655 million spread over 37 enterprises – wholly foreign-owned units or joint ventures. Profits are correspondingly enjoyed by foreigners. The point assumes severe dimensions under the following conditions:

1   where the profit rates are far higher than the rates of interest applicable to the amounts of investment;
2   where the enterprise enjoys monopoly power and the profit rates are not controlled by the government;
3   where the major proportion of foreign investment in the context of divestiture pertains to the more profitable segment of the public enterprises divested;
4   where the most profitable enterprises divested attract foreign investment wholly or substantially;

5   where the foreign investor receives very generous concessions from the government through tax and customs reliefs, the like of which are not easily available to local capital;

6   where the foreign owner pursues policies of managerial hiring bordering on 'delocalization' as well as excessively generous compensations for foreign personnel; and

7   where, through transfer pricing and other techniques of relationships with foreign trading or consultancy firms, the enterprise unduly syphons off profits as cost items, as found in the case of the Guyana Telephone and Telegraph Ltd. This case is so revealing that the findings of the Public Utilities Commission of Guyana in the context of a request for rate increases are cited extensively in Appendix 2.

This section neither represents a comprehensive review of foreign capital in the context of divestitures or otherwise, nor intends to pass judgements on its place in divestiture transactions. Its purpose is merely to indicate the probable disadvantages to the national economy from the distributional angle. There could be many advantages, on the other hand, which such investments might bring in – e.g. technologies, development of ancillary industries, export markets, import substitution, and cost efficiency. From out of such developments certain other and good distributional results might emerge through new employment opportunities, price reductions, output availability and improvements in the balance of payments position. Conclusive inferences should be drawn only after a rigorous study of the trade-offs implicit in a given case.

Managerial emoluments   Let us turn to the issue of managerial compensation consequent on divestiture. There is an obvious tendency for steep increases in the emoluments of managers. The reasons, briefly, are that:

1   their former earnings bore poor comparison with those of their counterparts in the private sector and should hence be enhanced;

2   the new emphasis on profit orientation seems to justify devices of boosting managerial incentive;

3   the managers have opportunities of capturing the acquiescence of the new owners who might be enterprises, institutions or a highly dispersed multitude, none seriously interested in, or capable of, adjudging managerial salaries as long as profits are on the up swing;[91]

4   to the extent that the managerial group is foreign in origin, there is a general notion that very high emoluments are indispensable; and

5   most importantly, there may be no public policy on managerial compensations in the country, within which one may question their propriety in individual cases or in general. In fact the view gets round that, since the divested enterprises are private, it is for the owners of those enterprises to decide on managerial salaries.

The most notorious examples of salary increases come from the UK.[92] We are not concerned here with whether the high salaries that managers in divested enterprises begin to receive are justified or not. Our limited point is that, in an economy where income disparities are high, they are likely to be resented on distributional grounds. Besides, in many countries in the developing world and in Eastern Europe where the public sector has been relatively large, if not dominant, and top salaries were subdued, the new salary trends might appear to be especially distasteful. (Incidentally, there has been a tendency in recent times for shareholders voicing protests at steep increases in managerial emoluments – chief executive officers' compensations in particular – in developed economies themselves.)

Social benefits   Privatization – in particular, divestiture – has impacts on the social benefits which an enterprise, while in the public sector, was yielding. The simplest definition of social benefits in the present context is that they are the benefits that one enjoys either by paying less than what the due costs imply or by receiving more than what is due to be received on commercial criteria. Prices lower than related costs and wages higher than at market rates are examples. By placing the operations on a commercial footing or by bringing them within enterprise disciplines under the sway of market forces, privatization tends to minimize, if not eliminate, the flow of social benefits as defined here. As a result, certain distributional impacts ensue, implying that some groups or regions, which were recipients of such benefits, will suffer a deprivation.

In examining this proposition we have to distinguish between the category of benefits which, on macro grounds, it would be desirable to scale down, if not eliminate, and the other category which it would be undesirable to lose. In other words, the distributional results would be good rather than bad in the former case, while they would be unfavourable in the latter case.

To the first category belong the following changes:

1   Wage incomes get linked with performance; and employees cease to get paid for inputs not provided by them.
2   Expenditures popularly termed 'social expenditures' on employee housing, recreation, etc., which used to be heavily subsidized, if not free in some cases, get scaled down, except for providing genuine incentive for employee effort.
3   Price concessions which used to be enjoyed by undeserving groups of consumers, along with or more than by the target groups, will cease to be available. Low electricity tariffs for agriculture in India are an interesting example. They do not even cover the marginal costs in several cases, and the benefits accrue disproportionately to the rich land owners. Similar have been the inordinate benefits of subsidized prices reaped by urbanites as against the rural poor from the operations of CONAPSU of Mexico.[93]
4   Unwise investment decisions, in terms of product, region and technology,

which have no intended justification on social grounds, tend to be curbed; and the benefits that certain persons or regions might have received from such decisions will cease to be available.

5   Benefits traceable to patronage and bureaucratic or political power will disappear as the officials and ministers (or members of parliament) cease to have any formal relations as owners with the divested enterprises.

While the loss of benefits belonging to the foregoing category is an acceptable result on distributional grounds, losses which fall into the following categories contain elements of disadvantage.

1   Low and stable prices in respect of certain commodities and services, which have the characteristics of basic needs, might give way to profit-maximizing price policies. Either all consumers or some needy groups of consumers in particular might suffer from such a development.

2   The availability of an output might shrink on grounds of commercial calculation on the part of a divested enterprise, whereas its continued availability at a given level might be deemed socially desirable. Examples include telephone call boxes, off-peak bus services, food supplies in all seasons, and drinkable water in all inhabited areas.

3   Operations and expansions will be limited in regions where profits are likely to be low or negative. As a result, the prospects of economic activity, income and employment in those regions are affected.

4   A privatized enterprise would like to feel free on decisions regarding the development of ancillary industries, which might have been imposed on it as a matter of national policy during its public sector days. Where such an obligation is uncommercial or affects its own commercial interest while trying to benefit the incomes of the ancillary occupants, it prefers to keep away from undertaking such activities; and the former beneficiaries in the ancillary sector begin to experience a loss of benefits.

5   While as a public enterprise it may have undertaken investments on government-inspired grounds of anti-cyclical policy, as a divested unit it will not be obliged to act in a similar way, if that does not suit its own commercial calculations. Thus there will be a loss of benefits expected of such investments.

There are two second-round factors which have a bearing on the distributional results mentioned above. The first relates to the way in which the divestiture proceeds are utilized. If the government looks at them as a resource for social expenditures designed to improve the living conditions of the lower-income brackets, there can be an ultimate good result from the distributional angle. Provision of water, irrigation, rural electrification, free hospitals and primary education centres are examples of such expenditures. Incidentally, there is another good point to be noted in this connection. The expenditures can be so organized that the benefits accrue to target groups and regions, identified broadly on welfare criteria; whereas the social benefits which public enterprises were yielding were linked to specific consumer or employee groups.

To illustrate the possibility of an opposite effect through decisions on the use of divestiture proceeds, we may refer to decisions by the government to treat them as an occasion for reduction in personal taxation. (This is not a hypothetical proposition. This happened in the UK for two years in the early stages of privatizations.) The benefit goes to the income tax payers. Unlike in the UK, income tax payers are a minority in developing countries; and the benefits of tax reduction disproportionately accrue to the relatively well-to-do sections of the population.

The other factor relevant to second-round effects concerns the government's budget measures intended to assuage the loss of social benefits, on a selective basis. The government may persuade divested enterprises to undertake certain operations, uncommercial but socially desirable, on promise of adequate compensation from the public exchequer. The compensation is expected to relieve the financial burdens sustained by the enterprise in undertaking the operations. This policy, however, requires careful deliberation and rigour in implementation, so as to ensure that only the desired and deserving social benefits are subsidized, that the subsidies tend to be minimal rather than finance enterprise inefficiencies, and that the choice of the enterprise for a given subsidized operation depends, as far as possible, on competitive tendering. Where this is not possible, strict scrutiny of the costs of the operations would be necessary.

This analysis is relevant to non-divestiture options also. Even where the organizational and operational options are applied, involving the privatization of management or enterprise disciplines, the effects attributed to divestiture are likely to unfold themselves, though on a somewhat smaller scale. There could be some difference in practice. In the case of a divested enterprise commercial criteria would be overriding and exceptions on social criteria are only possible through positive interventions from the government. Such exceptions would be far easier under non-divestiture options, since continuing government ownership exaggerates the assumption of 'publicness' of the enterprise. The right course of action would, however, lie in enforcing hard constraints on the enterprise managers; and exceptions to commercial decisions should, by and large, result from deliberate instruction from the government, followed by a compensation formula. (The British Government tried such a technique in the 1970s. It was good in intention but proved inadequate in practice.)

Employment effects   Here our discussion is limited to analysing the distributional implications of the employment effects earlier delineated.

First, privatization would generally be followed by a desire on the part of the new entrepreneurs to go in for the most economical production function. Where this involves the substitution of capital for labour, they might not hesitate to opt for it. From the standpoint of enterprise efficiency as well as consumer interest, this cannot be criticized. However, it can have the effect of increasing the share of profits, as against wage incomes, in the enterprise sector. Thus the process is in favour of the investors as against the employees in aggregate terms. It can have a distributional implication if it can be assumed that the former are the richer group.

Second, if privatization results in improved mobilities in the labour market and competitive wage rates, it is likely that in heavily populated and surplus-labour economies the wage rates at which workers can be hired would be biased in the downward direction. The pre-privatization situation of sheltered labour rewards, coupled with relatively low productivity, would change substantially.[94] It is also possible that trade union strength is weakened. On the whole, the wage potential of the labour force would be somewhat lower than under public enterprise, the more so if lay-offs resulting from privatization continue over a long period.

Third, business failures due to enterprise sickness would force privatized units to go into liquidation, unlike in the generality of public enterprises. Thus the chances of periodic loss of jobs, redeployment, relocation, and variations in wage rates, tend to be high, within the limits of the laws governing the closure of units. National employment insurance schemes and other safety nets can moderate the severity of this factor, but the situation itself is inherent in the case of enterprises fully exposed to market forces.

These implications no doubt arrest one's attention, as they are witnessed in the wake of privatization. But one has to judge them in light of enterprise efficiency which results from the effectiveness of market forces, with benefits of reduced cost and price structures. The latter certainly benefit the consumers concerned, both end consumers and intermediate consumers. And in course of time they might help expand economic activity and create the conditions of new demands for labour. Herein lies a logical trade-off.

Tax effects   Here the discussion is limited to the distributional implications of the tax effects traceable to privatization, and to divestiture in particular.

If we assume that the divestiture incomes are treated as a means of balancing the budget, i.e. if they are used for meeting current expenditures, as in India[95] and in the Philippines,[96] there may be no immediate tax effects. Such might be the position as long as divestiture incomes keep flowing in. But one day they will dry up and the problem of budget imbalance will recur. Tax enhancements will be probable.

If we assume that the divestitures relate to profitable enterprises more than to losing enterprises, the current revenues situation tends to deteriorate. Subject to the point mentioned in the preceding paragraph, there are likely to be tax enhancements.

If we assume that loss-making enterprises are divested, the current budget position improves; and tax enhancements are unlikely as a consequence of privatization.

The extent to which the budget balance will be affected depends also on the incidental costs in which the public exchequer is likely to be involved prior to, during and after divestiture – a point discussioned on pp. 33–6. To the extent that they are material, tax enhancements are likely.

Our assumption underlying the likelihood of tax enhancements is that neither public borrowings are resorted to, nor is deficit financing preferred. This is a reasonable assumption, given the conditionalities of international agencies.

The distributional consequences of tax enhancements depend on the nature of taxes enhanced. In general the tax incomes in developing countries are derived predominantly from indirect taxes. These are well known to be regressive; and tax enhancements, therefore, aggravate the regressivity of the tax burdens. The lower-income brackets suffer relatively more than the others.

An interesting possibility as regards import duty enhancements is worth mentioning at this point. If their purpose is raising a sizeable revenue, it will be necessary to create conditions for the continuous inflow of the imports in question. If these imports are intermediate goods necessary for local production activities, the end prices of the latter may have to be higher. The consumers concerned will bear the burden. The relative spread of the burden among the richer and poorer consumers depends on which groups of consumers are the predominant users of the products. If the imports are end products, the permitted price ceilings may have to be raised in order to enable the imports to sell, despite the increased import duties, in the face of competition from local products. Now the local producers begin to realize rental profits. Once again profit incomes rise, while the consumers bear the brunt of the increased import duties.

The increase in profits can be arrested if the government imposes an excise duty on local production simultaneously with the import duty. This erases the chance of local producers snatching away the entire market as against the imports which become dearer because of the import duty. Incidentally, the public exchequer has the additional benefit of excise revenues.

Roughly similar distributional effects flow from the measure of eliminating or reducing subsidies – as against levying tax enhancements. The consumers concerned are affected through subsidy contractions; and the budget balance is similarly influenced through reduced expenditures, rather than increased revenues. In practice, subsidy contractions are likely to be a more immediate measure than tax enhancements in many countries.

This brief section is not intended to examine tax policies *per se*. Its focus has been on the distributional consequences of possible tax measures owing to the impacts of privatization on the public exchequer.

Conclusion

We may conclude the analysis with the following observations. First, privatization has substantial macro impacts in countries with low incomes, large population, considerable unemployment, wide income disparities, and regional differences in development. Limited market sizes often aggravate the problems.

Second, implicit in the analysis of the impacts – both micro and macro – is the problem of measurement. This is the more complex, the more difficult it is to identify the impacts definitely attributable to privatization.

Third, the processes of privatization warrant monitoring, in order to establish how effectively the objectives of privatization attached to individual cases or categories of cases are being realized, how transparent the processes of privatization happen to be in practice, and what basic changes in the structure of the national economy are being brought about by the processes of privatization.

Fourth, the impacts of privatization constitute such a wide range that they do not all produce a uniform result. The concept of trade-offs deserves attention. Certain direct and immediate results need to be considered alongside certain others which might be less direct and immediate, before the net benefit or cost to the economy is established. Of course, one has to decide on how far to go in identifying the results beyond the first-round effects.

Fifth, privatization calls for preparedness in the area of regulation aimed at exorcizing the unwelcome impacts.

Sixth, in many developing countries and centrally planned economies in transition the role of the state in steering economic development will not cease to be important – though it has to be different from what it has been – or else the impacts of privatization can be too anarchic to sustain distributional equity and social stability.

It would be desirable for analysts, policy makers and practitioners to focus attention on establishing the impacts of privatization, on monitoring privatization, on regulation post-privatization, and on redefining the precise role of the government in the development strategy specific to a country. These items should have high priority in work programmes relating to privatization.

NOTES

1 OECD Document DCD/DAC (92) I, February 1992.
2 OECD Development Centre paper for the Commonwealth Secretariat Conference on Privatisation, Islamabad, March 1992.
3 Christopher Adam, William Cavendish and Percy S. Mistry, *Adjusting Privatisation: Case Studies from Developing Countries*, Oxford, 1992: 35, 66.
4 'The divestiture of public enterprises in Ghana has proceeded at a much slower pace than many of us would have hoped' (W.A. Adda, 'Managing the privatisation process: the case of Ghana', Commonwealth Secretariat Conference on Privatization, Islamabad, March 1992.
5 Since the impetus to thinking gained in favour of privatization by the Report of the Working Party on Government Expenditures, in 1982 in Kenya, which was accepted by the government, too little has been done, barring the announcement of the most important step taken so far – the listing of non-strategic investments to be divested, 'which was made by the little known CMAA (Capital Markets Authority)' (John H.N. Kosieyo, 'Latest developments in privatisation process in Kenya', Meeting of UN Center on Transnational Corporations, Geneva, 1991).

6 'Capital privatization' targeted 308 enterprises; but 'only 26 to date actually have been fully privatised'. (Ryszard Rapacki and Susan J. Linz, 'Privatisation in transition economies: case study of Poland', Southern Conference on Slavic Studies, Jacksonville, March 1992).

7 'Major enterprise privatisations have not been quick enough or mistake-free' (Minister Madl, Workshop on Privatisation, Institute of Industrial Economics, Budapest, January 1992).

8 Adda, op. cit.

9 *Privatisation and Commercialisation Decree No. 25 of 1988*, Lagos, July 1988.

10 Brian Van Arkadie and Vu Taj Bui, 'Managing the renewal process: the case of Vietnam', UNDP Management Development Division (MDP) Colloquium, London, March 1992.

11 Summary: *The Seventh National Economic and Social Development Plan (1992–1996)*, Bangkok, Section 3.4.2.

12 *A proclamation to provide for the encouragement, expansion and coordination of investment*, Proclamation No. 15/1992, Addis Ababa.

13 Gao Shangquan, 'The process and basic experience of China's economic system reform', MDP Conference, London, 1992.

14 Statement of Minister of Economy, Gjergi Konda, at MDP Colloquium, London, April 1992.

15 Anton Andonov, 'Managing the transition from the centrally planned economy: the case of Bulgaria', MDP Conference, London, 1992.

16 Mario Blejer *et al.*, 'China: economic reform and macro economic management', IMF, 1991.

17 Koba, K., *Comments on Manfred Balz's lecture on 'Privatisation in Germany'*, CERGE, Prague, 20 December 1991: 25.

18 World Bank, *Transition 3 No (2)*, Washington DC, February 1992.

19 In Ghana the problem originated in the fact that confiscation was not backed by the law (W.A. Adda 'Privatisation in Ghana', in V.V. Ramanadham, *Privatisation in Developing Countries*, Routledge, 1989: 319).

   In Pakistan law required that a 'taken-over' enterprise had to be offered first to the previous owners. This constituted a 'legal lacuna' which later amendments sought to rectify (Riyaz Bokhari, 'Privatisation in Pakistan', in Ramanadham, op. cit.).

20 Manfred Baez, *Privatisation in Germany: The Experience of the Treuhandanstalt*, CERGE, Prague, December 1991: 3.

21 Jiri Bilek's comments in Baez, op. cit: 15.

22 Adda, op. cit.

23 'Hungarian economy', *Vilaggazdasag* (daily paper) 14 January 1992 Supplement, Budapest.

24 'Majority of the members of the business community are unable to properly comprehend the actual benefit of associating themselves with the stock market system', *Economic Survey 1990–91*, Finance Division, Economic Adviser's Wing, Government of Pakistan, Islamabad, 1991: 38.

25 UN Centre on Transnational Corporations, *Review of important current developments at the global level in the field of accounting and reporting by transnational corporations*, Report of the Secretary-General, E/C. 10/Ac.3/1992/2, New York, 23 December 1991.

26 The revaluations varied between 30 per cent of net book values of assets in the case of Exbud and 94 per cent in the case of Krosno. 'Accounting problems arising during privatisation in Poland', *Commission on Transnational Corporations*, New York, C/C.10/Ac.3/1992/5/Add.6, 25 November 1991: 33).

27 *Economic Survey of Europe*, UN Economic Commission for Europe.
28 Cited in the *Guardian*, London, 31 March 1992.
29 Rima M. Khalaf, 'Privatisation in Jordan', in V.V. Ramanadham (ed.) *Privatisation in Developing Countries*, London, 1989: 248.
30 Uganda Development Corporation, *Corporate Plan 1988–91*, Arusha: 1.
31 For instance, the President of the People's Republic of Korea stated: 'Our Party's line in the building of heavy industry was to create our own solid bases of heavy industry which would be able to produce at home most of the raw materials, fuel, power, machines and equipment needed for the development of the national economy by relying on the rich natural resources and sources of raw materials in our country' (*Korean Review*, 1988 edition: 114).
32 *The New Vision*, Kampala, 12 August 1991: 11.
33 Rapacki and Linz, op. cit.
34 Data on the finances of public sector banks in India for 1990 indicate that, in the aggregate, about a third of their advances (about Rs 20,000 crores out of about Rs 64,000 crores) were in the nature of bad debts. (*The Economic Times*, New Delhi, 13 February 1992: 12 and 13.)
35 The following observations referring to Pakistan are applicable to many other developing countries:

> Privatisation hardly puts in any risk capital these days, particularly in large projects.... DFIs are suffering as many units in the private sector go sick again and again.... Private sector is still choosing fields, which can yield quick and high returns and where risk capital involved is not large.... Private sector has not shown much inclination in the balanced development of the country.... Private sector continues to fight shy of basic manufacture, new fields, sophisticated technology and mineral exploitation work.

(Mohammad Anwar Khan, 'Private sector's process of development', *Frontier Post*, 28 September 1991.)
   Any generalisations about the superior efficiency of private sector are not borne out by Pakistan's experience. (V.A. Jafarey, 'Privatisation: a mixture of patronage and desparation', *Muslim*, 2 January 1992).
36 The fear is expressed in Uganda that its entrepreneurial class is 'small and relatively poor', and that many of them are 'no more than struggling agents of foreign companies' and 'may indeed be the medium through which foreign capital will gain dominant control over Uganda's modern economic sector' (J.W. Okune, 'The long-term well-being of the country and the costs of privatisation policies', Orientation Programme on Privatisation, Kampala, August 1991.)
37 The inaugural address of the President of Nigeria, International Conference on the Implementation of the Privatisation and Commercialisation Programme – An African Experience, Lagos, November 1990.
38 Bimal Jalan, 'Some lessons in the management of privatisation – with special reference to India', Commonwealth Secretariat Conference on Privatisation, Islamabad, March 1992.
39 Frank Rampersad, 'The rationalisation of the state enterprise sector', Conference of the Trinidad and Tobago Economies Association on Privatisation, November 1991.
40 Cited in *The Straits Times*, Singapore, 30 January 1992.
41 Rapacki and Linz, op. cit.
42 W.A. Adda refers to the constraint of socialist attitude against priority for selling profitable enterprises. He also refers to 'the importance of attitudes, values and perceptions ... also of the broader public whose interests governments exist to serve' (Adda, op. cit: 17).

43 It is said, with reference to Albania, that 'the intimidation that was used in the past to dominate the population has led to a situation where individuals are now unwilling to accept personal responsibility for their actions' (Gjerj Konda, Artan Dulaku and Ross Bull, 'Albania – moving from a command to a market economy', MDP Colloquium, London, April 1992).

44 With reference to Poland, Ryszard Rapacki and Susan Linz refer to 'social perceptions, labour–management relations, egalitarian attitudes, distorted work ethics, pervasive risk-averse behaviour, vested interests, rent seeking and second-economy activities, and the prevalence of monopoly in the economic bureaucracies of the former socialist economies' (Rapacki and Linz, op. cit.).

45 Aftab Ahmad Khan, 'Privatisation: background, limitations and hazards of ad-hoc implementation', *Pakistan and Gulf Economist XI* (4), 25–31 January 1992: 8.

46 For instance, the Executive Director of the State Privatisation Agency on Hungary observed: 'I protest against the overweight of the budget' (*Nepszabadsag*, socialist daily newspaper, 13 January 1992).

47 Koba, op. cit.

48 Andonov, op. cit.

49 Muncef Bal Hadj Amor, 'A report on the experience of the Democratic Popular Republic of Laos', MDP Colloquium, London, April 1992.

50 Mohd. Shah bin Abdullah, 'Privatisation in Mayalysia – MIMB's experience', Commonwealth Secretariat Conference on Privatisation, Islamabad, March 1992.

51 *Economic Survey of Europe*, UN Economic Commission for Europe.

52 Louis Emmenj, 'The costs of free market economy', Inter Press Service, as reported in *Indian Express*, Hyderabad, India, 16 March 1992: 9.

53 It is proving difficult to move away from guaranteed jobs, fixed wages and life-long official positions in China (*International Herald Tribune*, Hong Kong, 11 June 1992: 14).

54 'The experience here suggests that even a gradual weaning away from central planning can lead to widespread fear and sometimes fury' (Nicholas D. Kristof, *International Herald Tribune*, Hong Kong, 12 June 1992: 1).

55 World Bank, *Transition*, Washington DC, February 1992.

56 Adda, op. cit.: 320.

57 *The Windhoek Advertiser*, Namibia, 30 November 1991.

58 Carl B. Greenidge, 'The Privatisation of Guyana', Commonwealth Secretariat Conference, Islamabad, March 1992.

59 Tissa Jayasinghe, 'Sri Lanka's first privatisation', Commonwealth Secretariat Conference on Privatisation, Islamabad, March 1992.

60 J.W. Okune, op. cit.

61 *Accounting Problems Arising During Privatisation in Germany*, Report of the Secretary-General, E/C/10/Ac.3/1992/5/Add. 3, 16 January 1992: 24.

62 *Vide* the allegation of the National Confederation of Officers Associations of Central Public Sector Undertakings: disinvestment is 'made so far at throw-away prices' (*The Economic Times*, New Delhi, 8 July 1992: 3).

63 *Identification of accounting problems arising during privatisation and their solution*, Report of the Secretary-General, E/C/10/Ac.3/1992/5, 17 January 1992: 5.

64 *Review of important current developments at the global level in the field of accounting and reporting by transnational corporations*, Report of the Secretary-General, E/C/10/Ac.3/1992/2, 23 December 1991: 35–6.

65 *Trinidad Guardian*, Port-of-Spain, 13 November 1991: 1.

66 *Adjusting privatisation*, op. cit.:59.

67 Second Report from the Committee of Public Accounts, Session 1985–6, Departments of Transport, Trade and Industry, and Energy, 1985. *Sale of Subsidiary*

Companies and Other Assets, London, HMSO, 34, 1985, Note 5: vii, note 2: xiv, and note 3: vi.

Rover was sold at a price which fell 'significantly short of the real value of the company' (The National Audit Office Report, DTI: *Sale of Rover Group plc to British Aerospace plc*, HMSO).

Also see Trades Union Congress, *Stripping Our Assets*, London, p. 7; Hamish M. Rae, 'The tax payers are having their assets sold too cheaply' (*The Times*, London, 20 May 1987).

68 French Treasury Report, December 1988: 19, quoted by Reuters, 7 December 1988.
69 Some evidence from Sri Lanka:

> In regard to the Buhari Hotel, it is alleged that it changed hands at the mere value of land alone on which it stands. Likewise, it is alleged that the property belonging to Ceylon Oxygen was valued at Rs 6.8 million but it was sold to the Norwegian company at Rs 17 million.
> (*Ravya*, 4 August 1991, cited in Saman Kelegama, *Privatisation: The Sri Lankan Experience*, Colombo, 1992: 27)

> The Oils and Fats Corporation was sold at a much lower price than its actual value and the purchaser was given the benefit of paying the cost on deferred payment terms.
> (Wijitha Nakkawita, *The Island*, Colombo, 18 January 1992: 3)

> The Thulhiriya Textile Mill, valued at over US $100 million on a current replacement value basis, was sold to the Koreans for US $ 7 million.
> (*Textiles Today*, a publication of the Ceylon Textile Manufacturers' Association, Colombo, June 1991)

70 See S.R. Mohnot, in this volume, p. 288.
71 Hussein Mullick, 'Robbery in the stock exchange', *Pakistan Observer*, Islamabad, 22 February 1992.
72 Masood Abdul Karim, 'Performance of public and private sectors – an analysis', *Nation*, 3 August 1991.
73 Greenidge, op. cit.
74 For evidence and further discussion see V.V. Ramanadham, *Public Enterprise and Income Distribution*, London, 1990, Chapter 2.
75 For the special terms of shares offer to employees in the UK see Appendix 7 on p. 70 in Ramanadham (ed.) *Privatisation in Developing Countries*, Routledge, London, 1989.
76 Commission on Transnational Corporations, *Accounting Problems Arising During Privatisation in France*, Report of the Secretary-General, E/C10/Ac.e/1992/5/Add.2, 20 December 1991.
77 Commission on Transnational Corporations, *Accounting Problems Arising During Privatisation in Poland*, Report of the Secretary-General, E/C.10/Ac.3/1992/5/Add.6, 25 November 1991, paragraph 31.
78 Branko Vukmir, 'Privatisation in Yugoslavia', in V.V. Ramanadham, *Privatisation: A Global Perspective*, London, 1993.
79 For instance, *Sunday Observer*, Colombo, 3 May 1992, reports how a foreman in Ceylon Oxygen received free shares worth Rs 557,000 in the market; an electrician in Lanka Milk Foods received free shares worth Rs 399,271; and a clerk in Hotel Lanka Oberoi received free shares worth Rs 676, 720; and so on – quite large sums in the local context.
80 It is relevant to note here the suggestion of the National Audit Office in the UK in favour of some claw-back provisions aimed at giving the taxpayer a share in the

benefit arising from subsequent sale of surplus assets by the privatised enterprise. (National Audit Office Report: *Sale of Rover Group plc to British Aerospace plc*, HMSO, London).

81 E.g. India, vide *Public Enterprises Survey*, Annual Report by Bureau of Public Enterprises, New Delhi.

82 Reference may be made at this point to an interesting exercise recently made by the Philippines International Trading Corporation to reflect its developmental costs as an intangible asset in the divestiture (floor) price. It calculated the expenditure incurred in developing each foreign market over a period of years by adopting techniques that included the valuation of human capital inputs, and arrived at a total figure of an intangible asset entitled 'goodwill' (Louis Yulo, *ASTRO Workshop on Restructuring/Privatisation of TRPEs*, Manila, June 1992).

83 The Presidency, Technical Committee on Privatisation and Commercialisation, Half-yearly Progress Reports, Lagos.

84 A.M. Touray, 'Privatisation and divestiture strategy of the Republic of the Gambia', Commonwealth Secretariat Conference, Islamabad, March 1992.

85 Adda, op. cit.

86 Committee on Privatisation, *1991 Annual Report*, Manila, December 1991.

87 Lajus Csepi, Gusztav Bager and Erzsebet Lukas, *CEEPN/EDI Second Annual Conference on Privatisation in Central/Eastern Europe*, Ljubljana, November 1991.

88 For instance, an analysis of the shareholders' holdings showed that as at 15 May 1989 out of a total number of 338,350 shareholders in British Airways plc 97.82 per cent held between 1 and 1,000 shares each and accounted for 10.26 per cent of the share capital (British Airways plc, *Annual Report and Accounts*, 1988–89: 47). Shareholders owning between 1 and 500 shares in British Gas plc accounted for 13.8 per cent of the total share capital (British Gas plc, *Annual Report and Accounts*, 1989: 45).

   In Sri Lanka, shareholders with less than 500 shares each accounted for 4.86 per cent of the share capital as at 31 March 1991 in the recently privatized Pugoda Textiles Lanka Ltd (Pugoda Textiles Lanka Ltd, *Annual Report for the period ending 31st March 1991*, Colombo: 6).

89 For example, British Airways had 1.1 million subscribers on flotation in 1987; but by 1990 the number 'dwindled' to 314,000. 'The same pattern is true of the other major privatisations' (Ruth Kelly, 'Wooing the new shareholders', *Guardian*, London, 8 April 1991: 11.).

90 A.M. Touray, op. cit.: 21.

91 'Why should they – small investors and City institutions alike – complain about the big rewards for bosses so long as their companies are performing well? ... The institutions are more shy; their own chief executives are some of the most highly rewarded men in British finance' (*Weekend FT*, London, June 29/June 30 1991, Section II: 1).

92 Pay rises at the top level in British privatized enterprises attracted almost uniform criticism from all sides. The Chancellor of the Exchequer, Mr Lamont, termed them as 'excessive and unjustified'; Mr John Major, the Prime Minister, made his opinion 'perfectly clear' regarding the 'undesirably large increases'; and Mr George Foulkes, Labour MP, referred to the 17 per cent increase in the salary of the Governor of the Bank of England on the top of an already large salary, 'overtaken by the boss of British Telecom, 43 per cent; the boss of National Power, 58 per cent; the boss of British Gas, 66 per cent; in a fat cat's greed race' (*Daily Telegraph*, London, 28 June 1991: 13).

   Anger at rising top salaries was 'particularly vehement against a background of what many regard as excessive profits in some groups, and larger than expected price rises for consumers' (*Guardian*, London, 13 June 1991: 13).

93 William P. Glade, *Entrepreneurship in the State Sector: CONAPSU of Mexico*, No. 203, Offprint Series, Institute of Latin American Studies, Austin, 1979.

94 For a full discussion as well as evidence from India, Kenya and Peru, see V.V. Ramanadham, *Public Enterprise and Income Distribution*, London, 1988, Chapter 2.

95 Note the criticism by the National Confederation of Officers' Associations of Central Government Undertakings that disinvestment was merely to overcome current revenue deficits (*Economic Times*, New Delhi: 3).

To cite another case: the recent privatization attempts in Spain are believed to be connected with the budget-deficit situation (*The News International*, 29 February 1992: 16).

96 In the Philippines it is widely believed that 'the government had been counting on the proceeds of the privatisation to finance its expenditures' (*The Philippine Star*, Manila, 20 June 1992: 17).

APPENDIX 1

Policy statement on privatization

Brief review of the public enterprise sector and its performance
Objectives of privatization
Modality options
Criteria in the choice of privatization candidates
Macro implications:

- the distributional consequences
- the impacts on the exchequer
- compatibility with national development strategy
- relationship to policies of administrative reform, liberalization and deregulation

Efficiency capabilities of domestic private enterprise
Establishment of a high-level Privatization Advisory Body
Creation of a technical cell with adequate resources
Publicity for privatization decisions and techniques of implementation

Source: *Guidelines on Privatisation*, United Nations Development Programme, New York, 1991: 18.

APPENDIX 2

G T & T's practices

The Public Utilities Commission in Guyana expressed concern with the following practices of Guyana Telephone and Telegraph Ltd:

The Company accepts for payment invoices made out in the name of two affiliated companies, ATN and VITELCO, in respect of which no documentary evidence has been provided to show that the goods or services to which the invoices relate have been received by G T & T.

Payments have been made to individuals and companies with which G T & T has no proven business relations.

G T & T has entered into an Agreement with ATN providing for loans by G T & T to ATN and its affiliates without the approval of its Board of Directors.

G T & T has entered into an advisory contract with ATN under which G T & T pays a fee of six per cent of gross revenues per month to ATN regardless of the amount of service provided during the month or whether any service whatever has been provided. This fee is in addition to full re-imbursement of all expenses (including the cost of overheads) for personnel provided and materials used in connection with such services.

The Commission has been unable to find any satisfactory justification for the six per cent advisory fee in terms of benefit to G T & T.

The Commission finds that the failure of G T & T to conduct its business with affiliated companies on an arms-length basis has brought seriously into question the conduct of its financial affairs.

Of particular concern to the Commission is the fact that the financial management of G T & T is in the hands of ATN with the officer in charge of G T & T's finances being the Chief Financial Officer in ATN and in the second in command being the Assistant Financial Controler of VITELCO, even though neither of these officials is in the employment of G T & T.

Source: Public Utilities Commission, 'Application of the Guyana Telephone and Telegraph Ltd. for rate increase decision,' Georgetown, November 1991.

2

PRIVATIZATION IN THE UK

George Yarrow

THE EMPIRICAL CONTEXT OF PRIVATIZATION

The pre-privatization structure of the public sector

British privatization policies have encompassed enterprises at both the central and local government levels. The analysis here will concentrate on the former, which is the area of policy that has attracted the most international attention. Collectively, state-owned enterprises that are controlled by central government are/were known in Britain as nationalized firms. They typically take the legal form of a public corporation (see Vickers and Yarrow, 1988), an institutional device that seeks to combine managerial autonomy in day-to-day decision making with political control of strategic policy decisions.

In 1979, the year which marks the beginning of the UK privatization programme, the public corporations' sector of the economy accounted for around 10.5 per cent of gross domestic product, 8 per cent of the labour force, 17 per cent of the industrial capital stock and 15 per cent of gross investment. The shape of the sector at that time is readily explicable in terms of the original motives for state ownership. These include the following.

Political ideology

The Labour Party has a commitment to public ownership that is enshrined in Clause IV of its constitution.

Utilities/networks

Public ownership is one regulatory device that has been used when attempting to correct the market failures that are likely to characterize utilities or network industries. Classic issues in these areas include the natural monopoly question and the spatial pricing structures produced by economies of density (which may adversely affect some regional and local interests).

National security

In times of emergency or perceived threats to national security, nationalization has been motivated by a desire to obtain state control of certain key resources.

Industrial strategy

Governments have frequently taken the view that a number of sectors of the economy are of particular importance in meeting public policy objectives. Where market failures are perceived in these sectors, nationalization has sometimes been the regulatory option chosen.

Declining industries and financial failure

Here government have used public ownership to slow down the rate of decline in output and employment or to forestall the bankruptcy of a major firm.

In general terms, the socialist commitment to public ownership had, in the first three-quarters of the twentieth century, generated pressure in the direction of increasing the relative size of the state-owned sector, but the *pattern* of nationalizations was much more a function of the other motives in the above list. Indeed, even in respect of the determination of the overall size of the sector, these latter motives have probably been the more important influence. For example, postal services have been publicly owned since their inception in the nineteenth century, well before the foundation of the Labour Party, and it was Winston Churchill who was the minister responsible for the nationalization of British Petroleum.

Another feature of nationalized firms in Britain, shared with many other countries, has been their concentration (in terms of assets, if not of numbers) in a relatively small number of industries. These are energy, communications, transport and water. Thus, by categorizing enterprises by industrial group and by motives for public ownership, it is possible to present a summary picture of the overall shape of the nationalized sector (see Table 2.1).

The classification of enterprises to a particular cell in the matrix is not free from ambiguities. In several cases, the motives for nationalization were mixed. Thus, for example, an ailing industry or firm was much more likely to be a candidate for public ownership if its continued existence was considered important for reasons of national security or industrial strategy. The classification therefore reflects judgements as to what was the primary motive in such cases.

Public sector performance

In the period up to 1975 the profitability of the public corporations was signficantly below that of private industry and the state sector showed a

Table 2.1 Nationalized industries and firms in 1979

	Monopoly networks	National security	Industrial strategy	Decline/ failure
Energy	Electricity Boards British Gas	British Petroleum	British National Oil Corporation	British Coal
Communications	Postal service Telecoms	Cable and Wireless		
Transport	British Rail National Bus Airports		National Freight Corporation British Airways	
Water	Water Authorities			
Other		British Sugar	National Enterprise Board British Aerospace British Steel	British Leyland (vehicles) British Shipbuilders Rolls-Royce

persistent and substantial financial deficit. Moreover, the trend in profitability between 1965 and 1975 was downwards (see Table 2.2.). Particularly large downward movements tended to occur in general election years (i.e. 1970 and 1974, and note also that a similar effect occurred in 1979). Unsurprisingly, incumbent governments, charged to exercise their stewardship in the public interest, tended to feel that the public interest would not be well served by state-sector price increases that improved the electoral prospects of the political opposition!

The difficulty in interpreting indicators of financial performance is, however, that they tell us little directly about either the internal efficiency of the enterprises concerned or the more general contribution of the nationalized industries to economic efficiency as a whole. For example, poor financial performance may be consistent with high levels of internal efficiency if the former is simply the result of government-imposed price controls. Alternatively, the financial results may be the result of implicit and explicit subsidies aimed at correcting divergencies between social and private costs. Put another way, since public ownership is frequently a response to perceived market failures, in situations where public

Table 2.2 Public corporation financial indicators as a percentage of net capital stock at replacement cost

	Gross trading surplus net of subsidies	Gross trading surplus net of subsidies & depreciation	Financial surplus net of subsidies
1985	2.6	−0.2	−2.5
1984	3.4	−0.5	−3.4
1983	4.8	0.6	−2.1
1982	4.8	0.6	−2.5
1981	4.0	0.1	−2.4
1980	3.4	−0.3	−3.3
1979	3.6	0.0	−3.4
1978	4.4	0.5	−2.4
1977	4.9	0.9	−2.9
1976	4.8	0.9	−4.5
1975	3.1	−0.3	−6.3
1974	2.4	−0.7	−5.6
1973	4.3	0.1	−4.4
1972	4.6	0.0	−4.4
1971	5.3	0.3	−4.9
1970	5.6	0.6	−4.5
1969	6.5	1.3	−3.3
1968	6.3	1.2	−5.1
1967	5.6	0.8	−7.4
1966	6.2	0.9	−7.1

Source: UK national accounts

ownership is observed, profitability and related measures are unlikely, on their own, to be reliable indicators of performance.

Turning, then, to other measures of performance, the evidence is incomplete and somewhat mixed. Where it *is* available, data on productivity movements tend to suggest that, in aggregate, between 1960 and 1975 publicly-owned enterprises did relatively well in comparison with the private sector. Table 2.3, for example, summarizes some of the results of an extensive study by the National Economic Development Office (NEDO), and includes those enterprises for which data were available for all, or almost all, of the 1960 to 1975 period.

Figures of this type have to be handled with great caution. Airways, gas and telecommunications all experienced rapid demand growth, and much of the measured improvements was almost certainly due to the realization of economies of scale rather than to shifts in production functions. More importantly, productivity *movements* are not necessarily a good indicator of the *level* of internal efficiency. Thus, it is entirely possible that the cost-efficiency of the public corporations was poor while, at the same time, their relative productivity performance was improving.

Table 2.3 Productivity increases in nationalized industries 1960–75

	Output per head	Total factor productivity
British Airways	150%	145%
British Gas	242%	116%
Electricity	127%	28%
National Coal Board	25%	n.a.
Postal Service	−6%	n.a.
Telecommunications	169%	125%
All UK manufacturing	51%	28%

Source: NEDO 1976

Unfortunately, there is little convincing evidence on this last issue. Since many of the major public corporations were monopolies there were no very obvious benchmarks (i.e. similar privately-owned British companies) against which their performance could be evaluated. International comparisons of performance with industries overseas tended to show lower productivity for the British enterprises, but precisely the same sorts of results were obtained from studies of the relative performance of the private sector.

Turning to wage rates, the NEDO study results indicate that both the level and movement of earnings in the nationalized industries were broadly in line with those in the private sector in the 1960s, but that public sector earnings then moved ahead in the early 1970s (see Table 2.4). A significant fraction of this later increase was contributed by the coal industry, where a national strike had brought forth major government concessions in 1974 (and forced an early general election), just after the world oil price shock had greatly increased the mineworkers' union's bargaining strength. Even excluding the coal industry, however, there was a clear upward trend in relative wages in the public sector between 1970 and 1975.

A similar picture emerges from evaluations of the relative prices of the nationalized industries' goods and services (see Table 2.4). Between 1960 and 1970 these moved very closely in line with consumer prices, but then jumped ahead in the mid-1970s. The latter movement is, however, unsurprising in the light of the upward pressure on energy prices from 1973 onwards and the concentration of energy industries in the public sector.

The second half of the 1970s witnessed a major shift in public policy towards the nationalized industries. Starting with the sterling crisis of 1976, governments began to place much more emphasis on financial performance in general, and upon the implications of public enterprise behaviour for the central government public sector borrowing requirement (PSBR) in particular. Of special concern was the problem that the PSBR – which is linked to, but not identical with, the fiscal deficit – had grown substantially during the first half of the decade in both

Table 2.4 Earnings and prices in the nationalized industries 1960–75

	1960	1970	1975
Earnings of full-time male manual workers relative to UK manufacturing	99.2	96.1	110.2
Price index relative to final expenditure price index (1960 = 100)	100.0	100.0	109.4

Source: NEDO 1976

absolute terms and as a proportion of gross domestic product.

In addition, the Conservative governments of the 1980s have also sought to increase the competitive pressures operating on a number of the nationalized industries. Thus, there has been a sequence of pieces of legislation designed to reduce entry barriers and facilitate the emergence of privately-owned competitors to incumbent state-owned firms in road transport, telecommunications, gas and electricity.

As Table 2.2. shows, there was some recovery in profitability from the low levels in the mid-1970s (and it should be noted that (a) the 1980 figure is depressed by the deep recession experienced in that year, (b) the 1984 and 1985 figures are depressed by the year-long coalminers' strike in that period, which seriously affected the results for coal, electricity and steel, and (c) data for the years from 1984 are influenced by the shift of major public corporations to the private sector). There was also a rather larger effect on the public corporations' financial deficit, indicating that the tighter financial constraints led to significant cut-backs in investment programmes.

The aggregate figures in Table 2.2 do, however, mask a number of very substantial changes in relative performance among the nationalized industries, which in turn provide important evidence relevant to the question of the economic impact of changes in ownership. To explore this issue further Tables 2.5 and 2.6 provide data on four of the major corporations that were retained in the public sector throughout the whole of the 1979–87 period (but note that British Steel was privatized at the end of 1988).

Each of these corporations had relatively poor productivity and profit performance in the 1970s and the tables show what has happened in the more recent period. The picture is somewhat erratic, largely as a result of a series of strikes in the industries as labour unions resisted the cost-cutting pressures induced by tighter financial controls. Thus there were major strikes in steel (1980), rail (1982) and coal (1984/5), the last of which was particularly serious and had major impacts throughout the state sector in general and on the electricity, rail and steel industries in particular. It can also be noted that the profit figures quoted in Table 2.6 are calculated on the basis of treating some

Table 2.5 Steel, coal, rail and postal services: annual percentage changes in labour productivity since 1979

Financial year ending in:	Steel	Coal	Rail	Post Office
1980	8.3	3.1	–	–
1981	−9.0	0.4	1.7	–
1982	54.3	3.5	−6.4	–
1983	1.5	1.6	12.8	2.8
1984	31.0	−1.3	*	1.7
1985	1.4	−13.6	3.7	4.0
1986	11.1	30.7	2.8	3.7
1987	1.6	20.9	2.1	3.5
1988	24.0	10.0	8.3	2.8

Note: *Change in accounting year
Source: Corporation reports and accounts

Table 2.6 Steel, coal, rail and postal services: real profits before interest and tax, £ millions at 1980 prices

Financial year ending in:	Steel	Coal	Rail	Post Office
1980	−395	51	−7	47
1981	−463	95	34	25
1982	−194	−20	−72	78
1983	−224	−64	68	123
1984	−82	−261	*	102
1985	−31	−1143	−184	105
1986	91	436	42	98
1987	153	250	50	88
1988	307	141	74	111

Source: Corporation accounts

government grants and subsidies as corporation revenues. Particularly in the cases of coal and railways, the financial position would be considerably worse in the absence of these payments (in 1988, for example, British Rail received a grant worth over £500 million in 1980 prices).

Nevertheless, some clear patterns do emerge from the statistics. All of the industries covered achieved better productivity performance than in the 1970s. The turnaround was most dramatic, and occurred earliest, in steel, where the consequent improvement in profit performance can be seen in Table 2.6. Rapidly increasing productivity in coal has been observed only since the end of the 1984/5 strike (and note that profit performance since that year should be interpreted in the light of falling energy prices).

Significantly, the improvements in rail and postal services have occurred at a slower and less erratic pace. These are industries less subject to competition than steel and coal, so that tighter, government-imposed financial constraints could be more easily met by raising prices. The ability of monopolistic state-owned firms to behave in this latter manner highlights one of the defects of the reformed control system for the public sector. If pricing policy is constrained by competition, the imposition of stricter financial disciplines can be expected to lead to firms focusing upon cost-cutting strategies (as it has in steel and coal). On the other hand, where demand for a corporation's outputs is less sensitive to price the effect will be more diffuse: higher financial targets can be met also by significantly increasing prices. Evidence from other nationalized industries such as electricity and water supports the hypothesis that the impact of stricter financial targets on productivity performance has been much weaker for state monopolies than for more competitive state enterprises.

PRIVATIZATION: THE CONSTRAINTS

The major programme of privatization of state-owned enterprises in Britain commenced in 1979 with the sale of a tranche of stock in British Petroleum (BP), a company that was already in part privately owned. This sale followed a precedent that had been set by the previous Labour administration which had likewise sold a tranche of stock in the company, largely as a funding exercise stimulated by what at the time was a relatively large public sector fiscal deficit. However, from 1979 onwards, privatization of state-owned enterprises was quickly established as a major component of the government's economic policy and a whole series of flotations followed the BP issue. The major asset sales to mid-1992 are shown in Table 2.7.

The British privatization programme was developed and implemented with remarkable speed, and is perhaps most notable both for the relative absence of major constraints (at least in comparison with many countries) and for the vigour with which the UK Government tackled the constraints which did exist. Thus, by 1992 only three of the major nationalized industries featured in Table 2.1 were still in existence, namely coal, rail and postal service, and, as a result of pit closures in the 1980s, the coal industry was of significantly lesser economic significance than it had been in 1979. Plans to privatize parts of the railways and of the Post Office were announced in July 1992.

Nevertheless, although obstacles to privatization did not substantially prevent the implementation of a fairly rapid divestiture programme, they did affect the timing and form of certain aspects of the process in significant ways. A number of these effects are considered below.

Capital markets

Despite the size and sophistication of the London stock market, there was concern in the early 1980s about its capacity to absorb new equity issues on the

Table 2.7 Major asset sales 1979–91

Company	Year(s) of share issue
British Petroleum	1979, 1981, 1983, 1987
British Aerospace	1981, 1985
Cable and Wireless	1981, 1983, 1985
Amersham International	1982
National Freight Corporation	1982
Britoil	1982, 1985
Associated British Ports	1983, 1984
Enterprise Oil	1984
Jaguar	1984
British Telecom	1984, 1991
Trustee Savings Bank	1986
British Gas	1986
British Airways	1987
Royal Ordnance	1987
Rolls Royce	1987
British Airports Authority	1987
Rover Group	1988
British Steel	1988
The ten water authorities	1989
The twelve electricity area boards	1990
The two Scottish electricity boards	1991
Non-nuclear electricity generation	1991

scale required by divestitures of companies the size of British Telecom. Thus, the early sales of equity by the state were considerably larger in financial terms than had been the typical new equity issues of privately owned companies in previous periods.

The result was a tendency to conservatism in the packaging and pricing of the British Telecom divestiture in particular. A relatively unintrusive regulatory environment was put in place, the offer price was set relatively low, underwriting provisions were extensive, and a tranche of shares was made available overseas (see Tables 2.8 and 2.9).

The immediate implications of this were effects such as significant under-pricing of the offer relative to market prices (and hence government revenues foregone), windfall transfers of wealth to overseas nationals, and high transactions costs of the sale.

Administrative complexity

One option available to the government in privatizing publicly-owned monopolies such as British Telecom and British Gas was to break up the existing corporations, with a view both to assisting with the goal of promoting

Table 2.8 Pricing of shares (£)

Company	Gross proceeds	Offer price	First instalment	Opening price	% gain	Value of gain
BT	3,900m	1.30	0.50	0.93	86%	1,290m
Trustee Savings Bank	1,360m	1.00	0.50	0.85	70%	476m
British Gas	5,600m	1.35	0.50	0.625	25%	518m
British Airways	900m	1.25	0.65	1.09	68%	317m
Rolls Royce	1,360m	1.70	0.85	1.47	73%	496m
British Airports	920m	2.45	1.00	1.46	46%	172m

Source: *Financial Times* various dates

Table 2.9 Costs of major assets sales

Company	Expenses (£ million)	Expenses as % of proceeds
Cable and Wireless	7	3.1
British Aerospace	6	3.8
Amersham	3	4.6
Britoil	17	3.2
Associated British Ports	2	11.2
Enterprise Oil	11	2.8
BT	263	6.8
British Gas	360	6.4
British Airways	42	4.7

Source: National Audit Office

competition and to establishing a more effective regulatory structure (e.g. by allowing the regulators to compare the performance of different utilities and make use of 'yardstick' competition).

However, in addition to the problem that capital market investors would have been less enthusiastic about purchasing newly created companies with no previous commercial track record, the organizational restructuring of the industries prior to privatization would have been a task of some considerable administrative and legal complexity. It would, therefore, have delayed the flotations.

In the early 1980s *rapid* privatization was a key policy target, not least because one of the underlying objectives of the programme was to improve the overall financial position of the central government which, in that period, had a substantial fiscal deficit. Hence, administrative and legal constraints were a significant factor in decisions not to attempt major pre-privatization restructuring of the telecoms and gas industries.

By the late 1980s the position had changed somewhat. The central government was running a financial surplus and the impact of privatization on the public finances was a less pressing consideration. In the cases of both the electricity and water industries a much greater amount of administrative effort was expended in developing appropriate organizational and regulatory structures.

For example, the initial plan to privatize water, announced in a White Paper in 1986, was abandoned because of objections to the planned retention by private companies of many of the (environmental) regulatory tasks previously entrusted to the publicly-owned water authorities. A new scheme, based upon the separation of environmental regulation and commercial operations was eventually implemented late in 1989.

Similarly, electricity is the one example thus far of a major utility industry that was restructured prior to privatization, among other things with a view to promoting competition in the industry. Development of the new organizational and regulatory structures was a highly complex administrative and legal task, but this was preferred to a quicker route to the private sector.

Profitability

Perhaps the major constraint on privatization in the UK has been the profitability of some of the public corporations. This explains, for example, why state monopolies such as telecoms and gas (with strong cash flows) were privatized well ahead of much more natural candidates for private ownership such as steel, coal and vehicle manufacture. The problems in the latter cases were the heavy losses being made by the firms concerned.

Arguably, private owners should be willing to take on loss-making concerns if there is a reasonable prospect of future profit and provided, of course, that the price is right. Thus, the parcels operations of the Post Office are currently loss-making activities, but plans for their privatization were nevertheless announced in July 1992. If, however, the losses are substantial and the period required to turn the situation around is relatively long, then the 'right price' may involve promises of continuing state subsidies for some given period. The 'agency' costs of such an arrangement may then make privatization a less attractive option.

In the case of the steel industry, then, privatization did not occur until 1988, by which time the industry's financial performance had been radically improved *within the public sector*. A similar story occurs in the case of the privatization of the Rover Group, the state-owned car manufacturer. At the time of writing, the coal industry is still in the public sector largely because of the difficulty of reducing it to a size where it will be profitable at world market prices for coal. And the plan to retain the rail track and signalling infrastructure within the public sector for the foreseeable future is based largely on the difficulties of making these activities profitable (unlike railway stations which, with their property assets and retailing opportunities, clearly offer profit opportunities).

Finally, and perhaps the clearest example of the operation of the profitability constraint, it can be noted that the government's plans to privatize nuclear power, announced in the 1988 White Paper on the privatization of the electricity industry, had to be abandoned in the face of the reluctance of private investors to take on the potentially very large contingent liabilities surrounding the technology. Even the attempt to compensate investors by bundling the nuclear stations with an attractive portfolio of thermal power stations failed to overcome the problem.

Social and political influences

Although the UK privatization programme marked a sharp departure from the prevailing political consensus that Britain was to continue to be a 'mixed economy', the divestitures were achieved without having to overcome major social and political barriers. The Labour Party opposed most of the larger privatizations, as did the trade unions in the industries concerned. In steel and coal there were major strikes, but these were directed at pre-privatization policies of retrenchment, rather than at privatization *per se*. In both cases the strikes were defeated.

On the other hand, managements of enterprises being privatized do appear to have placed significant constraints on the programme. Given that the co-operation of incumbent managements was important in enabling governments to proceed smoothly and swiftly with divestiture, these managements were, in many cases, able to extract favourable concessions from the politicians. One pay-off here was a government willingness, particularly in the earlier stages of privatization, to allow organizations to be sold off without major structural surgery (see also pp. 72–3). Another was the use made of 'golden shares' and limits on the size of individual shareholdings.

Such devices were aimed at protecting the newly privatized firm from early takeover, and were justified in terms of the advantages of allowing the enterprise a chance to adjust to its new position as a private company. Whatever these advantages, however, golden shares and limits on shareholdings served to protect incumbent managements from one of the disciplines that confronts the managers of most large privately-owned companies.

Another possible motive for steps to hinder takeovers is that such measures also serve to protect the government from the political reaction that might occur if some of the former nationalized industries came under foreign control. In this context it is worth recalling that some at least of the nationalizations were influenced by national security objectives and others by consideration of national industrial policy.

Other factors

A miscellaneous range of other factors have served as minor constraints on the privatization programme. For example, Her Majesty the Queen is thought to be opposed to the privatization of the *Royal* Mail, and this may help account for the fact that the Post Office is the only profit-making nationalized industry that has not yet been privatized. Another important influence on this outcome, however, is the difficulty of reconciling universal service obligations with the promotion of competition. While government could directly subsidize a private company to serve unprofitable (usually remote) areas of the country, the agency costs of public subsidies of this kind reduce the attractiveness of the privatization option (see p. 74 above).

In the case of British Airways, privatization was delayed by litigation in the courts over airline conduct on North Atlantic routes. Thus, uncertainties surrounding the possible liabilities that British Airways might have to face in the event of an unfavourable legal outcome made pricing the shares a difficult exercise. Moreover, leaving aside the technical problems, the possibility of smaller investors eventually facing substantial capital losses was not politically attractive.

IMPACTS OF PRIVATIZATION

Efficiency

Despite the diversity of economic conditions associated with its constituent asset sales and the limited nature of the evidence that is currently available, it is nevertheless possible to draw some general lessons from the British privatization programme. However, while the results are generally unsurprising in the light of established economic theory, they are at odds with some of the more simplistic views concerning the impact of changes in property rights. In particular, the hypothesis that privatization *per se* will quickly lead to substantial improvements in the performances of inefficient state-owned enterprises is not well supported by the data.

It is true that, in many cases, there has been a history of improving profitability and labour productivity since privatization, but, over the relevant period, the same is also true of both the private and public sectors more generally. At the end of the 1970s, virtually all parts of British industry were lagging behind their international competitors across a series of dimensions of economic performance. And, over the last decade, most sectors have significantly improved their relative performance. Indeed, the most spectacular improvement of all has been by the publicly-owned British Steel Corporation which, from a position well down the international league table, had become the least-cost major steel producer in the world by 1988.

Although, when judged against the appropriate benchmarks, it is difficult to find substantial and general performance improvements that are *directly* attributable to privatization as such, it is nevertheless possible to advance arguments in favour of the British programme that are based upon more indirect consequences. In particular, it can be argued that (a) the desire to privatize itself acted as a spur to improving the performance of state-owned enterprises in preparation for flotation and that (b) although it is possible for a determined government to provide strong efficiency incentives for public enterprises, this outcome is a matter of discretionary choice and is not compelled – as it is after privatization – by competitive pressures in the marketplace.

The implication of (a) is that, but for the privatization programme, the profit and productivity performance of state-owned enterprises in the 1980s would have been rather poorer than they turned out to be, while the implication of (b) is that, in future, a government less committed to reducing state subventions to public industry would allow the enterprises to return to less efficient modes of operation. Put another way, privatization, while not strictly necessary for the introduction of enhanced performance incentives, is an effective way of establishing commitments to those changed incentives which, because they are not easily reversed, are likely to be relatively durable.

Both lines of reasoning have merit, and are supported by the data on enterprise performance *before* privatization and by the more general history of government interventions and policy reversals in respect of British nationalized industries since 1945. They are, however, subject to a number of major caveats.

First, substantial improvements in the efficiency of major nationalized industries appear to have taken place without the immediate prospect of impending privatization. British Steel in the early 1980s is one case in point (it was only in later years that transfer to the private sector came to be viewed as a feasible prospect), and the Post Office, which has never been on the privatization list, is another.

Second, argument/hypothesis (b) assumes that once firms are in the private sector they will be subjected to strong and persistent pressures to perform efficiently, which in turn assumes that they will face substantial competitive pressures. This assumption is warranted for a number of the smaller asset sales in respect of product market competition, but the government has deliberately sought to weaken capital market competition by offering managements initial protection from unwanted takeover bids. Given that, again as a matter of deliberate policy, share ownership in these companies is highly dispersed, political discretion has partly been replaced by managerial discretion. And managerial discretion has, in a number of cases, led to policies of growth via acquisitions which, from the perspective of shareholders, appear often to have been of doubtful merit.

Third, in those cases where the relevant state enterprise enjoyed substantial product market power, privatization was typically not accompanied by radical measures to increase competitive pressures. The most extreme example of this outcome occurred in respect of British Gas, but the BT and BAA flotations can also be criticized on similar grounds. Thus, preoccupation with ensuring a rapid transfer of ownership led to relatively little effort being applied to finding ways of opening up markets to greater actual and potential competition: state monopoly was replaced by private monopoly.

Finally, the privatizations of telecommunications, gas, water, electricity and airports have been accompanied by the establishment of new regulatory regimens which, *inter alia*, include systems of price controls. This raises the problem that such industry-specific regulatory institutions may themselves become all too easily available instruments for future *ad hoc* political interventions in the industries. That is, the barriers to the exercise of political discretion that have been created by privatization may not in fact be very great, and future political disagreements about how the industries should be run may focus less on *ownership* and more on *control* (i.e. regulation) than in the past.

This last point is of particular significance when viewed from a longer-term perspective. Before nationalization, many of the major industries discussed above were extensively regulated, including coal, steel and rail as well as utilities such as gas and electricity. And the experience of that earlier period offers little encouragement for the view that extensively regulated private enterprise is substantially more efficient than public enterprise. For the future, then, the success of the British privatization programme is likely to depend crucially upon the extent to which further steps are taken to strengthen the operation of competitive forces in a number of the relevant industries.

The public finances

Much of the initial impetus for rapid privatization in the UK came from its anticipated effects on the public finances. Thus, in the very early stages of the programme, many of the flotations were of oil companies, and these sales represented to a large extent the disposal of government stakes in oil reserves under the North Sea. Similarly, the first of the major utility privatizations was of an enterprise, British Telecom, whose large investment programme was implicitly making large calls on the exchequer (since BT's only sources of finance were internal cash flow and the exchequer).

In addition to receipts from sales of shares and the removal of requirements to finance investment programmes from government budgets, the public finances have also been significantly affected by the increase in corporation tax receipts from privatized companies. Although the state gave up rights to future income flows in return for lump sum payments from investors, it did not give up *all* rights in relation to those flows. Thus, with corporation tax for large companies at a rate of 35 per cent, the state continues to lay claim to over a third of future profit flows, even when the divestiture is complete.

When divestiture is only partial, the state's interest is, of course, even larger than this. For example, between 1984 and 1991 the government continued to hold a shareholding of nearly 50 per cent in British Telecom. Combining this with the corporation tax factor then, it can be seen that approximately two-thirds of British Telecom's profits over the period were claimed by the state.

Particularly in the cases of the utility industries, which contained very substantial elements of monopoly in their activities, the post-privatization periods are marked by quite rapidly increasing profits. Corporation tax receipts from these sectors have therefore been particularly bouyant.

Impact on labour

Workers in the industries and enterprises shown in Table 2.1 have been very considerably affected by public policy reforms in the 1980s. It is, however, arguable that the major impacts have been the result not of privatization as such but rather as a consequence of the increased priority attached to financial objectives over this period (indeed, privatization itself can be interpreted as an effect of this change in objectives).

Many of the industries and enterprises concerned reduced employment considerably during the 1980s, including British Steel, British Coal, British Airways, Associated British Ports and British Rail. Although some of this reduction in employment occurred after divestiture, the bulk of it occurred before flotation, and in some cases appears to have been largely unrelated to any immediate plans for asset transfer.

Nor is there any indication that privatization has had a great deal of effect on wage rates, other than on the salaries of senior managers which have increased very sharply to bring them more into line with the salaries of senior executives in other parts of the private sector, often to the considerable political embarrassment of the government. Where workers have taken up options to acquire shares in their enterprise on favourable terms they have, of course, tended to benefit from the general increase in value of the privatized enterprise. The most spectacular example of this effect occurred in the case of the National Freight Corporation, which was privatized via a management/employee buyout: those who purchased shares in 1983 saw their value increase over fortyfold by early 1990 (see Table 2.10).

Table 2.10 National Freight's share price (£)

1982	1984	1985	1986	1987	1988	1990	(March)
0.05	0.16	0.35	0.78	1.35	1.75	2.23	

Sources: Company reports and accounts; *Financial Times*

Distribution

The redistribution of wealth that has occurred as a result of the pricing of shares at the time of flotation has attracted a good deal of comment in the UK. The typical pattern, particularly for utility privatizations, has been for the shares to be underpriced relative to the expected market equilibrium. Thus, while some degree of underpricing is a general qualitative characteristic of new equity issues by privately-owned companies, the discounts have been much higher than normal for privatization issues (see Table 2.8).

Those successfully acquiring firms at the offer price have therefore been able to make significant short-term capital gains, which represents a redistribution of wealth to them and away from taxpayers in general. Since the number of successful investors, albeit in millions, is considerably lower than the number of taxpayers the redistribution is characterized by an average loss to each taxpayer that is much smaller than the average gain to successful investors. Moreover, whereas the gains have been highly visible, the losses have tended to be less obvious (taxpayers do not see money disappearing from their bank accounts!).

This redistribution of wealth has been a highly effective political weapon in the hands of government, which has been able to point to the financial benefits its policies have brought to a highly important and influential part of the electorate. Indeed, many of the offers have been specifically targeted at small investors who have received priority treatment in the allocation of shares.

Privatization in the UK has had a variety of other distributional effects, one of the most important of which has been the change in price structures in industries such as telecoms and electricity. While in the public sector, the price structures of a number of public corporations were such as to cross-subsidize supplies to the domestic sector at the expense of the commercial and industrial sectors. Since privatization, there has been considerable tariff 'rebalancing' in telecoms, so that, while average prices have fallen considerably in real terms since 1984, the bulk of those price improvements has been accounted for by business accounts. More precisely, there has been a substantial increase in the price of domestic telecoms services *relative* to the price of business services. Similarly, since the announcement of the industry's privatization in February 1988 there has been a substantial increase in domestic prices of electricity relative to commercial/industrial prices of electricity (see Table 2.11).

Table 2.11 Index of domestic electricity prices relative to industrial electricity prices

1986	1987	1988	1989	1990	1991
101	104	104	104	112	120

Source: *Energy Trends*

REFERENCES

NEDO (1976)

Vickers, J. and Yarrow, G. (1988) *Privatization: An Economic Analysis*, Cambridge: MIT Press.

3

PRIVATIZATION IN EAST GERMANY

Dieter Bös

THE POLICY OF THE TREUHANDANSTALT

As of 31 May 1992, in East Germany 3,775 out of a total of 11,759 (32 per cent) industrial enterprises have been transferred from public into private ownership, i.e. have been privatized. In 3,838 further cases, enterprises were partially privatized; in most of these cases, however, the majority of the companies' shares are still publicly held.[1] In official publications the numbers of full and partial privatizations are often added together to impress the general public. These reveal some 7,613 cases of privatization.[2]

However different the ways of counting the cases of privatization, it can be stated that no other country has ever privatized so many industrial enterprises in so short a time. (Recall the date of the German unification: 3 October 1990!) It is hoped that at the end of 1992, only 2,500 East German industrial firms will still be fully or partially owned by the government. It is also thought that at the end of 1993, no East German industrial enterprises in public ownership will be left which could be candidates for an immediate privatization.[3] (Privatizing small shops, restaurants or hotels is comparatively easy in East Germany, as in any other former communist country.[4])

The agency in charge of privatization is the Treuhandanstalt (THA). Originally founded by the Government of the German Democratic (GDR) in December 1989, it was further restructured in June 1990. The activities of THA depend on the viability of their 'client' firms:

1   privatizing firms which could be viable in a market environment,
2   governmental restructuring of firms to make them viable, or
3   liquidating firms which are non-viable.

Such a catalogue can be meaningful only if precise definitions of the relevant terms are given. With respect to the *viability* of a firm, an often-quoted definition was given by Akerlof and his group in Berkeley in their empirical study on East German industrial enterprises.[5] They obtained cost data, previously used for GDR planning, which they adjusted to the present situation by:

81

1   removing all profits, interest and depreciation in excess of repairs necessary for current operation, and
2   taking account of changes in the tax structure, in the cost of imported intermediate inputs, and in wages.

The resulting modified short-run average variable costs were then compared with the respective world market prices. Consequently, a firm was denoted as 'non-viable' if, at world market prices, it could not cover the short-run average variable costs. However, a firm considered to be 'non-viable' cannot be sold by the THA. Akerlof and his co-authors calculated that, as of October 1990, only 8 per cent of the East German industrial labour force was employed in viable firms as a result of the price-cost squeeze. Obviously this calculation grossly underestimated viability, otherwise the THA could not have sold as many firms as it did. Hence, viability of an industrial enterprise obviously must be defined so as to include the restructuring by the private investor who buys the enterprise. The best definition would then be as follows: viability is decreed if the present value of revenues from sales minus the present value of costs, including costs of restructuring, is positive. In this definition revenues and costs are as calculated by the private investor, not by the THA.

In contrast to the above definition of viability, there is also the possibility of governmental restructuring, i.e. by the THA alone or in co-operation with one of the East German states. Governmental restructuring has sometimes been postulated for the following reasons:[6]

1   If private investors restructure an enterprise, they will not take account of externalities, productivity spillovers, etc. From a general economic point of view, the explicit consideration of these effects may be worthwhile and restructuring by the THA would be the adequate instrument.
2   The THA may enjoy economies of scale and of scope in restructuring. The THA can pool the risks of restructuring many firms, including environmental damage to be repaid, property claims by previous owners, and unexpected demand developments. The THA can also hold out until the necessary infrastructure has been developed and the administration has become more reliable.
3   Western private investors are better informed on western markets and on the organizational aspects of a firm to be privatized. However, the THA might possess informational advantage with respect to the East German environment, for example, how to treat East German employees, etc.[7]
4   The THA may have political advantages in restructuring. As a government agency, it has direct channels to other government agencies and could, for example, arrange a better co-ordination between restructuring of firms and developing the infrastructure. It could also exert political pressure to modify laws that inhibit the restructuring of firms.

These arguments look convincing from the point of view of second-best theory.

One could easily think of theoretical models where the above advantages of the THA more than outweigh its being trapped in a principal–agent relationship with the firm to be privatized. However, in my opinion, the second-best economic theories simply miss the point, which is eminently political. I do not think that a large state-owned holding company is a good instrument for expediting restructuring. The second-best arguments restore the theories of planning which we want to eliminate.[8] It would be like moving from Marx I to Marx II. Moreover, a THA in full command of restructuring would not act according to a second-best model. It is to be feared that under political pressure, the THA would try to preserve firms which should otherwise be liquidated. 'Restructuring' is often used as a label to disguise subsidization of non-viable firms. In particular, the THA would try to preserve jobs because that is the government's mandate. For these political reasons, I think that restructuring should be removed from the responsibilities of the THA.[9] Its activities should be reduced to privatization or liquidation.

CONSTRAINTS

High-wage policies[10]

East German expectations are often excessively high, be it the 1:1 conversion of East and West German marks, or be it the rapid increase in East German wages to reach the West German level in a few years. West Germany, on the other hand, may bail out non-viable East German firms for too long, where the non-viability is precisely brought about by high wages which significantly exceed East German productivity. A country like Poland could not afford to pay such high wages *and* keep the firms alive; hence Polish workers have to accept low wages. Only a rich country like West Germany can opt for a policy of high wages *and* intense subsidization of non-viable firms. Such a policy is extremely costly because it ignores the trade-off between wages and jobs.

The background of such a policy is the special German internal migration problem. There are two types of migration which German policy makers fear. The first is a high unemployment migration, brought about by high East German wages. Although the unemployment benefits are high, East Germans seem to be quite averse to lasting unemployment, even in spite of the difficulties they would have to face if they moved to the West.[11] The second type of migration is a low-wage migration, for which the wage differentials between East and West Germany are the main driving force. This type of migration makes it difficult to adjust the East German wages to the development of labour productivity.

However, any policy of moderate unemployment coupled with moderate wage increases was made impossible by the trade unions who used the argument of imminent high migration to advocate a policy of high minimum wages. Unfortunately, the trade unions met no resistance on the employers' side.[12] This shifted the responsibility for the employment policy to the Federal government which, in turn, pushed the Treuhandanstalt to rank job preservation quite high on the scale of its objectives.

It should be stressed that the policy of retraining and thus promoting human capital should be intensified in order to increase labour productivity and allow it to catch up with increasing wages. Labour productivity will, of course, increase because of the recent influx of investment capital into East Germany. The scale effect of capital incentives (investment premiums, tax credits, accelerated depreciation) makes them an alternative to wage subsidies, implying a tendency toward increased employment. However, capital subsidies increase the relative price of labour which, in the present situation of very high East German wages, leads to an even more extensive substitution of capital for labour. The obvious consequence is then overly capital-intensive industries[13] and a tendency toward reduced employment. This is an imminent danger in East Germany since quite generous capital subsidies have recently been provided for investment purposes.[14] It is the hope of government and trade unions that eventually the scale effect of capital subsidies will outweigh the substitution effect, thus solving the employment problem in spite of the high wages. This hope is overly optimistic.

Property rights – the problem of restitution in kind[15]

In the treaty on German unity, the original owners whose individual property was expropriated by either the Nazis or the GDR were explicitly entitled to plead for restitution in kind.[16] However, former owners may be given monetary compensation instead of restitution in kind, if this is in the interest of prompt economic recovery.[17] For political reasons, there is no in-kind restitution for properties nationalized in the Soviet-occupied zone of Germany (1945–9). However, as the constitutional court in Karlsruhe ruled in 1991, in these cases, the former owners may claim a monetary compensation.

The 1945–9 nationalizations, however, constitute an important part of East German nationalizations because, during this time, the large estates in the Soviet-occupied zone were taken away from their owners. Approximately a third of land property was nationalized during that time. In my opinion, many Germans, even in the West, would oppose restitution in kind in these cases. However, in other cases of nationalization, the idea of restitution in kind seems quite natural. Take, for instance, any of the small- or medium-sized enterprises which were nationalized in 1972.[18] In 80 per cent of these, the former owners still work as managers of their former firms. In such cases, the German lawyers' principle of restitution in kind seems equitable and appealing.

From the economic point of view, the principle of restitution in kind should not be applied as the general rule in a transition from planned to market economies. Restitution in kind takes time. Claims for restitution must be carefully examined, although the relevant documents and registers, in particular land registers, are not easily accessible. The final decision has to be made by government officials who typically do not want to make a decision because often they still sympathize with the old regime. Moreover, and equally often, they simply feel uncertain as to how to decide on the basis of the new West German law and hence try to shirk responsibility for such decisions. In fact, uncleared property claims are a major obstacle for the transition of the East German economy. Although an investor can be given the property unless the original owner offers a comparably good investment- and job-guarantee plan, this legal provision has been applied in only a few cases. The whole 'reprivatization' of small enterprises has nearly come to a stop since the unification, although this policy flourished in the last months of the former GDR.

Other constraints

It is impossible to render an extensive treatment of all the various impediments which hinder the more rapid development of the East German economy. However, a catalogue of the most important changes which must be orchestrated is given in the following. These are relevant both for the successful privatization of existing firms and for the establishment of new firms. They include:

1   improvement of the infrastructure;
2   improvement of the public administration;
3   increase in bank flexibility for loan-grants to potential new enterpreneurs;
4   training of East German managers to promote entrepreneurial spirit;
5   retraining of East German employees to stimulate occupational changes;
6   replacement of minimum wage provisions; and
7   weakening of labour market rigidities.

IMPACTS

To evaluate the impacts of privatization in East Germany, we should first briefly describe how the THA proceeds when privatizing an enterprise. The enterprise is sold not at an auction, but on the basis of negotiations between the THA and bidders who are willing to take over the enterprise. In these negotiations three basic problems must first be cleared:

1   ownership risks (is there a claim from a former owner?),
2   environmental problems (problems of contaminated soil, etc.), and
3   firm's indebtedness to the state (formerly an important part of financing the government's budget).

The THA shares with the investor, or even fully bears, environmental and ownership risks. It also enters into some agreement with respect to servicing former company debts. The agency sells firms at a low price, sometimes at even DM 1; however, these sales are coupled with investment pledges and job guarantees (with penalties to be paid by those investors who do not abide by their commitments).

This particular procedure has been chosen by the THA to guarantee the development of an industrialized economy in East Germany. It had been feared that West German investors would buy the East German potential competitors, not with the intention of innovating the outdated technology, but with the intention of closing down production and using the land for storage houses for the western products to be sold in East Germany.

As a result of this policy, the THA reports investment pledges of DM 138.5 billion and job guarantees of 1.17 million employees (as of the end of May 1992). Unfortunately, however, only some 40 per cent of jobs in East German industrial enterprises could be secured when the THA decided on the existence or non-existence of such jobs. For details see Table 3.1.

The concentration on investment and jobs has led to high deficits for the THA, as shown in Table 3.2. The deficit is financed by borrowing in capital and

Table 3.1 Reduction in employment in THA-owned firms (in thousands)

	Employment in THA firms (1)	Decrease in employment (2)	Number accounted for by employment guarantees in THA firms sold (as % of (2)) (3)	Number accounted for by labour-shedding and closures (as % of (2)) (4)
1/7/1990	4,000			
1/1/1991	2,937	1,063	201(18.9%)	862(81.1%)
1/7/1991	2,115	822	338(41.1%)	484(58.9%)
1/1/1992	1,565	550	384(69.8%)	166(30.2%)
1/4/1992	1,235	330	155(47.0%)	175(53.0%)
Total (end of March 1992)		2,765	1,078(39.0%)	1,687(61.0%)

Source: Updated version of Table 3 in Carlin and Mayer 1992: 7; based originally on Kühl 1991: 682–3.

Table 3.2 1991 budget of THA (DM billion)

Revenues		Expenditures	
Privatizations	15.8	Interest and repayment of debt	13.8
Others	1.1	Restructuring of firms	12.9
Deficit (debt financed)	20.8	Cost of sale of firms	4.8
		Others	6.2

Source: Informationsdienst des Instituts der Deutschen Wirtschaft, No. 26, 37, 43, 1991.

money markets. According to the treaty on German unity, the borrowing limits for 1990 and 1991 amounted to DM 25 billion. For 1992, borrowing of DM 32 billion is expected. Since the THA is a government agency, the Federal government is obliged to pay the THA's deficit. After a closure of the THA the Federal government will be responsible for repayment of the debt principle and interest.

It is a legitimate fear that in the next few years the THA's deficit will remain in the DM 30–40 billion region. This could occur in response to political pressure not to liquidate non-viable industrial enterprises, but to keep them artificially alive. In Bös (1992)[19] I argued that by the end of 1993 the THA will be left with firms which private investors are unwilling to take over because they are considered to be non-viable, even after restructuring. In particular, shipyards, steel, coal and chemical industries will constitute the core of the doomed remnants of the former GRD economy. THA is unlikely to liquidate all those firms in the next few years. On the contrary, it is to be feared that by subsidizing such firms for the next ten or so years, the mistakes of West German industrial policy makers with respect to shipyards in Bremen or coal mining in the Saarland will be repeated.[20] Of course, the clear-cut recipe for the THA is to liquidate those firms which have not been sold by, say, end-1993. But how can we make sure that such a policy is actually applied? Unemployment in East Germany will be high in December 1993, even without closing all of the remaining THA firms, and the Federal government will be eager to capture votes for the end-1994 election of the German Bundestag. Given this situation, the THA then will be under pressure not to liquidate too many firms.

At that stage, the THA will have become a liability. What can be done to abolish the THA in due course? In Bös 1992 I suggested a sunset provision: the annual borrowing limits of the THA should be set for the next seven years such that the limits continually decrease over time and equal zero by the year 2000, thus signalling the government's determination to end the THA's activities by that time. Of course, the government's ability to commit itself credibly to such a financial policy can be seriously called to question, particularly since the credibility of the present government has severely suffered from broken promises such as the introduction of an income-tax surcharge in spite of earlier pledges that German unification would take place without tax increases. The financial means to be distributed by the fund on 'Germany unity' were also intended to decrease from 1991 to 1994. Meanwhile, however, these financial means follow a non-decreasing pay schedule.[21] Would not the same happen to the planned financial means of the THA? Unfortunately, this is a real possibility. However, even then the original law on decreasing THA's funds would have signalled the government's intention not to let the THA go on forever and would have presented a political barrier against easy increases in its funding.

CONCLUSION

Privatization in East Germany has been a big-bang policy. In contrast to the policy applied in other post-communist states, no gradualist strategies were chosen. At the moment of unification the idea prevailed in West Germany that the 'big brother' could bail out the poor relative through a short-run policy. Meanwhile the advantages and shortcomings of such a policy can clearly be seen.

The main advantage, undoubtedly, is a more rapid convergence of the economic status in East and West Germany,[22] which seems expedient due to the internal migration problem.

However, the shortcomings of this myopic policy can also clearly be seen. The quick sale of firms implies lower revenues from privatization and hence makes the process of economic unification more costly. In spite of all the job guarantees, the Treuhand policy is one of the reasons for the high East German unemployment of approximately 14 per cent (compared to the 5.5 per cent in West Germany).

A considerable part of the East German population has become embittered in recent months. The rapid privatization policy is one of the more important reasons for this embitterment; first because many East Germans see the privatization as a rapid sell-out to West German investors. For the East Germans, this implies losing their own economic identity. Second, problems have arisen as a result of the rapidly increasing high rates of unemployment. (One should never forget that being unemployed is a totally new traumatic experience for someone who never had much in terms of material wealth, but who was at least 100 per cent certain of a secure job.) However, it is fair to state that a large part of the embitterment has its roots in the unrealistic expectations of East Germans. (Unfortunately, West German policy makers are partly responsible for raising false hopes.)

In spite of this growing embitterment, I do not see any policy that the THA might have applied which could have proved better. Proceeding more slowly would have cost taxpayers billions of DMs just to keep East German firms alive before privatization. Moreover, reducing the rate of unemployment would have implied a costly policy of subsidization of East German industrial firms.

NOTES

1 This holds for 3,283 out of these 3,838 cases.
2 Source: *Monthly Bulletin of Treuhandanstalt* (THA), 31 May 1992. For details on these and other data see the statistical appendix to this chapter.
3 Interview with B. Breuel, the chief of the Treuhandanstalt, as quoted, for instance, in *Die Zeit*, 22 May 1992.
4 As of 31 December 1991, a total of 22,300 small enterprises of that type were privatized by the Treuhandanstalt (THA). Source: *Zahlen zur wirtschaftlichen Entwicklung der Bundesrepublik Deutschland* 1992, Institut der Deutschen Wirtschaft Köln, Table 9.
5 Akerlof *et al.* 1991.

6   See Bös 1992: 16–18.
7   See Möschel 1991.
8   Not surprisingly, the October 1991 reform proposal of the union of the metal workers (IG Metall) speaks of 'volkswirtschaftliche Sanierungsfähigkeit' (restructuring which is justified from a general economic point of view, i.e. not necessarily profitable for a private investor).
9   This is the predominant opinion in Germany. See Sachverständigenrat 1991 and Beirat of the Bundeswirtschaftsministerium 1991. See also G. and H.-W. Sinn 1991: 85–6.
10 See Bös 1992:3, 15–16.
11 According to Akerlof *et al.* (1991) unemployment is more important than wage differentials for the East–West German migration.
12 The employers' side was presented by former East German officials and managers who themselves were interested in high wage increases (which also guarantee higher unemployment benefits). Moreover, the West German employers' representatives did not interfere, most probably because they are not interested in low-wage competitors located within Germany.
13 See G. and H.-W. Sinn 1991: 165–70.
14 This is similar to the policy which Italy applied to the Mezzogiorno.
15 See Bös 1991:190–1; Bös 1992:7.
16 See Article 41 (1) and the joint declaration of FRG and GDR of 15 June 1990, which is part of the treaty on German unity.
17 See Article 41 (2) of the treaty on German unity, 'Vermögensgesetz' in the version of April 1991, and Zweites Vermögensrechtsänderungsgesetz (for the latter see Frankfurter Allgemeine Zeitung of 15 July 1992).
18 For a detailed treatment of the 'reprivatizations' of these firms see Freund, Kaufmann and Schmidt 1990.
19 See Bös 1992:19–21.
20 See Streit 1991:175–6. The same mistakes were also made in other countries; IRI in Italy is a good example.
21 See Informationsdienst des Instituts der Deutschen Wirtschaft (43) 24 October 1991.
22 How long it will take until East Germany catches up with West Germany is an open question. For a recent careful evaluation of this problem, see Dornbusch and Wolf 1992.

REFERENCES

Akerlof, G.A., Rose, A.K., Yellen, J.L. and Hessenius, H. (1991) 'East Germany in from the cold: the economic aftermath of currency union', *Brookings Papers on Economic Activity 1*: 1–87.
Beirat of the Bundeswirtschaftsministerium (1991) 'Probleme der Privatisierung in den neuen Bundsländern', *Studienreihe*, Bundesministerium für Wirtschaft, Bonn, *73*.
Bös, D. (1991) 'Privatization and the transition from planned to market economies: some thoughts about Germany 1991', *Annals of Public and Cooperative Economics* (Liège) 62: 183–94.
Bös, D. (1992) *Privatization in East Germany*, Washington, D.C.: IMF, Fiscal Affairs Department.
Carlin, W. and Mayer, C. (1992) *The Treuhandanstalt: Privatization by State and Market*, Mimeo, Cambridge, Mass.: NBER.
Dornbusch, R. and Wolf, H. (1992) 'Economic Transition in East Germany', *Brookings Papers on Economic Activity*.
Freund, W., Kaufmann, F. and Schmidt, A. (1990) 'Der Reprivatisierungsprozeß in den

DIETER BÖS

neuen Bundesländern', *Materialen des Institutes für Mittelstandsforschung* (Bonn) (79).

Kühl, J. (1991) 'Beschäftigungspolitische Wirkungen der Treuhandanstalt', *WSI Miteilungen*: 682–8.

Möschel, W. (1991) 'Ein Staatskonzern im Angebot', *Frankfurter Allgemeine Zeitung*, 26 January.

Sachverständigenrat (1991) *Marktwirtschaftlichen Kurs halten: Zur Wirtschaftspolitik für die neuen Bundesländer*, Sondergutachten (Wiesbaden), 13 April.

Sinn, G. and Sinn, H.-W. (1991) *Kaltstart: Volkswirtschaftliche Aspeckte der deutschen Vereinigung*, Tübingen: J.C.B. Mohr (Paul Siebeck).

Streit, M.E. (1991) 'Ordnungspolitische Defizite der deutschen Vereinigung', *Wirtschaftsdienst* (Hamburg): 71 (4).

APPENDIX

Table 3.3 Industrial enterprises of THA (numbers of enterprises)

Total number of enterprises which are currently or formerly owned by the THA	11,759
Privatized enterprises (total privatization)	3,775
Partial privatization (private majority)	555[1]
Reprivatization (returned to previous owners)	807
Transferred to local communities	187
Other (provisional transfer of possession through closure, merger or splitting up)	318
Currently being closed	1,480
Enterprises still to be privatized (either in full THA ownership or in majority ownership of THA)	4,637[2]

[1] In 3,283 further cases of 'partial privatization' the majority is still owned by the THA. These cases are included in the 4,637 firms which are still to be privatized.
[2] This figure will hopefully be reduced to 2,500 by 31 December 1992.
Source: *Monthly Bulletin of Treuhandanstalt* (THA), 31 May 1992.

Table 3.4 Size distribution of industrial enterprises which are still to be disposed of

Number of employees	Number of enterprises
0 to 20	1,364
21 to 50	920
51 to 100	785
101 to 250	835
251 to 500	411
501 to 1,000	170
1,001 to 1,500	54
> 1,500	98
	4,637

Source: as Table 3.3

90

Table 3.5 Foreign investors

Country	Cases of privatization	Investment pledges (DM mill.)	Job guarantees
Switzerland	69	682	14,148
Great Britain	68	1,629	14,387
France	51	2,703	18,350
Austria	48	503	9,015
Netherlands	33	912	5,854
USA	27	1,581	6,168
Sweden	19	89	3,351
Denmark	16	372	2,524
Italy	15	377	2,920
Belgium	9	87	2,804
Others	35	2,623	27,105
	390	11,558	106,626

Source: as Table 3.3

Table 3.6 Management buy-outs

Thuringia	211
Saxonia	340
Saxonia-Anhalt	229
Brandenburg	238
Berlin	62
Mecklenburg-Vorpommern	271
Total	1,351

Source: as Table 3.3

Table 3.7 10 largest enterprises for which various forms of liquidation have been instituted

	Jobs in the enterprises	Jobs preserved	
		Number	%
FEDI – Reisebüro der Gewerkschaften	13,500	0	0
Robotron Büromaschinen AG, Sömmerda	8,650	1,255	14.5
Sächs.Baumwollspinnereien und Zwirnereien AG	8,600	950	11.1
AWE – Automobilwerke Eisenach	7,047	2,373	33.7
Pentacon GmbH Dresden	4,833	434	8.9
Ascota AG, Chemnitz	4,473	3,840	85.8
Pneumant Reifenwerke Fürstenwalde AG	3,830	480	12.5
Robotron Telecom GmbH Radeberg	3,450	640	18.6
Elektromat GmbH Dresden	3,390	1,000	29.4
Simson Fahrzeug GmbH, Suhl	3,048	1,200	39.4
Total for the 10 largest enterprises	60,821	12,172	21.4
Total for enterprises to be liquidated	245,686	72,120	29.4

4

PRIVATIZATION IN HUNGARY

Gusztáv Báger

THE EMPIRICAL CONTEXT OF PRIVATIZATION

Hungary is experiencing radical political and economic changes which are leading to the energetic pursuit of privatization. The privatization strategy of the government (the programme of privatization) is based upon a four-year (1991–4) programme for the transformation and development of the Hungarian economy aimed at realizing a socially responsible market economy and macro-economic stabilization.

Hungary has registered during 1990–1 significant progress toward the realization of an efficient social market economy. The balance of payments showed a surplus of $ 287 million, compared to a deficit of $ 1.314 million in 1989, and to a surplus of $ 156 million in 1990. This favourable result was due to a larger than expected influx of external capital (US$ 1.5 billion). As a consequence, the net foreign indebtedness has marginally declined (see Table 4.1).

It is particularly important that during 1991 the rate of inflation did not exceed the forecast 32 per cent as measured by the industrial price index, and has exceeded the forecast 34 per cent, as measured by the consumer price index (CPI), by only 1 per cent. Results are even more significant if one considers that the average monthly increase of the CPI is declining: it was 3.8 per cent during the first half of 1991, but only 1.2 per cent during the second half. The successful application of tight monetary policies has considerably contributed to the present declining tendency of prices and has prepared the ground for declining interest rates during 1992. The National Bank of Hungary, having kept the central rate for a long time at 22 per cent, has reduced it, during March 1992, to 18 per cent. Simultaneously, it devalued the forint by 1.8 per cent, as a small signal to exporters that the central authorities are still considering exports as the main driving force of the economy.

The Hungarian industry, agriculture and services reacted with extraordinary and unexpected flexibility to the sudden loss of non-convertible (CMEA) markets, by shifting their exports to convertible payments. While in 1991 total exports increased by 24 per cent in current prices, compared to 1990, which

Table 4.1 Representative data on the development of the Hungarian economy, 1989–90

	Unit	1989	1990	1991 (plan)	1991 final*
Gross National Product	% of prev. year	−1.0	−5.3	−4.5	−12.0
Gross Domestic Product	"	0.0	−3.3	−4.0	−10.0
Domestic use	"	0.0	−4.0	−5.0	−9.5
of which: household consumption	"	2.0	−3.6	−5.0	−7.5
Import	"	0.0	−5.5	−6.5	−8.0
Export	"	−1.0	−4.5	−5.5	−9.0
Industrial producers' price index	"	15.0	23.5	32.0	32.0
Consumer Price Index (CPI)	"	17.0	29.0	34.0	35.0
Unemployment	"	0.1	1.7	5.0	8.5
Balance of payments	US$ mill.	−1.314	156	−1.200	287
Budget deficit	HF bill.	−54	−1	−79	−114

* Subject to minor change

corresponded to a decline of about 9 per cent in constant prices, exports to the western trading area increased by 52 per cent in current (or by about 14 per cent in constant) prices, and exports to the former CMEA countries shrank to 14 per cent in current (and to about 50 per cent in constant) prices as compared to the previous year.

Important legislative activity, concerning the economic underpinning of the country's economy, characterized 1991. Legislative Acts concerned the Central Bank; financial institutions, including the banking sector; unified accounting practices; bankruptcy procedures; Church properties; state concessions; compensation for formerly nationalized properties; investment funds; the transfer of state property to municipalities, and various tax laws. A new law on co-operatives and one on the Employee Share Ownership Programme (ESOP) were enacted early in 1992. A privatization law package, including laws on companies remaining under state control, on the State Property Agency (the privatization organization of Hungary) and on the needed modifications of the laws establishing the crucial legal framework for privatization (the Transformation Law, the Companies Act, the Law on the Protection of State Assets, etc.) was enacted in June 1992. Among the important legal/institutional changes the State Holding Company deserves special attention. It is to be set up to act as a custodian and manager of those shareholdings the government intends to keep under control in the long term. The new holding company also has the right to sell off stakes in enterprises the state will not own completely.

As a consequence of the state's increasing withdrawal from economic activity, both producers' and consumers' behaviours became increasingly market oriented. Foreign trade is *de facto* liberalized; so is foreign exchange for commercial purposes. For non-residents the Hungarian forint is convertible on capital account as well. Non-residents can repatriate both capital and profits at will.

Under the influence of market factors personal savings have significantly increased. At present, they represent about 10 per cent of disposable income. This high savings rate is due to the positive real interest rates, the newly developing confidence in financial instruments, especially government bonds, and the anticipation that savings could eventually be converted into homes and durable household goods or form the basis of new small enterprises and of participation in privatization.

This progress has been achieved at a considerable economic and social cost. One of the victims of the transition process was the GDP which has declined by 10 per cent in 1991 as compared to 0 per cent and 3 per cent declines during 1989 and 1990, respectively. About half of this decline was due to the collapse of the eastern markets; a quarter to the closing of inefficient production facilities; and a quarter to the shrinkage of the domestic market, caused by the previous two factors.

As a consequence of dropping output, unemployment has rapidly increased, reaching 8.5 per cent by the end of the period, as compared to 0.6 per cent and 1.7 per cent at the end of 1989 and 1990, respectively. As a result of declining GDP and increasing unemployment, the domestic use of the GDP has declined by 9.5 per cent, as compared to 4.0 per cent during 1990. Within domestic use, the private consumption has declined by 7.5 per cent, as compared to a decline of 3.6 per cent in 1990, and the investments have declined by 5.5 per cent, as compared to a decline of 9 per cent in 1990.

As per expectations, the Hungarian privatization has proceeded with a relatively high speed under the influence of some favourably changing macro-economic conditions, e.g. the balance of payments situation and the availability of foreign exchange resources, deregulation, high but declining inflation, and fast export market reorientation, particularly in the second half of 1991. Up until the end of 1991 about half of the 1,897 state-owned enterprises belonging to the State Property Agency were involved in some phase of privatization, representing about 35–40 per cent of the total book value of HF 1,900 billion to be privatized (see Table 4.2). A total of 218 of these enterprises were transformed during the privatization process into normal shareholding corporations; 88 per cent of these transformations took place during 1991. The transformed enterprises represented 18.1 per cent of the total book value to be privatized. In 126 cases it was not transformation, but the creation of completely new corporations that was the chosen venue; 64 per cent of these new corporations were created during 1991, and 45 per cent of the 126 new corporations were funded with foreign participation. The privatization process has been completed in corporations and organized by the State Property Agency representing 10.8 per cent of the book value of HF 1,900 billion to be privatized. It might also be taken as the rate of privatization attained so far.

However, in order to arrive at the real rate of privatization the change in the

Table 4.2   Selected data on privatization, 31 December 1991

	No.	HF bill.
Transformation of firms into corporate form	865	
by book value		654.58
Application for transformation, refused	11	
by book value		5.04
Application for transformation, accepted	218	
by book value		345.07
by value of contracts		465.20
In the new corporation foreign ownership (%)	8.26	
Transformation in process	636	
by book value		304.47
Transactions, involving the protection of state property	364	
Number of refused transactions	31	
by book value		2.57
Approved transactions	333	
by book value		29.93
by value of contracts		54.41
Approved rapport with domestic partners	70	
by book value		3.73
by value of contracts		9.10
Approved rapport with foreign partners	56	
by book value		17.61
by value of contracts		28.20
Sales or other methods of protection of property	207	
by book value		8.59
by value of contracts		17.11
Value of foreign participation in transactions		58.68
Proportion of foreign participation in joint ventures (%)	42.14	
Shops sold in the pre-privatization process	2120	
Income from privatization		40.12

ownership structure of investors' equity should also be taken into account. After transformation of the companies, the state (State Property Agency) remains the main shareholder (86 per cent) reflecting the fact that in the Hungarian privatization scheme the idea of issuing coupons to the population at large is rejected. Consequently, 14 per cent of investors' equity of the transformed companies might be taken as subject to real ownership change, according to which the real rate of privatization is only 3 per cent. From the investors' equity the share of local councils is 3 per cent and that of foreign capital is 8 per cent. Although the share of foreign capital is significant it is lagging far behind the target figures (25–30 per cent) of the privatization strategy of the government.

CONSTRAINTS

Despite the progress achieved in the Hungarian privatization it is somewhat lagging behind the desired pace as suggested by the government's four-year economic programme. Over a four-year period, the programme postulates a share of less than 50 per cent of public enterprise in the national economy, as a result of privatization and the creation of new corporations.

Apart from the growing political and economic uncertainties in Eastern Europe, some elements of the macro-economic situation, the queuing up phenomenon, the bankruptcies and particularly the deteriorating state budget situation (see Table 4.1), and consequently the high taxes and unusually high social security contributions, have an unfavourable effect on both the supply and demand sides of the privatization process.

The supply constraints have been impinging on privatization actions, due to the fact that there is a significant number of public enterprises either making a loss or operating at very low levels of efficiency. The attractiveness of these companies to investors appears to be rather low. The investors' greater interest in efficient enterprises might be illustrated by the larger difference between the book value and the contract value of transformed corporations in 1990 (55 per cent in favour of the latter) than in 1991 (33 per cent in favour of the latter only), due to the first choice of efficient companies. Although several options (decentralization, sale at a low price, etc.) have been tested to find a solution to the privatization of insolvent and loss-making corporations, no real solution has been found so far. According to Hungarian experience, a lasting solution can be reached only through the radical reorganization of these companies. Such a task is mainly to be fulfilled by the newly established State Holding Company.

Another supply constraint is connected with infastructural considerations. Many practical considerations come into conflict with the rigidity of legal regulations. They (e.g. on the purchase and development of real estate by foreigners) are far from perfect. A well-defined ownership situation is still missing. Laws concerning the protection of the environment have not yet been developed. Another problem is the lack of a well-functioning banking system and that of other financial institutions such as investment funds, insurance companies and pension funds. Due to the lack of a developed capital market the possibility of sale in the stock market is very limited. Finally, the lack of updated and complete information on the Hungarian economy, both on the macro and micro levels, particularly on sectoral development policies, has an unfavourable effect on the privatization process. Record keeping with regard to land and real estate is a complicated affair, while the condition of the environment is completely unclear. Because of this, the sale of Hungarian companies to foreign investors is extremely time consuming and requires the extensive and expensive use of expert consultants.

On the demand side, the main constraint is the restricted volume of investment capacity, particularly as far as domestic private investors are concerned. Up until now, most property (8 per cent) has been purchased by foreigners. The share of purchases by all domestic owners is about 5 per cent, in which the share of banks is 1.3 per cent only. The small Hungarian participation in the privatization process is a result of both the lack of accumulated capital and the limited credit facilities. The government has assisted privatization and the formation of small businesses in several ways. One of these is the E-credit construction (E for Existence), which has provided HF 1.8 billion in credit facilities for new enterprises. A somewhat similar construction is the S-credit programme (S for Start), which supplied HF 3.8 billion for almost the same purpose. The government has decided upon the creation of a new guarantee fund to speed up the utilization of existing credit facilities. Compensation bonds and the ESOP will also assist the strengthening of domestic investment capacity and entrepreneurship in the future. Large-scale investment activity, however, can be developed only gradually.

THE IMPACTS

In general, the expectations from privatization are very high, almost Messianic. The collapse of the former economic system and the success of developed market economies have established the truth of the need for an economic system based on private ownership. Consequently, privatization appears to be a key element for solving all problems inherited from the former economic system. In the long term, it might be so; however, in the short term, the results could be vitiated by the side effects of privatization and the time needed for the manifestation of new behavioural patterns. Because of the short span of experience the possible impacts of privatization can only be indicated.

In order to illustrate the possible impact of privatization on efficiency, the economic indicators of 100 transformed companies have been analysed on the basis of balance sheets. When these are compared with the average values of indicators of a given branch of industry, the differences appear to be material only in the case of industries where the share of foreign ownership in transformed companies is high. Here, the efficiency indicators of transformed companies are much more favourable than the average ones, e.g. in the tobacco industry (see Table 4.3).

Table 4.3 Comparative indicators of the tobacco industry, 1991

	Branch as a whole	4 transformed corporations
Net value of fixed assets as % of gross value of fixed assets	67.3	67.5
Total exports as % of production	2.9	3.3
Net operating surplus as % of net capital stock	16.3	25.9

When the wage increase of 25.7 per cent of 100 transformed companies in 1991 is compared with that in the national economy, the difference seems to be very small. However, the amount of personal income tax of 100 transformed companies increased by 57 per cent, much faster than in the economy as a whole, indicating that wage increases appeared to be rather in the high income brackets during 1991. This is the result of a more efficient labour force policy according to which the corporations tend to compensate the workers of higher qualifications and dismiss the excess labour.

From such developments it is becoming increasingly evident that privatization would contribute to creating efficient resource allocation and income distribution. However, such a contribution might be seriously jeopardized by the survival of monopoly positions after the privatization, too.

The impact of privatization on the export performance has proved to be pronounced. In 1991 total exports of 100 transformed companies increased by 50 per cent in current prices, and exports to the western trading area by 73 per cent, faster than the increase of exports of the economy as a whole (24 per cent and 52 per cent respectively). In the light of these results it seems to be justified that the privatization can be an engine of export-led economic growth, in harmony with the four-year economic programme of the government.

As regards the impact of privatization on the aggregate demand, one of the original options was that privatization could reduce the excess demand. As the Hungarian economy was essentially characterized by demand constraints, due to the near collapse of the eastern market, decline in private consumption and investments, increase of domestic savings, tight monetary policies, etc., such a role of privatization has become less important. For example, privatization played a minor role in the significant increase in domestic savings. On the other hand, some elements of privatization, the influx of external capital, preferential credit facilities and compensation vouchers, tended to increase the aggregate demand which, however, could be kept under control. As far as the compensation vouchers are concerned, the government, instead of restitution, proposed partial compensation in the form of securities, which can be used for buying new properties. In line with the Compensation Act the State Property Agency ensures the redeemability of compensation vouchers by creating an adequate privatization supply.

The positive impact of privatization on aggregate supply is lagging behind expectations. It has not counterbalanced the fall in production. One reason is the narrow range of privatization accomplished so far. Another is that some aspects of privatization appear to work against the growth of production, for example:

1   the new owners' preference is to buy market rather than capacity;
2   the monopoly positions survive after privatization; and
3   the rationalization programmes are set up for short-term periods only and the rationalization process, in most cases, starts with a cut in production.

The low supply effect, of course, has a direct impact on employment by reducing the demand for labour. Its magnitude depends on the size of surplus employment existing within the companies. According to a forecast, the privatization of some 40 per cent of state assets during three years might result in a 10–15 per cent reduction of labour force. However, one has to take account of its job creation effect – due to growing private entrepreneurship, the small ventures, in particular – though this effect appears to be lagging behind the surplus labour resulting in a further increase in unemployment. Such a forecast is supported by the following underlying facts:

1 the pace of privatization has not yet reached the planned speed;
2 the number of real (private) owners is still not large; and
3 the share of foreign capital is still small.

From the sale of shares and shareholdings, as well as from pre-privatization (i.e. the privatization of the retail, catering and service industries), an income of HF 676 million was realized in 1990. More than two-thirds of this income was in convertible currency. HF 511 million of this income, after deducting expenses, was used to reduce the national debt. Privatization expenses for which limited companies may not be held liable, for example the cost of maintaining a shareholding or advertising, and privatization costs related to the introduction of shares on the stock market, amounted to HF 3.2 billion. As a result of the acceleration of the privatization process, the State Property Agency realized an income of HF 40.1 billion in 1991; 72 per cent of this income was in convertible currency. The revenues obtained from privatization have been used for reducing the national debt (HF 23 billion), and for covering transfers to the state budget (HF 13 billion), to the local councils (HF 1.3 billion) and to the corporations (HF 2.8 billion). Although Hungarian decision-makers have been bent on retiring national debt, in the light of the increasing financial needs for reorganization processes, it can be stated that revenues from privatization do not seem to be enough for a significant reduction in, or liquidation of, the national debt.

CONCLUSIONS

In the Hungarian macro-economic policy and programming great attention is given to privatization as a key element in the transition to a market economy system. Yet, there is need for further measures to improve the macro-economic situation and to remove the constraints which have been impinging on privatization actions. In doing so, greater attention should be given to the policy harmonization of the requirements of privatization, new private entrepreneurship (the creation of private firms) and restructuring of firms earmarked for long-term state ownership.

Although Hungary's privatization process is quick in comparison with that in other countries, it is somewhat lagging behind the desired and potential speed. In order to speed up further privatization, beyond the removal of constraints discussed above, there is need for a flexible use of various privatization methods of both divestiture and non-divestiture types. In Hungary's privatization process too much emphasis was put on the so-called 'active' privatization programmes (the First and the Second Privatization Programmes, the Construction Industry Privatization Programme, etc.), the aim of which was, with the active participation of the state (State Property Agency), the acceleration of privatization by attracting new circles of investors into the Hungarian economy. However, the speeding up of privatization in 1991 could be attributed not to these programmes but rather to a new, investor-initiated privatization method and to the so-called self-privatization method extending the range of participants. The latter makes possible the transformation and sale of companies without direct involvement from the state, but with one of the independent consulting and property evaluating companies to be selected by the State Property Agency through competition. Furthermore, greater attention should be given to methods like the breaking up of monopolies, leasing, management contracts and worker and management buy-outs, as well.

Foreign capital can also play an important role in speeding up the privatization process given the shortage of domestic capital. Its role is also crucial in the transfer of technical and managerial knowhow.

From among the impacts of privatization the large labour redundancies resulting from the restructuring of firms deserve special attention and call for active employment and social policies.

There is need for intensive future activities in estimating likely impacts, both favourable and unfavourable, *ex ante*. Without such activities a 'culture' of privatization in the widest sense can hardly be built up.

5

PRIVATIZATION IN POLAND

Jersy Cieslik

INTRODUCTION

This paper summarizes recent experiences in the privatization of Polish state-owned enterprises.

From the author's perspective three issues are worth mentioning at the very beginning. The first one relates to the notion of privatization. Poland, as well as other post-communist countries in Eastern Europe, is currently undergoing radical transformation of her socio-political and economic systems, of which privatization, although crucial, represents only one component. This makes the overall environment for privatization completely different from that of several developed and developing countries where privatization has been confined to a relatively small public sector.

A second comment relates to the relatively short time span of the privatization in Poland. The Law on Privatization of State-Owned Enterprises was passed by the Polish Parliament only two years ago – on 13 July 1990. Without a doubt, two years of privatization attempts do not allow a thorough examination of impacts and constraints. What is possible, in the author's view, is only a preliminary assessment of the privatization process with clear understanding that firm trends have yet to emerge.

Third, it is important to note that the analysis of experiences, constraints and impacts contained in this paper has been undertaken from a consultant's perspective. The author of this paper has been involved in privatization since the very beginning of the process, acting as an adviser even prior to the official announcement of the programme. Obviously, the conclusions drawn are very much affected by this and might significantly differ from those formulated either by government officials or management and employees of the privatized companies.

EMPIRICAL CONTEXT

In two years' time since Poland headed down the road to the western market capitalism, the economy has undergone radical changes. The share of the state-owned sector, which dominated Polish economy for more than forty years after the Second World War, has declined significantly. The change resulted from a rapid expansion of private businesses, privatization of state-owned enterprises, and the reclassification of the co-operative enterprises, the majority of which ceased to be a part of the state-owned economy in 1989.

The private sector in Poland essentially consists of small- and medium-sized companies. The other pertinent characteristic of this sector is its significant growth. The number of private incorporated enterprises increased from less than 2,000 in 1988 to almost 60,000 as of 30 June 1992 (see Table 5.1).

At present, over 55 per cent of Poles are employed in the private sector, and including those unofficially employed the share of the private sector in total employment of the country amounts to some 60 per cent.

In addition to these changes in number of companies and employment, there were also marked shifts in the different sectors' shares of total value-added. Table 5.2 illustrates shares of value-added generated by the private sector in the main areas of economy in 1990 and 1991.

A third of the Polish GNP was generated by the private and co-operative sectors in 1990 (see Table 5.3). As compared with the previous year, the share increased by 13 percentage points, partly due to the above-mentioned reclassification of co-operatives. During 1991 private sector investment outlays

Table 5.1 Number of incorporated companies, by ownership in 1990–2

	1989	1990	1991	end June 1992
State-owned companies	7,337	8,454	8,604	8,830
Co-operatives	16,691	18,575	17,374	18,135
Private businesses a/	12,963	32,157	50,660	59,557

a/ including joint ventures and foreign small-scale companies. In addition, there are about 1.43 million non-incorporated private small businesses in Poland by the end of March 1992.
Source: Main Statistical Office Report, July 1992

Table 5.2 Share of private sector in the value-added, by sector in 1990–1

Industry	Share of the private sector (%)	
	1991	1990
Retail/domestic trade	83.0	n.a.
Construction	55.2	32.0
Transportation	23.7	14.0
Industrial output	21.4	16.8

Source: Gazeta Wyborcza, 30 June 1992

Table 5.3 Ownership structure of GNP in Poland in 1989–90

	1990 (%)	1989 (%)
State-owned sector	67.7	80.8
Private sector a/	32.3	19.2

a/ including co-operatives
Source: Main Statistical Office Report, 1991

continued to grow and as the public sector investment declined, the private sector's share in total outlays rose from 35 per cent in 1990 to 40 per cent in 1991.

In the last two years, the state-owned sector of the Polish economy encountered serious financial difficulties. Despite this, the public sector continued to supply 81 per cent of revenues to the state budget in 1991 versus 19 per cent coming from the private sector. In other words, while employing almost 60 per cent of the labour force, producing over 20 per cent of industrial and almost 75 per cent of agricultural output, dominating in trade and occupying a significant position in transportation, construction and services, the private sector does not make a proportionate contribution to the state budget. A liberal fiscal policy towards the private sector, especially firms involved in trade and imports, had the effect of increasing the state budget deficit and the inflation rate.

Even while the private sector is growing, the Polish economy is suffering the pains of its transition to a market economy. Unemployment, unknown three years ago, is growing. In May 1992, official unemployment reached 2,228,000 people, or 12.3 per cent of the labour market. Fifty-two per cent of these are women. 'Hidden unemployment', made up of those people who remain employed in state enterprises but are in fact not necessary to maintain current levels of production, may be as high as an additional 2 million people, 900,000 of them in industry.

PRIVATIZATION PROSPECTS AND POLICY

Privatization has been viewed by the Polish government as the best way to rationalize operations in those still-public industries. The structures are in place, although progress remains slower than expected. The Privatization Law for State-Owned Enterprises provides for a multi-track approach to privatization, with three main mechanisms for privatization:

1 privatization by equity transformation;
2 privatization by liquidation, and
3 mass privatization.

Reprivatization, which is meant to provide legal recourse for former owners of land and other property to regain or be compensated for their family holdings, is the subject of ongoing and heated debate in the Polish parliament. Politicians are trying to address the questions of who has rights to reprivatized property, what criteria should be used in deciding claims, and how the property should actually change hands. Unfortunately, the budgetary problems and political differences will make agreeing on the necessary legislation a slow process.

Privatization by equity transformation

This method of privatization is meant for those large state-owned companies which are found to be financially viable. These firms are first 'commercialized', transformed into limited liability or joint stock companies, whose equity is temporarily held by the National Treasury. This transition phase is intended to allow a clear decision-making and control structure to be implanted, while adjusting the legal status to the requirements of potential buyers. During this commercialization the entity should start to respond to market forces, and its potential as a private company should start to be realized. This theory has not always been borne out in practice, though, as the commercialized firm often has the same management under a different guise.

After commercialization, enterprises may be privatized individually or as part of the mass privatization programme. Under the first scheme, the employees should be offered 20 per cent of the equity in their company on preferential terms. The rest of the shares go to the public in a public offer or are sold to domestic and foreign investors after individual negotiations.

The ministry has recently developed the concept of privatization through restructuring. Because foreign investors were not showing much interest in buying inefficient and heavily indebted companies, the ministry intends to restructure businesses fully before seeking buyers. This new approach was tried in the sale of the Szczecin shipyard, one of the three largest shipyards in Poland. It is too early to ascertain the success of this new approach to privatization.

Privatization by liquidation

Originally this route of privatization was meant for smaller companies that were not estimated to be financially viable on their own. These companies would be liquidated, and their assets would be sold off to individuals, investors or their managements and employees.

In practice, the liquidation route has become the most popular form of privatization in Poland, as it offers several distinct advantages over the more formal transformation method. In a liquidation, a company's assets are transferred and directly invested in a new enterprise, while under the transformation route, the proceeds of the sale would go to the state budget, and not to the enterprise itself. Another distinction relates to the transformation route's requirement that 20 per cent of the equity of the company be offered to employees on preferential terms. This requirement does not hold for liquidated companies, often raising criticism from their employees.

The liquidation method does have certain difficulties, though, as it requires the consent of the Privatization Ministry and the consent of the founding ministry of the enterprise (i.e. in most cases the Ministry of Industry). At times, government bodies involved may disagree on the valuation of the assets or the terms of the sales, delaying any action on the part of the would-be investor. Reinforcing this difficulty is the fact that this method of privatization was meant for smaller enterprises (i.e. less than USD 10 million annual turnover).

Mass privatization

Poland's mass privatization plans are similar to those under way in Czechoslovakia and Hungary. Several hundred enterprises are being selected to be included in the programme. These will be transformed into joint stock companies, and their shares will be distributed as follows:

national investment funds	60 per cent
employees	10 per cent
state treasury	30 per cent

There are plans for ten national investment funds (NIFs), usually managed by foreign security firms and organized along the lines of joint stock companies, i.e. having supervisory and management boards. Fund managers are currently being selected. NIFs are expected to be closed-end investment funds. Each fund will have a portfolio of shares of the newly transformed state-owned enterprises, and ownership will be limited to under 33 per cent of any one enterprise. Initially, the NIFs will be owned by the State Treasury.

At the same time, every adult Polish citizen will have the right to buy one 'share-holding certificate' representing his/her stake in all NIFs. The fee paid for these shares (or participation in the mass privatization programme) will probably amount to 5–10 per cent of average monthly earnings. Poles will pay cash for 'share-holding certificates'. Their contributions should cover part of the costs of the mass privatization programme. The certificates will be tradeable. In about one year's time holders of certificates will be given an opportunity to buy shares of the NIFs.

But, although urgent, the mass privatization scheme is experiencing delays and it could be as late as autumn or winter 1993 before the NIFs are established. The delays are caused, *inter alia*, by the scarce funds of the Ministry of Privatization. However, the World Bank is considering lending USD 25 million to cover the initial costs of the scheme and the EBRD is now approving a USD 40 million loan for the same purpose.

Sectoral privatization

In August 1991, the government began to look at the Polish economy in terms of sectors in order to develop privatization strategies. This was an attempt to co-ordinate privatization efforts so that activities in one part of an industrial sector would not negatively impact other areas. The Ministry of Privatization contracted consulting firms and investment banks to analyse 21 sectors of the economy (see Table 5.4), including over 400 enterprises.

The ministry hoped that the sectoral approach to privatization would have the following benefits:

1   provide the ministry with up-to-date information, as the basis for better decisions on specific privatization and offer economies of scale in gathering information;
2   indicate the best way to approach the privatization of the various firms within a sector, and ensure a more consistent effort among firms in one industry;

Table 5.4   Sectoral privatization projects in Poland

Sector	Lead adviser	No. of enterprises	No. of employees	Turnover
ball bearings	Kleinwort Benson	4	3,127	625 bn
breweries	Sankt Annae	27	13,860	3,264 bn
cement and lime	IFC	19	16,365	2,251 bn
commercial vehicles	Maison Lazard	6	27,400	1,498 bn
cosmetics, detergents	Bain & Co	14	7,418	2,450 bn
electronics	Bain & Co	n.a.	n.a.	n.a.
household glass	IPG	34	26,035	1,747 bn
industrial gases	Samuel Montagu	n.a.	n.a.	n.a.
machine tools	Company Assistance Ltd	28	16,350	725 bn
motor components	BZW	n.a.	n.a.	n.a.
meat processing	Ernst & Young	67	82,500	12,210 bn
paint and lacquer	J Henry Schroder Wagg	7	2,643	735 bn
passenger cars	CSFB	n.a.	n.a.	n.a.
polymer synthesis	Bankers Trust	n.a.	n.a.	n.a.
potato processing	Ernst & Young	16	6,229	548 bn
power engineering	Samuel Montagu	5	7,200	900 bn
pulp and paper	Hambros	10	15,671	2,611 bn
rubber/tires	LEK	11	11,809	5,542 bn
shoes	Company Assistance Ltd	36	22,500	2,060 bn
surgical instruments	Bankers Trust	n.a.	n.a.	n.a.

Note: The number of employees by the end of 1991 and the turnover for 6 months of 1991 in bn zlotys; except cosmetics and detergents which indicates employment by the end of 1990 and turnover for 1990.
Source: Ministry of Ownership Changes

3   help the ministry understand cross-company effects of privatization, i.e,
     impact of a sale of one enterprise on the rest of the industry; and
4   improve the ministry's bargaining position, as all potential investors and
     companies in a given industry are channelled through one adviser.

The sectoral privatization started with sectors which seemed to be the most
interesting for foreign investors. But by mid-1992 only three sectors had
witnessed more than one transaction; meat-processing, detergents and breweries.
For many reasons, especially the difficult and complicated political situation and
delays in market-oriented reforms, fewer foreign investors than expected have
proved to be really interested.

While progress in sectoral privatization has been slow and has not been
uniform among sectors, the process is expected to accelerate this year. Eight
breweries, four meat processing factories, five machine tool companies and ten
textile plants are poised to be sold in the very near future.

INITIAL RESULTS

From the beginning of the privatization programme up to the end of May 1992,
284 companies decided to take the transformation route to become private, of
which only 35 reached their goal and were sold to domestic and foreign
investors. They brought revenues amounting to about USD 160 million to the
state budget.

Among the 35 enterprises which were privatized individually, 11 were sold by
public offer of shares, 2 by employees' leveraged buy-out, 3 went on auction and
19 were sold to domestic and foreign investors through a public invitation to
negotiations.

In addition, 168 companies have been commercialized so far, i.e. transferred
into joint stock companies owned by the State Treasury, in order to be included
in the mass privatization programme.

The most popular route to privatization has proved to be liquidation (the
reasons for which were mentioned above). This route was followed by a total of
527 companies.

Figures for the first quarter of 1992 are rather disappointing. They seem to
confirm the fact that the privatization process has slowed down. Only 29 state-
owned enterprises were turned into joint stock companies owned by the Treasury
during the first quarter of 1992, as compared with 30 in the fourth quarter of
1991 and 152 in the third quarter. Only six companies were fully privatized
during January–March 1992, i.e. the same amount as in the final quarter of 1991
and one company less than the total for the third quarter of 1991.

Table 5.5 breaks down, by industry, those enterprises undertaking the first
step towards privatization, i.e. transformation into joint-stock companies owned
by the State Treasury.

Table 5.6 may shed more light on the progress of the privatization process,

Table 5.5 Transformation of state-owned companies in Poland into joint stock companies, by branch in 1991–2

	Number of state-owned companies transformed into joint stock companies owned by the State Treasury					
	31 May 1992			31 Dec. 1991		
Branch	Total	For individual privatization	To be included into the mass privatization scheme	Total	For individual privatization	To be included into the mass privatization scheme
Total economy	452	284	168	309	245	64
Industry	373	233	140	256	201	55
Construction	62	46	26	39	31	8
Agriculture	1	1	0	1	1	0
Forestry	2	2	0	2	2	0
Transportation	10	8	2	8	7	1
Telecom.	0	0	0	0	0	0
Trade	1	1	0	1	1	0
Other sectors	2	1	1	1	1	0

Source: *Bulletin of the Ministry of Privatization*, Warsaw, June 1992

and the routes that are being used most often. At the end of May 1992, 12.4 per cent of Polish state-owned enterprises started the privatization process.

CONSTRAINTS

In general, the experiences accumulated so far have clearly indicated that the privatization process in Poland has been and will be much more complex and difficult than originally envisaged when the Privatization Law was passed two years ago. The fundamental constraint seems to be the lack of clarity as to the ultimate goals and objectives of the privatization. This has been aggravated by very concrete macro- and micro-economic factors, and a weak administrative infrastructure for the programme.

Confusion as to the objectives of privatization

When the Privatization Law came into effect in 1990, there was not a clear ideological orientation about the process. Some important actors saw it as simply a legal transformation of certain enterprises, rather than a radical metamorphosis of the entire economy. The law itself calls for the transformation of enterprises from centrally controlled to market driven, but builds in the maintenance of

Table 5.6 State-owned enterprises which started the privatization process

	31 May 1992	31 Dec. 1991
Total number of state-owned enterprises	7,869	8,228
Enterprises transformed into joint stock companies owned by treasury to be privatized individually:		
in number	284	245
in percentage	3.6	3.0
Of which enterprises fully privatized		
in number	35	30
Enterprises transformed into joint stock companies owned by treasury to be included into the mass privatization scheme:		
in number	168	64
in percentage	2.1	0.8
Enterprises privatized by liquidation[1]		
in number	527	416
in percentage	6.7	5.1
Total: enterprises which started the privatization process		
in number	979	725
in percentage	12.4	8.8

1 excluding enterprises liquidated due to bankruptcy.
Source: Bulletin of the Ministry of Privatization, Warsaw, June 1992

certain social goals, for example, by requiring that companies offer 20 per cent of their equity to employees at preferential rates. This type of compromise between a thoroughly capitalist ownership structure and some kind of employee ownership structure has been confusing to employees and buyers alike.

A similar contradiction is found in attitudes towards foreign investors. On the one hand, foreigners represent a necessary, even critical, source of finance and business know-how in Polish firms; however, even as one hand of the government is courting foreign investors, the other hand discourages their investment by certain actions or comments. For instance, the parliamentary debate if foreign investors should be allowed to establish and own casinos in Poland, after the casinos were already opened, was perceived by the foreign investing community as a signal that the instability of Polish politics could spill over to the economic sphere. And, in fact, the general public's fear of foreign investors does influence the Polish decision-making process.

Macro-economic obstacles

Macro-economic factors have also proven a serious constraint to the privatization process. In a poor and deteriorating macro-economic environment, the privatization options of both the government and the general public are severely curtailed. First, the financial reserves that would ease such a transformation are simply not available during a time of economic crisis. Neither domestic private investors nor the government have the cash that would speed the process along. The dire economic straits of the average Pole or Polish company during the last two years have made it almost impossible for positive results to come about in any kind of short-term period. Also, the high inflation rates, underdeveloped capital markets, low levels of individual savings and other economic difficulties have limited the range of privatization tools and mechanisms that can be implemented. For example, low interest rate loans to encourage acquisition of shares are not an alternative in a highly inflationary environment such as the Polish economy in 1990 and 1991.

Micro-economic obstacles

Compounding the problems found in the Polish economy as a whole are the problems within individual companies. The vast majority of Polish companies, even the most successful ones, are just not ready for immediate privatization and should be thoroughly restructured first. The most dramatic example of this is evident within those companies that made up the pilot privatization programme in autumn 1990. The most promising Polish companies were selected for this programme, in the hope that their successful privatization would build confidence and demonstrate the positive consequences of participation. However, without adequate preliminary restructuring these companies have found the process extremely painful, and many are still in very difficult circumstances, even after their privatization. The pilot programme was necessarily a learning process, but these companies' predicaments have negatively impacted the general perception of the privatization process.

The initial restructuring needed by most companies is extensive. The companies generally have far too many employees and more equipment than they need, and are production rather than market oriented. In addition, the companies frequently own holiday homes, blocks of flats and other 'social' assets common under the centrally planned economic system, which need to be divested. In addition, the enterprises often suffer from legal complications; some of them are unable to produce titles to their own land and buildings, or they are the subject of property claims by former owners. Privatization needs to be delayed until such murky structures can be clarified, and the companies can be properly structured.

Other problems result from the actual sale of shares of the companies. Domestic investors have a limited purchasing capacity. While the first few public issues were well received, there is reason to believe that in the future it will be more and more difficult to find domestic buyers for large-scale privatization. So far, foreign investors have not filled this gap. They perceive that the investment climate is unstable; furthermore, the official privatization route is often seen as the less efficient way to invest as compared to the joint venture formation during the pre-privatization era. If they create a joint venture, their investment goes to the company, while under the privatization programme, they must pay the State Treasury for the shares that they acquire. Clearly there are incentives for them not to participate in the privatization programme if there are other options.

Employees and managers often question the fact that they should pay for shares of their companies. Their confusion has been reinforced by the recently announced alternative version of mass privatization originating from the President's Office that every Pole should be granted a kind of loan in the equivalent of USD 10,000 for buying such shares. In addition, employees are afraid of the new demands of working for a privatized company or, worse yet, unemployment. They are concerned about the loss of social benefits that they received through their state-owned companies, and the decline of workers' influence through Employee Councils, etc. Management has been the driving force in some transformations, but many managers fear that their management skills will not be sufficient for a private company and that they will be replaced. They, too, stand to lose the control and influence that they had in the company under the old system.

Weak infrastructure

Added to the general macro-economic malaise and the problems of privatizing individual companies is the weak administrative infrastructure that should be supporting the privatization process. Privatization of formerly communist countries was a brand-new process when the programme began, and the people at the Ministry of Privatization were necessarily inexperienced; very high turnover, due to low salaries and political instability, within the Ministry has exacerbated this problem. Foreign experts and consultants, whose experience was gained in contexts very different from that of Poland, had to be brought in as a temporary measure. Local consultants lacked analytical and restructuring skills early on, although this has been resolved somewhat as a number of new Polish and international consultancies with the requisite skills have been established.

In addition, the close co-ordination and co-operation needed between the Ministry of Privatization and Ministry of Industry were not always there.

The lack of developed capital markets and the investment banks and other companies that work in them also proved a serious problem. As a result, the idea of large-scale public offerings has been stalled.

These infrastructural and administrative weaknesses continue to hinder the development of the mass privatization programme. Companies do not have the expertise to restructure themselves effectively for the upcoming privatization. Foreign-run investment management funds are to oversee that the necessary changes take place eventually, but the lack of internal skills will make the process very slow.

IMPACTS

The impact of the privatization programme is the subject of intense debate in Poland. However, it is still too early to draw serious conclusions about the programme's effects on the efficiency, competitiveness, or market orientation of the economy. The results of one survey of employee and management perceptions of privatization is attached as an appendix to this chapter.

We can say that the number of companies privatized (not just transformed into joint stock companies owned by the Treasury) has been significantly lower than was expected. At the enterprise level, there are clear signs of disillusionment as employees and management expectations of immediate positive results have not been borne out. The changes that have been witnessed so far can only be very short-term effects, and as might be expected they are not overwhelmingly positive as yet.

That said, there are some potentially positive indications for the long-term impacts of the privatization programme. Among Polish employees, there is a growing conviction that privatization is inevitable; this leads to a major shift in attitudes in the work place, as people begin to change their work habits and their expectations. Companies, too, are abandoning their 'wait and see' attitudes for a more proactive approach to their eventual transformation into private companies. Employees and management understand that acting quickly to acquire new skills and retrain for increased flexibility may spare them the more painful adjustments of restructuring. Many companies are performing some initial, internal, pre-privatization analysis, and for the first time they are understanding exactly what their position is relative to the market. This may prove to be a very important positive, if indirect, impact of the privatization process.

These impacts, neither tangible nor quantifiable, should nevertheless prove to be critical in laying the groundwork for a well-planned and successful privatization programme.

APPENDIX

Results of privatization questionnaire

A recently prepared study (conducted by the Center for Trade Union Research NSZZ 'Solidarity' Mazowsze Region in autumn 1992), based on questionnaires sent to and interviews made with representatives of 100 privatized companies provides for closer look into mechanisms and typical behaviours during the transformation process. Of the 100 companies, 40 were privatized by transformation and 60 by liquidation. In most cases, the privatization process had been driven by company management. In far fewer cases, privatization processes had been initiated by employees and workers' councils. Only a few companies started privatization due to action of the Ministry.

Why do the management and employees want privatization? The main reason in the case of privatization by equity transformation and individual sale, mentioned by 38 per cent of respondents, proved to be a wish for exemption from the tax on excessive wage increase and tax on fixed assets applied to state-owned companies only. Companies transferred into joint stock companies owned by the State Treasury cease to pay these two taxes.

The second most important reason to go private, mentioned by 28 per cent of interviewed companies, was a desire to be independent; 23 per cent believe that privatization will improve the financial status of the company and give it new development possibilities.

In the case of companies which decided to follow the privatization by liquidation route, the most important reason for that was a desire to give new development possibilities to the company. As the second most important factor, companies mentioned a wish to improve the financial status of the company, and as the third – the wish to increase payrolls.

The study indicated that the process of privatization is a long one, taking three to six months in 36 per cent of the companies, six to twelve months in the case of the next 36 per cent and more than 12 months in 22 per cent of the companies. The main reasons for the long privatization process and delays proved to be first of all bureaucracy and reluctance of the Ministry of Privatization and the founding bodies, difficulties connected with valuation of assets, clarification of legal rights to the occupied land and property, and complicated legal acts.

What typically happens after privatization? About 80 per cent of companies privatized by transformation and 50 per cent of those going private by liquidation initiated adjustment and restructuring programmes. Typically such programmes involved organizational changes, development of business range, and better sales promotion. The organizational changes were intorudced by 44 per cent of companies transformed and by only 19 per cent of companies liquidated. The former in most cases laid off employees, whereas the latter only in a few cases decided to limit employment.

A third of companies privatized by transformation and 40 per cent of companies liquidated said that the financial situation of the company improved as a result of ownership changes. However, as many as 38.5 per cent of companies transferred and a third of companies liquidated said their financial status actually deteriorated.

The study clearly indicates that privatization typically limits employees' influence on the functioning of the company, number of trade unions, etc.

6

PRIVATIZATION IN CZECHOSLOVAKIA

Olivier Bouin

INTRODUCTION

The Czechoslovak transition towards an open market economy represents one of the most dramatic changes brought about by the 'Velvet Revolution' of November 1989. Debates over the scope, speed and sequencing of economic reforms were carried inside Civic Forum, the leading political force that gained nearly 60 per cent of seats in the Federal Assembly after the June 1990 elections. These debates rapidly led to the victory of the most radical reforming approach supported by Federal Minister of Finance, Vaclav Klaus, and consequently to the disintegration of Civic Forum in February 1991. Since then, the Czech Civic Democratic Party (the influential conservative party created and presided over by V. Klaus) has been deciding upon and implementing radical reforms.

In order to break with forty years of centrally planned socialism, priority was given to a legal framework adaptation. Fundamental laws on private property, private business and foreign participation in the economy have been approved since 1990 (see Appendix 1). During the same period, a restrictive monetary and fiscal policy has been implemented to avoid major macro-economic imbalances. The Czechoslovak 'big bang', i.e almost complete freeing of prices and the beginning of small privatization, occurred in January 1991. So far (September 1992), positive results have been obtained as regards inflation, the state budget and the trade deficit in the context of a deep recession (see Table 6.1). In this 'stabilized' environment, the first wave of large-scale privatization is likely to be completed before the end of 1992.

This chapter is organized as follows. The first section examines the interaction between governmental objectives and existing constraints in defining privatization strategy. The second section presents the multi-track approach adopted for privatizing the Czechoslovak economy. In the third section, emphasis is put on *voucher* privatization as a key component of Czechoslovakia's ownership transformation policy; and the final section looks at the impacts of large-scale privatization on the restructuring of firms and the emergence of the financial sphere.

Table 6.1 Main economic indicators

	1990 (Actual)	1991 (Estimate)	1992 (Programme)
Gross Domestic Product	−1.7	−14.4	−5.0
Consumer price index	10.1	57.9[1]	12.0
Unemployment rate	1.0	6.6	9.5
Budget[2]	0.1	−2.0	−2.9
Current account[2]	−2.9	2.1	−1.7

1 1st quarter: 40.9%, 2nd quarter: 5.8%, 3rd quarter: 0.2%, 4th quarter: 2.7%
2 in per cent of GDP
Source: Federal Statistic Office

GOVERNMENTAL OBJECTIVES AND EXISTING CONSTRAINTS

Widespread state ownership was the cornerstone of centrally planned socialism. In Czechoslovakia, almost all private property had been eradicated before 1989. In the middle of the 1980s, Czechoslovakia's state sector represented 97 per cent of Net Material Product (NMP), 11 points more than in Hungary – where the private sector benefited from gradual legal recognition – and 15 points more than in Poland – where the agricultural sector was dominated by private farmers.[1] Czechoslovakia's state sector contribution to NMP was equal to that of the Soviet Union.

It is difficult to provide precise figures of the total number of state-owned enterprises (SOEs) in Czechoslovakia. Table 6.2 presents a sectoral estimation of this number based on various official documents. It shows that 5,600 enterprises controlled by central authorities and sectoral ministries in Czechoslovakia[2] composed the state sector along with more than 120,000 small businesses in retail trade, local services or craft industry and 1,800 agricultural co-operatives.

Because of its inability to allocate resources efficiently enough to satisfy consumers, to give economic agents appropriate incentives, and to keep up with western technological innovations, central planning was dismantled overnight by the new political regime. As a consequence, the transformation of ownership patterns became a crucial issue. It was argued that any delay in this field would endanger the whole reform process for at least three reasons:

1   The absence of radical change would signify the perpetuation of bureaucratic control over large parts of economic activity and would encourage anti-reform coalitions.
2   The systemic vacuum left by the dismantling of central planning was not an appropriate environment for undertaking measures in favour of enterprise restructuring.

Table 6.2 Distribution of state-owned enterprises and other state equity participations controlled by Republican ministries

Czech Republic	Number of Entities
Ministry of Industry	1,501
Ministry of Agriculture	1,095
Ministry of Trade and Tourism	230
Ministry of Economic Policy and Development	362
Other Ministries (Environment, Finance, Culture ...)	391
Total	3,579

Source: This table is based on data presented by Czech government, July 1991

Slovak Republic	Number of Entities
Ministry of Economics	287
Ministry of Food and Agriculture	364
Ministry of Water and Forest	111
Ministry of Industry	181
Ministry of the Interior	71
Ministry of Construction	359
Ministry of Trade and Tourism	101
Other Ministries and State Agencies	426
Total	1,900

Source: This table is based on data presented by Slovak government, October 1991

3   Micro-economic adjustment in the enterprise sector (including liquidation decisions) should be decided on and carried out under the vigilant control of new private owners.

The authors of Czechoslovakia's privatization programme had to square a circle. The task was to privatize in a short time period thousands of SOEs in all sectors, different in size and financial situation. For these purposes, nearly 37,000 small businesses were readied for privatization in the course of 1990, and 70,000 were involved in the small restitution process. In the third quarter of 1991, Czech and Slovak governments separately published lists dividing SOEs into four categories: those to be privatized in the first wave of large-scale privatization (about 40 per cent of the total number of SOEs); those to be privatized in the second wave of large-scale privatization (about a third of the total number); those remaining under state control for the next five years (mainly schools, universities, hospitals, selected public utilities and industrial firms); and those to be liquidated by governmental bodies. The precise distribution between the four categories in the two Republics is presented in Table 6.3. More than 3,000 SOEs in the Czech

Table 6.3 Distribution of state-owned enterprises and state participations controlled by central authorities according to Republican government decisions

	Czech Republic	Slovak Republic	Total number
Privatized (first wave)	1,777	623	2,400
Privatized (second wave)	1,177	562	1,739
No privatization within 5 years	584	672	1,256
Liquidated	41	43	84
Total	3,579	1,900	5,479

Source: Czech and Slovak Ministries for the Administration of State Property and its Privatization. SOEs controlled on a federal level should be added. However, increasing tensions between the two Republics led to a Republican control over firms formerly controlled on a federal level. It is therefore difficult to give any precise evaluation.

Republic and 1,200 in the Slovak Republic were thus earmarked for large-scale privatization within the next two years!

The country was, however, unprepared for radical privatization. Before 1989, local entrepreneurs had been constantly discouraged, if not openly prohibited, thus limiting the financial resources of potential local buyers. According to different estimates, domestic savings were insufficient to cover more than a fifth of public sector assets' book value. The banking sector needed institutional changes and write-offs of credits granted to industrial firms under central planning. It was unprepared to mobilise financial resources for privatization. Stockmarkets and other financial markets were almost unknown. Numerous industrial SOEs were plagued with obsolete technological processes, overstaffing, Comecon export-orientation, and over-indebtedness. . . . Finally, foreign investors were extremely cautious because of significant uncertainties about the real value of state assets, about recognition of property rights, and about Czechoslovakia's macro-stabilisation and country risk.

Objectives and constraints of privatization stategies in post-socialist countries are far different from those observed in developed or developing countries during the 1980s. These latter strategies aimed at achieving a better balance between the public and the private sectors using standard methods of divestiture (public offerings, direct sales, management/employee buy-outs). In post-socialist economies, privatization represents a way to (re)create from the far side a capitalist economy. This systemic transformation is unlikely to occur without the emergence of a capitalist class. A first best solution may be a spontaneous emergence of 'schumpeterian' entrepreneurs.[3] Some may rapidly prosper and accumulate enough financial resources to buy state property through standard methods. Such a scenario – even when assuming the active participation of foreign investors – may take decades to bear positive and visible fruits. It may also simply not occur because forty years of omnipotent state control have severely undermined individual initiative and responsibility. Attitudes inherited from the socialist period *vis-à-vis* competition, money and success represent another important obstacle to rapid economic transformation. Ownership transfers are supposed to re-motivate economic agents by inducing profit-maximizing behaviours and thus help create from scratch a class of genuine capitalists. In this respect, voucher privatization and the high degree of popular participation it generates are an important element of the pedagogic process of learning capitalism.

Given their objectives of massive and rapid privatization and existing constraints, Czechoslovak authorities attempted to define a strategy that might be socially acceptable. Any ambitious ownership transfer policy could not be implemented without clear support from the public opinion. Czechoslovak authorities have given priority to measures combining rapid implementation and socio-political feasibility. For example, Federal and Republican governments limited centrally approved and operated liquidations (only 84 SOEs earmarked for liquidation in the two Republics)[4] in order to preserve a social consensus for implementing its radical economic transformation policy. Undertaking massive liquidations might have triggered strong opposition from trade unions, opposition parties, managers and employees of liquidated firms and undermined the government's political credibility. On a more general level, it was considered that the post-communist state could not carry out optimal liquidations (in terms of speed, targets chosen, ways of implementing) of enterprises it owned; only liquidations decided by private owners under market conditions would be effective. This latter point is a feature of Czechoslovakia's radical large-scale privatization strategy. The state is considered incapable of divesting its property in a satisfactory way. Political interference (priority given to friendly buyers, importance of foreign buyers' nationality) and social considerations (employment, local or regional dimension) will divert the state from selecting the micro-efficient agent to buy state property. The same remark applies for appointing managers of National Property Funds, of Investment Privatization Funds, etc. State intervention should thus be severely limited because no institution other than the market is better able to allocate competence, reward motivated, active, competent managers and shareholders, and select winners of post-socialist privatization.[5] Consequently, Czechoslovakia's privatization strategy has been designed to leave as much room as possible for private initiative, popular participation and market intervention.

THE MULTI-TRACK APPROACH

As many Central and Eastern European post-socialist countries did, Czechoslovakia divided its ownership transfer policy into three parts to take into account the diversity of SOEs inherited from the socialist era. Leaving aside private sector development issues, we will concentrate on the three pillars of ownership transfer policy: restitution, small-scale privatization and large-scale privatization.

Restitution

Restitution of confiscated property to previous owners or their heirs raises a complex question. Is this form of re-creating the capitalist system economically, politically and socially desirable? This problem needs a clear solution because threats of subsequent claims on state property may deter potential local or foreign investors. The Czechoslovak government imposed a pragmatic solution: acceptable compensation should be sought to satisfy legal claims but the scope for legal restitution was limited to facilitate implementing small- and large-scale privatization programmes.

Four laws (see Appendix 1) enact restitution conditions depending on the nature of confiscated property (ecclesiatic property comes under Law 298/1990, land or other agricultural property under Law 229/1991 ...) and the way in which it was confiscated (violation of existing laws comes under Law 403/1990, in accordance with existing laws but in violation of civil rights under Law 87/1991). The first category is composed mostly of small businesses illegally confiscated after 1955 and is known as 'small' restitution. The second category comprises companies nationalized without compensation between 25 February 1948 (date of the communist *coup*) and 1 January 1990.

Three basic principles guide restitution operations. Property is given back directly to legally authorized persons (Czechoslovak citizens with permanent residence in the country) or to some institutions (religious orders, congregations, towns, communities). Restitution is made in kind and in current state. In some cases, financial reimbursement or company stocks may replace restitutions. Property is returned by present owners (which are often state holdings). Central state intervention is, therefore, limited to cases of direct responsibility.

By the end of 1991, about 55,000 restitution claims involving financial reimbursement had been addressed to central authorities. The Czech Ministry for National Property Administration and its Privatization – thereafter referred to as the Ministry of Privatization or the MOP – treated more than 10,000 applications and paid Kcs 90 million ($ 3.5 million) as financial reimbursement charges. The Czech Ministry of Finance, which is in charge of restitutions in compliance with Law 87/1990, received 44,000 restitutions claims. It is reasonable to suppose that the number of restitutions in kind addressed to due persons has been much more important. With a few exceptions, restitutions have not so far triggered outright discontent.

The co-existence of restitution with privatization operations has been prepared in several ways by Czechoslovak authorities to avoid problems and delays. First, units involved in 'small' privatization auctions would not include, in three-quarters of the cases, buildings because of possible restitution claims. Auction winners would subsequently be given preference to buy buildings in the absence of legal claims. Second, the borderline of 25 February 1948 set by law excluded *de jure* many SOEs from restitution. Most large companies were indeed nationalized under the Democratic government between 1945 and 1948. As a consequence, Law 87/1991 affected only 6 per cent of state assets. Third, restitution in kind of medium-size and large companies would be limited. In most cases, property value has increased while being state owned. Restituents have the choice either to pay the price difference or ask for financial reimbursement. Given their insufficient financial resources, they frequently choose the second solution. A Restitution Fund has been established for this purpose and has received 3 per cent of equity of all firms involved in large-scale privatization. Finally, property owned by enterprises with foreign capital participation, and commercial companies comprised exclusively of natural persons are exempt from restitution for ten years. Restitution in Czechoslovakia thus covers only 10 per cent of all former private property.

Small privatization

Small privatization began officially on 21 January 1991. The set target was to sell 50,000 units in the course of 1991. Sixteen months after its beginning, 'only' 25,000 units had been sold throughout the country out of 37,000 units approved for privatization. In the Czech Republic, by July 1992, 21,000 units out of 25,700 units scheduled for privatization were auctioned. The aggregate revenue for the state was approximately Kcs 26 billion ($ 900 million). In the Slovak Republic, by the end of 1991, 6,720 units out of 10,340 were sold and generated Kcs 7 billion ($ 250 million). This wave is, therefore, close to completion and preliminary lessons can be drawn. Decentralization of the process with district privatization commissions supervised by the MOP of each Republic has proven to be efficient. Simple and standardized auction procedures facilitated handling by district commissions and local magistrate offices. Global impacts on retail trade activities and services were positive and visible to the population, even if many shops are still closed and converting former activities is often a chaotic process.

Three problems emerged, however, as the programme developed. First, financial resources of auction winners have frequently been suspected by the population. Small privatization auctions have undoubtedly laundered *grey money* accumulated by former 'apparatchiks'. Furthermore, as far as shops, restaurants, services in touristic areas and particularly in Prague are concerned, foreigners with a Czech or Slovak figurehead participated in many auctions as silent partners.[6] Theoretically, only Czechoslovak citizens could participate in the first round of auctions. A second round open to foreigners was scheduled after unsuccessful first auctions. Investment opportunities in terms of attractive units and low selling prices were, however, to appear during the first round and thus triggered the interest of foreign 'participants'. The official position of 'no inquiries about the origin of funds' validated such practices to keep the process alive. Second, Dutch auctions, i.e. the possibility to sell units below the initial price (up to 50 per cent) encouraged some forms of collusion between potential buyers. This occurred mostly in the countryside where the number of buyers was very small. In the Czech Republic, 15 per cent of units (i.e. 2,100) were finally sold below their initial price. Third, many small-business managers tried to escape small privatization auctions by giving improper financial data on inventories, turnover, etc. They were reluctant to participate in the process because new owners usually coincided with new management. Better conditions for them could be obtained with a foreign partner under the law on joint-ventures. The proliferation in 1991 of small joint-ventures with partners from border countries illustrates this phenomenon. Germans and Austrians finalized, respectively, 883 and 839 deals and represented 80 per cent of the total number of joint-ventures. In two-thirds of cases, the amount of initial investment was less than Kcs 500,000 ($ 16,500).

So far, small-scale privatization in Czechoslovakia has not significantly contributed to the emergence of capitalism in the production sphere. In the Czech Republic, only Kcs 6 billion ($ 250 million) of property has been transferred to new owners[7] (here, property refers to *usus, usus fructus* and *abusus* of the assets by the new private owner). This figure should be compared, for example, with the value of property distributed through the voucher scheme (almost Kcs 300 billion). Moreover, especially shops and restaurants were auctioned and small manufacturing units represented only 2 per cent of all completed sales.

Large-scale privatization

The large-scale privatization process is what most differentiates Czechoslovakia from other post-socialist countries of Central and Eastern Europe. Insufficient financial resources of local private sector and difficult evaluation of SOEs' assets representing binding constraints when considering medium and large-scale privatization.[8] This helps to explain the slow progress of divestiture using standard methods in 1991. Only a few dozen firms were privatized in the whole country. Significant direct sales always involved foreign investors. Foreign companies increased threefold their investments in Czechoslovakia in 1991 ($ 600 million compared to $ 180 million in 1990; see Table 6.4 on biggest foreign investments approved in Czech and Slovak Republics). Most economists consider that foreign participation in the Czechoslovak economy should be higher and benefit a wider range of industrial sectors. However, massive denationalisation of SOEs – if economically desirable for privatized firms because of easier financial re-structuring, better access to foreign markets, technology transfers, input of managerial expertise and for the economy as a whole through diffusion of market-oriented rationality – has political limits. The omnipresence of German investors that realised 77 per cent of the total volume of foreign investment in Czechoslovakia may be seen in the future as a sign of economic dependence.

The Czechoslovak government therefore embraced, the idea of an unconventional privatization process based on active popular participation to achieve their ambitious targets concerning large-scale privatization. They supported a radical

Table 6.4 Biggest foreign investments in Czechoslovakia

Czech Republic

Foreign partner	Local partner	Activity	Transaction price (Kcs bill.)	Planned investments (Kcs bill.)
Volkswagen (Ger)	Skoda Mlada Boleslav	Car, motors	1	1
Copart (Nestlé-Bsn-Berd)	CS Cokoladony	Agro-industry	3.1	2.3
Dow Chemicals (USA)	CHZ Sokolov	Chemistry	2.9	4.5
Mercedes Benz (Ger)	Avia Liaz	Bus, motors	2.3	7.6
Glaverbel	Sklo Union Teplice	Glass	1.9	–
Air France (France)	CS Aerolinie	Airline company	1.7	4.4
Linde (Ger)	Technoplyn Praha	Gas	1.6	–

1 Total amount of new capital invested by Volkswagen: Kcs 9.6 billion
Source : Federal Agency for Foreign Investments

Slovak Republic

Foreign partner	Local partner	Activity	Transaction price (Kcs bill.)
Volkswagen (Ger)	BAZ Bratislava	Car, motors	1.1
Samsung (Sth-Korea)	Calex Zlate Moravice	Domestic appliances	0.67
Henkel (Ger)	Palma Bratislava	Detergents	0.35
Meisser Grieshem (Ger)	Chemicka Bratislava	Chemistry	0.3
Hoechst (Ger)	Biotika Martin	Pharmaceuticals	0.21
Alcatel (France)	Tesla Liptovsky Hradok	Telecommunications	0.2

Source : Federal Agency for Foreign Investments

strategy which has taken the form of voucher privatization to supplement standard methods. The scheme has two specific objectives: to discredit traditional arguments of selling off state property and concentration among few local businessmen of privatization benefits, and to speed up the reintroduction of risk and profit as determinants of individual action. The participation of 8.6 million adult Czechoslovak citizens – threequarters of all eligible citizens – represented a major success for voucher privatization and for the governmental privatization programme as a whole.

LARGE-SCALE PRIVATIZATION AND THE VOUCHER SCHEME

Czechoslovakia's large-scale privatization is atypical on three levels. First, the scope is very wide to meet governmental objectives. No other post-communist country has so far unveiled such a radical scheme. As already mentioned, no less than 4,200 SOEs have been earmarked for privatization in two waves. All sectors of the economy have been included. Apart from a few exceptions in sectors such as armaments, nuclear power generation, coal industry and railways, no 'strategic sector' or 'strategic enterprise' escaped privatization.[9] Privatization involved some public utilities and natural monopolies such as water distribution, electricity or telecommunications. This radical privatization programme affected almost all industrial firms and three-quarters of the overall number of SOEs.

The first wave began mid-1991 with hopes that the process would be completed before the end of 1992.[10] It was planned to involve on a Czechoslovak level nearly 3,000 SOEs. This number has inflated because many SOEs submitted projects in order to participate in the first wave of privatization. In the Czech Republic, when taking account of the 523 public enterprises controlled by district authorities, an overall figure of 2,883 units participated in the first wave. Their total book value exceeds Kcs 770 billion ($ 26 billion). Two-thirds of these units will be privatized solely through standard methods of privatization in this first wave. The remaining third (i.e. 943 units) will take part in the voucher scheme and amounts to Kcs 362 billion (i.e. 47 per cent of the total book value). The scope of voucher privatization is unprecedented, involving 430 IPFs, 8.6 million coupon holders (2.5 million participating in the auctions on their own), 8.6 billion points and 299.4 million shares of 1,492 companies to be distributed. Units involved in the voucher privatization currently employ more than 1.2 million people (a sixth of total employment in Czechoslovakia).

The second feature of Czechoslovak large-scale privatization is the organization of its decisional process. According to the law of February 1991, 'basic' privatization projects submitted by the management of each firm and 'competitive' privatization projects drafted by local or foreign entities are the principal vehicles for ministerial decisions. Projects submitted by the management contained a detailed presentation of the firm with data on output, profit and export performance since 1989, an estimation of the value of assets to be privatized, a scheme for transferring total equity of the company.[11] When taking into account basic and competitive projects, four projects per company in the Czech Republic (three projects in the Slovak Republic) were submitted, on average. About 11,000 privatization projects were submitted to the Czech Ministry of Privatization before the final deadline of 20 January 1992. A quarter of this number were 'basic' projects drafted by companies' managers; three-quarters were competitive projects submitted by external entities. Among them, local and foreign bidders submitted nearly 39 per cent of the total of projects (i.e, 4,000 projects), reflecting their high interest in numerous Czech enterprises (the same phenomenon appears but to a lesser extent in the Slovak Republic). Table 6.5 details the origin of proposed projects.[12]

Considering the important volume of competitive projects, it is not surprising that the most frequently proposed privatization method (in 45 per cent of the cases) is direct sale to a pre-determined buyer. The methods that are pre-requisites for voucher privatization came second. In 23 per cent of projects, vouchers were proposed for transferring between 1 per cent and 97 per cent of the firm's equity. Table 6.6 presents the distribution of privatization projects by methods of ownership transfer in the Czech Republic. Other methods such as public auction, public tendering or unpaid transfers to municipalities represented altogether 27 per cent of projects but only a marginal part of the equity to be transferred in the first wave. It is interesting to note that, on average, one approved project combined two methods of privatization (see Table 6.7). For the first 1,044 approved privatization projects, the most frequent combinations were method D (commercialization into joint-stock company) with method C (direct sale) or method F (unpaid transfer).

Table 6.5 Distribution by origin of proposed and approved privatization projects in the Czech Republic

Entity drafting the project	in % of submitted projects (11,166)	in % of approved projects (1,044)
Bidders	39.1	7.4
Management of the company	25.1	81.8
Regional privatization committee	6.8	0.6
Regional office of the founder	3.9	0.2
Management of a subsidiary	3.7	5.7
Restituent	3.6	0.9
Consulting company	3.0	1.9
Founding Ministry	0.2	0.2
Trade union organizations	0.2	0.1
Others	14.4	1.2

Source: E. Klvacova (1992), 'Privatizace pod lupou', *Ekonom*, 25 June. Projects have been submitted for 2,883 units i.e. 2,360 SOEs and 523 firms owned by district authorities.

Table 6.6 Distribution of privatization projects submitted to Czech MASPP* by methods of ownership transfer

Proposed methods	Number of projects	%
A: Public auction	1,150	10.5
B: Public tender	872	8.0
C: Direct sale	4,905	44.8
D: Commercialization into joint-stock company	2,452	22.4
E: Sale of state-owned joint-stock company	432	4.0
F: Unpaid transfer to municipalities, pension funds …	887	8.1
Total	10,949	100.0
Voucher privatization (out of D and E)	2,523	23.0

Source: *Czech Ministry for the Administration of State Property and its Privatization

Table 6.7 Distribution of units involved in 1,044 approved privatization projects by methods of ownership transfer

Methods of ownership transfer	Number of units	%
A: Public auction	172	7.8
B: Public tender	103	4.7
C: Direct sale	336	15.2
D: Commercialization into joint-stock company	839	38.0
E: Sale of state-owned joint-stock company	168	7.6
F: Unpaid transfer to municipalities, pension funds …	592	26.8
Total	2,210	100.0
Voucher privatization (out of D and E)	943	42.7

Source: E. Klvacova (1992), 'Privatizace pod lupou', *Ekonom*, 25 June

All these privatization projects had to be evaluated by the founding ministry and then transmitted for final approval by MOPs. In each Republic, Funds of National Property (FNP) were set up in August 1991 to administer temporarily the extensive state property and to implement approved privatization projects. This decisional structure resembles very much that used under central planning (companies => founding or supervising ministry => centre, here MOPs). It has been argued that far from representing the most satisfactory structure it was the only possible one for implementing rapid privatization in a post-socialist economy.

Three measures have been taken to guarantee the best possible selection of projects (in terms of new investments, new competences, and corporate planning). First, a multi-level decision-making process for reviewing and approving privatization projects was set up to avoid coalitions between employees of ministries and managers or bidders. It involved founding ministries, the Economic Council, MOPs, and the governments of each Republic. Second, competition was openly encouraged. At least in principle, when many competitive privatization projects were submitted, public auctions or public tendering methods were automatically preferred. Former Czech Minister of Privatization Tomas Jezek postponed the final deadline for disposal and approval of competitive projects in order to increase the room for competition in the process. Third, a tight schedule was set to prevent a lengthy decision-making process. The official position was that one or two additional months for reviewing projects would have been ineffective. Existing structures even strengthened with foreign advisers would need decades to prepare a detailed auditing of each SOE. As a consequence, 6,750 projects have so far been reviewed by the Czech MOP in six months! For units participating in voucher privatization, 4,500 projects were reviewed between January and April 1992!

Selection procedures and severe time constraints have been criticized for leaving a decisive advantage to SOEs' management. Benefiting from an important information asymmetry, managers had many strategies to distort competitive tendering. Among them were restricting access to information or providing 'worsening-the-picture' information for 'unfriendly bidders'; submission of inconsistent and unattractive competitive projects by 'friendly bidders' in order to raise the number of projects artificially; submission of competitive projects by 'friendly bidders' in which the selling price is relatively low because current managers are shareholders in the competing joint-venture.... Some observers warned that this process might unduly benefit managers appointed under central planning.[13] Table 6.5 shows indeed that by mid-June, 80 per cent of approved privatization projects had been drafted by the management of the company. This figure is nonetheless biased upwards because MOPs dealt first with companies having only one submitted privatization project with a high percentage of vouchers.

The third feature of large-scale privatization is the voucher scheme. Often presented by the Czechoslovak government as one method of privatization among others, the voucher scheme is the necessary complement of its radical large-scale privatization strategy. It summarizes the whole philosophy of radical privatization in Czechoslovakia, a mixture of neo-classic textbooks, pragmatism, social and political considerations.[14] We have separated the demand side from the supply side to simplify the presentation of the voucher scheme.

Demand side

The demand side reflects the willingness of Czechoslovak government to promote 'popular capitalism'. The voucher scheme, i.e. the possibility for each Czechoslovak adult citizen to take part in the 'privatization lottery' (the term was given by its main architect, D. Triska), achieves a pedagogic mission to the millions of small shareholders it creates and, by extension, to the population. This pedagogic mission has three dimensions:

1 voluntary participation in the voucher scheme may help rehabilitate private ownership in the economy;

2 people will quickly find that their interest is to seek maximization of their portolio's value, such rationality requiring on the enterprise level efficient restructuring of newly privatized firms; and

3 people will have a chance to participate in an open game where asset and wealth concentration will reflect market decision and not state intervention.[15]

During four and a half months (from 1 October 1991 to 15 February 1992), coupon booklets were sold in Czechoslovakia through the Post Office network. Adult Czechoslovak citizens living in the country could obtain a booklet for a fee of Kcs 1,035 (about one week of average salary). This sum covered the booklet itself (Kcs 35) and the registration fee (a stamp of Kcs 1,000) to defray administrative costs. Each coupon booklet comprises fourteen cheques with a nominal value ranging from 100 to 1,000 points. Each participant could use his (her) 1,000 points to bid for shares of hundreds of firms earmarked for voucher privatization in the first wave and/or to acquire a participation in a legally constituted Investment Privatization Fund (IPF) that would bid on their behalf in the auctions. Nationwide public auctions have been organized under supervision of the Federal Ministry of Finance. Up to five rounds of auctions have been scheduled to find an equilibrium between demand of shares and supply.

The genesis of the registration phase is instructive. At the end of November 1991, two months after the process had begun, only about a quarter of people were willing to participate in the voucher scheme. The process was judged very complex and this impression was reinforced by awkward official terminology used in the information booklet available for the general population (references were made to waves, phases and rounds of privatization). By December 1991, official expectations stood at 2.5 million participants. Before Christmas, the situation changed overnight. A newly created IPF, named Harvard Capital and Consulting because its Czech founder held a BA from that university, promised to reimburse – after one year – ten times the initial investment of Kcs 1,035 to any coupon holder that would accept entrusting its points to the Fund. This promise initiated two dynamic reactions. Firstly, the 430 created IPFs tried to outbid their rivals in offering reimbursement guarantees up to Kcs 15,000 (14 times the initial investment). In December 1991, the total value of equity to be auctioned against vouchers amounted to Kcs 250 billion. With 2.5 million participants, 2.5 billion points would bid for equity. Thus, 1,000 points would permit to acquire equity for a face value of Kcs 100,000! Second, people reacted favourably to IPF's aggressive advertising campaigns. At the end of January 1992, the number of people willing to register tripled to reach three-quarters of the population! Closing registration dates had to be postponed by two weeks to reprint coupon booklets. Finally, an overwhelming 8.6 million Czechoslovak citizens bought their coupon booklets.

Supply side

This popular success had many consequences for the supply side. Czech and Slovak MOPs had to rush to approve enough property to be redistributed through the voucher scheme. They finally approved an overall amount of equity of Kcs 300 billion involving 1,492 enterprises (see Table 6.8). This figure was higher than the expected Kcs 250 billion to keep the lottery attractive after the rise in the number of participants. Nonetheless, the value of 1,000 points fell to about Kcs 35,000. Two technical constraints increased the bulk of preparative work. Every newly created joint-stock company (method D in Tables 6.5 and 6.6) had to be registered by one of the eight commercial courts in the Czech Republic. An exact ratio of property to be redistributed from Czech and Slovak Republics had to be applied. This property ratio was fixed at 2.29 following the registration ratio between Czechs and Slovaks. The first round of auctions suffered only marginal delays.

The 'quality' of supply of voucher privatization is an interesting question. Used as a supplementary method, the voucher scheme gave every SOE the possibility to participate in the large-scale privatization process and thus enlarged the process to those firms that would not have been privatized with standard methods. As mentioned earlier, two-thirds of enterprises involved in the first wave of privatization in the Czech Republic will not participate in the voucher privatization. What does this mean? It means that firms transferring a high share of their equity through coupons are those which were not able to find any local or foreign partner. In a sense, they are the less attractive SOEs of the first wave of privatization. The share of voucher in the capital becomes a sign of (un)attractiveness. For example, the fact that Slovak enterprises participating in voucher privatization contributed on average a higher share of their capital to vouchers (74 per cent) than did Czech firms (62 per cent) has been interpreted as a sign of less attractiveness. On a national level, out of the 1,492 enterprises involved in the voucher privatization, 55 per cent of them (i.e. 827 enterprises) are transferring more than 95 per cent of their equity through coupons. Only 164 enterprises proposed less than 50 per cent of their capital for coupons. Detailed

Table 6.8 Voucher privatization in the CSFR

	Czech Rep.	Slovak Rep.	Federal	Total CSFR
Number of enterprises	943	487	62	1,492
Total book value (bil. Kcs)	362.2	133.6	72.8	568.6
Total equity	232.1	114.4	25.4	463
Total value of property to be redistributed through vouchers	200.8	85.1	13.5	299.4
Total employment (in thousands)	864.4	344.2	49.8	1,258.4

Source: K. Cermak, Czech Ministry of Privatization

distribution of firms by the share of coupons in total equity is presented in Figure 6.1. According to my calculations, foreign participation in equity of firms contributed to a marginal 1.1 per cent of the total value of equity to be redistributed through coupon (see Table 6.9). Domestic participation was not significantly higher, standing at 2.2 per cent of the total value of equity (see Table 6.10). Some well-known hotels, breweries or industrial firms were nonetheless put in the voucher process in order to keep the lottery appealing.

The Czechoslovak auctioning process is not a typical Walrasian allocation process, particularly because only limited recontracting is possible.[16] Before the first round, general information about the 1,492 units involved in voucher privatization was published in most Czechoslovak newspapers. Specialized press burgeoned, information about the progress of voucher privatization was omnipresent and numerous financial lectures on how to invest points wisely were broadcast. Most people have become familiar with the national auctioning process. It is difficult, however, to conclude about the achievement of voucher privatization's pedagogic objectives (a real understanding of what stocks, trading, quotations mean).

The auctioneer, here the Federal Ministry of Finance, set before the first round a single conversion rate: 100 points will 'buy' 3 shares of any enterprise proposed in the voucher scheme. The first round lasted from 18 May to 8 June. Orders were centralized and computed by the auctioneer who published the results at the end of June.[17] According to the ratio of demand to supply for each firm, the conversion rate has been modified to create conditions for an equilibrium. Three basic principles were defined before the auctions had begun. In case of massive oversubscription (demand exceeds supply by more than 25 per cent), no distribution of shares would occur. A higher conversion rate would be calculated for the next round. In case of equilibrium or marginal oversubscription, shares would be allocated on a basis of full allocation for individual applicants and

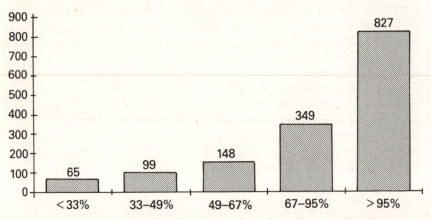

Figure 6.1 Distribution of firms by the share of coupons in total equity

Source: Author's calculations based on data from the Federal Ministry of Finance

Table 6.9 Foreign participation in equity of firms involved in the coupon privatization

	Number of firms	in % of total equity
No foreign participation	1,440	98.9
Foreign participation less than 33%	24	0.4
Foreign participation between 33% and 50%	9	0.2
Foreign participation more than 50%	16	0.5
Total	1,489	100.0

Source: Author's calculations based on official lists published before the first round of auctions

Table 6.10 Domestic participation in equity of firms involved in the coupon privatization

	Number of firms	in % of total equity
No domestic participation	1,367	97.8
Domestic participation less than 33%	53	0.6
Domestic participation between 33% and 50%	20	0.2
Domestic participation more than 50%	49	1.4
Total	1,489	100.0

Source: Author's calculations based on official lists published before the first round of auctions

reduced allocation for IPFs. In case of undersubscription, shares applied would be allocated to applicants. Remaining shares would be proposed for the next round at the lower conversion rate. Unsuccessful applicants could reapply in subsequent rounds of the first wave with unused points. Figure 6.2 presents the results of the first round of auctions. In only 48 cases, demand was equal or marginally superior to supply. However, about 30 per cent of shares were sold during this first round. When considering that 92 per cent of total points were used (95 per cent and 84 per cent of points possessed respectively by IPFs and by individuals), the first round of auctions seems to be a technical success and a satisfactory beginning. New conversion rates are ranged from 100 points for 10 shares for undersubscribed enterprises to 300 points for 1 share for over-subscribed enterprises. Results of the following rounds (the incremental percentage of shares sold at each round, the elasticity of demand to conversion rates' variations, the evolution of the distribution of unsold shares between undersubscribed and oversubscribed companies) will be extremely important for the convergence of the auctioning process.

FORESEEABLE IMPACTS

Voucher privatization is an unconventional and unprecedented process. It raises many questions about the viability of recreating *ex nihilo* an economic system

131

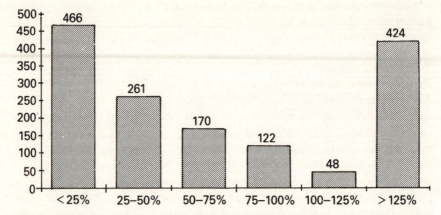

Figure 6.2 Distribution of firms by ratio of subscription after the first round of auctions
Source: Author's calculations based on data from the Federal Ministry of Finance

dominated by private ownership. The Czechoslovak scheme has been designed to encourage as much as possible private initiative (maximum choice was left to individuals, spontaneous creation of IPFs was welcomed, etc.). Unexpected evolutions are therefore the rule. Nobody expected IPFs to guarantee any financial reimbursement; nobody expected almost all eligible citizens to participate. Governmental authorities in charge of the process must therefore react quickly to these new configurations in order to maintain the credibility of the process. So far, they have been able to control the process without significant problems and scandals. The following remarks on enterprise restructuring and on the emergence of the financial sphere will help explain some of the challenges that Czech and Slovak authorities will soon be facing.

Radical privatization is based on the assumption that enterprise restructuring should be undertaken by new private owners. Everywhere in the world, restructuring is a painful and difficult process. This is particularly true in Central and Eastern European countries where most industrial firms need to liquidate loss-making activities, to cut employment, to begin new production, to raise dramatically their productivity, and to increase their price competitivity and product quality. Successful enterprise restructuring and modernization crucially depends on competent and motivated managers. Ideally, their business plan should be monitored by rational private owners/shareholders. In case of a convergence of interest, managers would receive strong backing for implementing costly measures and for financing enterprise modernization (through raising capital, new banking credits, partnership with a local or a foreign investor). Efficient micro-restructuring is therefore positively correlated with the existence of a core group of shareholders.

Most firms that are privatized by standard methods have local or foreign partnership prospects. The situation is more complex for firms privatized through the voucher scheme. As already mentioned, it aims at providing a privatization prospect for the numerous firms that have been unable to find partnerships. The success of the voucher scheme will be measured in the real sphere by its effective impact on enterprise restructuring. A summarized typology of firms involved in the voucher scheme is helpful.

The first category comprises those firms (whatever their size or activity) that introduced minority or majority foreign or local investors in their capital. For them, voucher privatization was a way to transfer remaining shares to the private sector and thus escape from any state or public tutelage. The second category is composed of small and medium-sized firms that contributed a high percentage of their equity to vouchers. In their cases, spontaneous emergence of core shareholders (sectoral or regional oriented IPFs, groupings of small shareholders) is not unlikely to occur. Voucher privatization may thus appear as a genuine privatization method. The third category comprises large firms that had no other option than to rely heavily on voucher privatization. According to my estimates, 118 firms with more than 1,000 employees integrated vouchers up to 95 per cent of their equity and cover, in 1991, 277,000 employees.

What are the prospects for the firms belonging to this third category? Will voucher privatization give these firms an opportunity to form a stable and motivated new ownership? After the first round of auctions, demand for equity reached less than 3 per cent of the supply for 15 per cent of these firms. Points to shares conversion rate has been lowered to 100 points for 10 shares i.e. thirty times less than for massively oversubscribed firms 300 points for 1 share. Will it be sufficient to attract individuals or IPFs? Results of the second round may be decisive. Two scenarios are possible: first, conversion rates may be lowered in a way to find shareholders for these firms 100 or 200 points for 100 shares in the fourth or the fifth round). These shareholders may be interested in closing down firms they received for free and in selling the company's assets. The voucher scheme may thus create the conditions for market decided liquidations. Second, the state may withdraw these firms from the auctions before the fifth round (this possibility is envisaged by decree) and transfer them to Funds of National Property of each Republic for liquidation. This second scenario may prevail if the first one fails. The state will argue that liquidating these firms is unavoidable because no private party was interested in them even for free. This measure may nonetheless go against the overall philosophy of the process to reduce state operated restructuring and liquidations. By reflecting private rationality and private expectations, the voucher scheme also intends to decentralize re-structuring and liquidation processes.

Questions about spontaneous emergence of core shareholders and ability of small shareholders to provide efficient monitoring of managers remain. In the post-socialist context, to what extent private owners will promptly adopt capitalist rationality and how they will effectively impose their rationality on managers are open questions. This classic principal/agent problem is unlikely to be solved in the case of widespread distribution of shares. Scheduling a shareholding assembly to dismiss current managers and to appoint new managers and new boards of directors may be problematic. Furthermore, restructuring measures and corporate strategy need strong supervision that small and inexperienced shareholders may not be able to ensure. Finally, small shareholders may not be able or may not be willing to invest their limited financial resources in enterprise modernization. Problems of recapitalizing companies and financing modernization investments may be left unresolved by voucher privatization.

The role of IPFs is, therefore, crucial. They collected in the pre-round of voucher privatization about 72 per cent of the total points. As a consequence, IPFs will be important shareholders in many firms involved in the voucher scheme. How many of these funds will behave as *institutional investors* (the biggest IPF, Ceska Sporitelna – the main Czech savings bank – which owns about 10 per cent of the total of points will surely fall in this category), as *speculative entities* (many small IPFs may try to take advantage of share prices' volatility on the burgeoning secondary market) or as *industrial holdings* (Harvard Fund, second largest IPF, claimed that it prepared business plans for each company it targeted and would bring foreign investors in)? How much will their reimbursement promises hurt them?

It is true that the largest IPFs have been created by well-known national or foreign financial institutions. In the case of the Harvard Fund, its director was able to convince thousands of voucher holders that his fund had close contacts with foreign investment banks. These large IPFs have to some extent a solid financial backing. However, many investment companies that created IPFs have no track record. In this respect, conditions for approving IPFs' creation set by the Federal Ministry of Finance seem to be very loose. Before the new Business Code took effect on 1 January 1992, IPFs had to have a minimum capital of Kcs 100,000 ($ 3,400). Later, this minimum capital requirement was raised to Kcs 1 million. As a consequence, even if only close-end funds were created, many IPFs are vulnerable. Many of the 430 registered IPFs rushed to propose Kcs 15,000 to individuals who entrusted their points to them.[18] In January 1992, they were considered to have a comfortable security margin between the value of equity they would get with 'their' points and the guaranteed Kcs 15,000. However, this margin shrunk as the number of participants surged and in any case was a risky calculation. The average Kcs 34,000 of equity distributed for 1,000 points is calculated on the unreliable book values of companies. Some IPFs may, therefore, have a negative asset value and face insolvency problems. Third, in absence of a sound secondary market, liquidity problems may arise for IPFs as many individuals will ask for financial reimbursement. The Prague Stock Exchange will open only a couple of weeks before the end of the auctioning process. It is supposed to ensure trading and quotations for any company involved in the voucher scheme. In many cases it may, however, be difficult for IPFs to cash their equity participation. Fourth, this one-year reimbursement guarantee put a short-time pressure on many IPFs that may deter them from undertaking long-term measures of industrial restructuring. Czechoslovak authorities may have to bail out selected IPFs to maintain people's confidence in other IPFs and thus circumvent a financial crash.

Only basic rules have so far been unveiled to regulate IPFs:

1   one IPF cannot invest more than 10 per cent of its assets in a single company;

2   it cannot bid for more than 20 per cent of the shares of a single company; and

3   it cannot, altogether with its subsidiaries, bid for more than 40 per cent of the shares of a single company.

Moreover, major uncertainties remain – even after the first round of auctions during which millions of shares were distributed – about the nature, the form and the trading of shares.[19] All required regulations – according to various government officials – will be unveiled before effective trading of shares begins. The lack of clear and straightforward regulations is a feature of the privatization process. Governmental bodies regulate or directly intervene when market forces are threatened or when the process cannot properly develop. Government reaction thus follows the dynamics generated by private agents, reflecting the general philosophy of state intervention in the privatization process in Czechoslovakia. The biggest drawback of this *ad hoc* approach is that IPFs, individuals and potential local or foreign investors do not know the rules of the game. This may encourage short-termist behaviours, generate endogenous uncertainty and instability and endanger the whole process. The government will thus have to scrutinize the factors affecting the expectations and the reactions of the population, the financial stability, and the supply-side response to clinch the success of large-scale privatization in Czechoslovakia.

NOTES

1   Data presented in B. Milanovic (1989) *Liberalization and Entrepreneurship: Dynamics of Reform in Socialism and Capitalism*, London: M.E. Sharpe. Other data presented in the Economic Survey of Europe (1992) Chapter 6, *On Property Rights and Privatization in the Transition Economies*, United Nations Economic Commission for Europe, Geneva, June, show that according to Czechoslovak statistics the share of the socialized sector stood at 99.3 per cent in 1987. However, it is reported that national statistics were often biased upwards, since most governments were willing to show the highest possible degree of 'socialization'.

2   Hereafter, the term 'SOEs' refers only to those firms controlled by central authorities or supervising ministries. In the sole Czech Republic, more than 2,000 firms controlled by district authorities should be added to the 3,600 SOEs. Unless otherwise mentioned, figures presented in the text are given for SOEs.

3   See, for example, J. Kornai (1990) 'The Affinity between Ownership Forms and Coordination Mechanisms: the Common Experience of Reform in Socialist Countries', *Journal of Economic Perspectives* 4 (3).

4   They represent only 0.2 per cent of the overall number of SOEs. Estimations of Czechoslovak industrial firms' economic and financial viability generally reached the conclusion that around a quarter of industrial firms are technically bankrupt or

economically unviable under new conditions. For example, G. Hughes and P. Hare (1991) consider that 19 per cent of the total output of manufacturing industry shows negative value-added at world prices, in 'Competitiveness and industrial restructuring in Czechoslovakia, Hungary, and Poland', *European Economy*, special edition (2): 83–110.

5 Recent conceptual articles by Pelikan are useful for understanding radical structural reforms in Czechoslovakia; see, for example, 'The Dynamics of Economic Systems, or How to Transform a Failed Socialist Economy', *Journal of Evolutionary Economics* (1), 1992.

6 The average auctioned price of business units in small privatization reached Kcs 1.2 million and was 60 per cent higher than the starting price. In central quarters of Prague, the average auction price reached Kcs 34 million, 15 times the starting price!

7. For a detailed analysis of the small-scale privatization programme, see E. Klvacova *The current situation of privatization in Czechoslovakia*, Prague, October 1992, mimeo.

8 Little attention has been paid to methods of privatization introducing mortgage loans. Up to now, the Czechoslovak banking sector could not assess correctly the risks generated by these operations. Different scenarios for alternative methods of privatization in Czechoslovakia are presented in V. Kluson (1992), 'Alternative methods of privatization', *Polticka Ekonomie* (1): 23–38.

9 For a detailed discussion of the concept and reality of 'strategic sectors' in developing countries, see O. Bouin and C.-A. Michalet (1991) *Rebalancing the Public and Private Sectors: Developing Country Experience*, Paris: Development Center Studies, OECD.

10 Up to now, in spite of a tight calendar, the voucher process does not suffer significant delays. See note 15 and Appendix 2 for the calendar of voucher schemes of the first wave. The second wave of large-scale privatization is already under way. The final deadline for submitting basic and competitive privatization projects was 16 June 1992. The completion of the second wave is scheduled for autumn 1993. Doubts remain, however, about the Slovak participation in this wave.

11 However, several problems arose: lack of reliable information and items about restitution, poorly elaborated business plans, limited understanding of the current legal situation of the company after constant changes in the legislation, etc.

12 It is noteworthy that trade unions proposed only 0.2 per cent of the total number of submitted privatization projects. We could have expected a higher participation because no special provisions were made in the Czechoslovak privatization programme for employees. Submitting competitive privatization projects might have been a way to compensate for this situation.

13 Nonetheless, to a lesser extent than in other post-communist economies where this phenomenon is known as 'spontaneous' or 'wild' privatization. The fate of current managers is a complex question with political, social and economic dimensions. Viable solutions – if any exist – are related to the more general problem of liquidation of former elites.

14 It is interesting to note that the end of the first round of voucher privatization (8 June 1991) coincided with Czechoslovakia's general elections (6/7 June 1992). The popular success of the voucher scheme provided a strong political support to the Civic Democratic Party (ODS) and to its President, V. Klaus, who was Federal Minister of Finance and thus responsible for implementing the voucher scheme. ODS gained 35 per cent of votes in the Czech Republic, 10 percentage points more than expected according to pre-election opinion polls.

15 This point is of theoretical importance. The voucher scheme aims at increasing the number of privatization participants to put market forces in a position to make the best possible allocations of talents and competence. Thus, the overall process may be

economically efficient and reach the highest level possible of welfare. Apart from theoretical reservations, adverse selection of privatization projects may impede the realization of this scenario.

16 Scholars expressed doubts about the ability of such auctions to converge to an equilibrium and to provide relevant information about the relative situation of privatized companies. These auctions are not exactly of Walrasian type: the number of rounds is determined (5), buyers are not atomistic (the main Czechoslovak savings bank owns about 10 per cent of the total of points), shares are allocated before demand equals supply. These features of Czechoslovak auctions could reduce the likelihood of a market-clearing equilibrium. See J. Brada (1992) 'The mechanics of the voucher plan in Czechoslovakia', *RFE/FE Research Report 1*, (17): 42–45 and O. Bouin (1992) *The Voucher Privatization's Auctioning Process: Basic Mechanisms and Foreseeable Results*, Prague, mimeo.

17 Each round takes seven weeks to be completed. According to the auctioneer's main objective – to continue the auctioning process till an acceptable percentage of shares remain unsold is reached (10 per cent, 5 per cent or less?) or till the (financially and economically) weakest firms have sold a significant share of their equity to IPFs and individuals – ending voucher privatization by the end of 1992 could be a realistic objective.

18 The biggest commercial bank, Komercni Banka, did not promise any financial guarantee. The biggest savings bank, Ceska Sporitelna, promised credit facilities (up to Kcs 10,000) to coupon holders who might entrust their vouchers to its fund.

19 The Securities Act was still under discussion at the end of September 1992.

APPENDIX 1

Table 6.11   Approved laws concerning privatization

Restitution	Law 298/1990 on amendment of some proprietorship of Monk Orders and Congregations and Olomouc Archbishop Law 403/1990 on mending of some ownership harms Law 87/1991 on extrajuridical rehabilitations Law 172/1991 on conveyance of some property from Czech Republic ownership to communities proprietorship Law 229/1991 on amendment of ownership links to land and other agricultural property
Small privatization	Law 427/1990 on assignment of state property to other legal or physical entities Law 500/1990 on the scope of Czech bodies' control in the state ownership of some objects assigned to other legal or physical entities
Large privatization	Law 92/1991 on conveyance conditions to state property to other entities Law 171/1991 on the scope of Czech bodies' control in the state ownership of some objects assigned to other legal or physical entities
Co-operatives transformation	Law 42/1992 on amendment of ownership relations and settlement of proprietorship claims in co-operatives

Table 6.12   Main approved laws concerning private sector development and foreign participation

---

New Joint Stock Companies Act, legalizes company limited by shares, April 1990.
Amendment to CSFR Economic Code, legalizes commerical companies, April 1990.
Foreign Exchange Act, November 1990.
Act for the Protection of Economic Competition, January 1991.
Act on Bankruptcy, July 1991.
New Commercial Code, November 1991.

APPENDIX 2

Table 6.13   Time implementation of the first wave of coupon privatization

---

1 October 1991	Selling of voucher booklet begins
31 October 1991	Collection of basic privatization projects ends
20 January 1992	Collection of competitive privatization projects ends
15 February 1992	Selling of voucher booklet ends
17 February 1992	Pre-round of auctions begins
16 April 1992	Final list of firms involved in the first wave published
27 April 1992	Pre-round of auctions ends
11 May 1992	Registration of new Joint-Stock Companies in courts ends
18 May 1992	First round of auctions begins
8 June 1992	First round of auctions ends
29 June 1992	Results of first round are published in the press
8 July 1992	Second round of auctions begins
28 July 1992	Second round of auctions ends
18 August 1992	Results of second round will be published in the press

---

7

PRIVATIZATION IN CENTRAL AND EASTERN EUROPE

John Howell

INTRODUCTION

Although over the last twenty years there has been considerable experience in privatization in a number of countries throughout the world, in many ways the transformation which is taking place in Central and Eastern Europe is vastly different. The privatizations which have been carried out in the UK, for example (which has had an active privatization programme now for close on fifteen years), took place over a long time span and were restricted to a limited number of public utilities and nationalized industries which were privatized under detailed plans closely monitored at all stages by the government and within a highly regulated environment including consumer protection. The situation in Central and Eastern Europe is radically different. The speed and scope of privatization plans (for example, mass privatization programmes in Poland and Czechoslovakia) would have been considered impossible only three years ago.

Not only is the speed and scope of change radically different, but the environment in which privatization is being carried out is also radically different. It is an environment where no official private sector has existed for the last forty to seventy years; none of the normal infrastructure which supports a market economy has existed or yet exists; few related elements of the market economy have thus far been introduced; and the environment for the protection both of consumers and shareholders is very poorly regulated and not considered a high political priority. The aims are to attract investment and to achieve political goals. Regulations are seen as a distraction from and a slowing down of this process regardless of the certainty of impending public scandals.

The underlying financial infrastructure, along the lines, for example, of that which has developed in western economies, has had to be built from nothing. Investment mechanisims such as stock markets, capital markets and money markets still need to be developed. The banking systems, despite some reform, must still be decentralized, upgraded and at least partially privatized. Business support services including the law and accountancy and related infrastructure such as professional training must also be developed and that training must be instituted on a continuing basis. While most countries introducing a privatization

139

programme recognize this, the reality is that insufficient funds exist to develop the underlying financial structure within a short time period and the commitment to carry these developments through is often not as widely held amongst the public as reformist politicians would like. Privatization has often been developed ahead of the financial infrastructure which can make a success of it in order to satisfy the political objectives of giving ownership back to the people. The impetus for this has been the high political temperature of the recent general elections across Central and Eastern Europe which has required something tangible and high profile to be done to counteract the effects of growing recessions. This has the effect of never quite allowing the privatizations to become success stories or producing public confidence in the minds of a cynical population that they will see a return on their money.

Although most countries have developed western-style publicity campaigns to sell privatization these have, with the exception of Czechoslovakia, not been successful in convincing the public to apply for shares. The belief is still widespread:

1   that only the worst companies are being privatized in order to dump them; and
2   that advertising is required only for goods that will not otherwise sell, i.e. the advertising itself is often counter-productive.

Almost all politicians responsible for privatization have recognized the need to make the pilot privatizations a success regardless of what they need to do to rig the system to achieve this. Few, however, have actually been able to carry this through.

It is not only the lack of infrastructure and institutions which creates a situation where the privatization process is fraught with difficulties. It is also the fundamental gap of understanding created by the concepts on which a centralized system is based compared with those of a market economy. Add to this the political instability inherent in such a radical change of ideology, and the scene is set for the unique political and economic environment in which privatization is taking place.

To a large extent, the advisers whom these governments have retained must share in the blame for the mistakes. Both Poland and Russia, for example, have appointed such a breadth of economic advisers that conflicts between them and their academic approaches are inevitable. There is more than a suggestion that old academic rivalries are being settled on the battlefields of Eastern Europe. What is particularly unsatisfactory about this is that:

1   there has been no attempt to distill western experience and thinking into a workable plan. The East Europeans have had and still have no real means or cultural disposition to synthesizing conflicting views; and
2   short sharp shock plans have been put forward in a rarified macro-economic environment without any thought for the micro-economic realities.

There is also more than a little absence of intellectual integrity in much of the advice being given. No one has had direct experience of the scale and scope of the task being undertaken in Eastern Europe. We are all working to greater or lesser degrees in the dark. To admit this would at times be useful. Not holding out a quick-burning match as the light at the end of the tunnel would be even more useful.

In the euphoria of the initial political changes which began the reorientation to market economies, neither western advisers and investors, nor the governments and business communities of Central and Eastern Europe, conceived the size of the problems that needed to be overcome. The local governments, particularly, planned privatization programmes which aimed to move high percentages of state assets into the private sector within three to five years: objectives which were clearly unobtainable.

In addition to the other misconceptions which I have already touched on, misconceptions which arose from the gap in understanding between East and West created unrealistic expectations in the minds of government officials in Central and Eastern Europe as to the level of support which would come from western governments and investors. The misunderstanding was rooted in the lack of understanding on the East European side of what motivates a western corporation's strategy – in particular, the profit motive. This can be illustrated all too clearly, for example, in the speeches of President Walesa of Poland.

However, despite the general lack of understanding of the essential motivations within a market economy throughout Central and Eastern Europe, it has been recognized that privatization is central to the process of transformation. There is more or less a consensus on the main direction, but the speed of the process and the method are frequently changed in response to political or academic pressure. Although everywhere privatization is always a political issue, in Central and Eastern Europe the political factor is aggravated because of the high expectations of the local populations for change and the resultant pressure brought to bear on new and inexperienced politicians.

The communist ideology exercises an important constraint on this process. In many Western European countries, the privatization process created political opposition on the grounds that:

1   nationalized industries were already 'owned' by the people; and
2   the 'family silver' was being seen to be sold off at too cheap a price, i.e. the state was not generating sufficient sales income for what were perceived as key national assets.

The effect of a communist ideology has been to intensify these feelings in Central and Eastern Europe amongst significant sections of the population who retain a left-of-centre (i.e. socialist) mind-set. There has, therefore, been considerable resentment:

1   that assets have been sold off too cheaply; and

141

2   that they have been sold off to foreigners who are still often perceived as exploitative and uncaring, if not actually amoral.

It has been the political climate in each country which has had the most powerful effect on the process of privatization and which has created the diverse approaches which have been introduced. All too often, however, the political climate has had to deal with xenophobia and intense nationalism.

In order clearly to understand the effect of the transformation in each of the countries and the role they are likely to play in the future for a wider Europe, it is necessary to gain an understanding of the political climate and the process of transformation as it has developed in each country.

CZECHOSLOVAKIA

In Czechoslovakia, although the process of change came late, the parties which gained political power after the 'velvet revolution' have maintained a high degree of stability despite the ongoing question of the split of the Czech and Slovak republics. This stability has resulted more from the strength and decisiveness of certain individuals, through whom the approach to transformation has remained focused despite fragmentation of political parties, and it is these individuals who have maintained popular support. Vaclav Klaus in particular has been the driving force behind the unique approach which has been taken to privatization and specifically the main privatization (or voucher) programme.

The mass privatization scheme has at times been heavily criticized within Czechoslovakia but there has always been a refusal to bend to criticism or to abort the focused approach without which such a unique scheme would have no possibility of success. It remains uncertain as to how successful the scheme will prove to be in the long run, but it is now acknowledged that the scheme may potentially privatize a high percentage of the economy with unprecedented speed and stimulate some practical experience of the workings of a market economy for a large percentage of the population. This may well result in a flourishing stock exchange with a high level of activity. Nevertheless, the speed with which the mass privatization programme has been introduced has meant that the necessary regulatory environment in which the privatization will operate has lagged behind. This is expected to cause difficulties later and may produce a backlash if investors feel that their interests are not protected and advantage is taken of their commerical *naïveté*. Probably one of the most important effects of the approach, however, is its potential ability to undercut the sense of being stripped of the 'family silver'.

In parallel with the main privatization programme, local companies in whole or in part are also often eligible for direct foreign investment. While few large direct investments have so far been made, this process is expected to increase despite the result of the recent general election.

A clear constraint on this process is the poor state of many Czech and Slovak businesses which have seen their traditional markets in the former USSR eroded and have been unable to reorientate the business to new markets. Many of these face inevitable liquidation. Others will have to undergo a thorough process of restructuring in advance of privatization if the state is to have any asset of value left to sell.

Although the restructuring process is difficult it is not impossible, as evidenced by tremendous success in this respect with energy companies.

HUNGARY

The results of free elections in Hungary have created a comparatively high level of political stability despite the inexperience of all of the new politicians in both the governing and opposition parties. Hungary's historical approach to reform has also meant that, within the political sphere, the continuing influence of the old regime has remained a minor factor and has resulted in a strong consensus for reform which has limited the debate as to the approach. Also, the economic situation was not such that it required the same level of shock therapy as has been needed in countries such as Poland and Russia.

Privatization began spontaneously at the instigation of managers of companies. In response to public pressure the State Property Agency (SPA) was set up to oversee the sales of state assets. Although this body has sometimes been a useful facilitator of individual privatizations, it has more often impeded the process due to a lack of understanding and imagination of individual bureaucrats within the SPA. The SPA has also been used as the political scapegoat in order to relieve criticism levelled at the government. This has resulted in many members of the SPA being unwilling to make decisions which might be considered controversial and has frequently led to frustration on the part of foreign investors.

In order to speed the process of privatization, particularly of larger companies, the government introduced formalized government controlled programmes. These programmes were singularly unsuccessful as there was a lack of clear direction from the SPA and a lack of understanding on the part of company managers. At the same time, privatization by public flotation was also becoming an unattractive route as overvaluation and excessive expectations of the performance of some of the few earlier issues has resulted in a seriously depressed stock market.

In recent months the government has again retreated to a position of encouraging spontaneous privatizaion. The approach overall has been one of putting the appropriate legislation in place and allowing the business community to move ahead with minimal government direction and interference unless an issue became politically uncomfortable. The process of transformation has been allowed to happen rather than actively being controlled and directed by the government.

The government's *laissez-faire* approach has allowed the privatization of many medium-sized companies, usually through trade sales to foreign investors. It has also resulted in some unexpected bonuses for the economy such as the ability of a surprising number of Hungarian companies to reorientate exports westwards after the collapse of Comecon. However, it has done little to raise public awareness of the underlying rules governing a market economy and has left a sense of disillusionment for much of the population in both the transformation process and the government. It has also resulted in a split in society as a small number of managers and entrepreneurs take advantage of the open situation whilst the vast majority of the population have found themselves unable to participate except to suffer the effects of the transformation. This has included the liquidation of many Hungarian companies.

Most people have found themselves worse off and many are facing unemployment for the first time. There is a rising tide of resentment towards the government for 'allowing the situation' and resentment towards the minority who have been able to take advantage of the situation and have become well off in the process. The politics of envy are very much in evidence. Resentment is exacerbated by the sense of powerlessness arising from non-participation which in turn has increased the apathy which was an inherent part of the old centralized system.

POLAND

The initial government which took power in Poland as the communist system began to collapse resulted from negotiations between Solidarity and the previous regime. This created a government with strong union support for radical economic transformation but with the impediment of the continuing strong influence of the previous communist party undermining transformation. However, the government was able to move ahead with a shock therapy reform programme because of popular support based on the assumption that there would be quick and tangible results from political and economic change and as the only way in which much needed international funding would be made available.

The first full free elections came at a time when severe disillusionment had set in resulting from the pain of the transformation process. The strength of the unions resulted in a stronger and more widespread expression of dissatisfaction compared to the more apathetic responses in other countries. The election process permitted a large number of small parties to be represented in the parliament and disillusionment with the previous government led to a large number of disparate views being represented. This has destroyed the possibility for consensus and the lack of clear government is fast destroying the gains made by the previous government.

During the period of shock therapy, the government also took a strong approach to privatization. In order to control the process and ensure that individual privatizations were not detrimental to the industry as a whole, sectoral privatization was introduced whereby all the companies in a particular industry sector could be assessed and appropriate privatization plans put forward in the context of the industry as a whole.

Although spontaneous privatization instigated by management is permitted in Poland, in practice there have been few successful trade sales on this basis. Foreign investors have frequently found that, on the one hand, foreign investment is encouraged, but in practice it is difficult to bring deals to fruition. This has mainly been as a result of ambivalence on the part of individual ministries arising from the undermining influence of former communists who still retained political power. It has also resulted from the often open hostility between rival politicians. The investor also has had to contend with the political differences between the industry ministries, which favour leaving existing management in control and for any cash generated to stay in the business, and the privatization ministry whose chief interest is in meeting the wholly unrealistic targets of the Polish budget for privatization proceeds.

Meanwhile there is no real control over the economy, and the environment allows little possibility to progress the restructuring of the large state-owned industries. However, Poland's saving grace may well be its flourishing private sector which is not caught in the recession which bedevils the state sector. According to official statistics, private companies account for 40 per cent of the country's output and are expected to make up more than 50 per cent of GDP by 1994. Unfortunately, foreign investors see only the political chaos and continuously encounter new faces in the relevant ministries. As a result, they are hesitant about proceeding with investment. If further foreign investment can be attracted so that further privatization can take place, Poland may well become one of those countries where the economy flourishes despite ongoing instability in government. In this respect, there may be more than a little comparison between Poland and the way in which Italy has developed in the post-war years.

Consideration is also being given to carrying out similar programmes as are being used in Central Europe, in particular the type of mass privatization similar to that being implemented in Czechoslovakia. This type of scheme is being considered in both Russia and the Ukraine.

RUSSIA

Since coming to power, President Yeltsin has provided a strong focus for the reform process and has gathered a team of reforming economists who have had the courage to implement tough reform measures in the face of strong criticism from elements of the former communist party in the parliament and fears of violent social unrest. Three main factors impede the process of reform:

1 the continuing influence and power of former communists;
2 the total chaos of the economy which creates a fertile breeding ground for mafia elements and widespread abuse and discontent; and

3   the power wielded by large companies which control all major industry
     sectors and threaten mass unemployment if government sudsidies are
     withdrawn.

The government has been actively encouraging privatization, beginning with
small enterprises, and the intention is now to progress to mandatory privatization
of those large state enterprises which are impeding the progress of transformation
of the economy as a whole due to inefficiencies.

The government appeared to have a strong hand and a strong stomach for
tackling the reform of the economy. However, recent changes in members of the
government have reintroduced conservative elements less favourable to dramatic
reform who have forced a number of U-turns in policy, for example, the
liberalization of energy policy. In addition, the underlying bureaucratic structure
is frequently made up of old communist elements which are also resistant to
change and undermine government policy, making it impossible for the
government to maintain control over the process of reform. Although overall
direction is being given for the privatization process and for the participation of
foreigners in that process, investment in large state enterprises continues to be
negotiated on a deal by deal basis.

However, foreign investors are hesitant to buy into enterprises which are
heavily overmanned, provide huge social benefits for their employees such as
schools and health services and over which they are unlikely to have any control.
There has been some discussion of introducing special exchange rates for
foreigners to try to prevent discrimination against Russian participation in the
privatization process due to the weak rouble. At present, however, this plan has
been dropped.

The major enterprises are also forcing compromise on the government's
strong monetary policy by using the threat of mass unemployment to demand the
retention of subsidies. The potential for serious unrest as a result of the decline in
living standards and the constant threat of unemployment cannot be ignored, but
the government recognizes that these problems cannot be overcome without
continual efforts to break the power of state property and the centralized system
of planning and distribution which is still such an inherent part of the country's
economy.

Only privatization on a massive scale can do this but it remains to be seen how
successful the programme will be. An entrepreneurial spirit is beginning to
emerge throughout Russia and change may well develop in ways that have not
yet been seen despite the experiences of Central Europe.

UKRAINE

Although the Government of the Ukraine was freely elected there is widespread
disenchantment because of the slow pace of reform. The Ukraine Government is
widely seen as not yet having reached even the level of reformist zeal which

existed under former President Gorbachev's administration. Although privatization legislation is in place and the government has stated intentions to privatize 65 per cent of large and medium-sized enterprises within five years, very little has taken place in practice.

To date the government has been preoccupied with establishing and defending the national interests of the Ukraine as it emerges as a new country and has only peripherally addressed the problems of the economy. As in Russia, a tight monetary policy is needed but has not yet been introduced. Market regulations need to be liberalized and privatization must be encouraged. As yet the government has not faced any of these issues except at the level of legislation or in response to moves by Russia.

Until the government moves from words to action it is difficult to assess how the transformation will progress and it may be that the government will move only in response to the growing popular pressure.

ROMANIA

Romania has embarked on a privatization process funded largely by PHARE with some assistance from the UK Know How Fund (KHF). Twelve companies were selected for privatization. Ten, funded by PHARE, were principally to be sold via trade sales. Two, funded by the KHF, were to be sold by public offer.

The advisers selected came from the UK, France and Germany in an effort to show that PHARE was representative of the EEC. In fact, as can be expected, the style and standard of the work has varied enormously broadly in line with the underlying experience of those three countries in privatization programmes on their home territory.

It is too early to say whether these privatizations will be successful. Ultimately, their success will depend on the speed with which other aspects of the reform process can take place. With an election in late September, the emphasis will undoubtedly be on high profile political results over the next few months rather than on economic results.

BULGARIA

Bulgaria now has a workable privatization law and is developing the infrastructure to push privatization through. It is therefore too early to comment on the experience to date.

Nevertheless, it is clear from the attitude both of major local enterprises such as Balkan Bulgarian Airlines and Balkancar and the attitude of senior ministers that greater emphasis will be given to spontaneous privatizations rather than large government programmes.

8

PRIVATIZATION IN GUYANA[1]

Carl B. Greenidge

INTRODUCTION

The success of Guyana's privatization efforts has tended to be overshadowed by the severity and initial fall-out of the structural adjustment programme and from the political liberalization process being undertaken by Guyana.

Privatization has been a crucial element of Guyana's Economic Recovery Programme (ERP) which has been in place over the last three years. This exercise has probably been the most successful of its kind in the English-speaking Caribbean, which is not to say that it has been unproblematic. Precisely because of the size of the public enterprise (PEs) sector in Guyana and the extent of the privatization exercise, there is a range of experiences which can provide useful insights into the impact and constraints associated with privatization. Although entities were privatized prior to 1989 they were not part of a programme to constrain and reduce the size of the public sector.

EMPIRICAL CONTEXT

The sectoral composition of the public enterprise sector

As of 1990 the bulk of the PEs were located primarily in the agricultural and forestry (29 per cent), commercial and transport (21 per cent), manufacturing and food processing (19 per cent), banking and financial services (17 per cent), utilities (10 per cent) and mining (4 per cent) sectors.[2] These include five regional PEs in agriculture (3), financial services (1) and transport (1) (see Greenidge 1982).

The size distribution of public enterprises

The enterprises as a whole accounted for the employment of 44,300 persons in 1990. This represented over 50 per cent of public sector employment. The largest of the enterprises in terms of employment was the sugar company, Guysuco (29,000 in 1990). The next in line were the bauxite (5,000), the electricity (1,500) and the telecommunications (1,440) companies.

148

Table 8.1 Employment distribution among PEs

No. employed	No. of enterprises	%
Over 5,000	1	2
2,000–4,999	1	2
1,000–1,999	5	11
500–999	7	16
250–499	9	20
0–249	22	49
Total	45	100

It can be seen from Table 8.1 that the bulk of the enterprises employed less than 250 persons. The modal employment level (24 per cent) was 50–100 employees. Relative to the private sector, however, these are large enterprises.

In terms of fixed capital formation, the largest of the enterprises are in mining, sugar, agriculture and manufacturing. Similarly in terms of annual turnover as at 1990 the largest of the enterprises were the sugar enterprise, the bauxite company, a commercial bank and a trading entity followed by the telecommunications utility. These five enterprises alone accounted for 57 per cent of total PE turnover in that year.

Public ownership in terms of equity participation (excluding subsidiaries)

Seventeen of the PEs are subsidiaries of one or other of the main government-owned PEs. The partners involved in those partially owned range from PEs to trade unions and from co-operatives to private insurance companies.

Organizational structures

Two of the PEs, Bidco and GLC, are formal holding companies. The central government employs a variety of devices to control and monitor those enterprises. The Public Corporations Secretariat which is responsible for the 'non-independent' entities has that function *de facto* also. The Guyana Pharmaceutical Corporation (GPC), Guyana Sugar Corp. (Guysuco), and Construction Management Combine Ltd. (CMLC) also have subsidiaries, some of them more than one. Some companies such as Guymine also have subsidiaries. One minister has policy responsibility for the entities falling under the PEs. The other PEs except the financial institutions are the responsibility of the President.

Profitability record

No exhaustive information is available on the financial performance of all the public enterprises in Guyana. During the latter part of the 1970s, there was a

Table 8.2 Government ownership

Govt equity share in 1990 (%)	$	%
75–100	37	82
50–74	2	4
25–49	1	2
0–24	6	13
Total	47	99

decline in dividend payments relative to net after tax income (Greenidge 1982). Since 1982 the fiscal performance of these enterprises has declined and has necessitated guarantees and transfers from the central government as well as claims on the banking system.

This trend has been most evident in the case of the major enterprises such as the Sugar Company, Guysuco, and the bauxite companies, BIDCO and Guymine.

Between 1976, when the sugar enterprise was nationalized, and 1990, nationalization payments by the state amounted to £12m. Over that period, the state received no dividends, was paid negligible amounts of corporation and property taxes, remitted $ 1,200m in levies payable and, in addition, invested $ 593m to keep the industry alive.

Similarly, over the 14 years from 1977 to 1990 the bauxite company, Guymine, paid income and corporation taxes in only four years. No dividends have been declared or paid to the government by the Holding Company Bidco since 1979. Between 1980 and 1989, G$ 775.9m of current transfers from the Treasury were effected to clear the overdrafts accumulated by the company.

Between 1978 and 1987, some G$ 703m was provided by the Treasury to the Guystac corporations. In the following three years, 1988–90, the current transfers rose from G$ 59m to over G$ 600m. That to the electric utility, GEC, alone amounted to $ 836m. Whilst the current transfers to the Guystac corporations, other than the rice group (GRMMA, GREB and NPRGC), did not match that dramatic increase, there was a similar increase in capital transfers. In 1985 these amounted to about $ 31m. By 1989 the figure stood at roughly $ 190m. In 1990 companies with over G$ 30b of government shares paid less than $ 100m in dividends representing under a third of 1 per cent of the former investment. Only ten entities contributed to that payment.

At the end of December 1990, the external debt contracted by the PEs or by the Government of Guyana on behalf of PEs was US$ 285m, of which US$ 197m was still outstanding. So, the traditional central government deficit on the current account, instead of being offset by dividends and operating surpluses of the PEs, was compounded. In the absence of measures sufficiently strong to correct this situation, the overall deficit on the current account of the public sector quickly assumed outlandish proportions.

Central government and state government enterprises

Strictly defined, very few enterprises are operated by municipal agencies. By and large the services provided by these agencies do not cover the full cost of provision of the services and it is debatable whether this has been the intention of such charges as are levied.

Share of public enterprises in the national economy

In 1990 PEs accounted for 44.4 per cent of Guyana's GDP. This reflects a decrease in their contribution relative to 1980. The importance of PEs varies from one sector to another.

The most important sectors in GDP terms were agriculture (14.4 per cent), services (13 per cent) and mining and quarrying followed by manufacturing (5.8 per cent). One would expect this importance to decline as the privatization gets under way. This has been the intention of the ERP.

THE SETTING

The relevant political and administrative structures

Responsibility for privatization was initially assigned to the Public Corporations Secretariat (PCS) which was required to report to an economic sub-committee of the Cabinet. Subsequently, the Minister of Planning was given responsibility for overviewing that aspect of the work of the PCS. A standing committee of economic ministers and senior officials was set up to approve final recommendations. The PCS is charged with vetting applications, undertaking the relevant analysis and making recommendations to the Minister of Planning for all but the rice, bauxite and sugar entities. A Divestment Unit headed by a very senior official and reinforced with UNDP/UNIDO experts was established in the PCS to undertake the tasks and the Attorney General's Chambers and the Auditor General's Department were to provide special support to the Unit.

The divestment of the rice milling entities (GRMMA) was handled by the Office of the President, and more specifically the Economic Adviser, whilst the others were the responsibility of the Chairman of the State Planning Board (who was during part of this period in question also the Minister of Planning) and the relevant managements assisted by some other agencies.

Responsibility for divestment of the financial agencies has rested with the Chairman of COFA who is also the Minister of Finance. The flotation of shares in the two formerly private banks was undertaken by a team or task force under the aegis of the Ministry of Finance.

These arrangements, informed by the distribution of skills and interest, appear to be unexceptionable relative to other countries. Many of the latter have utilized the kind of combination employed in Guyana. Brazil, for example, uses the

National Development Bank (BNDES), the Economic Planning Unit and the relevant policy or executing ministries.

In some countries such as Germany and Hungary, on the other hand, specialized agencies, the Treuhandanstalt and the State Property Agency (SPA), respectively, were specifically established to implement privatization. Nigeria established the Technical Committee on Privatization and Commercialization (TCPC) for this purpose.

Clearly there is something to be said for each of the institutional forms. There are also problems associated with each. Many problems were encountered with the structure employed in Guyana. Among these was striking an acceptable balance between speed of decision making and completion of technical assessments. From time to time this would give rise to tensions between the relevant agencies. The weight to be given to financial considerations such as the bona fides of the applicants, the fiscal concessions to be granted and the price have also been the sources of problems. The fact that privatization was largely fiscally driven, while the priority assigned to financial problems and issues was frequently determined by the Planning Agency or Office of the President, not only gave rise to tensions between the agencies but contributed to decisions that did not appear transparent to the public.

The lack of a clear separation of responsibility between the policy and privatizing agencies can be very much a problem. The role of the policy minister and the minister responsible for divestment is a case in point. In that regard, mention should be made of the need to identify the most appropriate channel of communication to affected employees and the lack of a conflict-resolution mechanism particularly when matters pertaining to fiscal policy arise.

Since the preparation of information on the PE itself is a time-consuming exercise it may well be appropriate to free senior managers of the burden of routine management if they are responsible for privatization. The possibility of conflict of interest should not be overlooked either. In many instances managers seek to secure favourable post-privatization treatment of themselves by passing inside information to potential owners. Indeed, a similar phenomenon was also experienced during the course of nationalization.

Policy statement on privatization

The factors responsible for the acceleration of privatization in Guyana have been outlined elsewhere (Greenidge 1992a). A formal commitment to step up the pace of privatization was made in the latter part of 1989 following recognition of the need to further improve the fiscal performance in the light of the unwillingness of the Support Group to provide adequate financial support for the Economic Recovery Programme. However, the commitment to privatization can be said to have been signalled in the State paper on investment (1988). It was underpinned to a large extent by the recommendation of an Advisory Group (Kuhn Loeb Lehman 1983). The latter report had set the PEs on the road to non-divestiture

152

privatization. The policy, therefore, on privatization was cast and structured in a very specific context outside of any ideological considerations.

Indeed, insofar as ideology exercised an influence it was ambivalent. There was still a commitment to the democratization of capital. There was now to be divestiture of PEs with no 'sacred cows'. The private sector would not be debarred from any economic activity. There was, however, some hostility to an unregulated market economy. Government policy statements on privatization were in this sense, therefore, quite narrow and can be found in the annual budget statement 1990 and 1991 and the Policy Framework Papers of the same year. The PFP statement proposed a two-pronged approach to privatization by way of the divestment of some enterprises to the private sector contemporaneously with the strengthening and structuring of other enterprises through their association with foreign investors.

Economic recovery programme (ERP) and its relevance to privatization

In 1989 Guyana embarked on a wide-ranging programme of economic liberalization. The basic objective of this programme was to resuscitate the economy and reverse the decade of economic decline and deterioration which the economy had suffered. At that time Guyana's per capita GDP was SDR 297; its external debt/GDP ratio at 902.7 per cent was the highest in the world; net international reserves minus US$ 500m, and overall public sector deficit was minus 47 per cent of GDP. This was not a situation which could be corrected without external help; nor would the then current solutions such as the Brady Plan be of the least relevance.

The intention of the ERP was to restore the economic vibrancy of the economy by converting it from a regulated market system with extensive administrative and price controls to one based on the vibrant operation of the market. There was an extensive liberalization of foreign exchange, trade and domestic pricing regimes. At the same time the policy aimed to enhance the role and capacity of the private sector.

The impact of this programme on incomes, particularly on wage incomes, was severe during the first 27 months. The exchange rate depreciated from G$ 10 to G$ 130 to US$ 1.00: that resulted from foreign exchange shortages and inadequate support from the international community. Accelerated inflation severely eroded real incomes. Referring to the proposed transfer of resources from the public to the private sector, one commentator observed that it was probably the most ambitious programme of adjustment ever to go before the IMF Board of Directors. This was the background against which privatization was implemented.

CONSTRAINTS

Privatization progressed far more slowly than had been anticipated or promised by the government. Implementation eventually picked up pace in the latter half of 1991 partly as a result of the inclusion of profitable enterprises not on the original list of eleven. The programme is currently very much ahead of the schedule which the government embraced in 1989. Nineteen enterprises have been either fully or partially privatized. Two of the entities on the original list have yet to be privatized.

Until the process gained momentum, there was public criticism of this slow pace and the commitment of the government to the process was questioned. As the number of privatizations started to increase, however, criticism switched to the excessive pace of the exercise as well as the low prices at which settlements were effected. It would appear that this is a classic catch 22 no-win situation. Additionally, public dissatisfaction was voiced about two or three transactions. These have tended to dog the entire programme.

Political and social factors

Given the political background prevailing in Guyana during the 1970s and most of the 1980s it should hardly come as a surprise to learn of political resistance to privatization. In addition to that ideological resistance, the general circumstances of economic crisis and recession in domestic economic activities in which privatization has had to be effected did not help. Guyana, like Brazil, for example, is attempting to privatize during the course of one of the worst economic recessions since the 1939–45 War.

As a consequence, political tempers flare and as happened in Poland, Hungary and Czechoslovakia recently, may be serious enough to stop economic reforms. Some part of the hostility may be aimed at foreigners because of the growing public resentment over real or perceived give-aways to foreigners. The asymmetrical impact of rapid exchange rate depreciation and monetary imbalance on domestic relative to foreign incomes is the prime catalyst here. It may mitigate against domestic participation in the privatization process.

Furthermore, in Guyana that process is evolving against a background of a radical liberalization of the economy. Those charged with implementing the process find it necessary to review and modify the rules almost daily. This has also been the experience elsewhere, particularly in Eastern Europe.

Recognition of these very real problems has given rise to research into the relationship between capacity to implement harsh adjustment policies and forms of governance. One recent study concluded that dramatic changes in economic management including privatization might most effectively be undertaken by an autonomous state which is both benevolent and intelligent. Such a state can fashion and implement sensible reforms without the need to seek consensus, an exercise which is difficult in fledgling democracies or countries in the process or throes of rapid economic change (Lall 1990).

In some countries, the politicization of the work place has led some governments to embrace privatization. In Guyana it may be said that some work places, such as sugar and bauxite, are so politicized. There is some evidence to suggest the widening of this process. The political party which has controlled the sugar unions has been resisting the initiative of privatizations of these industries because they perceive in it a threat to their political muscle *vis-à-vis* the government.

Considerations of national development strategy

An important constraint to privatization is the state of socio-economic infrastructure. It is widely recognized that, depending upon the stage of a country's development, private sector initiative may not be forthcoming within a reasonable time span and at a reasonable cost in relation to some activities. This is believed to be true in some infrastructural projects particularly in the lowest income countries or those with a markedly uneven incidence of development across geographical regions. To some extent privatization makes difficult, if not impossible, planned development led by innovative investment. In pursuit of facilitating some such undertakings, the inadequacies of the market, in a situation where new initiatives need to be taken in sectors characterized by high risk, is widely recognized. Governments, therefore, sometimes attempt to assign higher priorities to privatization proposals which are consistent with national development strategy. Governments may favour companies which promise to address such areas. The same may be done in relation to encouraging technological advancement. The use of such criteria, however, may mask the transparency of the decision.

Additionally, the financial and operational state of the enterprise in question can be important constraints to the extent that both the Treasury and the enterprise are in very difficult financial straits. In such circumstances it would be difficult to privatize or, if privatization takes place, to receive a decent return for the assets since prospective buyers are likely to discount heavily for risk.

Macro-economic situation

In the light of what was said above about the economic background under which Guyana embarked on privatization, it should be obvious that privatization is likely to be more profitably pursued in more buoyant economic circumstances. All experiences in depressed economic circumstances point to the attraction of basement bargain seekers.

The financial situation and managerial capacity of individual enterprises, if very poor, can be a deterrent to joint ventures. If the enterprise could be restructured in a timely manner, the prospects of a better price as well as a partial divestiture option would be greater. The problem of the restructuring of the enterprise is essentially one of the opportunity cost. Would the use of the money for that purpose yield the required result within a reasonable time span? Would that result spawn greater returns than an alternative use of the funds (Greenidge 1992b)? This is another reason why privatization is best conducted in more stable and non-crisis ridden macro-economic circumstances.

Nature and efficiency of private enterprises in the country

The employment policies and related practices of many of the private companies in Guyana have served to make some of the members of the public wary of an increased role for them. By and large concerns about efficiency of the sector have not loomed terribly large in the debate. Far more important have been concerns about discriminatory sales and employment policies and unconscionable pricing practices.

The contribution of Guyana's private sector to GDP is very significant especially by way of agriculture where rice, forestry, livestock, fisheries, ground provisions, fruits and coconuts are dominant. Trading activities are notable, with manufacturing accounting for a relatively small share of activities. This latter sector, which initially suffered most grievously from the structural adjustment measures, has expanded significantly in recent months. The most notable segments of the sector are textiles, food and beverage processing, matches, insurance and mining.

The remarkable 1991/2 upturn in economic performance which saw the economy return to a large and positive growth rate after a decade of almost unmitigated decline was attributable in large measure to improved performance and investment by the private sector. Major actors in this regard were the rice and gold mining sectors. Non-traditional agriculture, especially the export of fruit and the production of all types of foodstuff, has performed well over the years notwithstanding the crisis.

It would be true to say that six characteristics are noteworthy in relation to the Guyana private sector:

1. outside of agriculture and the grey economy, local businesses have tended to be very conservative and less than innovative;
2. the leading technological sectors are under foreign ownership and control, e.g. industrial gold mining and shipping, forestry and sawmilling;
3. foreign investors and Guyanese emigrants are increasing their influence and control of the economy;
4. most of the locally-owned companies are closely-held family businesses;
5. there is a high incidence of tax evasion not limited to local firms; and
6. employment policies have tended to be community based and very narrow.

156

Infrastructural considerations

Capital markets

In Guyana, the cost and time associated with privatization have been considerably increased by the absence of a capital market. In any case private share issues in recent years have, with one notable exception, been markedly undersubscribed, although at the same time, the banking system is characterized by excessive liquidity.

The efficiency of share issues is limited by the narrow volume of stock trading and the absence of a stock market. In recent times a few large issues have been floated, thereby restricting the prospect of other large issues within the near future.

Legal instruments

Whilst legal instruments have not been a particular problem, the untidy financial and legal arrangements associated with many public enterprise operations have without a doubt slowed the pace and increased the cost and complexity of the process of privatization. The legislation has been modified in order to facilitate the orderly and timely transfer of PEs to the private sector and to stop creditors holding up the process.

Regulatory structure

Few regulative structures exist for the purpose of safeguarding the public interest. The Public Utility Commission (PUC) established after the transfer of the telecommunications entity is understaffed and short of funds. It may well be argued that the skills required of the agency for purposes of carrying out its mission exceed those of managing the company itself. More importantly, however, the attack mounted by the private telecommunications company against the members of the Commission, the recruitment of the Consumers' Association and the suborning of prominent public and private Guyanese has served to weaken the public support and understanding for the role and activities of the Commission.

In the absence of the types of regulatory structures which exist in the United Kingdom, for example, the negotiation of a privatization agreement may be unnecessarily side-tracked by attempts to substitute safeguards concerning the public interest in the agreement. In the United Kingdom some sectors, in addition to having recourse to the Serious Fraud Office and the Monopolies and Mergers Commission, also have specific regulatory agencies such as OFEL in the electricity sector. In the absence of regulatory structures, it becomes difficult to assuage the concerns of the public.

Privatization is very demanding in terms of skills, especially in those areas such as marketing where the public sector has generally not been terribly active, and this is one of the primary reasons why both the preparation of profiles of enterprises tends to be slow and sometimes inappropriate, and the assessment of applications tends to be less than perfect (Greenidge 1992a).

In Guyana, the attitude of the public to privatization was favourably influenced by the declining level and quality of services being provided by the public enterprises. It does appear, however, that *ex post* report on the negotiations and the outcome appears not to be sufficient for the public. Where the media are not taken fully on board they can do immeasurable damage to the public confidence in the process. For this reason governments may be well advised to give early consideration to devoting resources to supplementing the work of the privatization agencies with a carefully co-ordinated and adequately resourced press campaign. Indeed the director of the Treuhand in Germany pointed to the fact that the bulk of the time of her staff was taken up in dealing with the press.

Even as obvious and necessary an exercise as the operation of regulatory agencies for utilities can be thrown off the track. In Guyana the PUC finds itself at the brunt of ill-informed and unwarranted criticism about its role, 'helped' by a hostile or suborned press.

It needs to be said that in the last analysis the effectiveness of the privatization programme will turn in large measure on the context in which the privatized entities are operating. The model of extensive privatization is, for example, consistent with widely accepted principles of social equity and justice, only if it is supplemented by strong and effective government as well as active and financially robust charities and non-governmental organizations. The general experience in developing countries such as Guyana is that these conditions are far from being met to any extent. The public attitudes to and perceptions of the costs of privatization are already coloured by the absence of these supporting structures.

The constraints on non-divestment options

It may be observed from Table 8.3 that there has been relatively limited resort to non-divestment options. Looking at the cases since 1984, over a quarter were closed or liquidated primarily because they were unviable and constituted a heavy drain on financial resources or were of marginal production significance.

The lease or rental option has been quite effective in the solitary case where it has been tried. Whether the state receives a net benefit from it will depend, of course, on its ability to ensure that the assets are maintained in good order.

There have been only two management contracts. The management contract is an attractive proposition. Again not many private sector businesses seem interested in pursuing it perhaps because they prefer outright acquisition. To be effective it requires the government to be able to have a capacity to independently

Table 8.3 Privatization options employed

Modes of privatisation	No. of PEs	%
Liquidation	1	4
Closure	6	22
Share issue	6	22
Lease/rental	1	4
Sale	8	30
Management contract	2	7
Total	27	99

assess targets and to judge a reasonable fee for the attainment of the targets. Where some major industry with an international market is involved, the state may find itself without the independent advice. In fact, the arrangements have tended to result in a switch of employees' allegiances to the new managers. There is the obvious temptation to exaggerate the difficulty of achieving the targets. In Guyana's case, there is the possibility that the contractors may be interested in taking equity eventually. In such circumstances, care needs to be taken to ensure that funds are not directed in a manner intended to save the future owners from part of the burden of areas of expenditures – areas that will not necessarily be reflected in the valuation of assets.

Finally, where industries may be international in nature, small and highly competitive, conclusion of a management contract may well scare off other interested partners because they feel that the incumbent contractor may have an 'inside track' in any future search for an equity partner.

The choice of the other means was influenced by objective circumstances.

IMPACTS

By and large the results of privatization have been positive. It needs to be said, however, that in public discussions of this matter, between this reality and the perception lies a very wide gulf.

The nature of post-privatization ownership

This is the case, for example, with ownership. Guyana was, prior to 1976, so dominated by foreign enterprises in general, and Booker McConnell in particular, that the acronym B.G. was popularly used to describe 'Booker's Guyana'. In these circumstances there was a fierce debate about the desirability of facilitating stronger foreign influence in the economy through ownership by means of privatization. The conditions of recession and the steep devaluation of the currency which have characterized the initial phase of the economic recovery programme reinforced such concerns. In reality, however, privatization has not been a device for providing foreigners with a bonanza or for the recolonization of the economy. From Table 8.4 it may be seen that some 56 per cent of the entities privatized were acquired by Guyanese, resident and expatriate. Leaving aside the commercial banks, all but two of these privatizations which did not involve the sale of assets on a piecemeal basis went to the traditional, culturally-based entities. In the exceptions, shares have been issued and have been reasonably widely taken up. Naturally, this was conditioned by the recession. Employees have also tended to be allocated a preferred place in the queue.

Although the bulk of the smaller businesses were acquired by Guyanese, they were not alone in such acquisitions. Guyanese buyers secured 40 per cent of the number of entities that fetched prices in excess of US$ 5m. Most of the assets sold as a result of the closure of enterprises were acquired by Guyanese. Furthermore, where privatization has been associated with marketization, in the sense of the contracting out of services, Guyanese provided the bulk of such services, e.g. transportation of all types, installation of telephones. It needs to be added that the bulk of the acquisitions by Guyanese has been by individuals or closely held private companies. This has implications for the pattern of employment associated with privatization since traditionally such companies tend to recruit skills within their cultural communities.

Changes in efficiency

The impact of privatization on efficiency may be separated for analytical purposes according to the micro and macro context. It would require a great deal more information than is currently available in order to make an assessment of privatization on the macro-economic indicators.

It would be difficult also to be definite about relative efficiencies in an economy so little studied in depth. If it is any guide, a recent report prepared for the Government of Guyana and financed by the IBRD suggested that the competitiveness of the private sector manufacturers was relatively low and accounted for price levels of as much as 40 per cent in excess of free market prices (Crittle 1991).

Table 8.4 Categories of buyers acquiring PEs

	< US$ 1m	1.01–2m	2.1–4.1m	> US 5m	No.	%
C'com Cos.	3	–	1	1	5	31
Extra-regional Cos.	–	–	–	2	2	13
Local closely held Cos.	2	1	–	1	4	25
Individuals & misc.	2	1	–	1	4	25
Local public cos.	1	–	–			6
Total	8	2	1	5	16	100

The most visible impact of privatization in Guyana has been on output, employment, wage income, investment levels, and management styles. It should also be added that the fiscal impact of privatization has been largely achieved in accordance with the original intention of the programme. The most dramatic area of improved efficiency has been in the output of commodities such as rice and sugar. The Minister of Finance pointed out in his budget statement of 1991 that the record first crop in that year was probably the result of the conjunction of privatization and increased availability of imported inputs.

Additionally, problems over the payment of rice farmers which had been a persistent matter of contention between the state-owned rice agencies and farmers seemed to have been attenuated to some extent. It should be added, however, that the euphoria generated by the early and timely payments during 1991 has now given way to complaints about bounced cheques and late payments by private millers. In reality, however, the burden of adjusting to market vagaries have been transferred from the millers, or rather from the Treasury, to individual farmers. Those millers who pay on time whatever the circumstances are more likely to take farmers' rice only when convenient.

This twist serves to highlight the dangers of drawing too facile a conclusion about differences in perceived patterns of behaviour with reference to one indicator only. Similarly, there can be no doubt that the management contract currently being executed in relation to the sugar industry has contributed significantly to an increase in the technical and financial efficiency of the company. The capacity of the contractor to acquire skills on a contractual basis or to draw on support from Head Office has enabled them to capitalize on the fortuitous changes in the weather and the arrival of inputs under external financial programmes.

At the same time some of these privatized entities, whilst perhaps more efficient than their public sector counterparts, have not been efficient enough to overcome the objective circumstances of environment in which they operate. Thus, the fishing entities have in recent months found it difficult to operate with an adequate level of profit in the face of falling yields and probably inadequate research and survey work. Some entities have had their efficiency enhanced by the nature of the privatization. This has probably been the case with SAPIL, a container manufacturer. As part of a debt-for-equity arrangement, its major and influential customer in the market characterized in recent years by over-expansion, overinvestment and fierce competition, acquired shares in the company.

In other instances, it has also been difficult to make an objective assessment of the extent to which privatization *per se* has been a major factor in improving efficiency. An example is provided by the commercial banks which have been very profitable since privatization, but, unlike their counterpart which remains in the public sector, exhibit the benefits of not having to work under the constraining hand of the government. Their interest rate spreads have been quite phenomenal, achieving levels as high as 18 percentage points. In one case, the pursuit of profits by the aggressive pricing of foreign exchange has at times contributed to unnecessary fluctuations in the exchange rate.

It is sometimes difficult to disentangle management efficiency from the benefits accruing to a company which has substantial capital injections. In fact, it has been widely recognized and acknowledged that one of the main difficulties facing Guyana's PEs since the mid-1980s has been undercapitalization. Many no doubt would have been in a position to improve their efficiency had the state been able to remedy this problem and to provide them with working capital. Capacity utilization had on average fallen to levels of 30 per cent by 1989.

Changes in the profit record

No systematic or extensive work has yet been undertaken on the financial performance of recently privatized entities. Part of the reason for this has, of course, been the fact that privatization is of recent vintage. It could be said as a general rule, however, that to date there have been no demonstrable financial failures, although the fact that some entities have received or are seeking exceptional fiscal concessions should be borne in mind. Doubtless some companies are in difficult financial straits and these do not only include the very small local companies. There have been spectacular profit increases or performances in some cases such as the privatized telecommunications company, the sugar company and the commercial banks, to name but a few.

Employment effects

In Guyana, privatization, excluding pre-sale closures, has not been associated with redundancy, or any form of widescale frictional employment. On the contrary, unlike the experience elsewhere in the region, the exercise has led unambiguously to increases in numbers employed. This is a reflection, in part, of the nature of the difficulties including inadequate working capital, underutilized capacity, as well as the chronic shortage of skills. Just as importantly, many entities have been able to increase wages and salaries substantially after privatization.

Impacts on technology

We are not in a position to say a great deal about the impact of privatization on the level and extent of technological developments in the new entities. From the reports received, and as would be expected, given the access of many of the enterprises to management support, the management of technological change has improved.

Second, the considerable increases in fixed capital formation taking place in many of the enterprises, such as in the forestry and sawmilling sectors, telecommunications, sugar, and container manufacturing, will bring them technological advances. In some instances, the introduction of new technologies have been the subject of controversy and intervention by the regulative agencies. The dispute between the Public Utilities Commission and the GT&T Corporation is a case in point and turns on the price at which such technologies are introduced. The nature of the technology and the priority of technological change in a situation where the basic services have not been provided to consumers and where the new technology does not aim to address this issue, are likely to pose a greater conceptual and regulative problem in the utilities than elsewhere.

Foreign involvement in ownership and management

As has been observed earlier, a majority of entities have been acquired by Guyanese owners. Foreign involvement in ownership has been significant in the direct purchases but the extent of foreign ownership is understated in Table 8.4 to the extent that foreigners have been in a position to purchase shares issued by companies such as Demerara Distilleries Limited. Additionally, in the case of the share issues, many local shareholders who received priority under the divestment in the commercial banks may have subsequently sold their shares to foreigners. In these latter cases, however, foreign ownership has not impacted in any clear and discernible way.

Where entities are partially owned by foreigners other than as majority shareholders, there appears to be a willingness to retain Guyanese managers, providing them with the necessary technical and institutional support of the foreign partner. In the larger companies, however, there has been a tendency to bring in foreign chief executive officers and, in particular, financial and accounting managers. In some instances, the recruitment of foreigners goes beyond what are discernible areas of local deficiency. The recent exchanges between the PUC of Guyana and GT&T points to concern in some quarters over this development. Indeed it was contended in this particular case that unskilled and semi-skilled staff who could be recruited in Guyana were passed over in favour of foreigners who were then paid exceptionally high emoluments. Some of these very skills were being employed in the mining sector which, when unable to find such skills, provided training.

This therefore remains something of a controversial area and it is to be expected that it will feature as a point of contention between the foreign owners and Guyanese labour representatives and commentators. There is a recognition that such patterns of recruitment are aimed at weakening the hold of local labour and making the accounts less transparent.

Post-privatization national investment spread

One of the characteristics of Guyana's economy since the late 1970s has been the declining share of the private sector in fixed capital formation. Whereas over the years 1970 to 1979, roughly 20 per cent of total investment was contributed by the private sector, in the 1980s as a whole it was substantially less than 15 per cent and by 1985 had fallen to 10 per cent. By 1989 and 1990, however, this ratio had started to climb. Privatization has contributed to increased investment and has been facilitated by the repatriation of balances held abroad by the Guyanese.

Effects on the public exchequer

In some instances, enterprises have been acquired on an instalment basis and in yet others rental and leases rather than outright sale have taken place. In the case of debt-for-equity swaps, a phenomenon which has been countenanced in only two cases, some part of the price is lost to the Treasury.[3]

By the middle of 1992, some US$ 61.5m plus G$ 1.2b had been generated by the privatization initiative. These proceeds have been paid into a special account at the Ministry of Finance. Some portion has been approved to meet the expenses associated with privatization; these include legal conveyancing and consultancy fees, liquidating debts incurred by PEs, etc. This category of expense has been relatively insignificant. Additionally, a more significant quantity has been approved for the payment of specific debts associated with privatized companies. Such liabilities include outstanding indebtedness to the Commissioner of Inland Revenue, and contributions to employees as a result of the privatization process itself, in other words in lieu of employees' pensions where there had been no pension fund.

All the remaining sums deposited in the account have gone towards helping to restore fiscal balance. The latter in Guyana's case is quite staggering and, as a consequence, the government has as a matter of policy agreed to, and kept faith with, arrangements to utilize the funds for two purposes only. In the first place, the most important priority is to reduce the stock of debt. The second priority is to facilitate the financing of the Public Sector Investment Programme (PSIP). Forty per cent of the proceeds have been allocated for the latter purpose and the PSIP is agreed with the World Bank independently of the availability of this sum. This formula, reflected in the Policy Frame Work Paper, can be said to have contributed in a very crucial way to reducing the imbalances which have characterized Guyana's fiscal accounts.

Some idea of the importance of this can be gleaned from the fact that the proceeds from three years of divestment activities are equivalent to more than 30 per cent of Guyana's GDP in any of the years in question.

Only one enterprise is now in receipt of current transfers from the Treasury. Privatization can be seen to have relieved the Treasury of the burden of meeting annual losses of PEs. The extent to which the privatized enterprises contribute relative to their predecessors is a matter that is reasonably easy to ascertain in normal circumstances for the bulk of the companies. It appears that improved financial performance has enabled some to make higher tax contributions. Many others, by virtue of new investment being undertaken, enjoy tax holidays or waivers of import duties and consumption taxes. With the exception of the bauxite enterprise and to a lesser extent the sugar company, the government has no continuing commitment to meeting current operating costs for any but a few of these entities. It should be added that assistance with the financing of capital programmes continues to be provided by the Treasury. In most cases, however, these funds are to be on lent from multi-lateral financial institutions.

Conclusion

Privatization in Guyana has been implemented under very difficult circumstances. With the benefit of hindsight some commentators now deem the speed and effectiveness of Guyana's economic recovery programme to be without parallel in recent times. The background that the early months of the programme generated was not conducive to a smooth implementation of privatization. The dramatic liberalization of the economy contributed to uncertainty and a depressed economic situation. However, the programme has so far achieved, in a rather remarkable way, the targets set. The most critical of these are fiscal, since, as has been pointed out, privatization was itself fiscally driven. Notwithstanding this success, there is a lack of appreciation of the concrete results of the process. Inadequate attention to public relations and two or three problematic cases have been responsible for this. The experience of Guyana suggests that, as far as possible, privatization ought to be pursued outside of a situation of economic crisis.

Now that the worst aspects of economic crisis are behind Guyana, the ERP has begun to yield significant positive economic growth. It would be interesting to contrast the experience of privatization in this phase with that of the first phase which can be considered to have just been completed.

NOTES

1   This paper draws on the findings contained in Greenidge 1993.
2   Excluding CARICOM ventures, and subsidiaries, the numbers for which are in some cases merged with those for the relevant Holding Companies.
3   This needs to be taken into account when estimating the proceeds of privatization.

REFERENCES

Crittle, J. (1991) *A Study of Consumption Taxes in Guyana*, Georgetown, Guyana: UNDP/IBRD.
Greenidge, Carl B. (1982) 'An overview of public enterprises in Guyana', *Social and Economics Studies*, U.W.I. Jamaica: Institute of Social and Economic Research.
—— (1992a) 'The privatisation of Guyana', Commonwealth Secretariat, Conference on Privatisation, Islamabad, March.
—— (1992b) 'The fiscal impact of privatisation', *Bulletin IV (1) Interregional Network on Privatisation*, New York, sponsored by UNDP.
—— (1993) 'Privatisation under structural adjustment', in V.V. Ramanadham (ed.) *Privatisation: a Global Perspective*, London: Routledge.
Lall, D. (1990) *The Political Economy of Poverty, Equity and Growth in 21 Developing Countries: a Summary of Findings*, Paper presented to AEA annual meeting.

9

PRIVATIZATION IN ARGENTINA

Alejandro E. Rausch

INTRODUCTION

The relative weight and size of the public enterprise (PE) sector in Argentina does not differ from that found in both indistrialized and developing countries (see Short 1984). However, the structural crisis faced by the economy in the early 1980s, together with the PE's financial and economic mismanagement, operational and investment inefficiencies, politicized bureaucracies and trade unions, amidst the protracted setting – by government – of non-commercial objectives and goals, established the ground for the privatization process which started in 1989.

Given the debate and growing concern with the problems related to macro-economic impacts, management and reform of state-owned enterprises, this chapter, based on empirical evidence of the completed or ongoing privatization process in Argentina, will try to describe and analyse briefly the following aspects: economic, financial, institutional, legal and political background; the socio-political, external, technical, market and other constraints faced by this process; the actual and expected outcomes, results and impacts. To illustrate and provide further information on the sector itself, the Appendix contains a list with basic data, charts and graphs at the enterprise or agency level.

BACKGROUND

Since the 1930 world crisis, despite the fact that the new conservative governments were still willing to pursue their liberal trade policies, they gave the state a significant role in economic and industrial development, compensating for market failures, and setting a new pattern for the accumulation process. By the mid-1940s, the Argentine Government had bought assets from foreign investors and established new enterprises. Thus, the size of the productive public sector towards 1950 was significant, contributing to 7.2 per cent of the labour force and 6.7 per cent of the Gross Domestic Product (GDP).

In 1976, research aimed at determining a total inventory of PEs concluded that there were 347 entities in which the state held a major interest, and about

400 in which it had a minor or passive role (Consejo 1976). By 1982, the Central Bank (BCRA) made an official inventory, estimating 297 financial and non-financial enterprises, of which 148 were national; there were also some minor shareholdings not included in this survey. This decline in the number of PEs was due to a piecemeal privatization policy started in 1976, which emphasized the reduction of employment, the reprivatization of over 120 small or medium-sized firms – which had been rescued or bailed out by the state – and the liquidation of several others (Del Campo and Winkler 1991). It was implemented amidst decentralization and contracting-out policies, as a means of downsizing the state.

Towards the 1980s the Public Works Ministry (MDSP) PEs and some within the aegis of the Ministry of Defence (MD), particularly petrochemicals, were starting important investment programmes in the hydrocarbons and electric energy sectors. The average capital productivity of PEs dropped, although there was an increase in net investment and a reduction in employment, with a rise in labour's average productivity (see Table 9.5). This situation can be explained, partially, because of the inadequate and deficient programming, evaluation and implementation of projects driven by available internal and external financing as well as earmarked funds. The aforementioned poor allocation of investment funds was also followed by a flawed management of project execution, operation and maintenance.

During the early 1980s Argentina faced the external debt crisis, having increased its external debt fivefold since the early 1970s to US$ 36 billion. Specifically, PE's financial management was stymied, due to forced heavy external borrowing which was imposed on them between 1976–82, and used to compensate balance of payments deficits and capital outflows. This debt was not offset by the state, as was the case with private foreign debt in 1982.

The overall weight of the Argentine public enterprise sector, before the extended privatization process started in 1989, was approximately 7 per cent of the GDP, an average of 30 per cent of the gross fixed investment (GFI), accounting for 56 per cent of public sector deficit, 26 per cent of external debt – US$ 58.5 billion – and 2.8 per cent of the total labour force (see Tables 9.4–9.7, 9.10, 9.17 and graphs). By July 1990, FIEL had counted 69 national PEs, of which 3 were financial institutions. The 1993 (proposed) National Budget mentions 55.

Public enterprises were concentrated in: hydrocarbons and energy (73 per cent), transport and communications (14 per cent) and water resources (2.7 per cent), within the aegis of the public works sector and consisted, mainly, of public utilities which were about 90 per cent of the overall sector, and productive industries, dominantly Ministry of Defence enterprises, which were about 10 per cent of the total sector – mainly steel, metalmechanics, chemicals and petrochemicals. Employment was concentrated heavily in the railway company Ferrocarrilos Argentinos (FA), which accounted for about 30 per cent of sectoral employment.

The new constitutional government took office in 1983 amidst a profound

167

recession, drop in per capita income, de-industrialization process and an increase in the relative weight of the large diversified national economic groups, many of which had developed as public works contractors or due to industrial promotion and other incentives. The rising and persistent inflation gave way to policy shifts and successive adjustment episodes. After the first hyperinflation in 1989, different sectors perceived the structural constraints and exhaustion of the state-centred matrix as the 'engine of growth' and the deterrent 'crowding out' effect on private activity as well as on social commitments – such as the social security system and equity. Bringing the state back in demanded its profound reform.

Nevertheless, this administration started liberalization, deregulation and privatization policies. Privatization, which began in 1985, comprised firms that had previously been rescued – SIAM S.A. Electromechanical by Decree 1228/86; Opalina Hurlingham S.A., tile plant, by Decree 216/85; Austral Lineas Aereas, domestic airline carrier, by Decree 1720/86, Resolution ME 461/87 and Decree 2066/87; and others in which the state had a minority share. Atanor S.A. was sold; and there was a signing of a Letter of Intent between ENTEL (telephone company) and Telefónica of Spain, and a Letter of Understanding between Aerolineas Argentinas (national airline carrier) and SAS, to proceed with negotiations for partial divestiture of 40 per cent of stake of these enterprises.

This first stage, although fiscally driven, was also concerned with the productive and economic efficiency of PEs, but lacked a consistent institutional, legal and regulatory framework and policy. Thus, some transactions were tackled through competitive bidding, and others through preferential rights and by direct negotiations to sell minor stakes of financially rescued enterprises. However, the small size of the capital market and the adverse political and economic context annulled any possibility of a consensus to provide the conditions required for the major sales.

In 1983 the Ministry of Public Works and Services (MOSP) was responsible for the main PEs through its four sectoral secretariats that were directly held accountable for each area. In 1985 the Secretariat of Growth Promotion was supposed to increase divestiture options, but due to its negligible effect was eliminated in 1988. During that year, the Secretariat of Control of Public Enterprises (SECONEP), which was supposed to advise the government on PE policies and control, was also dissolved.

The Directorate of Public Enterprises (DEP) was created in 1986. During its first stage (until late 1988) it was supposed to promote the institutional reform of PEs by means of decentralization, restructuring and privatization. The latter phase centralized power and decision making in DEP (and MOSP) which appointed directors and management staff; it tried to implement deregulation and demonopolization policies with limited success and was eliminated in 1989. The control bodies are the Syndic General for PEs (SIGEP) and the Accounts Court (Tribunal de Cuentas), which are independent audit agencies. Particularly SIGEP analyses legal, accounting and management procedures by participating in PE's Board Meetings. There were different regulations on expenditures, revenues and the legal, statutory and institutional framework which affected PE's decision making process and conditioned PE behaviour.

The new administration which took office in July 1989 emphasized the need to advance towards a profound state reform, economic emergency, fiscal adjustment, liberalization, the Central Bank's Statutory reform and decentralization presenting an ambitious legislative programme to Congress for its enactment and implementation. President Menem's initial address to Congress on 8 July 1989 stated that:

> All that the private sector can undertake by themselves will not be done by the National State. Everything which the provinces can do autonomously will not be done by the National State. All that can be done by the municipalities, will not be done by the National State.

The State Reform Law 23.696, enacted on 17 August 1992, refers to the following:

Chapter I: Administrative Emergency of public services and state. Authorizes appointment, by Ministers and Secretaries, of intervenors in PEs for limited periods and determines functions and responsibilities. Determines Control Agencies and authorizes changes in legal and institutional status of PEs.

Chapter II: Privatization and Participation of Private Capital. To privatize, PEs have to be declared 'subject to privatization', according to this law, except for minority stakes which are subject to their statutory provisions. This will be established by the National Executive Branch (PEN), with Congress (HCN) approval for others than those listed in the appendix. The scope is: total, partial, concession, firm, unit or plant and allows to eliminate any statutory condition that establishes monopoly/regulations/privileges and/or conditions which might affect the privatization/deregulation/demonopolization of services. PEN will establish by decree the alternatives, modalities and policies to be pursued, based on the state's share. In case it is in provincial (state) territory it will require their consent. A Congress Committee formed by 6 Senators and 6 Representatives will supervise and follow up the process.

Alternatives: transfer, establish or reform, liquidate, permits, licenses and concessions, tax incentives, deferred payments, etc.

Preferences: employees, consumers (ESOP or Cooperatives) and suppliers.

Modalities: sale of assets, sale of shares, rental/administration with/out purchase option, concession/license or permit. May use debt-equity swaps.

Selection Procedure: Public bid, public competition, public auction – all with/out base, share offer and direct contract.

Previous assessment: by public, international or private agencies.

Control: by Sigep or Tribunal de Cuentas (Accounting Court).

Share Ownership Programme: for employees (ESOP), consumers and users. There are also other provisions concerning the work force, contracting, concessions and emergencies.

Main emphasis is given to future reduction in public expenditures, by the state's present participation in this procedure through the intervenors. Towards this purpose, the state is supposed to assume PE's total liabilities to enable the privatization process. There is no explicit concern about the future operation and regulation of the sectors or enterprises involved at this stage.

The Minister of Public Works (MOSP), main author of these laws, expressed that without privatization no economic policy was viable; that they had to proceed very rapidly through sales or concessions, selling everything possible, and deregulate, with competitive bidding procedures. The recommendations concerning the labour force are general and establish intentions but do not set patterns to be dealt with in the process.

The State Emergency Law 23.697 was enacted in August 1992. This law has different aspects referring to temporary suspension of incentives and benefits related to the fiscal constraints and other structural reforms such as autonomy of the Central Bank (BCRA), equity for foreign investors, reschedules internal debt, eliminates nominative powers of private shares, authorizes dismissal of high echelons of public service personnel and tax penalties for evaders.

In February 1990, rumours of dollarization triggered new fears of hyperinflation. In March authorities responded with a new massive programme which was based on structural and emergency fiscal initiatives (Decree 435). Its main elements were announced as: reduction of public sector employment; suspension of payments due on public sector contracts; and extension or partial suspension of the regional industrial subsidy programme. Direct control was taken of PEs' cash-flows. The progress in structural reforms to date ranged over enhanced fiscal accounts which started by reducing tax subsidies; improved tax collection, downsizing the state and deregulation; improvement and proposal of new laws for programming and control of public expenditures and procurement; financial sector reform and new Central Bank Charter; labour flexibility; liberalization and further privatization of PEs, now focused on the energy and transportation sectors.

CONSTRAINTS

The economic coercion provided by hyperinflationary processes was a major factor which helped overcome resistance within civil society, particularly that of trade unions.

Entrepreneurs, who had developed their economic base as contractors for PEs, were aware of the limits faced by the previous development paradigm and considered seriously the possibility of diversifying towards the public service sectors. PEs in Argentina are of two very distinct types: public utilities, which operate in non-tradable and, sometimes, non-competitive markets, appropriate for rent seekers; and industrial enterprises which are subject to domestic and international competitive markets.

The previous administration had not been able to develop either divestiture or non-divestiture options for PEs, although it tried. It even had most of the large concentrated national entrepreneurs participate in diagnosis work to determine the conditions and reform strategies for most of MOSP's PEs. The macro-economic and political circumstances did not encourage such a procedure. The relevant economic and social actors that have so far been involved in the implementation of this policy are the private entrepreneurs and trade unions.

The state has not defined any strategy concerning the areas and sectors involved and has considered restructuring only those which, due to size or concurrent interests or conditions, required such consideration. Meanwhile, consumers have not had voice, except in Congress where the fiscal emergency has been the dominant factor and the application of privatization proceeds for social sectors has become a *quid pro quo*. Surprisingly, in most cases significant changes in tariff and price structures have not had the inflationary impact which could be expected and may have provoked regressive distributive effects. Notwithstanding, before the reforms, firms considered tariffs as expenditures and now they consider them as part of their cost structure.

The Argentine privatization policy has been fiscally driven and has also had a significant role in servicing external debt as well as increasing its value in the secondary market – from 12 per cent to 47.5 per cent, improving relations with external creditors.

This comprehensive and two-year deadline process has had two distinct phases: first, from mid-1989 to 1990 when, based on the urge to have a politically demonstrative effect, privatization was done at a rapid pace with insufficient consideration of the regulatory framework; and second, which started in March 1991, with the Convertibility Plan, in which due to the nature of the sectors and possible impacts, further regard has been given to the market aspects to provide adequate conditions for investors, competitors and consumers within each sector.

In this process the state has taken over most of the debt burden which PEs had. It has also assumed, and is negotiating, loans with the World Bank to finance the dismissals and severance payments in PEs, given that in most cases retrenchment is a condition for privatization. The Employee Share Ownership Programme has also been an issue which created expectations, at an early stage, but by now, although it is still supported by trade union bureaucrats, workers know that it is not feasible in most cases, given the present income structure.

Macro-economic conditions and abrupt changes in the relative price structures create an adverse environment towards investment, augmenting the internal discount rate and deteriorating asset values.

The overall and protracted fiscal restraint very rapidly damaged the technological and operational conditions of most enterprises. This policy, together with cuts in recurrent costs – particularly salaries – left only divestiture as the option for PE reform.

The economic recovery has permitted the development of the capital market – emergent market – at a very interesting pace. Probably part of these resources belong to local investors and represent a reversal of capital flight through capital inflow. However, the basis most investments are built on will probably set a ceiling to future growth in this market as a source of financing.

The legal instruments consisted of an array of laws, decrees and resolutions, most of which have been enacted with timeliness, adjusted and modified as needed.

Most regulatory frameworks and structures have encountered problems for their correct design and implementation and to date none is operating fully.

External financing has provided funding for international and indigenous consultant firms and individual consultants for all phases of the process. Notwithstanding, there is a lack of commitment and competence in some key areas to be able to interact and develop absorptive capacity for the technical assistance, advice, assessment and marketing provided. Probably the overall state reform process with very strict deadlines and goals has weakened the state's management capacity in the short and medium run. The sectoral political authority and institutional turnover, and the fragile audit and control capacities confronted with the diversity of sectors and enterprises involved, merit serious notice.

IMPACT

This part will review the major privatizations to date as well as their overall impact. Given that this is at a very preliminary stage and the period involved does not comprise a full business cycle, this analysis should be considered carefully.

ENTEL (telephone company)

The privatization of this company, which was monopolistic in providing telecommunication services, in a rapidly innovative technological sector, led to the sale of 60 per cent of the state's assets to foreign parastatals (Stet, France Telecom and Telefónica Española). The price was determined by a discounted cash flow, which considered a tariff that was later augmented significantly. The price was above the established base of US$ 214 million cash and US$ 3,500 million in debt papers, since the final price that was paid was US$ 214 million and US$ 5,000 million in debt papers. The 30 per cent which was left to the state was sold on the stock market for US$ 2,000 million, while the ESOP has not been agreed on. The price received for the shares can be analysed under different circumstances, related to conditions in the international and domestic markets; but by no means does it reflect an improvement in performance of both telephone companies. The total debt was assumed by the state and is presumed to be close to US$ 2,500 million, which means that the privatization management increased the outstanding debt by approximately US$ 1,500 million or more.

The company was split into two main areas: Telconorte S.A. and Telesur S.A. which provide basic telecommunications services; and Teleintar that renders international services and Startel which provides the so-called competitive services (cellular phones, data transmission, telex, etc.). The shares in each are as follows: Telecom: 30 per cent Stet, 30 per cent France Cable, 30 per cent Perez Companc and 10 per cent Morgan Bank; Telefónica: 33 per cent Telefónica; 57 per cent Citibank and 10 per cent Techint. Perez Companc supposedly bought 15 per cent of Telefónica at the offering (Herrera 1992). Both banks are important creditors from Argentina.

The licensees have monopoly rights for seven years with an option for extension to 10 providing all basic and long-distance services. There is an investment schedule for a five-year period which considers about 600,000 lines for each firm, 13,000 public phones and quality standards in other services, met in the first year with technical reserves and previous investments made partially by ENTEL. The monopoly given on the other value-added services and long-distance calls will be a cross-subsidy used to finance the network expansion. During the privatization process tariffs were increased from less than 1.5 US cents per unit to 4.2 US cents and now is close to 3.82 US cents. There are cross-subsidies among services and consumers, and monopoly in all services except cellular phone; the service has deteriorated significantly since it was privatized; and there still is not an effective regulatory framework nor authority after close to two years. The industrial impact is difficult to assess yet. Employment has been reduced from about 45,000 to 33,000 employees and ESOP has not been implemented yet. Most of the legal, investment and service goals have been disregarded.

Argentine Airlines (national airline carrier)

Argentine Airlines S.A. was purchased through a bid (in which there was only one tender) without having complied with bidding conditions: 8.5 per cent was sold for supposedly US$ 260 million and US$1,600 million in debt notes; 10 per cent was for ESOP and 5 per cent for the state. The bidding process would have been useful to compare investment and operative plans. After the purchase one of the partners, Cielos del Sur, owner of Austral, the domestic carrier, sold out and gave a monopoly of 95 per cent of domestic services to AA S.A., keeping domestic tariffs very high. The main partner for AA is the Spanish line Iberia which is a parastatal with a majority interest. The down payment, guarantees, financed debt and debt papers have always been subject to disputes, because of differences in inventories, outstanding debt and a possible lease-buy-back operation done to finance the purchase and the guarantees.

Operation plans were non-viable, the routes have served as collectors for Iberia and other European carriers in Europe and American ones in Miami. Quality of service and security conditions have deteriorated; and due to non-compliance of contract conditions, disputes about the reliability of balance sheets and other matters the state has recovered 28 per cent stake and the liabilities involved. ESOP conditions and agreement have not been established.

ALEJANDRO E. RAUSCH

Ferrocarrils Argentinos and Femesa (railway company)

The 35,000-km long railway system had carried 20 billion traffic units in ton–km, had 92,000 employees – now 50,000 – and received an annual subsidy of about US$ 600 million. There are three different business units into which the company has been split: freight, intercity passenger and suburban passenger in the Buenos Aires Metropolitan Region. The integrated restructuring programme agreed that the freight business (14 million tons) was financially viable. Privatization would be with concessions for 30 plus 10 years and split into six lines to make it technically and financially viable, while developing competition. This would go through a bidding process or declaration of interest for each line. Conditions are: 30 year concession plus 10 years; may run or give way for intercity passengers; employ part of FA's workers; present maximum fare for approval as a ceiling and allocate an amount of rolling stock.

For the Buenos Aires Metropolitan Region Suburban passenger services a firm called Femesa was created to cover the seven lines and metro (subway), free to negotiate new working conditions with the union; government will define maximum fares, minimum frequencies and operational standards and capital plan, and provide only the property required to operate the trains and subsidize the lines. This segment will be offered in at least four packages for 20 years. There are intercity linkages for passenger service for at least two lines (Buenos Aires–Mar del Plata and others). It is also possible to transfer the service to the provinces which will have to finance the service to run the trains. The strategy chosen is to set tariffs for the Metropolitan area and freight ceilings for the rest. The suburban traffic will be subsidized, while the cargo will pay a nominal fee, given that the rolling stock is covered by subsidy. The provinces (states) that want to run local passenger services may do so at their own cost.

So far three lines have been awarded and there is scarce information regarding the operations. The suburban lines have as one of the bidding groups the City Bus Transport Federation, which has the monopoly of all ground transportation in the city.

Gas del Estado (gas company)

The gas sector (natural monopoly) will be broken into two basic segments: transmission and distribution. The transmission will be provided by two operators on an open access basis, and the distribution will be dispensed by eight operators awarded concessions for 35 years. The bids will be without a base. There is a regulatory framework which contemplates a specific agency; there will be provision for an adequate profit and two kinds of tariffs: firm and cut-off ones; the agency will set a ceiling and threshold to avoid monopoly or predatory practices; investment and operation costs will be covered. Provided the bidder complies with the technical conditions, the award will be given on an up-front fee payment.

The adequate profit criterion involves risks of inefficiencies; there are also risks involving cross-subsidies between consumers and producers. The key issue is related to how to simplify the mechanisms, supposing that regulators always lack accurate information to determine monopoly or predatory practices.

Electric Energy Sector – SEGBA, AyEE, HIDRONOR

The electric energy sector has been divided into three segments: power plants (competitive), transmission grid (natural monopoly) and distribution (natural monopoly). So far awards have been given for power plants and distribution in the SEGBA area which comprises more than 5 million industrial, domestic and commercial consumers. Many of these projects were awarded to Chilean, Spanish and other foreign groups, together with local partners. It is presumed that, given the size of the market and condition of the network and plants, there are most likely to be possibilities of improving the capacity and reducing losses easily and financing future investment commitments from productive and operative improvements. The new power plants which are going to be bid for can also have a reasonable performance. The regulatory authority will presumably have an audit function and the new energy firm to be established will run the national grid.

YPF S.A. (national petroleum company)

The petroleum sector was always a mixed sector where the private sector participated. However, YPF has lately given two concessions, to produce in marginal areas, four central areas, joint-ventures and has plans to sell the main distilleries. Prices have been deregulated and there has been installation of service stations. The government intends to sell together with the provinces most of its stock in the newly created corporation. These proceeds will supposedly be used to finance the debts due to the structural problems faced by social security. Here, as in other cases, the policy of selling everything, to be left only with subsidiary activities, may be very dangerous. The greatest wealth and potential is in this sector and there is a problem of stocks and flows that should be addressed properly during this divestiture process. High yield sectors such as oil, telecommunications and gas might require a competent operator to make them profitable but selling out all participation can be a long-term mistake.

DNV (national road directorate)

There has been concession of 10,000 km of roads to be operated on a toll fee basis. The original proposal was to pay US$ 600 million a year; and because of toll reductions the state is giving a US$ 58 million subsidy. DNV considers its projects as highway building instead of operating a transportation project. There are still two other proposals for the Metropolitan Access to Buenos Aires and

3,200 km of trunk roads. These roads are the main national highway system into which all feeders go.

Industrial PEs

The firms which have been sold so far have been of various types. The petrochemicals were mixed enterprises with state minority shares and were mainly sold to the partners. The steelwork was sold to a French group with local partners (Citibank) at a price below the cost of land; it is expected that they will manufacture special steel with high technology under very competitive conditions. Others such as Tandanor (shipyard) were bought for the land, although they have important assets.

Somisa, the state-owned steelmill, is an unbalanced plant which has been in severe trouble for the last years. Most likely, one of the two competitors will buy the plant at a reasonable price waiting for the depressed market to improve. The problem can be the accumulated debt that Somisa is developing.

SUMMARY AND CONCLUSIONS

The extended privatization process in Argentina is mainly fiscally driven and used to service the external debt. The proceeds from this mechanism so far seem quite impressive – US$ 5 billion cash and US$ 6.7 billion in debt papers. However, there are serious doubts about this short-term narrow view if one considers the cost that this procedure has had in terms of net liabilities, loans to attend to severance payments and transfer of equity among others.

Regulation has been disregarded as a key issue for privatization in non-competitive sectors, and political and fiscal objectives have preceded market conditions and changes. Privatization *per se* is a very weak instrument if it does not provide competition and thus productive and allocative efficiency. Special attention should be given to environmental issues in future operation of utilities and industries. International experience shows that these operations have a very severe environmental impact.

Sequencing a privatization process might be very useful within an administrative, provincial, fiscal and sectoral reform process. Changes entail transition periods when there are weaknesses which are difficult to overcome. Given the negotiation and management capacities involved in this procedure, it may be wise to move on a step-by-step approach.

Changes in market conditions to depress prices when sold, through liberalization and then resorting to protectionism, can also be a risk in many cases. The policy shifts and conditions that have occurred (such as with toll and fees) should be carefully accounted for.

The fact that there are local economic groups which have participated in most privatizations quite successfully and are diversified in roads, telecommunications, electric energy, hydrocarbons and most likely steel merits recognition.

Given the domestic and international economic conditions, further thought should be given to policies when such large amounts of public sector workers are dismissed. The small and medium-sized industries are naturally more labour intensive and retain their work force better during the different phases of the business cycle. It would be useful to consider, as part of the public sector and structural reform process, the development of a framework to integrate industrial policy on a competitive basis for this endeavour.

Expatriate expertise cannot substitute indigenous skills in this process. However, it can be very useful when there are team work and technological transfers.

REFERENCES

Consejo Empresario Argentino, (1976) 'Las Empresas Públicas en la Economía Argentina', Buenos Aires: FIEL, December.
—— (1990) 'El Gasto Publico Social en Argentina 1960–1988', Buenos Aires: FIEL, September.
Del Campo, A. and Winkler, D. (1991) *State Owned Enterprise Reform in L.A. PSM TD. LAC.* LATPS Occasional Paper Series, Washington D.C.: World Bank, July.
Herrera, A. (1992) *Revolución Technológica, Reregulación y Privatización: Alcances y límites del Milagro: El Caso Argentino*, New York: Columbia Business Schools.
Short, R.P. (1984) 'The role of public enterprises: an international statistical comparison', in R. Floyd, C. Gray and R. Short. *Public Enterprises in Mixed Economies: Some Macroeconomic Aspects*, Washington D.C.: 1984.

APPENDIX

Table 9.1 Public works PEs subject of privatization

Sector/Company	Revenue MM Convt.$	Surplus/ Deficit	Employment	Instit. and Legal Structure	Public Ownership	Market	Strategy for transfer
Fuels & Energy							
Fuels Y.P.F.S.A. Petroleum Company	5,206	(35)	36,935	Stock Corporation Law 19.550 MEyOSP SSC	100%	Legal Monopoly	Conces. Joint-Venture Restruc., reduce share dist. to 50%. Sole proc. to passive sec. State and Prov. sell stock golden share 20% only modif. law. Vol. retirem.
Gde E S.E. Gas Company	1,384	(280)	10,564	State Company Regulated L24.076 MEyOSP SSC	100%	Integrated Natural Monopoly	Open-access to trans. operators 70% share 20% state 10% ESOP Investment commit. and expansion of 20%. 8 regional distrib. Restructure/ Priv. concession
Y.C.F.S.E. Coal Company	78	(56)	2,967	State Company MEyOSP SSC	100%		
Electric Energy AyEE S.E. Water and Energy Co.	836	(247)	11,276	State Company ME yOSP SSC	100%	Legal and Nat. Monop.	Priv. Power Stations Concession transm.

Company				Legal Form		Market Status	Notes
S.E.G.B.A. S.A. Energy Power and Dist. Company	1,485	(295)	20,271	Stock Corporation MEy OSP SE	100%	Legal Monopoly	Priv. Power Stations Concession of metrop. distrib. in 2 zones
Hidronor S.A. Hydroelectric North Patagonian Co.	136	(625)	1,264	Stock Corporation MEyOSP ST	100%	Legal and Nat. Monop.	Privatise/Concessions 60% priv. 30% State 10% ESOP
Transports & Communic.							
1. Transports & Communic.							
1. Transports F.A. S.E.	403	(854)	86,856	State Company	100%	Competitive	Cargo Lines 30 yrs conces., invest. fees Conces. intercity viable lines decent. others Conces. suburb. passang. and metro. 20 yrs based lowest subsidy
FEME S.A. National and Urban Railway Companies			(15,000)	Stock Corporation	100%		
A.A.S.A Argentina Airlines	660	6	10,722	Stock Corporation	100%	Legal Monop.	Privatise
A.G.P. S.E. Port Administration Co.	101	6	3,080	State Company ME y OSP ST	100%	Competitive	Legal status priv. ports. Federalize medium and small admin. decentralize 6 main ports. Debureauc. promote private invest.

Table 9.1   continued

Sector/Company	Revenue MM Convt.$	Surplus/ Deficit	Employment	Instit. and Legal Structure	Public Ownership	Market	Strategy for transfer
E.L.M.A. S.A. Shipping Company	288	(61)	4,645	Stock Corporation	100%		Private Concessions
2. Communications ENTEL S.A. Telephone Company	1,077	(504)	46,040	Stock Corporation	100%	Natural Monopoly	Privatize Concession
ENCOTE S.A. National Post Office Co.	363	18	35,991	Stock Corporation ME y OSP SOySP	100%	Legal Monop.	Priv. part. re-struc. 35% members UPU 14% ESOP
3. Water Resources O.S.N. S.E. Water Resources Co.	293	30	7,871	SOE	100%	Natural Monopoly	Concession/Priv. Regulat. frame-work for prod. and distrib. 30 yrs. 10% ESOP. Fee invest. internat. operat. Awarded best tariff and investment
D.N.V. Nat. Direc. of Roads	N/A	N/A	N/A	National Directorate			Conces. 10000 Km+320 metrop. access. 20 yrs
D.N. CVN Nat. Dir. Nav.							Concession of dredge and buoy maint.

Table 9.2 Privatized PEs (1988 to date)

| Sector/company | Terms of transfer | US$ millions | | Awarded to | Conditions Comments |
		Cash	Db. paper		
ENTEL (Telephone Co.) Personnel 45,000	Sale 60% 30% Telef shares 30% TELECOM promiss. note 10% ESOP	214.0 830.0 1,226.9 228.0	5,000	TELECOM S.A. STET FR. CABLE JP MORGAN PEREZ COMPA TELEFONICA CITY BANK INV. CATALINAS	License for 7 years plus 3 Basic services plus STARTEL Data transmission TELINTAR Long distance
AAR S.A. (National Airline) incl. optar and 55% share of Bs As Catering S.A. Personnel 10,000	Sale of 85% 10% ESOP 5% state (49% for and 51% local recent change 33% state and 10% ESOP	260.0 (130 in 10 paym.)	1,610 (+400 in due int) (real value 271m)	IBERIA BCO HISPANO-AMERICANO AMADEO RIVA DEVI CONSTRU	Purchased AUSTRAL-Cielos del sur (Changed) Having domestic market monopoly Inventory, lease-buy-back prob. Investm. US$ 683 million in 5 years
Television and Radio Stations Channels 11 and 13 3 Stations	Concessions for 15 years	19.6		Television Federal ARTEL RADIO LIB. Red Celeste y Blanca	

Table 9.2 continued

| Sector/company | Terms of transfer | US$ millions | | Awarded to | Conditions Comments |
		Cash	Db. paper		
YPF S.A.	Joint ventures 60% in 4 central areas	560.1		TECPETROL TOTAL	
	Increased private part. 4 centr. areas	200.0		PEREZ COMPA ASTRA BRIDAS	
	Joint ventures Austral Basin	44.0		BRIDAS	
	Joint ventures Austral Basin	143.5		CGC	
	Joint ventures Austral Basin	141.6		PEREZ COMPA	
	Conces. 28 marg. areas	238.0		PETROQ. Cdro Rivadavia	
	Conces. 28 marg. areas	172.0		TECPETROL	
Petrochemicals: ATANOR (1988) SAM 20.988% DGFM	Sale	18.6		Cia. QUIMICA Pref. Right	Purchased by main partner
POLISUR S.M. 30% DGFM	Sale	14.1	41	IPAKO	Local and international bid

Entity	Method	Detail	Value 1	Value 2	Buyer/Participants	Notes
PETROPOL S.M. 10% DGFM	Sale		4.5	12.1	INDUPA	Preference right
INDUCLOR 30% DGFM	Sale		17.8	50.6	INDUPA	Preference right
Monomeros Vinilicos	Sale		9.3	26.5	VINICLOR	Preference right
PETROQ. R.III S.M. 0.214% DGFM 1.023% ATANOR 0.766% YPF	Sale		7.3		EGERTON Finance	First and second bid without base
DNV (Highways)	Conc. 10,000K 20 years		(57.0)		12 Enterp. P. Works Part.	Orig. 600m fee. Later 59m subs.
FA (Railroads) 5,300 Km 15 Km 3,500 Km	Concession Rosario–Bahia Blanca Delta Borges Mitre		155.0		Only freight FERROEXPRES TECHINT COM. del PLATA DEHEZA NCA	30 years invest. plan and fee for rolling stock and retain part of the personnel
Hotel Llao Llao	Sale		3.7	12	Llao Llao, City Corp.	
Altos Hornos ZAPLA (Steelworks)	Sale		3.3	29.9	PENSA AUBERT DUVAL CITY	Retain 900 people, 1,700 voluntary retirement

Table 9.2 continued

Sector/company	Terms of transfer	US$ millions		Awarded to	Conditions Comments
		Cash	Db. paper		
SEGBA					
Central Puerto	Sale	92.2		CHILGENER CHILENA 5a Region	
Central Costanera	Sale 60% + pending debts 1,260 mw nominal cap.	90.1		ENDESA CHILECTRA COST. POWER ENERSIS	10% ESOP 30% state to be sold stock market adeq. service/exp.
Edenor (Distrib. Grid)	51% sold 39% state for stock market 95 yrs (15 + 10)	428 (Cash & notes)		ASTRA ELEC. FRANCE ENDESA (Spain) CHILECTRA	Minimun standard service, satisf. increase in dem. regul. tariff str.
Edesur (Distrib. Grid)	51% sold 39% state for stock market 95 yrs (15 + 10)	511		ENDESA (Chile) PEREZ COMPA DISTRILEC	Minimum standard service, satisf. increase in dem. regul. tariff str.
TANDANOR	Sale	59.8		Bco. Holandes Submarine Enterprices CIAMAR	
State-Owned Property Surplus to req.	Sale 372 buildings	91.6			Competitive bid
AyEE S.E. Alto Valle Power St. 95 MW	Sale	22.1 (liabil. 10)		Dominion Energ Neuquen Coop.	10% ESOP – 90% Private bid
Total		5,060.3	6,701.9		

Table 9.3 Ministry of Defence PEs subject to privatization–liquidation

Sector/company	Assets: US$ Mm	Sales US$ Mm	Personnel	Output capacity	Strategy	Market
SOMSA	1,890	597	5,500	2,200M Tn	Restructuring plan. Voluntary retirement of 8,500 workers. Sale of 80% private, 20% ESOP. Auction of land+building Base price. Due to duopol both can't bid together. Sizable steel operator. Minimum investment require	Local and External Pig Iron Tin Plate
Area Material Cordoba (aircraft parts and maintenance)			2,900		Subject to privat. Dec 899/91	
AFNE S.A.	60	24	2,191	30M Tn Naval Steel		
PGM SAJC 50% YPF – 50% FM		123	900	300M Tn Aromatics Olefine Complex		Domestic and external
PBB SAJC 17% DGFM – 17% YPF 17% Gas del Estado 21.23% PAKO, ect	340	120	377	245M Tn ethylene		

Table 9.3 *continued*

Sector/company	Assets: US$ Mm	Sales US$ Mm	Personnel	Output capacity	Strategy	Market
Direcc. Graf de Fabricaciones Militares (Military Directory of Military Factories)						
ECA		14	848	8,000 Tn Rods and cables	Asset Sale	Domestic
Fabrica Militar San Francisco	18	2	181	Metal-mechanics		Domestic and external
Fabrica Militar Graf San Martin	55	2	233	Civilian Vehicles		Domestic and external
Fabrica Militar de Toluena Sintetico	11	13	104	100M M3 Destil. Cap.		Domestic and external
Sidinox						
Satecna S.A. Military Prod:				tug boats		
FM Pliar			101			
FM de polvora y explos. AZUL			131			
FM Dgo Matheu			447	Pistols		
FM de polvora y explos. Villa Maria			461			
FM Fray Luis Beitron			584	Munitions		
FM Acido Sulfurico						

Metalurgy | Public bid

Submarines | Under review

Closed, non-viable

Forja Arg. S.A.
Carboquimica Arg.
AM Domeq Gracia

Sale of Assets:
  EDESA
  Aceros Holer
  Consultora S.A.
  ME. S.A.
  SIDNSA S.A.
  HIPASAM S.A.
  SIDINOX

Table 9.4   Share of GDP of PEs* in total GDP (in 1970 Australes)

Years	PEs GDP Factor costs	Total GDP market price	PE GDP /Total GDP
1980	606.3	11,291.9	5.4
1985	570.4	10,140.5	5.6
1990	619.1	10,229.6	6.1

*Public works enterprises (13 and since 1989 11) (since 1989 AA and ENTEL are not computed)
Source: SIGEP and BCRA

Table 9.5   Evolution of mean productivity of public works PEs (labour and capital index 1980 = 100)

Year Mean productivity	Capital	Labour
1980	100.0	100.0
1985	85.3	121.5
1990	90.4	146.5

Source: SIGEP

Table 9.6   Share of Gross Fixed Investment (GFI) and Public Works PEs' investment in GDP (as % of GDP)

	1961	1980	1990
Total GFI	22.1	23.7	8.1
Total public sector GFI	7.8	9.6	2.3
PEs' GFI	3.7	3.5	1.6
		(as % of total GFI)	
PEs' GFI/PS GFI	47.4	36.5	68.2
PEs' GFI/Total GFI	16.7	15.4	19.8

Source: Based on DNPP of the Secretariat of Finance and SIGEP

Table 9.7   Public works – PEs' external debt (U$S billions)

	1980	1985	1989
Short term	3.6	7.6	3.5
Long term	4.2	5.6	12.7
Total PEs debt	7.9	13.2	16.2
Total Ext. debt	27.1	49.3	63.3

Source: SIGEP and BCRA

Table 9.8 Structure of public works PEs' GDP at factor costs 1950–90 (as % of GDP)

Sector	1955–9	1975–9	1989
I. Hydrocarbons & Energy	25.3	58.7	81.1
1. Hydrocarbons	19.7	39.1	49.4
2. Electric energy	5.5	19.6	31.7
II. Transports	55.0	21.4	13.4
III. Communications	16.5	17.0	2.4
IV. Water resources	3.2	2.9	3.1
Total	100.0	100.0	100.0

Source: Based on SIGEP

Table 9.9 External debt of public works PEs ($ millions for December 1989)

	Short Term	Long Term	Total
Fuels & Energy	3,118.6	9,630.8	12,749.5
Fuels	1,958.8	6,273.5	8,232.3
Y.P.F	1,172.0	4,432.0	5,604.0
Gas del Estado	697.0	1,708.7	2,405.7
Y.C.F.	89.8	132.8	222.6
Electric energy	1,159.8	3,357.4	4,517.2
Agua y Energia Electrica	699.0	1,914.0	2,613.0
SEGBA	146.3	637.3	783.6
HIDRONOR	314.5	806.1	1,120.6
Transports & Communications	389.4	3,110.3	3,499.7
Transports	363.4	2,337.5	2,700.9
Ferrocarriles Argentinos	137.2	828.9	966.1
Aerolineas Argentinas	91.4	681.6	773.0
AGP	1.7	2.4	4.1
ELMA	133.1	824.6	957.7
Communications	26.0	772.8	798.8
ENTel	26.0	764.2	790.2
ENCo.Tel.	0.0	8.6	8.6
Total	3,508.0	12,741.2	16.249.1

Source: SIGEP

Table 9.10 Public sector employment (PSE)

	1965	1985	1990	1992
	(Thousand of Employees)			
National Public Administration	520	846	835	558
Provinces	383	839	1,094	N/A
Minicipalities	146	253	N/A	N/A
	394	304	223	*81
IPS employment	1,443	1,985	2,152	N/A
Total Pub. Sec. employment as % share of economic	(Percentage)			
active population (PEA)	18.1	18.0	19.7	N/A
PE's Employment as % of PEA	4.9	2.8	2.0	N/A
PE's Employed as % PSE	27.3	15.3	10.4	N/A

Source: Based on Consejo Empresario Argentino 1990, INDEC, SIGEP and Technical Operative Group

Table 9.11 Prices and tariffs for public works PEs
(1969/1985/1990; index 1960 = 100)

	1969	1985	1990
Paid by consumers (incl. taxes)	104.3	128.1	131.7
Collected by PEs (net of taxes)	102.4	99.6	107.7

Source: SIGEP

Table 9.12 Finances of PEs – 1983–92
(millions of convertible pesos)

Concepts	1983	1987	1992
Revenue	12,589	16,730	9,897
Expenditure (with interest)	19,136	20,395	10,493
Expenditure (without interest)	17,020	18,249	10,427
Deficit (with interest)	(6,547)	(3,666)	(596)
Deficit (without interest)	(4,431)	(1,519)	(530)
Government's transfer	5,811	3,379	995
Treasury	4,926	2,410	966
Others	885	968	29

Source: Technical Operative Group L 3292–AR

Table 9.13 Finances of public works PEs (cash basis) 1983–92

Concepts	1983	1987	1992
Revenue	11,249	13,766	9,897
Expenditure (with interest)	16,552	18,527	10,493
Expenditure (without interest)	14,317	16,545	10,427
Deficit (with interest)	(5,302)	(4,761)	(596)
Deficit (without interest)	(3,068)	(2,779)	(530)
Government's transfer	5,862	3,283	995
Treasury	4,955	1,989	966
Others	907	1,293	29

Source: Technical Operative Group L 3292-AR

Table 9.14   Public utility rates (in real terms) index December 1989 = 100

Year	1983	1987	1992(*)
Total	103.77	102.17	79.51
YPF	81.18	84.04	64.55
GF	135.08	136.35	90.52
YCF	65.06	80.99	69.64
SEGBA	120.20	105.73	100.83
AyEE	100.19	109.23	90.24
HIDRON	77.88	84.91	79.03
FA	129.27	124.67	110.62
AA	99.59	102.54	
AGP	106.14	101.74	38.23
ENTEL	226.19	153.18	
ENCOTE	45.40	89.09	128.23
OSN	83.17	109.16	86.41

(*) April
Source: Technical Operative Group (based on new estimated tariff structure) L 3292–AR

Table 9.15   Public unility prices and deficits (in real terms)
(millions of convertible pesos)

Year	Utility* public rates	Deficit
1983	104	(6,547)
1988	108	(6,263)
1992 (*)	80	(596)

(*) April
Source: Technical Operative Group L 3292-AR

Table 9.16 Estimated fiscal impact of privatization of Public Works PEs
(millions of convertible pesos)

Companies	Deficit (*)	Increased taxes (**) revenue	Total impact
YPF S.A.	66		66
Gas del Estado	260	357	617
SEGBA	244	210	454
Ay EE (*)	275	66	341
HIDRONOR	516	111	627
Aerolineas (1)	(8)	18	11
Ferrocarriles Argentinos	691		691
FEMESA			0
AGP	(8)		(8)
ELMA	45	6	51
OSN	(24)	12	(12)
ENTel	605	792	1,397
ENCOTel	(8)		(8)
Total	2,654	1,572	4,227

(*) Based on 88/89 average
(**) Based on estimates from 1993 and on
Source: Technical Operative Group L 3292-AR

Table 9.17 Share of public sector deficit in GDP (at market prices)

Years	Total PS	Total PEs	% share PEs/PS
1965	2.57	2.34	91.05
1983	10.69	3.77	35.27
1988	10.75	6.02	56.00

Source: based on FIEL

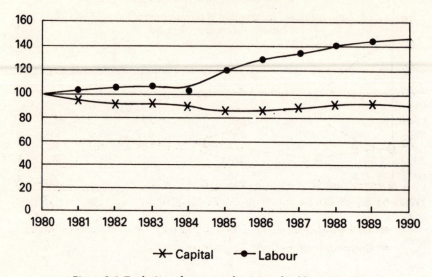

Figure 9.1 Evolution of mean productivity of public works PEs

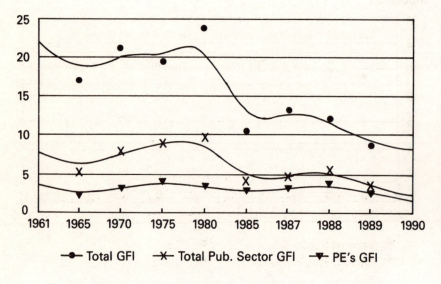

Figure 9.2 Share of GFI and public works PEs' investment in GDP

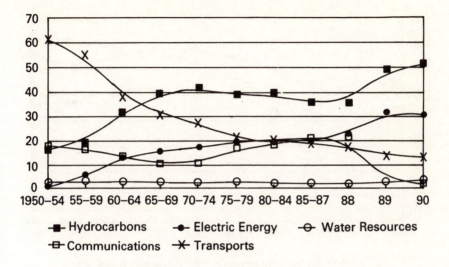

Figure 9.3 Structure of public works PEs at factor costs, 1950–90

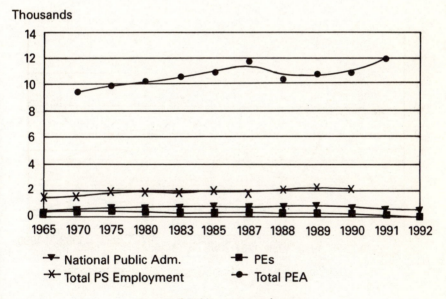

Figure 9.4 Public sector employment

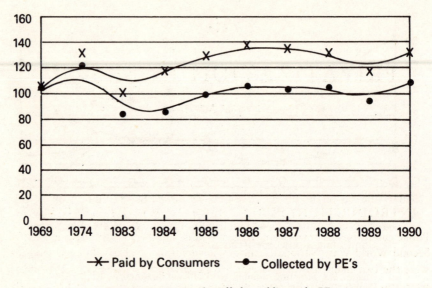

Figure 9.5 Prices and tariffs for public works PEs

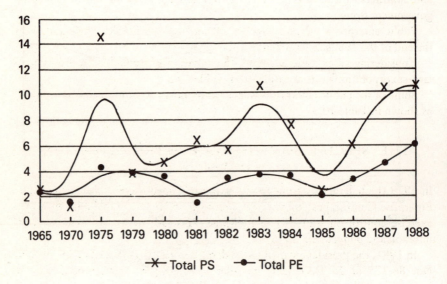

Figure 9.6 Share of public sector deficit in GDP

10

PRIVATIZATION IN BRAZIL

Enrique Saravia

INTRODUCTION: PUBLIC SECTOR WEIGHT AND SIZE

Public enterprises in Brazil were created in large numbers in the aftermath of the Second World War. National security considerations and development policies were the two main reasons. Several private enterprises with financial troubles were also transferred to the government in order to avoid unemployment or as a way of debt compensation.

At the end of the 1970s, public enterprises shared a big portion of the Brazilian economy. The private sector depended largely on state enterprises' sales and contracts as well as provision of public services and materials produced by government firms.

Public enterprises were reasonably efficient and profitable. The situation at the end of the 1980s is described in Tables 10.1–10.3.

Considering stockholder's equity, the situation of public enterprises among largest corporations was as displayed in Table 10.2.

Some of the public enterprises were among the most profitable firms in Brazil, as shown in Table 10.3.

THE 'SPECIAL COMMISSION FOR PRIVATIZATION' (1979–85)

In 1979 the federal government of Brazil established the Secretariat for Public Enterprise Control, best known by its acronym SEST. Its original mission was to exercise control on state-owned enterprises in order to control external debt, inflation and budget deficit growth.

In 1981, the President signed two federal decrees (No. 86,212 of 15 July and No. 86,215 of 15 December) in order to transform, transfer or deactivate enterprises under federal government control and to establish restrictions for the creation of regulatory agencies, wholly or partially state-owned enterprises and public foundations. Wide and detailed legal rules set up a special commission for implementing the regulations (Art. 6, Dec. No. 86,215).

The 'Special Commission for Privatization' began its activities listing all the

Table 10.1 PEs belonging to federal and state governments, among 500 largest enterprises in Brazil, Dec. 1990

Rank	Federal	Member states	Total
1 to 100	24	4	28
(1 to 10)	(6)	(0)	(6)
101 to 200	7	3	10
201 to 300	15	4	19
301 to 400	9	10	19
401 to 500	7	5	12
Total	62	26	88

Source: CEE-IBRE/FGV

enterprises amenable to being transferred to the private sector or to member states and local authorities, or whose activities could be performed by other agencies, or amenable to being totally or partially deactivated.

The first list contained 43 enterprises; all of them were former private enterprises that came under government control due to their owners' bankruptcy. In October 1981, the commission decided to withdraw three enterprises – an insurance company (Federal de Seguros), an engineering firm (ECEX) and a mining enterprise (Urucum Mineração) – and to include five others: a real estate firm, an insurance company, a petrochemical enterprise, a fertilizer company, and a dredging firm (Imobiliária Santa Cecilia, SOTECNA, Nitriflex, Fosfertil and Companhia Brasileira de Dragagem). The total number of firms listed was 48. At the same time, statute projects for authorizing two steel-industries privatization (COFAVI and COSIM) were concluded.

Decree No. 86,215 established a twelve-month term for the commission to conclude its work. A few days before the deadline the term was extended because the regulation had not been implemented on time. The commission's chairman reported the difficulties in transferring or ending operations of enterprises created by the government (*Folha de São Paulo* [newspaper], 23 June 1981: 21).

In 1983, the commission reported (*Folha de São Paulo*, 22 March 1983) the privatization of an insurance company (Federal de Seguros), a vegetable oil plant (Oleos de Palma), a paper plant (IMBRAPEL) and a petrochemical plant (Nitriflex).

Jose Olympio publishing company was transferred to the public sector on 16 April 1984 and in July 1984 it was decided to extend the commission's activities until 30 April 1985.

In three years, the Brazilian federal government sold to the private sector, through the commission, 18 enterprises. Nine enterprises were closed, 14 were merged with other enterprises and 3 were transferred to member states. Therefore, real privatization happened in only 18 cases. At the same time, 4 new enterprises were established, 6 government agencies became public enterprises

Table 10.2 Largest corporations by stockholder's equity, fiscal year 1990

Name	Sector	Type of ownership	US$ million*
ELECTROBRÁS – Centrais Elétricas Brasileiras S/A	Electricity	Federal-owned	13.252
TELEBRÁS – Telecomunicações Brasileiras S/A	Telecommunication	Federal-owned	5.875
PETROBRÁS – Petróleo Brasileiro S/A	Oil	Federal-owned	5.860
ELECTROPAULO – Eletricidade de São Paulo S/A	Electricity	Member state-owned	5.204
REFESA – Rede Ferroviária Federal S/A	Railways	Federal-owned	5.204
LIGHT – Serviços de Eletricidade S/A	Electricity	Federal-owned	3.439
SABESP – Cia. de Saneamento Básico do Estado de São Paulo	Water and sewerage	Member state-owned	3.096
CVRD – Cia. Vale do Rio Doce S/A	Mining	Federal-owned	2.849
COSIPA – Cia. Siderúrgica Paulista	Steel	Federal-owned	2.449
CST – Cia. Siderúrgica Tubarão S/A	Steel industry	Federal-owned	2.384
PETROQUISA – Petrobrás Química S/A	Petrochemicals	Federal-owned	2.194
CHESF – Cia. Hidrelétrica São Francisco S/A	Electricity	Federal-owned	1.979
METRO – Cia. Metropolitana São Paulo	Underground railways	Member state-owned	1.885
EMBRATEL – Empresa Brasileira de Telecomunicações S/A	Telecommunication	Federal-owned	1.720
FURNAS – Centrais Elétricas S/A	Electricity	Federal-owned	1.719
TELESP – Telecomunicações de São Paulo S/A	Telecommunication	Member state-owned	1.646
CESP – Cia. Energética de São Paulo S/A	Electricity	Member state-owned	1.474
CEMIG – Cia. Energética Minas Gerais S/A	Electricity	Member state-owned	1.456
AÇOMINAS – Aços Minas Gerais S/A	Steel industry	Federal-owned	1.178

* Cruzeiros converted into US dollar by 31 Dec. 1990 selling exchange rates: US$1 = NCr$170.06.
Source: CEE-IBRE/FGV.

Table 10.3 Largest corporations by net profit, fiscal year 1990

Name	Sector	Type of ownership	US$ million*
TELEBRÁS – Telecomunicações Brasileiras S/A	Communications	Federal-owned	676.32
PETROBRÁS – Petróleo Brasileiro S/A	Oil	Federal-owned	557.37
C.R. ALMEIDA – Construtora S/A	Engineering	National private	352.38
EMBRATEL – Empresa Brasileira de Telecomunicações S/A	Communications	Federal-owned	245.86
ELECTROBRÁS – Centrais Elétricas Brasileiras S/A	Electricity	Federal-owned	200.28
PETROBRÁS – Distribuidora S/A	Oil products	Federal-owned	126.13
DOCENAVE	Shipping	Federal-owned	122.78
EDIFICADORA S/A	Engineering	National private	122.33
CBPO – Cia Brasileira de Projetos	Engineering	National private	109.54
CVRD – Cia. Vale do Rio Doce	Mining	Federal-owned	109.25
TELESP – Telecomunicações de São Paulo S/A	Communications	Federal-owned	107.29
CONSTRUTORA NORBERTO ODEBRECHT S/A	Engineering	National private	92.08
TELERJ – Telecomunicações do Rio de Janeiro S/A	Communications	Federal-owned	85.60
Cia. SOUZA CRUZ – Indústria e Comércio	Tobacco	Foreign	85.46
Cia. Cervejaria BRAHMA	Beverages	National private	80.80

*Cruzeiros converted into US dollar by 31 Dec. 1990 selling exchange rates: US$ 1 = NCr$ 170.06.
Source: CEE–IBRE/FGV

and a failed private textile industry was taken over by the government (Tecidos Nova America).

The commission's achievements were not encouraging. Major difficulties hindering the commission's action came from other government agencies. For instance, several operations ready to be concluded were voided by the accounting court (Tribunal de Contas) – MAFERSA case – or seriously criticized by it – Federal de Seguros case. The same court said that privatization of textile firm Dona Isabel was harmful to public property.

In another case, private businessmen denounced as risky a copper-mining corporation privatization. They said it could produce a monopoly in copper supply.

THE 'INTERMINISTERIAL PRIVATIZATION COUNCIL' (1985–8)

In November 1985, The Interministerial Privatization Council (Conselho Interministerial de Privatização) was created by the new government (President Sarney's Administration). The privatization concept widened to include the possibility of capital stock partial subscriptions, minority stock alienation and enterprise closing (federal decrees No. 91,991 of 28 November 1985 and 93,006 of 21 November 1986 and Interministerial order No. 10 of 15 January 1986).

The above norms established mandatory procedures for the transfer of federal government-owned enterprises. The Minister of State who had a specific corporation attached to his ministry might be advised by a private consulting firm. The privatization operation had to be widely announced in all phases. Operations were analysed and assisted by external auditors. Transfer was implemented, whenever possible, through the stock market, and incentives were granted to employees to facilitate the acquisition of shares.

When the privatization operation was satisfactorily defined, the minister concerned submitted a detailed proposal to the council for approval. The inclusion of the enterprise in the privatization programme is implemented in the form of a decree of the President of the Republic.

Those rules did not modify some restrictions established by law as for example, the obligation of selling voting stocks only to Brazilian firms or citizens, although the subsequent maintenance of national control was not compulsory. Potential buyers were pre-qualified, having in consideration their experience, and financial capacity and, if necessary, technical or scientific capacity. Pre-qualified candidates might visit the firm, examine its books and audit its reports.

The council might choose among various bidding procedures: single offer to purchase through the submission by pre-qualified candidates of their respective bids; public purchase offer or auction; or direct negotiation.

Notwithstanding the flexibility introduced in the statute, the achievements were moderate. Five other enterprises were sold to the private sector and 6 were closed or merged. The new list included 54 enterprises for privatization and 4 firms for merging or closing. Nothing was done in regard to 4 enterprises a minority proportion of whose stock was going to be sold to private stockholders. Nevertheless, several enterprises were established or transferred from private to public sector.

The total amount of financial resources obtained by mid-1987 through the Privatization Programme was about US$ 190 million. This amount represented 0.6 per cent of total public enterprises' stockholders equity that was worth US$ 33,723 million in December 1985, and about 1.5 per cent of the market price of public companies whose shares were quoted in the stock exchange (US$ 13,100 million).

FEDERAL COUNCIL OF PRIVATIZATION (1988–90)

On 23 March 1988 the government decided to modify the privatization programme. Decree No. 95,886 established the 'Federal Programme of Destatization' and enlarged the concept of privatization contained in earlier policies. It included also the idea of deregulation and the possibility of granting concessions to private firms for delivering public services.

The 'Interministerial Privatization Council' was substituted, on 28 April 1988, by the Federal Council of Privatization.

Five enterprises were privatized in 1988–9. All of them were former private enterprises which became BNDE's subsidiaries due to financial troubles.

At the beginning of 1989 the President sent to the Congress a so-called 'provisional statute' (*medida provissoria*) proposing the extinction of three public enterprises (EMBRATER – a firm for rural extension and GEIPOT and CBTU – both for transportation planning and financing). The Congress rejected the proposal.

At the end of the period 1981–9, 38 privatization operations were concluded. They were predominantly 'reprivatizations'. The total amount obtained was about $ 1 billion.

PRESIDENT COLLOR'S PRIVATIZATION POLICIES
(1990–)

On 15 March 1990, one day after his inauguration, President Fernando Collor de Melo signed a provisional statute deciding to transform, transfer or deactivate several state-owned enterprises. The main objectives established for the new programme were to reduce the public sector debt, to promote wider share ownership and to increase competition.

Legal framework for privatization

The Congress passed an overall legislative authorization in the form of a general statute establishing norms and procedures to be observed in privatization

Table 10.4 Privatizations after Decree No. 91,991 (Nov. 1985 – Nov. 1989)

Enterprise	Sector	Date of sale	Sale price US$ mill.
Cia Nacional de Tecidos de Nova América	Textile	9 June 1987	15.8
Máquinas Piratininga do Nordeste S/A	Industrial equipment	23 July 1987	1.4
Máquinas Piratininga S/A	Industrial equipment	15 Sept. 1987	0.1
Siderúrgica N.S. Aparecida	Steel	10 Dec. 1987	12.9
Aracruz Celulose S/A	Pulp	3 May 1988	156.2
Cia. Guatapará de Celulose e Papel – Celpag	Pulp and paper	9 May 1988	72.7
Sibra – Eletrosiderúrgica Brasileira S/A	Iron	11 July 1988	47.6
Caraíba Metals	Copper	24 Aug. 1988	89.7
Cimetal Siderurgia S/A	Steel	21 Nov. 1988	59.0
Cia Brasleira do Cobre – CBC	Mining	29 March 1989	7.2
Cia Ferro e Aço de Vitória – Cofavi	Steel	12 July 1989	8.2
Cia de Celulose da Bahia – CCB	Pulp	17 July 1989	14.4
Usina Siderúrgica da Bahia – Usiba	Steel	8 Oct. 1989	54.2

processes (Law 8,031 of 12 April 1990, regulated by Decree 99,463 of 16 August 1990). Each process has to be preceded by at least two independent economic assessments made by private consulting firms, selected by bidding procedures. In addition, one of the firms selected will act as the privatization agent. The agent's fees will be proportional to the price obtained at the moment of the privatization. Independent auditors are selected by bidding procedures in order to monitor each operation, and a wide media coverage is required in all phases in order to ensure transparency and free access to information necessary to all parties.

The statute establishes also the institutional framework for privatization. It comprises two main actors:

1   the Privatization Committee, composed of four governmental members and seven members coming from the private sector. Their objectives are: to suggest the corporations to be included in the programme; to recommend sale conditions; and to control the observance o the programme's targets; and

2   the National Bank for Economic and Social Development (BNDES), that works as Programme Manager. The Bank has to supervise the work of the consultants and auditors, as well as carry out all the privatization processes.

Foreign capital participation comprises up to 40 per cent of voting shares and up to 100 per cent of non-voting shares.

Currencies for privatization

In order to ensure financial sources for the success of the programme, the following currencies are accepted for buying the privatized enterprises:

1   The cruzeiro, normal Brazilian currency.

2   The cruzado-novo, former Brazilian currency, coming from the temporary seizure of 80 per cent of private savings decided by the government in March 1991, and reimbursed to the owners in twelve monthly payments beginning in September 1991. The money blocked was worth over $ 110 billion.

3   Privatization certificates (CPs), that financial institutions and insurance companies were obliged to purchase in a total amount of $ 7 billion. banks were obliged to purchase in six months, beginning 15 June 1990 a total of CPs equal to 3 per cent of their assets or 18 per cent of net worth, whichever was lower as of 31 December 1989. (The government estimated the banks' share at $ 3.5 billion or half the total, but bank executives claimed they would end up paying around $ 2.5 billion.) The remaining $ 3.5 billion (or $ 4.5 billion according to bankers) was to come from other financial institutions including insurers (10 per cent of their assets), state employee pensions funds (25 per cent of their reserves), private pension funds (15 per cent) and stock brokers (10 per cent).

The controversial purchase rules established that if CPs were not used to buy shares as soon as the first company was put to auction, they were going

to lose value as their protection against inflation was gradually reduced.
4 Medium- and long-term debt of public enterprises and their subsidiaries.
5 Other government debt.
6 Brazilian foreign debt-for-equity swaps, through Deposit Facility Agreements (DFA)

Chronology for a privatization operation

As indicated in Table 10.5, about 240 days are required for the accomplishment of the whole privatization process.

Stages already concluded

The first four lists of enterprises to be privatized have already been approved by the President.

The companies already privatized or liquidated in 1991 and 1992 are shown in Table 10.6.

The privatization schedule for 1992 is shown in Table 10.7.

Privatized corporations: individual cases and their effects

Companhia Siderúrgica de Tubarão (CST)

Steel mill and the country's fourth largest steel producer (employing 6,150 people). It has as private partners the foreign groups Ilva and Kawasaki Steel.

Table 10.5 Chronology for privatization

Step	Average time for the step (days)	Total time (days)
1. The Committee recommends the enterprise and the President includes it in the programme		
2. Publication of public notices to recruit private consultants		
	15 to 45	15 to 45
3. Submission and approval of candidates' proposals		
4. Analysis of proposals, selection of consultant and contract signature	27	42 to 62
5. Consulting work carried out	90	132 to 162
6. Approval of sale method	10	142 to 172
7. Publication of sale notice	14	156 to 186
8. Public auction	60	216 to 246

Table 10.6   Companies privatized or liquidated, 1991–2

Company	Activity	Proceeds ($m)
USIMINAS	Steel	1,530.0
CELMA	Aircraft engines	93.0
MAFERSA	Railway rolling stock	51.0
COSINOR	Steel	14.2
SNBP	Shipping	12.9
INDAG	Fertilizers	9.2
PIRATINI	Steel	
PETROFLEX	Petrochemicals	244.0
COPESUL	Petrochemicals	800.0
ALCALIS		80.7
CST	Steel	305.7
ENASA	Shipping	liquidation
FRANAVE	Shipping	liquidation

The sale, through public auction, achieved a price of $ 305.7 million. The company's debt transferred to purchasers is $ 400 million. Investments to be paid until 1995, already contracted by the government and transferred to new owners, is $ 450 million.

Brokerage houses present at auction were 32. The company was purchased by a group composed by Unibanco: 18.30 per cent; CVRD: 20.79 per cent Companhia Bozano: 15.76 per cent; Banco Bozano: 10.04 per cent. The total of shares in auction was 91.3 per cent, about 64.9 per cent of equity. The final price obtained was 0.18 per cent above minimum price.

Companhia Siderúrgica do Nordeste (COSINOR)

Privatized in November 1991. The buyers were: Grupo Gerdau (local steel-making group). Price: $ 14.2m, above the minimum price of $ 12.6m.

Companhia de Navegação Lloyd Brasileiro

The biggest local shipping company. Contract with consulting firms selected in public offer was signed on 15 July 1992. They will prepare the privatization process.

Rede Ferroviária Federal S.A.

The state-owned railways company holds assets, including subsidiaries, that are valued at $ 20bn, while it has debts totalling $ 1.4bn.

Table 10.7   Schedule for 1992

Enterprise	Sector	Present situation	Date foreseen	
			Announcement	Auction
NITRIFLEX	Chemical	Sale	June	6 August
FOSFÉRTIL	Fertilizers	Sale	June	12 August
POLISUL	Chemical	Readying measures	August	10 September
PPH	Chemical	Readying measures	August	24 September
ARAFÉRTIL	Fertilizers	Readying measures	August	September
GOIASFÉRTIL	Fertilizers	Sale	August	September
ACESITA	Fertilizers	Preparation of announcement	July	22 October
ICC	Fertilizers	Readying measures	September	October
ULTRAFÉRTIL	Fertilizers	Readying measures	August	October
PETROCOQUE	Chemicals	Valuation in process	September	November
PQU	Chemicals	Valuation in process	October	December
NITROFÉRTIL	Fertilizers	Valuation in process	October	December
TRIUNFO	Chemicals	Readying measures	—	—
MINERAÇÃO CARAÍBA	Mining (copper)	Readying measures	—	—
COSIPA	Steel	Valuation in process	—	—
CSN	Steel	Valuation in process	—	—
EMBRAER	Aircraft industry	Valuation in process	—	—
AÇOMINAS	Steel	Valuation in process	—	—
LLOYD	Shipping	Valuation in process	—	—
REDE FERROVIÁRIA	Railways	Selection of consultants	—	—
VALEC	Railways	Selection of consultants	—	—
AGEF	Warehousing		—	—

On 12 March 1992 the government announced that it would be selling off the federal railway network (which runs on 23,000 km of track) in 1993. The entire process, perhaps the most complex in the privatization scheme, is expected to take between 12 and 18 months. The basic idea is to transfer to private hands the rolling stock and some installations, with the track and stations remaining in state hands.

In 1991 the government claims that it had balanced the books of the network, which had a turnover of $ 800m, by dismissing 11,000 of its 60,000 employees, selling off 3,000 properties, taking 1,000 km of track out of service, and halving the frequency of passenger services.

Five consortia of consulting firms were pre-qualified for consulting studies.

Usinas Siderúrgicas de Minas Gerais S.A. (USIMINAS)

Latin America's biggest steel producer, it was privatized in 1991.

Effects of privatization: debt shrinking: Dec. 1990 – $ 393 million; Sept. 1991 – $ 323 million. Net profit: 1st semester 1992 – $ 60.2 million; 1st semester 1991 – $ 59.6 million. Sales: $ 779.5 million during the same semester; 1991 – $ 1.27 billion.

Serviço de Navegação da Bacia do Prata (SNBP)

It is a shipping company working in the waterways of the River Plate Basin.

The purchaser was Companhia Interamericana de Navegação (CINCO). It was supported financially by the Bank of the State of São Paulo.

The privatized company made new investments of about $ 800 million and hired 60 new employees. After sale it was completely computerized. The fleet was operating at 20 per cent of its capacity; today it operates at 100 per cent.

Companhia Nacional de Ácalis

It was sold on 15 July 1992. The purchasers were Cirne Consortium (Grupo Frota Oceánica). Price: $ 79.5 million.

Government of the State of São Paulo

The first privatizations of the government of the State of Sao Paulo include:

1   Viacão Aérea Sáo Paulo (VASP): the commercial airline belonging to the state.
2   An infrastructure development programme (Water, electricity, roads, subway) launched in partnership with the private sector. The privatization of the operation is programmed.

Empresa Brasileira de Aeronáutica (EMBRAER)

The government reports that feasibility studies for the privatization of aircraft manufacturer EMBRAER will be ready in October 1992. Thus, the sale could take place in early 1993.

11

PRIVATIZATION IN MOROCCO

Alfred H. Saulniers[1]

INTRODUCTION

Morocco recently launched a major privatization programme. The constraints to getting that programme underway and its anticipated impacts may provide useful insights into the nature of the privatization environment. The first section reviews the setting for Morocco's privatization law; the second section surveys the mechanisms of privatization; the third section examines the privatizables; the fourth section examines special circumstances which mark Morocco's privatization; the fifth section looks at constraints to the current programme; and the sixth section examines its expected impacts.

THE PUBLIC ENTERPRISE SETTING FOR PRIVATIZATION IN MOROCCO

Origins

Morocco's public portfolio grew out of France's efforts, during the French Protectorate from 1912 to 1956, to accomplish two goals: to control natural resources and other key sectors of the protectorate's economy and to provide needed social and institutional infrastructure for French settlers.

To control key sectors of the economy, mining, exporting and transport were among the earliest firms in the government portfolio. For example, the phosphate mine and processor, the Cherifian Phosphate Office (Office Chérifien des Phosphates – OCP), currently and for many years Morocco's largest firm, was founded in 1920 as a public enterprise; the large mining holding company the Mining Research and Holding Board (Bureau de Recherches et de Participations Minières – BRPM) was similarly formed in 1928. OCP was justified on the basis of a government monopoly on extraction which pre-empted the possibility of non-French investment in phosphate mining. As agricultural exports and the needs for transport prospered and were developed, they too merited their own public enterprises, such as the Cherifian Office for Control and Exports (Office Chérifien de Contrôle et d'Exportation – OCCE) and the National Transport

Office (Office National des Transports – ONT), both created in 1937.

In an effort to provide needed institutional and social infrastructure for French settlers, two strategies were followed. First, public institutions were created, such as the Office for Industrial Property (a trademark registry) (Office de la Propriété Industrielle – OPI) in 1916 and the French Family Office (Office de la Famille Française) in 1928. Second, most concessions to provide such infrastructure as water, electricity and railroads were given to private sector firms, many of them subsidiaries of the French financial group the Banque de Paris et des Pays-Bas (PARIBAS). Clear exceptions were those of electricity and water entrusted to Electric Energy of Morocco (Energie Electrique du Maroc – EEM), 25 per cent of whose shares were held by the Cherifian state, and to the Industrial Works Government Corporation of the Protectorate (Régie des Exploitations Industrielles du Protectorat – REIP), created in 1929.

Distinct patterns of portfolio growth occurred during the Protectorate. The earliest ventures created by the French authorities laid the basis for French penetration of Morocco's economy. During the Great Depression, portfolio growth was virtually non-existent. Later, during the Second World War, the authorities created provisioning and supply agencies. After the war, the portfolio grew as the large holding companies took shares in mining or other ventures, seeking to reduce the risk for metropolitan, largely French, businesses. Thus, of the 25 portfolio additions from 1946 to 1955, 22 were via holdings, while only 3 were directly created by the government. The pattern of portfolio growth through subsidiarization set after 1946 later dominated the 1970s and is directly related to current privatization efforts.

After independence in 1956, the pace of portfolio growth increased. During the 1960s and early 1970s, Morocco created new firms to supply the essential services previously provided by private concessionaires and to direct industrialization. In the absence of a national private sector capable and willing to provide the levels of capital, risk taking or technical expertise deemed necessary by government authorities to achieve the desired industrialization, the government invested heavily in large, capital-intensive industries.

The period from 1973 to 1977 stands out in terms of portfolio growth with 215 new firms and subsidiaries, 69 of them in 1974 alone. During that period, 92 per cent of new public enterprises (PEs) were subsidiaries of existing ones. Existing public enterprises spun off subsidiaries, often to escape the central government's heavy financial controls over their operations; at other times, they bought into hitherto foreign-owned firms, thereby meeting the provisions of Moroccanization. Still more growth came from government investment banks or finance companies that took minority shares in private ventures with the intention of redeeming the shares, once the companies had shown the capacity to survive, and reinvesting the proceeds in new ventures. Such 'rolling privatization' of government shares lagged far behind expectations, with the result that the portfolio continued to grow.

One explanation of the massive portfolio growth from 1973 to 1977 is found in the high world market price of phosphates. Morocco, at this time, was the world's leading exporter and price setter, accounting for about 30 per cent of total exports. The windfall revenues accruing to the state via taxes and transfers from the public enterprise monopoly on production provided the means to invest in new firms. Until 1979, terms of trade effects were positive, namely the increased export earnings from phosphates far outweighed the increased import costs of petroleum products, making Morocco a net beneficiary of the primary product price rises. Indeed, phosphate revenues increased from an average of 24 per cent of exports for the period 1960–72 to an average of 41 per cent for 1973–7, while their amount more than tripled in constant terms. The mechanism that enabled this massive growth of the public portfolio was the recycling of phosphate earnings through a major increase in lending by the largely government-owned financial institutions.

Only part of the increased revenue was spent in linkage-related investments, such as the phosphoric acid plant Maroc Phosphore in 1973. The revenues also provided the catalyst to shift from a programme of gradual Moroccanization of capital and labour to a programme imposed by law. State holdings bought into formerly foreign-owned firms, while totally new firms were created to replace many firms that closed rather than conforming to the Moroccanization requirements.

The public enterprise creation process fell abruptly in 1978. While partly attributable to the drop in world phosphate prices, the fall is mainly due to internal factors. The King of Morocco, in announcing the new three-year plan, indicated his strong displeasure at the increasing number of public enterprises, wondering aloud if some of them should be eliminated. Thereafter, spectacular growth dropped.

The current, broad-based portfolio, with firms found in many sectors, consists of the remnants of the creation process going back to the beginning of the century. Some public firms were created for rational, economic or political motives. Others became public by accident, as subsidiaries of firms swept into the portfolio during Moroccanization. Others were created by public firms seeking to circumvent the heavy government control system.

The aggregate situation

In 1986, the last year for which complete figures are available, the public enterprise portfolio consisted of 682 directly or indirectly held firms (first-degree subsidiaries only). Firms with a 'small' state share or headquartered outside Morocco are excluded. The portfolio accounted for 17 per cent of GDP, 25 per cent of gross fixed capital formation, 17 per cent of employment and 27 per cent of wages and salaries.

Table 11.1 disaggregates the portfolio by sector.[2] Services comprise the largest group, 424 firms, with 89 in finance, 60 in commerce and 56 in transport and communications. Industry of all types accounts for 188, with agroindustry,

Table 11.1 Morocco's PEs by sector of activity, 1986

Sector of activity	Portfolio (No.)	Surveyed firms (No.)	Share of value added in sector
Agriculture	17	11	2
Mining, extraction	29	19	79
Energy, utilities	24	22	87
Industry	188	76	21
Services	424	127	n.a.
Building & public works	8	1	1
Finance	89	19	69
Commerce	60	15	+
Transports & communications	56	26	47
Other services	211	66	n.a.
Total	682	255	

Source: Portfolio data from Royaume, n.d.: 2; survey data from Roudies and Daoud, 1989: 41–2
+ <0.5%

including sugar processing and refining, the largest part. A survey of the largest firms details their importance across sectors. They account for about 90 per cent of value-added in energy, 80 per cent in mining, 70 per cent for the financial sector, and 50 per cent in transport and communications. Their contribution is minimal for agriculture, building and commerce. Few public enterprises are found other than at the national level, municipally-owned water and electric utilities excepted.

Holding companies

Morocco has traditionally employed holding companies to manage its public enterprise portfolio. The Ministry of Finance has identified 17 large groups, 11 of which had 20 or more subsidiaries in 1986 (Table 11.2).[3] The pension depository Fund for Savings and Management (Caisse de Dépot et de Gestion – CDG), has the lead, followed by the three financial/industrial holdings SNI, BNDE and ODI. These are followed by sector-specific holdings: BRPM and ZELLIDJA for mining, SOFICOM for marketing of agro-processed items, CMKD for tourism and hotels and SOMED, a joint venture with capital from the United Arab Emirates. Because of widespread, fragmented interlocking holdings, many firms are represented in more than one portfolio and some of them may be owned by up to six Moroccan public enterprises.

The privatization programme appears to repudiate the strategy of using holding companies to maintain the portfolio. Three of the largest holdings figure prominently on the privatizable list. Privatization of their assets and the 70 shares

Table 11.2 Principal holding companies in Morocco, 1986 (number of subsidiaries by share of equity)

Share of equity (%)	100	99.99–50	49.99–25	24.99 >	n.a.	Total	Privatizable
CDG	4	14	7	28	0	53	19
SNI	0	2	12	33	0	47	Firm on list
BNDE	0	0	2	15	27	44	Firm on list
ODI	0	11	14	10	1	36	24
BRPM	3	12	7	9	0	31	7
CMKD	0	16	6	7	0	29	6
OCP	13	4	3	7	0	27	3
CIH	3	2	3	19	0	27	3
ZELLIDJA	2	7	4	7	4	24	2
SOMED	0	3	3	16	0	22	6
SOFICOM	5	9	2	4	0	20	Firm on list
Total No.	30	80	63	155	32	360	
%	8.33	22.22	17.50	43.06	8.89	100.00	

Source: Portfolio data from Royaume, n.d., fascicule 4

in privatizables held by the other large holdings companies will account for half the firms held by the large holding companies.

The general structure of public ownership

Table 11.3 breaks down the portfolio by degree of government shares; 20 per cent of the portfolio, 134 firms, is wholly owned, either directly or indirectly. These include the public administrative establishments such as hospitals, training institutes and agricultural extension agencies. In total, 278 firms, or 41 per cent of the portfolio, are majority or wholly owned. The government share in 445 firms is less than 33.33 per cent, the amount needed under Moroccan law to block major changes at the level of the board of directors.

Profits of public enterprises

Available data, shown in Table 11.4, indicate that most of Morocco's public firms shown accounting profits. For 255 firms surveyed in 1986, 193, or 76 per cent, registered profits. As expected, the share of firms showing a profit drops as government ownership in the firm increases. The finding may be explained by the fact that, as wholly state-owned firms are more subject to central government scrutiny and control, they may be called on to fulfil a social role, or they may operate as heavily regulated monopolies.

Table 11.3   Structure of public ownership, 1986

State direct or indirect percentage	No.	(%)
100%	134	19.65
50 – 99.99%	144	21.11
33 – 49.99%	59	8.65
10 – 32.99%	136	19.94
0 – 9.99%	209	30.65

Source: Royaume, n.d.: 1

Table 11.4   Profitability of PEs, 1986

		<50%	50 – 99.99%	100%	Total
Profitable	No.	84	72	37	193
	%	86	73	64	76
Loss making	No.	14	27	21	62
	%	14	27	36	24
Total		98	99	58	255

Source: Roudies and Daoud, 1989: 40

THE MECHANISMS OF PRIVATIZATION

The Moroccan parliament authorized privatization on 11 December 1989. A broad consensus led to parliament's approving the law[4] by a vote of 78 to 45 with 3 abstentions. That law evolved from the long, on-going dialogue on the optimal mix between public and private sectors to bring about national development. The law lists specific enterprises and hotels slated for privatization before 31 December 1995.

The law provides the framework for the current privatization programme. It is implemented by a Minister of Privatization, who was named in October 1989, assisted by a five-member interministerial Transfer Commission. An independent Valuation Authority oversees the propriety of the evaluation process. Members of both groups are named by the king for their competence in economic, social and financial matters. To control future portfolio growth, the minister must approve the creation of all new public firms or subsidiaries except for those created by Act of Parliament.

In July 1991, the king named the Valuation Authority. Made up of seven 'wise men' outside the government, who are widely respected for their business and financial savvy, it sets the prices for privatizations on the basis of independent evaluations of company activity.

In September 1991, the king named the interministerial Transfer Commission, an event which marked the completion of the privatization structure. Basically, the commission provides greater transparency by associating those ministries concerned with the transfer of an individual firm in all decisions relating to the transfer. While the commission's role is mostly consultative, any proposal for private placement, to meet specific social, regional or employment goals, must have its concurring opinion.

The law fixes four privatization methods: financial market mechanisms; tenders; the combination of financial market mechanisms and tenders; and direct negotiation. To meet the law's social objectives, priority may be given for certain potential shareholders and special advantages are provided for the workers in firms being privatized.

Three social objectives have been assigned high priority in the law: to permit new social classes to buy shares while combatting increased concentration of wealth; to develop regional economies; and to safeguard employment. The mechanisms for meeting the objectives are specified in the regulations to the law. For employees, although no hard-and-fast rules have been set, the minister may reserve up to 10 per cent of a company's shares for those with at least one year's seniority. They may also buy discounted shares (maximum of 15 per cent reduction) that may not be sold for three years after their purchase. The privatization law makes no employment guarantees, Moroccan jurisprudence providing sufficient safeguards for labour.

The law favours local, regional buyers for those firms (or portions thereof) that are given regional priority. They include individuals residing, born or engaged in business where the firm is active, Moroccan workers living abroad who are native to the region, and certain firms or co-operatives based in the region. They may bid in a limited tender for two months; thereafter, if undersubscribed, the tender is opened to other bidders.

Further, co-operativized farmers who wish to buy shares in the agroindustrial concerns that buy their produce benefit from a similar limited tender process.

Regulations to the basic privatization law were approved by the cabinet on 15 September 1990 and by the Council of Ministers on 16 October 1990, and ratified by parliament on 26 December 1991.[5] The regulations fix the powers of the Valuation Authority, detail the methods of transfer and evaluation, and indicate special treatment for the favoured groups in the privatization process. Other decrees fix the powers of the Minister of Privatization and the Transfer Commission and detail special treatment for workers.

No privatizations have yet taken place under the mechanisms detailed above.

THE PRIVATIZABLES

The law lists 75 enterprises and 37 hotels to be privatized. Since the law's passage, two firms completed a merger which was already underway. The list of privatizables was the outcome of a political process. In the draft law submitted to parliament in October 1988, six firms were to be exempt from privatization for strategic reasons.[6] After long negotiations, the law included a positive list of firms and hotels to which privatization would be limited.

That list was the result of a deliberate effort by the government to choose firms that would be easy to privatize. The pragmatic choice was dictated on the basis of trying to maximize the probability of success of the overall programme. Six specific criteria were employed to reach this goal. The mix of large and small privatizable firms would be:

1 profitable or potentially profitable;
2 having a significant public participation;
3 already subject to competition, a criterion particularly applicable to industrial and commercial firms;
4 having a major economic role without having an important public service role;
5 without major overstaffing problems; and
6 having a regionally diversified basis.

Further, all firms chosen had a legal corporate form, *Société anonyme*, so that legal reorganization prior to the sale would be unnecessary.

The transfers will have varying impact in different sectors of the economy. The value-added by privatizable firms alone amounts to 6.0 per cent of GDP and their equity capital totalled US$ 1.8 billion in 1989. No estimates exist for the hotels.

According to data presented in Table 11.5, agriculture will have slight impact from privatization, whether gauged by firms, value-added or employment. In 1989, only 0.06 per cent of sectoral value-added and slightly more than 400 employees were accounted for by the public share of the three privatizables. A

Table 11.5 Sectoral distribution of privatizable firms, 1989

Sector	No.	Share of sectoral value-added	Employment
Agriculture	3	0.06	411
Extractive industry	5	6.25	1,543
Manufactures	41	6.12	19,837
Financial institutions	10	31.32	8,751
Commerce	9	4.23	3,285
Transport & communications	2	0.93	820
Services	4	0.27	1,279
Total	74		35,926

Source: Royaume, 1990: 7
Excludes privatizable hotels.

similar case holds for transport and communications and services, which also account for less than 1 per cent of sectoral value-added.

Industry (including sugar processing), however and finance have prominent positions among the privatizables. The 10 financial institutions weigh in for the strongest proportion of value-added, with 31.3 per cent and more than 8,000 employees; the 41 industrial firms have 6.1 per cent of value-added, but more than 19,000 employees, 5,541 of whom work in the sugar sub-sector.

The inclusion of several large financial holding companies on the list of privatizable firms will extend privatization's impact beyond the companies listed to their non-privatizable subsidiaries. Selling the holding company purges the subsidiary from the public portfolio, thereby reducing its size. Taking into account the portfolio holdings of all privatizables as part of their normal business assets, the privatization programme will encompass approximately 300 firms, in addition to the basic list. These include at least 86 firms at least half of which are held by privatizables, and a further 28 in which they own at least a third of shares outstanding. Not all the state's holdings in these 300 will be transferred to the private sector, but for those that do remain in the public portfolio, the state share will be diminished.

Only six of the privatizables receive subsidies: a livestock promoter, National Company for Livestock Development (Société Nationale pour le Développement de l'Elévage – SNDE), to cover costs of its extension activities, and five sugar refiners, half of those privatizable. A major reorganization is planned to eliminate the need for subsidies in the sugar sector prior to its privatization.

SPECIAL CIRCUMSTANCES OF PRIVATIZATION IN MOROCCO

This section details three particularities of the Moroccan privatization programme which set it apart from similar programmes in many countries.

First, privatization is not new to Morocco. Indeed, because Morocco's broad programme, underway for almost 30 years, has been largely devoid of ideological content, it is unrecognized at home and unknown abroad. Morocco has used many privatization methods at different times including capital dilutions to reduce the government share in firms, leases and management contracts, popular shareholding, asset sales, demonopolization of legal monopolies, liquidations, and portfolio restructuring by the major holding companies.[7]

Morocco's recent task of putting together a cohesive programme was simplified by the years of experience with different privatization paradigms. Some earlier procedures, liquidation for example, were rejected after an evaluation based not only on the issues of political feasibility, but also on Morocco's own practical experience. The most popular means which had the longest trial period, portfolio restructuring through the sale of shares and assets, has been accorded priority under the current approach. Morocco has also chosen to build on earlier experience in making popular shareholding – whether to employees, regional clients, or farmers – an integral part of the programme.

Second, in Morocco, privatization is a separate issue from financial or management restructuring. Privatization is the province of the Ministry of Privatization, whose minister was named in late 1989. Restructuring of public enterprises *per se* has traditionally been carried out by the teams at the Directorate for Public Establishments and Participations at the Ministry of Finance. Its staff members have carried out a number of successful restructurings, some of which have led to the firms' thereafter being included on the list of privatizables, as, for example, the CTM-LN bus company. It is expected that most firms on the current list of privatizables will not need any restructuring.

Other similar procedures are carried out in a decentralized fashion. Morocco has made extensive use of both management contracts and contract programmes. Thus, for example, since the early 1970s, management contracts for hotels have been negotiated by the holding companies that built them. Many contract programmes have been negotiated by the companies with a government team composed of the Ministry of Finance, the Ministry of Economic Affairs, and the sectoral supervisory ministry.

Third, in Morocco, privatization is a strictly local phenomenon. Contrary to the situation found in many other countries, privatization has not been imposed through agreements with the World Bank or the International Monetary Fund. Further, where the World Bank has intervened, it has had little impact on official thinking about privatization. For example, under the Public Enterprise Restructuring Loan (PERL), the World Bank lent $ 240 million to Morocco in 1987 to support restructuring of public enterprises. One of PERL's objectives, improving portfolio efficiency, was to be reached by developing a strategy leading to the medium-term programme to divest the state of those activities more effectively handled in the private sector.

The report, which was never made public, circulated among top administration decision makers as the privatization issue came to the fore. But, a measure of the marginal impact of the World Bank may be seen in that by the time the PERL-funded strategy had been defined, the Moroccan Parliament had already passed a privatization law and had already set a list of privatizables. The international agencies are, in Morocco, not a constraint on the content or the nature of the privatization process.

The strictly national nature of privatization may also be seen in the policy discourse which has repeatedly, through the speeches of the king or of successive prime ministers since the early 1970s, emphasized the transitory nature of state intervention in the productive sectors. The basic motive for state activity was to stand in for a private sector which, weakened under the Protectorate, found itself unable to take over after independence. As proof that the private sector has developed and prospered under the post-independence economic policies, privatization enables the state to reduce its role in an orderly fashion.

CONSTRAINTS TO PRIVATIZATION IN MOROCCO

This section will deal with three constraints to privatization in Morocco: the issues of timing, an inadequate capital market, and the principal–agent relationship.

The problem of timing

An important constraint to privatization in Morocco is its timing. It is no secret that the French programme, after the legislative elections brought Jacques Chirac to power in 1986, strongly influenced thinking in Morocco. Unfortunately, just one month after Morocco's Parliament had been invited by King Hassan II to reflect on privatization during the spring parliamentary session in 1988, new French elections led to a change in government and an abandonment of privatization. The abrupt stop to privatization in France was not propitious to speedy passage of the proposed legislation in Morocco. Further, when the legislative text was still being considered by Morocco's Parliament in 1989, the French National Assembly began hearings that were strongly critical of the conditions under which privatization had taken place. These hearings were followed in Morocco.[8]

The stop to privatization and the negative perspective of privatization reported by the French economic press came at a critical juncture for privatization worldwide. In late 1988 and 1989, Eastern Europe had not yet begun its massive swing away from the public sector. The resultant law adopted by the Moroccan Parliament in December 1989 has some intellectual links to the earlier French legislation, but with additional levels of safeguards to meet some of the objections raised in the French National Assembly hearings.

The first timing constraint for privatization in Morocco is that the law, because it is a forerunner in the current wave of worldwide privatizations, did not benefit from the transition to more supple systems of transfer. It provides for a centralized system with multiple layers of preventive safeguards. While the safeguards will certainly prevent many of the abuses of the privatization process found elsewhere, they mean that the process must move slowly.

A second timing constraint stems from the current political conjuncture in Morocco. In 1990, the scheduled parliamentary elections were postponed for two years after a nationwide referendum – to enable the United Nations to carry out a referendum on the future of the Western Sahara, thereby enabling all Moroccans to vote for their representatives in parliament. The two-year delay has expired and the United Nations referendum has still not been held.

To renew the democratically grounded representational system, parliamentary elections have been scheduled for late 1992. They will be preceded by elections for local representatives and a referendum on a new Constitution. The latter will give more power to parliament and the cabinet. Privatization has not been placed in abeyance until all stages of the electoral process have been completed, and the preliminary audits, evaluations and other steps prior to the actual transfers are going forward at a rapid pace.

However, the important issues linked to the electoral process make the competition for political attention, that the transfers would necessarily entail, difficult to realize at present. Continuation of the preliminary stages means that the transfers are expected to proceed at a rapid pace once the elections have been completed. The nature of the timing constraints detailed above, although broadly political in their origins, do not fit the major heading of attitudinal factors that Professor Ramanadham has assigned to political factors in his typology.[9] I suggest that another, more neutral and all encompassing, term be found.

An inadequate capital market

Overall, the capital market in Morocco falls far short of that needed to fully support privatization. Notably, a revitalization of the Casablanca stock exchange has been discussed for years. Stock exchange volume for 1991 was less than US$ 130 million of which less than $ 50 million was due to the sale of stocks, the rest mostly government or parastatal bonds.[10] In 1987, the Ministry of Finance established a working group to recommend improvements. Parliamentary action is needed on legislation arising out of those recommendations to improve the brokerage system, to increase the amount of available information, and to better protect potential stockholders. The privatization law does provide for alternative methods, such as worker participation and private placements, to tap financial resources in the absence of an adequate capital market.

The principal–agent problem

Privatization in Morocco has only one principal – the head of state. H.M. Hassan II has wholeheartedly embraced privatization. While the fact of having only one principal frees the privatization agents from the multiple pressures found at the level of the public enterprises, progress tends to be more sporadic, largely in function of competing issues on the national or international agenda.

Moreover, no political party has followed the lead of the head of state in pushing for massive privatization as part of the national agenda. The absence of such broad-based support means that the agents of the programme, notably the ministry and the other mechanisms detailed above, are not subject to the strong political pressures that would speed up the transfer process. Progress is, thus, slow in reaching the goals set forth in the privatization law.

EXPECTED IMPACTS OF PRIVATIZATION

This section details three impacts of privatization, the first of which is in the medium term, and the second two of which are in the long term.

No major changes should result from privatization

The first anticipated impact of Morocco's privatization programme is that, over the medium term, enterprise behaviour is not expected to change as a consequence of the transfers.

That the enterprises already operated in competitive sectors was a basic criterion for their inclusion on the list of privatizables. The major consequence of that criterion is that no major changes are anticipated in prices of the firms' products after their transfer to the private sector. The firms operating in competitive markets are price takers, hence their behaviour should not greatly influence prices after transfer. Moreover, under the privatization regulations no sale may be made to a person or group of persons if it thereby results in the creation of a monopoly. The regulations provide another safeguard against post-privatization price increases.

Further, in looking at the cost structure of the privatizables, the new owners should not undertake major cost restructurings through personnel reduction. On the one hand, the personnel criterion for inclusion on the list of privatizables was the absence of major overstaffing problems. On the other hand, the privatization programme needs 'early winners' – successful sales at decent prices to investors willing to bring in new capital and without major redundancies – to ensure its continued political viability. A key ingredient of the 'winner' strategy is that no major employment losses result from privatization.

Management style is also not expected to change. Of the 37 hotels, 35 are already managed by the private sector. In addition, 3 mines are under private sector management, while 3 textile firms, and 1 tyre manufacturer are not only under private sector management, but the public sector share of equity is so low (less than a third of equity) that decisions may not be influenced at the level of the board of directors. Currently, under private sector management, the firms and hotels are already operating efficiently and dynamically, and that behaviour is not expected to change as a result of a simple transfer of ownership from public to private.

Morocco's public enterprise portfolio will greatly contract

The privatizable list of 75 firms and 37 hotels represents just part of the firms in the public portfolio to be transferred to the private sector. The presence of large financial holdings on the privatizable list will extend privatization's impact to all their subsidiaries in the long term. Sale of the holding will remove its share in all its subsidiaries from the public portfolio. For those subsidiaries remaining in the public portfolio because part of their equity is held by other, non-privatizable public firms, the state share will decline following the transfers, resulting in a drop in the portfolio's overall economic importance.

Taking into account portfolio holdings as normal business assets, privat-ization will encompass approximately 300 firms, beyond the basic list. These include a minimum of 86 firms held at least 50 per cent by privatizables, and a further 28 in which they own at least a third of shares outstanding. Privatizing the large, healthy financial holdings will have important consequences in terms of paring the portfolio, bringing in revenues, and provisioning the stock market where many of them are already listed. But, for the subsidiaries, apart from the impact on the state portfolio, no change is expected in company behaviour because they are removed from the more direct means of state scrutiny and control and, consequently, are already run as private firms.

The role of foreign firms will increase in Morocco

Morocco welcomes foreign investment through privatization. Morocco sent an initial signal to foreign investors, in 1989, by abrogating regulations to the Moroccanization law as part of the groundwork for privatization. As a result, foreign investment in sectors previously reserved for Moroccans and found on the list of privatizables became possible. The sectors included: banking, real estate, insurance, certain industries, some transport, ranching, and some commerce. To send them an even clearer signal, in July 1991, a Ministry of Foreign Investment was created, which made even more obvious the government's strong desire for long-term foreign participation in the privatization programme.

CONCLUSIONS

Privatization is but one of Morocco's significant structural reforms undertaken since the early 1980s. Others have included the liberalization of much of foreign trade, the lifting of most domestic price controls, the gradual elimination of subsidies, the opening and welcoming of foreign investors, the reform of the fiscal system, and the promotion of exports. The gradually implemented liberalization measures laid the groundwork for the privatization programme by ensuring that some key policy changes were made prior to the programme's start.

Other measures linked to privatization's success are underway. These include the adoption of a modern accounting system, creation of a professional organization for accountants and auditors leading to improving overall enterprise management, and the stock market reforms. All these measures may be viewed as removing some potential constraints on the success of the privatization programme in Morocco.

Within this overall context, privatization has taken off from the diverse, uncoordinated actions to a fully fledged, well-oriented and co-ordinated programme implemented by a Ministry of Privatization. It is too early to look at the impacts of sales under the new programme for the simple reason that there have not yet been any sales. Nevertheless, it is expected that the impacts will be overwhelmingly positive.

NOTES

1 Only opinions of the author are expressed in this chapter, not those of any institutions associated with him. Comments by Hassan Amrani, Lhassan Belkoura, Najib Ibn Abdeljalil, Abderaffie Al Houari and Hans Pollan on this chapter or an earlier version are gratefully acknowledged but they are not responsible for any remaining errors.

2 The figures update those found in my earlier analysis of privatization in Morocco (Saulniers 1993).

3 The Ministry of Finance figures do not take account of the broad portfolios of two insurance companies, both privatizable: CNIA with holdings in 62 firms, and SCR with 29.

4 Royaume du Maroc, *Loi n° 39–89 autorisant le transfert d'entreprises publiques au secteur privé*, Adoptée par la Chambre des Représentants le 11 Décembre 1989, Promulguée le 11 Avril 1990 par *Dahir* n° 1–90–01, Publiée au *Bulletin officiel* le 18 Avril 1990.

5 Royaume de Maroc, Décrets d'application de la Loi n° 39–89 autorisant le transfert d'entreprises publiques au secteur privé: *Décret n° 2–90–402 du 16 octobre 1990 pris sur le fondement de l'habilitation prévue par l'article 5 de la loi n° 39–89 autorisant le transfert d'entreprises publiques au secteur privé; Décret n° 2–90–403 du 16 octobre 1990 relatif aux pouvoirs de ministre chargé de la mise en oeuvre des transferts des entreprises publiques au secteur privé; Décret n° 2–90–577 du 16 octobre 1990 pris pour l'application de l'article 7 de la loi n° 39–89 autorisant le transfert d'entreprises publiques au secteur privé; Décret n° 2–90–578 du 16 octobre 1990 fixant les conditions de fonctionnement de la commission des transferts prévue à l'article 2 de la loi n° 39–89 autorisant le transfert d'entreprises publiques au secteur privé*, Adoptés par le Conseil des Ministres le 16 Octobre 1990, Publiés au *Bulletin officiel* le 17 Octobre 1990.

6 Royaume du Maroc, Le Premier Ministre, 'Projet de Loi autorisant le transfert d'entreprises publiques au secteur privé', 1988. Text published in *Al Bayane*, 20 Oct. 1988 and *La vie économique*, 21 Oct. 1988. The six exceptions were: the phosphate holding (OCP); the water (ONEP) and electricity (ONE) utilities; the telephone company (ONPT); the railway (ONCF); and the airline (RAM).

7 For further details, see Saulniers 1993.

8 France, Assemblée Nationale, *Rapport de la Commission d'Enquête sur les conditions dans lesquelles ont été effectuées les* **Opérations de Privatisation de Enterprises et de Banques** *appartenant au secteur public depuis le 6 Août 1986*, Rapport remis à M. le Président de l'Assembrée Nationale, le 28 Octobre 1989. The one-volume report is supported by two volumes of hearings.

9 See Ramanadham 1992: 31–2.

10 'La Bourse de Casablanca: Situation, Insuffisances et perspectives de reforme', *CEDIES Informations*, 18 January 1992: 23–7.

REFERENCES

Ramanadham, V.V. (1992) 'Basic Working Paper – Privatisation: Constraints and Impacts', Paper presented at the Expert Group Meeting on Privatization: Constraints and Impacts, Geneva, Switzerland, 17–21 August, Doc. 5/EGM 1992.

Roudies, Brahim and Daoud Mustapha (1989) 'La Banque de données', in Royaume du Maroc, Ministère des Finances, Direction des Etablissements Publics et des Participations. *Actes du séminaire sur la reforme des entreprises publiques (Projet PERL II)*, Rabat.

—— (n.d.) *Etats statistiques sur les Entreprises et Participations Publics*, Rabat.
—— (1990) *Privatisation: Données économiques et financières (Exercice 1989)*, Rabat.
—— (1993) 'Privatization in Morocco', in V.V. Ramanadham (ed.) *Privatisation: A Global Perspective*, London: Routledge.

12

PRIVATIZATION IN TANZANIA

George Mbowe

INTRODUCTION

The purpose of this chapter is to examine the limited experience of Tanzania in its privatization policy and implementation. Specifically, the chapter surveys some of the constraints and impacts consequential to the adoption of the policy of the parastatal sector reform. The chapter attempts to provide in a nutshell the background to the government policy statement on parastatal sector reform of December 1991 which was issued by the Minister of Finance on 8 January 1992.

The minister's statement set out the background to a process of structural and institutional transformation which had already begun and had identified the need for parastatal sector reform including privatization as the focus of the government's development strategy.

In line with this objective, a World Bank IDA pre-appraisal mission visited Dar es Salaam in March 1992 in connection with the parastatal reforms and privatization component of a policy programme to be agreed under a proposed public sector adjustment credit. The mission's programme included work on:

1 the financial analysis of parastatal enterprises;
2 the institutional framework and capacity building;
3 fiscal and financial sector linkages and fiscal programming;
4 enterprise plans and the restructuring process;
5 parastatal financial restructuring and debt resolution;
6 the social costs of reform and labour redeployment;
7 the implications of concurrent industrial sub-sector restructuring studies;
8 the design of private sector development investment fund;
9 financial instruments, shareholding mechanisms; and
10 valuations for the privatization of parastatal enterprises.

The outcome of this mission's work will be submitted to the Parastatal Sector Reform Commission for review.

Reform strategy and objectives

In all, about 250 public enterprises have been identified by the government for either commercialization, partial or full privatization. It is estimated that over 95 per cent of medium and large enterprises, including some service enterprises, are in the public sector and the remaining 5 per cent are in the private sector. The objective, therefore, of government disengagement from taking an active role in the management of the public sector has twofold reasons:

Primary reasons

1   To reduce the ratio of public enterprises in the public sector from about 95 per cent to 5 per cent through commercialization and divestiture in the next five years; and
2   to liquidate immediately all non-performing enterprises that cannot be economically restructured.

Secondary reasons

1   To reduce the burden of loss-making parastatal enterprises on the government budget;
2   to improve the operational efficiency of enterprises that are currently in the parstatal sector and make them operate on commercial principles;
3   to increase and encourage a wider participation of the people in the running and management through equity ownership; and
4   to enhance the efficiency of enterprises through cost-efficiency, increased productivity and competition.

Steady implementation measures in the trade, pricing and exchange rate regime started in the mid-1980s. These changes have resulted in the virtual removal of much of the centralized system of controls and administrative allocation of resources that prevailed until 1984. This transformation in the structure of incentives and management has been a key factor in the turn-around in economic performance over the past five years or so.

However, it is evident that reforming pricing and trade incentives, while important for generation of supply response in the first stages of a transformation programme, would not be sufficient to thrust the Tanzanian economy into a sustained and equitable growth path. Redressing the deteriorated physical and social infrastructure and improving institutional performance are absolutely critical for Tanzania's objectives for the economy to be attained.

Disengagement of the government in the service enterprises started some five years ago. It was out of necessity that the government allowed private transporters to compete with the public transport system in the urban areas as well as in the rest of the country.

In the same vein, the government permitted the Tanzanian Tourist Corporation to lease its tourist lodges to Accor of France (Novehotel). Financiers to the rehabilitation programme of these lodges include SIFIDA, DEG and the East African Development Bank. Several private air charter companies operate in Tanzania today. Private luxury boat operators have been licensed to provide efficient services between Zanzibar and the mainland.

The crucial objective of the government has been to improve the efficiency of operations of all productive activities, including commercial services, by allowing competitive and market disciplines in all sectors. Thus, in order to accelerate the process of implementing the policy of the government's disengagement from the management of public enterprises, it was decided to establish a legal body which has been empowered to organize and supervise an orderly process of change. Hence the creation of the Presidential Parastatal Sector Reform Commission (PSRC), which came into existence in early January 1992.

The origins of the problems

The political considerations surrounding the establishment of public enterprises in Tanzania in the last two decades have given the government considerable trouble.

The obligation of the government to give subsidy to all non-performing enterprises was previously an important feature of the public sector policy. That clearly encouraged establishment of public enterprise which responded neither to the market demand nor to consumer tastes. The creation of most enterprises was to a very large extent politically influenced rather than based on strictly economic grounds. The high cost structure of the enterprises was aggravated by a pricing policy control system. Commercial pressures were negligible to induce competition and cost efficiency. A combination of political pressures, inadequate capital structure and laxity on cost control by management led to the establishment of numerous inefficient and uneconomic projects.

Need for change

The need for change in public sector management policy was triggered off by numerous issues which affected the economy and the business environment in general. After the overview of the performance of the parastatal sector by the government and other external agencies, it became necessary to introduce measures for economic change which were intended to produce an enabling competitive structure. In order to improve the supply of goods in the market, it was recognized from the outset that there should be substantial trade liberalization to encourage competition and to increase the availability of basic consumer and capital goods in the market. Decisions on the reform structure of the economy, the design of the financial instruments appropriate for the promotion of efficient enterprises and the advice of appropriate economic policies were made in the context of the wider process of economic change through the economic recovery programme.

CONSTRAINTS ON PRIVATIZATION

The experience of Tanzania in respect of the privatization programme has not been very long, but since the announcement of the policy of parastatal reform, there has been some apprehension or uneasiness about the process of change. The crucial objective of the policy is to improve the efficiency of operations of most of the enterprises in the public sector. The government's basic objective is to proceed with the process of change in terms of the comparative efficiency of all the enterprises in the productive sector and not merely a change of ownership of assets from the public sector to the private sector.

Serious question marks were recently raised by Members of Parliament during the 1992/93 Budget Session concerning the timing of the government policy to sell national assets to the private sector. In the minds of many people, privatization connotes the sale of public assets to foreigners at give-away prices. The workers are concerned that the new owners of these national assets may lay them off.

The root problem of the privatization process in Tanzania is that the announcement of the policy was not preceded by public discussions or education of the people regarding the reasons and the rationale of the new policy. A careful review of publicity of the new policy was necessary in order to enable the people to understand and support the implementation of a privatization programme.

It is important to note that the programme of parastatal reform in Tanzania was launched in the context of the structural adjustment programme. Broadly, there has not been much public discussion or debate on the best options to deal with the macro-economic problems which have crippled the operational performance of most public enterprises.

Specifically, the reform process in Tanzania has started experiencing a number of obstacles common to most countries whose socio-economic policies did not accommodate the principles of private enterprises. The process of change to market economy after two decades of public sector orientation certainly calls for a gradual process of assimilation of the virtues of private enterprises.

Bureaucratic arrangements

The establishment of the Parastatal Sector Reform Commission was preceded by the creation of sectoral restructuring units in the sectoral ministries. Each sectoral holding corporation has a number of subsidiary companies. Negotiations for divestiture options with potential investors involve several consultations. Sectoral ministries have now created some machinery for conducting negotiations and assessing the value of the assets (and for negotiating with the potential investors). The negotiation machinery is composed of a cross-section of experts from the key ministries who constitute a task force. These task forces, or management committees, are supported by executive committees and technical committees. The function of these task forces is to make recommendations to their ministers.

In future all these recommendations of the task forces will be forwarded to the commission for examination and final decision.

While the current system has attempted to achieve the objective of transparency, the lengthy process of screening these proposals has built in an element of protracted negotiations which is a source of irritation to some potential investors.

The problem of inertia or indecision

The objective of transparency through a bureaucratic structure has led to a tendency of inertia or indecision. A few transactions have fallen through because of inertia or indecision to take specific decisions at various levels of this bureaucratic arrangement. Prospective investors have expressed their disappointment with protracted negotiations.

Holding corporations' dilemma

Holding corporations were established in Tanzania on a sectoral basis in order to facilitate specialization, rationalization, co-ordination, R&D and promotion of new projects in each productive sector. The secondary function has been supervision and monitoring of the subsidiary companies. These holding corporations were established under the Public Corporation Act of 1969. The enactment of the Loans and Advances Recovery Fund Act of 1991 for the liquidation of non-performing assets in the books of the National Bank of Commerce, the amendment to the Public Corporations Act of February 1992 which provides general guidelines to the divestiture and restructuring process of non-performing assets and the Treasury Circular No. 1 of 1992 which has terminated the role of the holding corporations over their subsidiary companies have all set in motion a wave of potential constraints in conducting negotiations for divestiture options. Negotiations for divestiture of subsidiary companies require full participation of holding corporations. These corporations have a wealth of experience and expertise and all the vital information regarding their subsidiary companies. The interpretation of the two acts together with the Treasury Circular imply that the holding corporations have no further role over the subsidiary companies.

Uneasiness of management of subsidiary companies

An initial decision which the government took in respect of subsidiary companies concerns the liquidation of non-performing enterprises and divestiture of all other remaining ones. The latter depends on what is considered to be an appropriate divestiture option. Fear of the management being laid off has created a general feeling of apathy in the whole programme.

Buyers' (or vendors') inertia

Foreign buyers who had initially shown some interest to invest in the country seem to be in doubt to take decisions after visiting the enterprises. Some have offered very low prices knowing very well that those offers will not be accepted. Buyers' doubts seem to revolve probably around the following areas:

1 economic uncertainty about the success of the current structural adjustment programme;

2 uncertainty as to the commitment by politicians regarding the privatization programme;

3 inflation and currency devaluation which are still a worrying factor in Tanzania;

4 the problem of asset valuation and legal status of land titles;

5 repatriation of dividends for backlog funds, which still remains a problem; and

6 restriction of overdraft facilities granted by the National Bank of Commerce, which causes uncertainty over local funds being available for working capital.

Restructuring indecision

There are many ways in which restructuring of non-performing companies could be done. For instance, if the sale value of an enterprise is very low because of its indebtedness, restructuring could enhance its price. The majority of parastatals in Tanzania have enormous debts. Restructuring of these enterprises requires massive capital injection. The government is faced with two options: either it sells these enterprises at an agreed price less debts or it invests in restructuring the enterprises with a risk that it may or may not get a good buyer. Because of this gambling element, many decisions have been put in abeyance.

Determination of appropriate distribution of shares

One of Tanzania's major problems is to ensure that substantial shares are sold to indigenous people in a variety of ways – joint ventures, public issues, employee share ownership schemes etc. This is also intended to be an incentive to widen the share ownership. Therefore there is a conceptual problem to work out some equitable arrangements for share distribution in all forms of divestiture options. Because of lack of experience to develop some working options in this regard, decisions in some transactions have been postponed for one reason or another.

Establishment and problems of funds for acquisition of shares

At the moment no funds have been created in Tanzania for acquisition of shares in public enterprises. For privatization to succeed and to have full support of the

231

people, some basic nationwide funds must be established for acquisition of shares. Proposals have been made to create trust funds but no detailed studies have been made. The Commonwealth Secretariat has agreed to provide technical assistance to the commission to carry out a study on the creation of mutual funds. The creation of the trust funds again is not free from problems. There are four fundamental ones:

1 How would such funds acquire shares in public enterprises in Tanzania where there is no stock exchange market? In other words, what would be the acceptable basis? Will it be by bidding or allocation?
2 Does the country have local specialists in funds management? How will the funds be managed in terms of investment decisions?
3 What would be the appropriate life for such funds?
4 What percentage of shares should such funds acquire in any given company?

Lack of understanding of business valuation principles

The question of privatization is linked to the problem of asset or share valuation. Most of the public enterprises in Tanzania are loss making. This poses a serious problem of valuation. Finding suitable approaches which would be acceptable to the seller and the buyer will not be easy. Should the enterprises be valued on the basis of their net worth, net present value, depreciated replacement cost, book value or earning capacity of their assets? All this needs sorting out, and it will be necessary to understand these valuation methods and, most importantly, to agree on their limitations.

Fear of private companies

One of the main problems raised by politicians regarding privatization in Tanzania is the creation of monopolies of both local and foreign investors. When enterprises are privatized in favour of a few investors, it is feared that the concern of the new shareholders will be to maximize their profits. To some extent this can happen if there are no regulatory bodies. The programme in Tanzania envisages the creation of trade restrictions and control through some regulatory bodies to ensure that consumers are not exploited.

Fear of foreign ownership of national assets

A difficult problem concerns the arrangements for a mechanism for millions of citizens to acquire shares in the national assets. The question of privatization among many people is linked with the sale of assets to foreigners. The majority of Tanzanians cannot afford to buy these national assets. That is to say, the benefits of privatization will accrue to foreigners. It follows, of course, that the whole programme cannot be supported at the political as well as at the grassroots levels.

The commission has, therefore, a hard task in working out an efficient system that will guard against selling all national assets to foreigners.

Fear of failures because of poor selection concessions

One of the major considerations to be dealt with in privatization is how to formulate an equitable package of incentives that would attract buyers. The ability of the government to recover debts from the non-profit-making companies is dependent upon future profits and the cash flows of the companies which will be privatized. New capital to finance growth has to be attracted by an enabling environment and incentives. There is a limit to how many incentives can be granted to new investors. The government may well have to consider writing off some of the existing debts.

The first step in assessing the scale of concessions in a privatization exercise is to carry out a fundamental benefit–cost analysis. But the review should not be limited to the financial position of the business. It must consider the general policies and economic environment in which the business is operating.

Valuation of loss-making enterprises

Overall, 250 enterprises are under way for privatization – quite a large number. The factor of their indebtedness has caused a big problem in asset valuation.

Viability and capital adequacy

In their present form, many public enterprises suffer from capital inadequacy. This makes their viability questionable to buyers. Commercialization is, therefore, a crucial step which calls for an improvement in capital adequacy as a pre-condition for divestiture; and this will take a long period to privatize and will certainly cost the government millions of dollars.

Concentration of asset ownership

The selling of national assets offers a compromise between the need to promote popular capitalism and the desire to reduce the involvement of the government in the management of productive assets including commercial services. As currently seen, unless the process is carefully controlled, a few buyers or ethnic groups with concentration of wealth can acquire all the major assets in the country, which is not a tenable situation.

Limited capital market

As there is no developed capital market, the determination of share value of national assets will be questionable. A set of workable formulae will have to be determined to minimize revenue loss to the government.

Land valuation

As the country moves towards the market economy, there is a need to rethink the policy of land value. Currently, land in Tanzania has no price. Particularly in respect of enterprises which are situated on premium plots, valuation of the title deed land must be reflected in the valuation of enterprises. This is what has now led the government to consider revision of the existing land tenure policy. A task force has been established to review the situation and to make appropriate amendments to existing land legislation.

Absence of title deeds to property and major assets

There have been a few cases of transactions having been delayed because the enterprises in question have been operating their activities on plots of land which do not have title deeds. No deal can be concluded without them; and this is delaying the implementation of the programme.

High proportion of costs of building to direct machinery cost

Foreign companies have observed that there were in some cases unjustifiable capital expenditures on industrial buildings which were not necessary. But then it is difficult not to include the value of such assets.

Lack of dividend history

Here the issue is how do you determine the value of the companies as a going concern on the basis of their asset earning capacity. The evaluation process has to explore the option of other techniques applicable to the Tanzanian environment.

High levels of obsolete stock or inventory

Many enterprises do not have policies for providing provision against obsolete stock. In several cases this has caused many difficulties in determining the basis for the appropriate value of stock of both raw materials and finished goods.

Lack of appropriate legal procedures and administrative system

The existing systems of land laws, tax regulation, foreign exchange regulations and several other legislations were formulated several years ago. Ways around them have to be found through appropriate changes.

Risk of environment damage by private enterprises

Antagonists of privatization have raised exaggerated alarm that the country would be in danger if reckless privatization resulted in transferring all public enterprises to the private sector. Environment protection has now became a concern of many politicians. Cases have been cited of small private companies which are involved in woodcharcoal production and have seriously damaged Tanzanian forests and consequently affected the rainfall regime of several areas.

Insufficient competition in some sectors

The privatization programme in Tanzania intends to put a thrust on the need for developing a competitive environment. Evaluation of bids for direct sales will pay attention to this aspect in order to ensure that no single buyer is given a monopoly of acquiring majority shares in enterprises which are in the same sector.

The first barrier in achieving this objective is that the number of similar enterprises operating in the same sectors is limited. Perhaps competition can be encouraged only through trade liberalization policy.

Regulatory environment

There are bound to be conflicts in the objectives of the seller (that is, the government) and the buyers. There is, therefore, the need to protect the consumers as well as to encourage investors to be most efficient in the use of their resources. The need to establish an autonomous regulatory body is, therefore, imperative in monitoring and supervising acceptable trade practices. Potential investors from overseas need assurance or clarity of trade regulations, stability and predictability in the regulatory regime. To them regulation is fundamental to the determination of the value of their money. Similarly, consumers will need to be assured that the creation of private or public monopolies will not empower the owners to exploit them through overcharging or providing poor service quality. Employees are concerned with job security and any new employment rules that will affect their job security. The government is also concerned that the 'new' partners in investments operate within the law and that their activities promote economic and social development.

IMPACTS

A privatization programme is expected to have major impacts, of which some can be measured but others cannot easily be determined. For example, it is possible to estimate the fiscal impact of a divestiture programme on a year-to-year basis.

Some assumptions will have to be made such as:

235

1   the level of ongoing interim financial support for financially distressed enterprises;
2   increases in tax, dividends and lease rentals;
3   the minimum level of capital investment required; and
4   the likely proceeds from divestiture.

The fiscal impacts of restructuring, divestiture or liquidation of an enterprise will normally have to be assessed in terms of:-

1   net direct flows before restructuring or divestiture or liquidation;
2   net direct flows after restructuring, or divestiture or liquidation; and
3   net direct impact of restructuring, or divestiture or liquidation.

CONCLUSION

For privatization to work, a proper legal structure has to be in place. The macro-economic reforms needed to establish a market environment have been undertaken in Tanzania.

Competition for capital is an important factor that conditions the success of the privatization programme in Tanzania. There is an acute shortage of merchant banks, commercial banks and institutional investors who are experienced in investing funds in good bankable projects. These institutions need to be created. The Government has re-opened the banking sector to the private sector. Discussions about establishing stock markets have started.

To date Tanzania has privatized a few enterprises through joint venture and leasing arrangements. There are not enough savings in the country in the hands of the indigenous population to buy all the national industrial assets at full face value. Issuing vouchers at concessionary prices to citizens to enable them to buy some of the shares may be a solution for accelerating the pace of divestiture.

Foreign investment can, of course, play an important role, particularly with large and more viable enterprises. But the potential scale of foreign investment has serious political overtones.

13

PRIVATIZATION IN ISRAEL[1]

Eckstein Shlomo, Rozevich Shimon and
Zilberfarb Ben-Zion

GOVERNMENT ENTERPRISES IN ISRAEL

At the end of 1991 there were 161 government enterprises (GE) in Israel. Eighty-five GEs were business enterprises (53 per cent of the total) and the rest (76 companies) were non-business companies. In terms of economic activity the weight of the non-business enterprises was negligible. In 1990, GEs employed 75,292 workers; however 99 per cent of them (74,546 workers) were employed by the business GEs and only 1 per cent (66 employees) worked for the non-business GEs.

Table 13.1 provides the composition of GEs by economic branch. As can be seen from the table, GEs are present in all the major sectors of the economy. In some industries GEs are dominant, including water, electricity, sea and air transportation, telephones, oil refineries, mining and chemicals, and aircraft. In most of these, government enterprises are the major (if not the only) companies. The government holds all or a majority of the voting shares of 131 GEs. The other 30 GEs are 'mixed companies' where private investors hold most of the shares and the government has only a minority stake.

The business GEs vary widely in size. Table 13.2 shows the cumulative percentage of workers employed by the 10 largest business GEs. As can be seen from the table, the biggest 3 GEs employed half of the GE's labour force, the biggest 6 companies employed 74 per cent and the biggest 10 employed 87 per cent. Therefore, a meaningful process of privatization (in terms of its economic impact) must concentrate on these 10 companies. This does not mean that the privatization of other small GEs can be neglected. Selling GEs, regardless of their size, serves as a signal to the business community that the government is determined to reduce its involvement in the market. Such a signal has both a direct and indirect effect on the business environment and may facilitate the privatization of other GEs.

As of November 1992, the process of privatization has started in only two of these larger companies (Bezek Telecommunication and Israel Chemicals – ICL) and plans call for the sale of shares in two more big GEs (Zim Navigation Lines and Shekem Retail Stores) in the coming months. It should be emphasized that

Table 13.1 Composition of GEs by economic branch

Economic branch	No. of GEs	Thereof: mixed companies
Mining and chemicals	15	–
Water, electricity, transportation and communication	22	1
Industry and commerce development	12	5
Oil and gas	14	1
Defence	10	1
Agriculture	12	4
Housing and land development	13	–
Tourism	13	1
Culture and art	8	4
Study funds	12	3
Others	16	6
Inactive companies	15	4
Total	162	30
Business GEs	85	8
Non-business GEs	76	22

Table 13.2 Number of employees in the ten largest GEs

Company name	Number of employees	% of total GE's employment	Cumulative % of total GE's employment
Israel Aircraft Industries (IAI)	16,818	22.2	22.2
Israel Military Industries	10,996	14.5	36.7
Electricity Corp.	10,146	13.4	50.1
Bezek Telecommunications	9,746	12.9	63.0
Israel Chemicals (ICL)	4,276	5.6	68.6
El Al Airlines	4,176	5.5	74.1
Shekem Retail Stores[1]	3,663	4.8	78.9
ZIM Navigation	2,288	3.0	81.9
Water authority	2,102	2.9	84.8
Oil refineries	1,608	2.1	86.9
All other	9,924	13.1	100
Total	75,743	100.0	

[1] Started in early 1950s as army canteen and stores for soldiers' families; gradually became one of the country's leading chains of retail stores open to the general public.

even in the two big companies where privatization has started, the government still holds more than 75 per cent of the shares, although in both the government holdings are scheduled to decline to 50 per cent or less before the end of the year.

Some indicators of the economic performance of the GEs are presented in Table 13.3, which reports the rate of return on equity of GEs in the various sectors throughout the 1988–90 period. As can be seen from the table, GEs in mining and chemicals, transportation and communication, and oil and gas have had a positive annual return on equity ranging from 5 per cent to 18 per cent. Government companies in the defence and housing industries lost money most of the time. In the water and electricity industries, the rate of return on equity, while positive most of the time, was quite low. However, since these companies are natural monopolies, their profits reflect not just their economic performance but also government pricing decisions. These decisions, in the case of the water and electricity companies, have not been based on long-term policy reflected by a pre-fixed formula (as has been the case in the telecommunication monopoly since 1990). Instead, pricing decisions in these industries have been made *ad hoc* and are the outcome of intense lobbying (the agricultural lobby has been very powerful in keeping water prices below costs).

The profits of 8 of the biggest GEs over the 1987–90 period are provided in Table 13.4. These 8 companies, which account for 77 per cent of GE's employment, were profitable throughout the period. Thus, there is no pressure on the government to sell these companies because they are a burden on the budget, as is the case in many developing countries. Figures released by Dun and Bradstreet for 1991 (see Table 13.5), show that 5 out of the 10 biggest industrial companies in Israel are GEs; they account for 65 per cent of the sales of these largest 10 companies, and for 30 per cent of the sales of the biggest 100 industrial companies. In the services sector (see Table 13.6), there are 3 GEs among the 10 leading companies which account for 40 per cent of the sales of these 10 companies.

Table 13.3 GE's rate of return on equity, by economic branch

Branch	1988	1989	1990
Mining and chemicals	10.0	17.6	12.1
Water and electricity	1.2	4.7	(0.8)
Transportation and communication	5.0	6.8	7.6
Oil and gas	6.3	8.2	12.1
Defence	(14.0)	3.9	(2.4)
Industry and commerce development	0.0	(3.4)	4.9
Housing and land development	(27.1)	(15.7)	0.6
Total	1.4	5.7	3.3

Table 13.4 Profits in the largest GEs 1987–90 *($ million)*

Company	1987	1988	1989	1990
ICL	24.4	48.0	88.4	80.1
Bezek telecommunications	39.9	9.2	21.4	59.8
Oil refineries	17.8	28.3	28.2	50.3
Electricity Corp.	53.2	26.2	126.7[1]	(14.0)
Zim Navigation	12.1	25.3	29.5	29.1
Oil services	12.4	24.0	24.6	23.6
El Al Airlines	27.9	21.7	24.9	24.5
Israel Aircraft Industry[2]	10.3	8.8	12.1	13.2

[1] Includes a one-time $ 99 million project due to change in tax rates.
[2] Does not include loses due to the cancellation of the Lavi project.

Table 13.5 Sales of the 10 largest industrial companies, 1991

Company	Sales ($ million)	Type of ownership
IAI	1,607	GE
Electricity Corp.	1,400	GE
Oil refineries	827	GE
Tadiran	726	Histadrut
Tnuva	648	Histadrut
Dead Sea Works	558	GE
Scitex	430	Private
Elbit	410	Private
Rotem Import	323	GE
Teva	321	Private
Total largest 10	7,250	
Total largest 100	15,900	

Source: Dun and Bradstreet

The legal framework for the operation of GEs is provided in the Law of Government Companies passed by the Knesset (Israeli Parliament) in 1975. This law states clearly that a GE should operate according to business considerations applicable to private companies. A deviation from this guideline is allowed only by a government decision which must be approved in addition by the Finance Committee of the Knesset. However, one must recall that 76 government companies are non-business enterprises (non-profit organizations) and therefore business-like considerations are not applicable to their management.

The daily supervision of the GEs is entrusted to the Government Companies Authority (GCA), which is part of the Ministry of Finance. Government

Table 13.6 Sales of the 10 largest non-industrial companies, 1991

Company	Sales ($ million)	Type of ownership
Bezek	1,570	GE
Tnuva	1,540	Histadrut
Paz	1,170	Private
Zim Navigation	1,077	GE
El Al Airlines	785	GE
Delek	699	Private
Supersol	466	Private
Sonol	454	Private
Co-Op	435	Histadrut
Hamashbir Hamerkazi	365	Histadrut

Source: Dun and Bradstreet

enterprises are under the responsibility of the sectoral ministry most closely involved with their field of activity. Thus, for example, the Ministry of Transportation is responsible for Israel Airlines, while the Ministry of Commerce and Industry is responsible for Israel Chemicals. The responsibility includes the right to nominate directors of the GEs (including the CEO). However, these nominations have to be approved by the Minister of Finance and this gives him the power to include some of his nominees on the board of directors of every GE.

THE ISRAELI PRIVATIZATION PROGRAMME

The process of privatization in Israel can be divided into three stages. The first decision to sell GEs dates back to May 1970. The government decided then that the GCA would examine if there was a need for continued government ownership in the various GEs. A recommendation to sell the government's share in a GE required an approval of both the minister in charge of the GE and by the Ministerial Committee for Economic Affairs.

The GCA tried unsuccessfully to pass a decision in that committee that would define the criteria for selling the government's share in a GE. Some of the objections to the decision were ideological. During the 1968–77 period the government sold its holdings in 46 companies. However, these were small companies where the government had a minority stake.

The second stage of the privatization programme followed the Israeli elections of 1977. The Labour party had, until then, dominated Israeli politics since the pre-state era. The quasi-government institutions in the British Mandate period were controlled by the Labour party and this dominance continued when the state was re-established in 1948. The May 1977 elections brought a radical change: the 'right wing' party, the Likud, became the largest party in the Knesset for the first time in the history of Israel, and formed a coalition government. The Likud's platform specified that there would be an 'endeavour to establish a free economy based on efficiency, entrepreneurship and competition ... reduce government intervention and public bureaucracy in economic activity and gradually reduce government supervision on economic activity ...'. It is therefore not surprising that there were high expectations that the new government would pursue an active privatization programme. Indeed, in March 1978 the government decided to sell 48 companies, expecting revenues to total $ 100 million in 1978. The actual figures for 1978 were only a small fraction of that – $ 10 million. During the 1978–81 period only 16 GEs were sold with revenues totalling $ 42 million (see Table 13.7 for a list of these companies). In the next four years (1981–5), 5 more small GEs were sold with revenues totalling about $ 10 million.

The overall performance of the privatization programme in the 1977–85 period clearly lagged behind the expected and planned pace. The reasons for that lag are described in the next section.

The third stage in the privatization programme started in 1985 and has been far more successful than the previous stages.

Several factors contributed to the increase in the intensity of the privatization process. The first factor was that at the end of 1984 the Likud and Labour parties formed a national unity government. The new government enjoyed a very

Table 13.7 Sale of GEs, 1977–81

Company	Date of sale	% of ownership sold	Sale proceeds ($ million)
Maritime Bank	7/79	100	10.5
Haifa Chemicals	9/78	52	6.0
Trade Bank	8/78	95	5.0
Vitco Chemicals	11/77	40	4.2
Tefachot Mortgage Bank	9/78	17	4.0
P.B. Holdings	3/78	14	2.7
Electro-optical industries	7/79	50	2.5
Zion Cables	11/80	36	2.0
Orlite	79–80	100	2.0
Astoria	79–80	10	1.0
Turbo Chrome	8/78	50	0.8
Arkia Airlines	78–79	50	0.8
Makor Chemicals	3/78	60	0.2
Academic Printers	7/79	100	0.1
Iltam	3/78	100	0.1
Agricultural Spare Parts	10/79	100	0.0
Total proceeds			41.9

Note: With the exception of Zion Cables, the percentage sold by the government constitutes all of the shares held by the government.

comfortable majority in the Knesset; so it enabled the policy makers to take measures that were less popular with Labour.

A second factor was the worldwide trend to privatize, especially in the United Kingdom and other European countries such as France.

A third factor was the collapse of the Eastern European economic system and the attempts that were made there to move to a free market economy. This raised the level of awareness regarding the need to reduce government intervention among both politicians and the general public.

A fourth factor was the macro-economic conditions in Israel during that period. Following the 1973 oil shock and the Yom-Kippur War, rising inflation had been a major problem in Israel. Inflation reached an annual rate of 465 per cent in the first quarter of 1984. As a result, a new anti-inflation programme was implemented in 1985 by the national unity government. One of the key elements in the new programme was a substantial cut in the budget deficit. Selling of GEs was seen as a means to generate more income for the government and, not less important, a way to raise foreign currency from sales to foreign investors. Table 13.8 lists the GEs that were sold (partially or completely) since 1985. Overall the government sold shares in 11 companies through 16 issues. The total revenues from these sales reached $ 817 million, 20 times the amount received in the previous stages of privatization. However, like in the past, the third stage of privatization has lagged behind the planned pace. The reasons for that lag are the subject of the next section.

THE OBSTACLES TO PRIVATIZATION

The first reason for the slow pace of privatization is political power. In recent years, the most powerful political body governing the big Israeli parties has been

Table 13.8   Sale of GEs, 1985–91

Company	Date of sale	% of ownership retained by govt.	Sale proceeds ($ million)
Haifa Chemicals	86	0	14.7
Pericles	86,91	–	25.7
Jerusalem Economic Co.	87,89	0	54.7
Paz	87	0	96.7
Zion Cables	88	0	6.0
Industrial Bldgs	88,89	52	105.4
Nafta	87	–	18.1
Maman	89	72	32.1
Hanal	90	–	5.5
Bezek Telecommunication	90,91	75	213.0
ICL	92	80	250.0

the 'party's general assembly' which usually consists of a few hundred members. As was mentioned earlier, the minister in charge of a GE has the right to nominate its board of directors. This enables him to gain support in the party's assembly, by appointing his associates to the coveted posts of directors in the various GEs. These directors, in turn, can help secure more jobs for party members in their respective GEs. Obviously, selling GEs reduces the ability of the ministers in charge to gain political clout through the nomination of directors. Therefore, the first obstacle to selling GEs has been the reluctance of the minister in charge. Until the third stage of privatization, the consent of the minister in charge was a prerequisite to selling the company, so that the objection of the minister in charge was enough to stop the process. To overcome this obstacle the government decided in 1990 to appoint a special ministerial committee for privatization headed by the prime minister and including as its members only two more ministers: the finance minister and the minister of justice. This was a significant change from the previous committee which also included the ministers in charge of the GEs. It is interesting to note that the new Labour government announced on 19 July 1992 (only one week after its inauguration) that it would establish the same ministerial committee with the new ministers replacing the old ones.

The politicization of the GE's board of directors is reflected in the figures of Table 13.9, which shows the percentage of ministerial appointments in the board of directors of GEs. The GCA, which published these figures in its annual reports, has stopped doing so since 1983. Political appointments of GE directors were criticized by the State Comptroller in her thirty-ninth annual report (1989). In the introduction to the report she writes:

> The phenomenon (of political appointments of directors) is widespread and covers many years. It is not confined to one party and one time period. The phenomenon is prominent before elections to the Knesset and afterwards when different ministers take office. Political appointments

Table 13.9 The percentage of government appointees in the board of directors of GEs

Year	%	Total no. of directors
75–76	60	1,425
76–77	58	1,534
77–78	59	–
78–79	68	–
79–80	66	–
80–81	72	–
81–82	69	–

– figures not available
Source: Annual reports of the Government's Companies Authority

damage the purity of the appointment, the level of civil service and the morale of other workers.

Two years later, the phenomenon was criticized again by the State Comptroller. According to that report, as of November 1990, 65 per cent of the GE's public directors were members of the political parties' assemblies. Political appointments were made by both the Labour and the Likud parties. Some hope for an improvement in this area is given by the political changes inside the Israeli parties. The Labour party has recently adopted the primaries systems. This has reduced the power of the party's assembly considerably and thereby reduced the possible political gains from directors' appointments. It is very likely that other parties will follow suit and adopt the primaries system.

A second factor which contributed to the delay in the privatization programme is related to the first one. It is usually the case that a GE needs some restructuring before it is ready for privatization. This may include, for example, changes in contracts, updated estimates of real estate and other items that must be included in the prospectus. Most of these preparatory steps cannot be carried out without the co-operation of the company's management and its board of directors. Thus, while the company has no formal say in the decision to privatize the company, it can affect the pace of the privatization process through its involvement in the process. In many cases, political appointees who worry that they might lose their position if the company is sold to the private sector, do their utmost to slow down the privatization process. In many cases these are the very same persons who were nominated by the minister on their political merits. The paradox is that in companies with good management, where the need to privatize is less acute, management will usually co-operate in the privatization process. While it still faces the risk of being replaced under the new ownership, its good performance reduces that risk and raises hopes to earn more since the private sector pays much higher wages in the top echelon of management than GEs. However, in companies with poor performance, where the need to privatize is greater, management has a higher chance of being replaced by the new owners and as a result it will not co-operate with the privatizing agency (the GCA).

A third factor which contributed to the delay in the sale of large GEs at the beginning of the third stage of privatization was the fear that the Israeli capital market was too small to absorb the planned issue of the GE shares. Thus, for example, a report by Holzman and Shechter (1991) argues that 'raising large amounts of capital in a relatively short period of time may flood the market and cause a collapse and a crisis that will require a long period of time to recover'.

It should be emphasized that many economists did not share this view. They argued that the Israeli capital market was strong enough to absorb the planned issue of GEs' shares (see e.g. Eckstein, Rozevich and Zilberfarb, 1993). Later developments have supported this view, and there seems to be a general agreement nowadays that the capacity of the Israeli capital market can accommodate future flotations of GEs.

A case in point is the privatization of ICL. The initial plan, recommended by First Boston, called for the sale of 50 per cent of the company to foreign investors. The estimated value of ICL, according to the First Boston report, was $ 500–600 million. The choice of foreign investors was mainly justified by the claim that the domestic capital market was too small for the planned issue of ICL shares. This proposal was challenged by various sources on the ground that a higher price for the company could be obtained in the domestic market and that the Israeli capital market was large enough to absorb the planned issue of shares. The public debate delayed the privatization of ICL and eventually led the GCA to abandon its original plan. In January 1992 20 per cent of the company was sold on the Israeli stock market for $ 240 million – twice the estimated price recommended by First Boston.

A fourth obstacle to the privatization process was the result of turning to foreign consultants to advise the GCA on ways and means to privatize the various GEs. The foreign advisers, while being reputable and experienced in selling companies in the US and elsewhere, were not familiar with domestic 'sensitivities'. Thus, for example, they recommended selling ICL to foreign investors. This recommendation failed to take into account the public's objection to sell Israel's main natural resources (the Dead Sea Minerals) to foreigners. Indeed the GCA tried to follow the recommended method for selling ICL in 1990, but failed to do so because of public objection, and the resistance of ICL's employees. This resulted in a delay of about two years until a share of ICL was sold on the domestic market (in 1992). Had this sensitivity been recognized earlier, so would have been the privatization process of ICL.

It is interesting to note that in most cases labour resistance to the change of ownership has not been an obstacle to the privatization process in Israel. The reason is that most of the GEs that have been privatized so far have been profitable. Therefore, labour was not concerned too much with possible lay-offs. One case where labour objected to the privatization process was the case of Bet Shemesh Engines. The company has been a money-loser for years and prospective buyers have stated clearly that significant lay-offs would take place once they bought the company. Another case of labour objection to the privatization process is the first attempt to sell ICL. As was mentioned earlier, the government tried at first to sell the company to foreign investors. This raised fears among workers that the buyers, who own similar companies outside Israel, would transfer some of the local activities to the foreign companies, thereby reducing employment at ICL. Once it was decided that ICL would be sold to domestic buyers, labour dropped its objection to the sale.

THE IMPACTS OF PRIVATIZATION

As was described earlier, a meaningful process of privatization has started only in recent years. Since 1985 shares were sold in 11 GEs, but only in 4 GEs was the majority of the shares transferred to private hands. The short time that has elapsed since privatization in these companies took place does not enable an assessment of its impact on the individual companies. None the less, one can point at two areas with observable impacts of the privatization process: the effect of preparing a GE for privatization and the fiscal effect.

Impacts at the preparatory stage

There seems to be some evidence in the Israeli case that preparing a GE for privatization and selling even a minority stake in the company to private investors has a positive effect on the economic performance of that company. This is very prominent in the case of the Israeli telecommunication company, Bezek. Until 1984 all the telecommunication operations were conducted within the Ministry of Communication. The workers of what later became Bezek were government employees and the equipment belonged directly to the state. In February 1984 Bezek was converted into a business government enterprise. All the telecommunication equipment was transferred to the new company and the workers turned from state employees into the new company's labour force. The Ministry of Communication has retained the regulatory responsibility for the telecommunication sector and Bezek. In September 1990 9 per cent of company shares was sold on the Israeli stock market (for $ 94 million) and on May 1991 an additional 16 per cent was sold (for $ 119 million). The transfer of telecommunication services from the ministry to Bezek has resulted in a significant improvement in the quality of operations even before the first flotation. This efficiency gain, which is evident from the data provided in Table 13.10, helped to obtain a higher price for the company's shares and attributed to the success of the flotation which was oversubscribed. It should be noted that a similar experience is reported in other countries. Madsen (1989) notes that the very intention to privatize companies induced those companies to adopt changes that turned their profit performance around. Thus, for example, British Airways lost money five years before it was privatized, but showed profits when it was privatized in February 1987.

Table 13.10 Indicators of efficiency – Bezek telecommunication

	83–84	89
Workers per 100 tel. lines	7.9	6.1
Digital equipment (thousands)	39.8	550.6
No. of standing orders for tel. (thousands)	256.0	43.7
thereof: over one year	175.0	15.4
Average waiting time for tel. line (months)	36.0	12.0
Employment (thousands)	8.1	9.2
No. of tel. exchanges	87.0	242.0
No. of tel. lines	643.0	2,164.0

Unlike the British privatization process there was no attempt at 'popular capitalism' in the Israeli case. The GCA did not make even a minimal effort to distribute GE shares among more investors. In the first issue of Bezek shares there were 11,000 applications. In proportion to the size of population this corresponds to 200,000 applications for British Telecom shares. The actual figures in the British case were 12 times higher – 2.4 million. The lack of any attempt to distribute the shares more widely was criticized by Eckstein, Rozevich and Zilberfarb (1993). Their main argument is based on distribution effects. Since there is a problem in determining the 'right' price for a GE it is socially more desirable that in the event of under-pricing the gain should be distributed among as many people as possible.

The fiscal impact

One of the main goals of the privatization programme in Israel, if not the dominant goal, was its expected fiscal contribution. GEs, on the whole, have been well managed over the last decade and did not impose a fiscal burden on the treasury. However, a growing fiscal deficit and a threatening inflationary pressure, both kindled by a stagnant economy facing a massive immigration, inflated the value of any possible source of public revenue, even though this revenue has only a short-run effect, since it involves an internal transfer payment rather than a long-run incremental flow of net income.

However, even short-run achievements fell short of expectation. The projected sale of GE shares for $ 600 million in 1990 and $ 900 million in 1991 would have covered 20–25 per cent of the fiscal deficit. In fact, sales in these two years produced much less. Only in 1992 do the prospects of reaching the $ 900 million goal look better, with $ 225 million already raised by the February flotation of 20 per cent of ICL (Israel's leading chemical GE). The long-run fiscal balance is doubtful, however, even assuming that the whole revenue from GE shares sold is assigned to diminishing the outstanding public debt. ICL, for example, produced a real return of 5–6 per cent over the last couple of years. That is higher than the interest paid in real (inflation discounted) terms on government bonds. Most experts agree that similar amounts could be raised by selling additional bonds without straining the capital market. Other GE candidates for sale are perhaps less profitable, but on the whole divestiture is beneficial and necessary on other grounds, rather than for fiscal purposes.

SUMMARY

The decision to sell GEs in Israel dates back to 1970. However, only in the last seven years has the process gained momentum. Since 1985 about $ 820 million have been raised by the government through the sale of shares in its companies. This is 20 times the amount received until 1985, but it still falls short of planned revenues. There have been four main reasons for the slow pace of privatization:

1   Political resistance – ministers who can nominate their supporters to the coveted posts of directors in GEs do not want to give up this source of political power.
2   Management in some GEs resist privatization worrying that they will be replaced by the new owners.
3   The unfounded fear that the Israeli capital market was too small to absorb the planned issue of GE shares.
4   Foreign consultants who advised the government on ways and means to privatize were not familiar with domestic 'sensitivities'. Therefore their recommendations were met, in some cases, by strong public resistance.

It is interesting to note that in most cases labour resistance has not been an obstacle to the privatization process in Israel. There seems to be some evidence, in the Israeli case, that preparing a GE for privatization and selling even a minority stake in the company to private investors has a positive effect on the economic performance of that company.

NOTES

1   This research was supported by the Azrieli Institute for Research on the Israeli Economy and the Wolfson Chair in Economics and Business Administration at Bar-Ilan University.

REFERENCES

Eckstein, S., Rozevich, S. and Zilberfarb B. (1993) 'The privatization of government companies in Israel – history and future prospects', *Economic Quarterly*, March (Hebrew).
Holzman, Z. and Shechter, Z. (1991) 'Privatization in Israel' in 'Privatization of Government Companies', *The Economic Advisor*, Tel Aviv: Ministry of Defence, December.
State Comptroller Annual Reports (1989) (1991).

14

PRIVATIZATION IN BANGLADESH

Abulmaal A. Muhith

MEASURES FOR PROMOTION OF THE PRIVATE SECTOR

The first phase: 1973–81

Bangladesh emerged as a new nation at the conclusion of a nine-month long brutal war of liberation. The radicalized leadership of the liberation war and the circumstances prevailing in the devastated country virtually forced the option for a socialist state system. There was an immediate expansion of the public sector. Commitment to socialist transformation of the economy, however, was half-hearted and so there was not even the zeal and success usually associated with an initial revolutionary switch to a socialist mode of production and distribution. This transformation remained confined to public ownership of industry and public control of a large part of foreign trade. Agriculture or housing remained in the private sector and even domestic trade was not sought to be fully controlled by the public sector. But like the rest of the sub-continent, bureaucratic red tape and restrictive regulations were a prominent feature of the economic management system of Bangladesh immediately after liberation.

The early clear direction on private initiative in industry was provided in July 1972, fixing a ceiling of Tk. 2.5 million ($ 330,000) per private investment which could go up to Tk. 3.5 million through reinvestment of profits. In January 1973, a detailed industrial policy was announced. It confirmed the ceiling for private investment, allowed a five-year tax holiday provided 60 per cent of profits were reinvested in government bonds or business expansion, and provided a moratorium on nationalization for a period of 10 years. Foreign investment was permitted as long as local equity was 51 per cent; and fair compensation was assured in case of nationalization at the end of the moratorium period. Thus the private sector could undertake only small-scale industry.

There was no dedicated cadre in any of the political parties to support, not to speak of manage, large-scale nationalization. Boards of management initially set up for public properties (enterprises, real estate, transport, businesses, etc.) were soon superseded by administrators and managers, not all of whom were professionally qualified. The performance of the public enterprises tended to be

250

dismal. There was mismanagement, greed and cheating all around. There was no labour discipline; and labour productivity declined drastically while employment increased. There were problems with the supply of raw materials and finance which encouraged rent seeking. Scarcity of supplies enriched the pockets of favoured traders and agents. Some industries which lost the market in West Pakistan had marketing problems. Capacity utilization was low; it generally varied from 30 to 50 per cent. A number of sectors such as jute, sugar, paper and board, steel, and oil and gas suffered losses while a few like engineering and shipbuilding, fertilizers and chemicals and forest industries barely broke even. There was an over-all productivity decline.[1]

Liberalization efforts in Bangladesh began quite early in its history but lacked determination and long-term objectives. The industrial policy was first revised in July 1974. The new industrial policy raised the investment ceiling to Tk. 30 million or $ 3.4 million. Eighteen industries were reserved for the public sector and the others were thrown open to both domestic and foreign private investment; and guarantee on non-nationalization was extended to 15 years. Foreign investors could be equity partners of the public sector and the rigid limit on foreign equity participation was relaxed. The reserved list of industries has been amended from time to time. An important decision was in respect of the sale of abandoned units to the private sector.

Other liberalization measures were started in 1973 culminating in a new regime of trade and transactions in May 1975. A hefty adjustment of exchange rate took place in May 1975. Earlier reforms had established favourable rates for remittances by expatriate wage earners. Import liberalization was started in 1973, and in May 1975 the Open General Licensing system was introduced on a limited scale. Exports were given the facility of import replenishment in 1974. Adjustment of administered prices began in 1973 and the monopoly of TCB in many items of trade was abolished. Interest rates were liberalized in July 1974, and again in May 1975.

This liberalization process was further accelerated with the violent change of government in August 1975. In December 1975, the reserved list of industries was reduced to eight and 10 others were put on the concurrent list. The private investment ceiling was raised to Tk. 100 million or $ 6.7 million and a couple of years later it was virtually withdrawn. Guarantee against nationalization was no longer time-bound. The sale of abandoned units was expedited, and in order to encourage buyers black money was freely permitted to be used for investment. The industrial finance institutions were authorized to support the private sector. The Stock Exchange, closed in 1972, was reopened; and in 1976 the Investment Corporation was set up to provide bridge finance and underwriting facilities. In 1980 a liberal Foreign Private Investment Act was passed according the same treatment to foreign investment as that to indigenous private investment and assuring repatriation of capital and profits. At the end of the year an Export Processing Zone was opened in Chittagong welcoming both local and foreign investment for exports.

Other liberalization measures included privatization of retail marketing of fertilizers and irrigation equipment beginning in 1978. Rationing of foodgrains started giving way to open market sales of foodgrains to meet the price pressure in the lean periods. Subsidization of publicly produced or supplied goods also began to be reduced. Price control was eliminated from a large number of industrial products and consumer items. In 1980 the government also decided to open commercial banking to the private sector.

By March 1982, 374 industrial units were transferred to the private sector. At the same time a large number of new investment proposals were also sanctioned, not all of which, however, materialized. The efforts up to March 1982 can be termed as an attempt to re-establish the private sector and restore the confidence rudely shaken by the nationalization policy of 1972. There was also a move towards economic liberalization and diminution of government controls.

The second phase: from 1982 onwards

Another *coup* in March 1982 brought about further changes in industrial policy and the role of the government in economic activities. The announcement of the new industrial policy in June 1982 accompanied by a spate of liberalization measures actually carried the privatization policy begun in 1974 to its logical conclusion. A significant denationalization programme was rapidly executed and open economy measures characterized the economic policy of the new government. The global environment, the indirect pressures of international institutions like IMF and the World Bank and a genuine reconsideration of national priorities and strategies brought about this new approach. The military regime had the advantage of not countenancing any public resistance and undertaking fast measures. Privatization in a very broad sense began in earnest. Bangladesh easily fits into the mould described in the following quotation, 'Privatization in a very broad sense, which involved not only divestiture and sale of government asset, but a general decline in the interventionist role played by the public sector, constituted a noteworthy part of the new adjustment programme'.[2]

The policy announced in June 1982 withdrew all restrictions on the ceiling for private investment. Only six industries were reserved for the public sector. In the concurrent list the stipulation about a majority share for the public sector was withdrawn. The sanctioning procedure for investment was simplified and decentralized. Fiscal incentives were clarified and standardized. Improvements in debt servicing terms were stipulated. Rationalization of tariff rates and tax structure was promised and executed as well. The most salient features were expansion of the free lists of investments where no sanction was necessary and denationalization of the jute and cotton textile industry.

The policy also stipulated vigorous sale of abandoned units and offloading of 49 per cent of shares from selected public corporations. A total of 782 units were identified for divestiture which included 33 jute mills and 22 cotton mills. In actual fact 35 jute mills out of 68 and 27 textile mills out of 68 were denationalized within a period of a year and a half. The denationalization of the two banks was announced in June 1983, and the process was completed in two years. The private sector was soon allowed to undertake insurance business as well.

In 1986 the industrial policy was further liberalized in as much as the sanctioning procedure for many industries was eliminated and for others it was streamlined and simplified. This policy has been continued by the new government which came to power in 1991.[3]

The industrial policy of 1991 states as follows:

The new industrial policy will pave the way for rapid expansion of the existing private sector and for its transformation into a more competitive market economy. And, for this purpose:
(a) regulatory complications and controls will be reduced,
(b) a market based competitive price and interest rate structure will be developed and there will be a more equitable distribution of investible capital,
(c) a more liberal and harmonized industrial structure will be developed, and
(d) a competitive and efficient banking and financial system will be established.

The present policy of gradual divestment of public sector industrial enterprises to the private sector will continue. A smooth transition and divestment scheme will have to be evolved to this end.

The present policy is to divest all enterprises except in the six reserved industries and to do it through the tendering procedure, giving preference to Bangladesh investors willing to pay in foreign exchange.

THE CONTEXT OF PRIVATIZATION

The privatization process

Privatization began in Bangladesh well before the global popularity of the concept. It was mainly a reaction to the nationalization policy of 1972. That policy had virtually prohibited all private initiative in trade and industry. Instead it encouraged only promoters, agents and indentors for trade and industry. This created an intolerable situation and also promoted rent seeking in the economy.

When the World Bank initiated its structural adjustment programme in 1980 and when supply side economics took over the White House in 1981, Bangladesh was well poised for dramatic moves in privatization. Divestiture of abandoned units had gone on for a while. Various services and trades had been privatized including supply of input to agriculture. Trade liberalization had gone a long way and conservatism on exchange rate policy was waning. A mechanism for systematic consideration of trade and industrial policy reforms was in process in 1981.

In the last ten years there has been progressive liberalization in respect of investment sanction, import licensing and infrastructure services. The exchange rate is adjusted periodically in relation to a basket of eight currencies in which the main trade of the country is conducted and restrictions are very limited. Even in the area of interest rate and credit policy, which have traditionally been strictly regulated, the process of relaxation has begun in earnest. The trade and investment regime and the macro-policy framework are patterned very largely for an open economy.

Four methods have been followed in the privatization process in Bangladesh. For the sale of abandoned units under public management a procedure was developed in 1976 and it has been refined over time. For the reprivatization of jute and textile industries a special procedure was followed. For the reprivatization of the two banks a different procedure was adopted. For offloading government shares in enterprises another procedure is followed.

The jute and cotton textile mills 'owned by only Bangladesh citizens were returned to them on the same basis as was before independence'.[4] The erstwhile owners were indeed given the mills for a song as the compensation fixed in 1972 was treated as the price for re-acquisition of the mills. All former owners were persuaded to re-own the mills even though many of them had neither the experience nor the financial backing nor even serious interest in operating the mills. The mills were transferred as they were but their debt liability was not settled at the time of transfer. The creditors were not a party to the transaction and joint audit of accounts was left for a subsequent period. There was prohibition on transferring the mills till all dues were cleared. It was also stipulated that no retrenchment of labour could be made for one year.

The divestiture of the banks followed a different procedure. The valuation of the banks was made by auditors and then shares were issued for sale. A little over half the shares of both the banks were taken up by the previous owners. There was adequate preparation and no problems were encountered after denationalization.[5] This is not, however, to deny the myriad problems being faced by private sector banking in Bangladesh.

The sales of public enterprises follow a reasonably well-prepared procedure. A valuation of the enterprise is made on pre-determined principles to arrive at a National Reserve Price (NRP). The expectation is to recover at least the NRP, although even a lower price may be accepted if offers do not match it.[6] Enterprise profiles are provided to buyers and bids accepted from them. If necessary there would be retendering. The buyer makes a down payment of 20 per cent of the sale price and pays the rest in nine annual instalments and then only official transfer of the ownership would be final. The period by which full payment is to be made has now been revised to five years.

The government holds shares in some joint ventures with foreign investors and there are a number of companies where public ownership is in terms of shares. These shares are sold through the stock market.

The institutional arrangements for privatization have evolved over time. A Divestment Board was constituted in 1976 with the Minister of Industries as the chairman and it was assisted by an inter-ministerial Sub-Committee headed by a Joint Secretary of the Ministry of Industries. This Sub-Committee was later substituted by an Executive Committee constituted inter-ministerially but at a higher level; it was headed by the Secretary of the Ministry of Industries. In September 1991, an Inter-ministerial Committee on Privatization (ICOMP) headed by the Principal Finance Secretary was set up to carry forward denationalization of public enterprises. Simultaneously another Interministerial Committee on Industrial Reforms headed by the Secretary of the Ministry of Industries was established to deal with industrial policy, restructuring of public corporations and enterprises and management of public sector enterprises. Both these committees are now located in the Ministry of Industries and they put up their recommendations to the Executive Committee of the National Economic Council (ECNEC) for final decision. Presently ICOMP is considering a programme of divestiture involving 43 enterprises including 10 cotton textile plants. This divestiture will involve outright sale of enterprises, sale of 100 per cent shares of some enterprises as well as offloading of other percentages of shares.

One hundred and two units have been sold since 1982 giving a total of abandoned units sold to private parties of 497. As of the end of 1991, the sale value was about Tk. 1,763 million of which Tk. 1,323 million had been realized. Four hundred and ten units had cleared all their dues while 8 units were resumed by the government due to default. In another move the government had sold 49 per cent of shares of 12 enterprises to the public for a total of Tk 220 million.[7] In 1992, 18 out of the 75 enterprises which had not fully paid their dues have cleared their dues. On the whole the divestiture effort has so far been quite successful. In a way there was a great deal of reprivatization: units earlier nationalized from or abandoned by private owners were resold or given back to private parties. The Divestment Board, according to Eliott Berg, did an outstanding job.[8]

Public sector and its management

The public sector in Bangladesh today does not own much of industrial assets. From 92 per cent in 1972, it came down to 70 per cent in 1981, and it is presently estimated at 30 per cent. In the energy and water resource sectors the public sector has a virtual monopoly. Financial institutions are also largely in the public sector. In the transport and communication sector, railways, airports and airways, telegraph and telecommunication, broadcasting and television and postal service are in the public sector. The overall contribution of the public sector in the GDP can be placed at about 15 per cent. In 1990 Bangladesh had a labour force of 37 million of which about 23 million were regularly employed: 13

million were in the agriculture sector; 5.7 million in the industry, transport and energy sectors; and 2.6 million in the administration, financial and social services sectors. Public enterprises in industry, construction, transport and energy sectors employed about 350,000 people, while civil and military personnel of the government numbered a little over 1 million. Thus out of a non-agricultural employed labour force of 10 million the public sector accounted for 1.5 million.[9]

The public sector organizations involved in economic activities can be broadly classified as productive enterprises, service enterprises and financial organizations. A list is provided in the Appendix. The classification cannot, however, be very rigid because productive and service enterprises usually overlap in their functions. Although many of the public corporations were in existence before the emergence of Bangladesh, their management and operational efficiency suffered heavily in the aftermath of liberation. While government responsibilities expanded, the politicians, bureaucrats, managers, economists and planners were too inexperienced to cope with it. Centralization of decision making was so complete that autonomy of commercial or industrial units did not exist. The personnel policy, recruitment policy, compensation policy, sales and purchase policy, procurement policy and even staff deployment policy of enterprises and corporations were handled in the ministries.

At one time to ease things the heads of corporations were made Secretaries to Government to avoid the centralized exercise of power. Rules of business were to determine relations between the government, corporations and enterprises, but they were not formulated at all. In 1976 some guidelines were laid down to systematize relations between these entities. In 1983, as the public sector was considerably shrunk, more detailed rules of business were issued.[10] But rules or regulations seldom worked because of the arbitrary nature of the government where executive orders would always infringe on decentralized or delegated powers. For example, to undertake a sales mission, or to increase a price in response to increase in the prices of raw materials, or to purchase a vehicle, an enterprise or even a corporation supervising many enterprises would need presidential or ministerial approval. Interference in purchases and sales and contracting and ordering assumed scandalous proportions, especially during the last military regime. Recently the ICOR has decided to convert all the corporations in the industrial sector to holding companies and provide complete managerial and operational autonomy to the subsidiary units. This is intended not only to improve performance but also to facilitate divestiture; individual enterprises or shares in them in the event can be sold conveniently.

Some of these public corporations have long outlived their utility and some are a perpetual drain on national resources. In the transport sector privatization has made BRTC, BIWTC and even BSC nearly redundant. In agriculture, with privatization of input supply, BADC has almost no role to play. In the trade sector, the operations of BJC and TCB have largely shrunk. The railway, until the last military take-over, was an organization in small deficit but in the last few years, next to food, it needs the largest subsidy.[11] A number of other enterprises also depend on subsidy on a regular basis; notable among them are BJC, BJMC, BTC, BCIC and BSEC. REB and Post Office also need budgetary support. All these organizations have surplus labour in their pay-roll. But, ironically, while they have very little work to do there is no let-up in the spiralling labour demand.

In 1986-7 a System for Autonomous Bodies Reporting and Evaluation (SABRE) was introduced and it covers all public enterprises, although department-type large bodies are still out of its purview. This is an excellent MIS and provides useful information on public sector corporations and enterprises. In the Budget for Autonomous Bodies for 1991-2, information on 38 public corporations in the productive and service sectors was provided. From this it is observed that public investment in these enterprises is very substantial although the return is pretty dismal. The total investment in 1991-2 was estimated at Tk. 43 billion, distributed as follows: Tk. 9.7 billion of government equity; Tk. 22 billion of long-term loan from government or public financial institutions; and Tk. 14 billion of working capital funds usually from nationalized commercial banks. The expected return was only a paltry 2.8 per cent, which meant wasteful use of scarce resources.

CONSTRAINTS IN PRIVATIZATION

The twin aspects of divestiture and deregulation theoretically featured in the privatization effort of Bangladesh. Bangladesh was almost a pioneer in its early moves. But the great tragedy is the extremely slow progress and faltering steps, especially with respect to deregulation. There was obviously lack of conviction; and piecemeal measures were taken to meet immediate crises or to achieve specific objectives. Some intimate observers of the reform process have commented on the overall situation as follows:

> Unlike the reforms undertaken in Sri Lanka, Jamaica and Chile, the Bangladesh reforms were not motivated by a strong ideological commitment to a freer market economy. With few exceptions each major policy change had to be negotiated between proponents and opponents, so that logrolling and compromise were often necessary to win support for individual reform items; hence the reform agenda has followed no clear blueprint or schedule.[12]

The most serious constraint has been the bureaucratic opposition to the philosophy of privatization. The country 'inherited a tradition of state paternalism and a distrust of free markets'.[13] This distrust is all pervasive. Even among the actors in the private sector there is a preference for public intervention; they feel comfortable with securing advantages from a regulatory regime. Political commitment at the time of initiating reform measures has essentially been to specific steps or limited purpose rather than to the creation of an enabling environment for the free market. General Ershad needed to cultivate the erstwhile owners of jute and cotton textile mills and so reprivatization was rapidly and vigorously completed.[14] As it was not executed with proper planning and preparation, although it was effective in the short run it cost heavily in long-term efficiency.[15] As mentioned earlier, trade and industrial policy reforms were under consideration in 1980, triggered perhaps by a research study by Bangladesh civil servants in Boston University. A Directorate of Trade and Industrial Policy (TIP) was, in fact, created in 1982 and it functioned for nearly a decade doing very valuable work on all areas of policy reform for an open economy and free market. It not only studied and identified various problems but also recommended detailed corrective measures as well as their sequencing. It followed a politically prudent policy of establishing constituencies of support among the bureaucracy as well as the business and industrial community. It sought windows of opportunity in different crises that the economy underwent in order to promote reforms. Yet the achievements over a decade are tragically short of the potential. (This point will be further elaborated in the section on impact.) Control of foreign exchange allocations, control of import trade, control of investments and control of marketing were difficult for the bureaucracy to relinquish. It has been surmised that this was

> not only because controls were an important source of power and side payments, but because many controllers were convinced that markets in Bangladesh were fatally flawed and facilitated exploitation of the poor by the rich. Civil servants constituted an especially formidable barrier to decontrol because they traditionally enjoyed high prestige in the Indian subcontinent; no new policy could become effective without their help in implementing it.[16]

In Bangladesh there was also a financial constraint in privatization. Because of the low level of accumulation and endemic poverty there were very few buyers for even moderate-sized enterprises. The extremely low domestic saving rate is a positive constraint on privatization. The Gross Domestic Investment rate in the recent past has hovered around 11 per cent with the domestic saving rate never more than 3.5 per cent and usually around 2 per cent.[17] The bulk of investible resources has been external assistance and then savings of expatriate Bangladesh citizens. The preference given to expatriates in the divestiture policy is only natural. Recently ICOMP has been considering permitting foreign investors to take advantage of divestiture and bid for units on sale. The impediment in the past has been a deep suspicion of direct foreign investment as an instrument of exploitation.

A further constraint is the absence of a functioning security market and it is also related to the low saving rate. The stock market is very small. Presently only 144 companies are listed and daily transactions are at the paltry level of about Tk. 1 million or US $ 25,000. It is alleged that the private owners of the stock market, acting as a cartel, manipulate it and stand in the way of the growth of a vibrant market. The government has been facing difficulties in offloading shares of significant value in this market. It is expected that the stock market would attract small investors but it cannot happen if the market is controlled by a few speculators who combine the functions of issuers, brokers, traders, buyers and financiers.

Another constraint concerns the planning and sequencing of privatization in Bangladesh. As a matter of policy the government was interested in selling only losing concerns. Units in dilapidated condition, units with large debts, or units with labour or title problems were the favoured ones for divestiture. In the reprivatization move the erstwhile owners were asked to take back the mills with all their liabilities and assets, but no accounting was actually done. The debt liabilities of the reprivatized mills are still an unresolved issue and it has badly affected the overall environment for efficiency and financial discipline. Very few of the reprivatized mills have been restructured or modernized. The divestiture of the losing concerns also had an adverse effect on the investment climate. In 1982 the policy about selling only losing concerns was theoretically changed but the genuine implementation seems to have become possible only now. Surely some profitable units were sold after 1982; but the clear-cut decision now to privatize all enterprises except those in the reserved sectors of industry bodes well for the future. The present policy of adequate preparation before selling units altogether or even shares in units also looks sound.

Political uncertainty has also been a serious constraint. Until a few months ago the manifesto of one of the major political parties had reservations on privatization. While the Bangladesh Nationalist Party, which came to power in 1991, favoured privatization the Awami League, which secured the same percentage of popular votes in the election, had, until recently, quite different ideas. Privatization policy was mainly pursued by unrepresentative military regimes. Four years ago converting public corporations into holding companies and giving operational autonomy to subsidiary enterprises were opposed by the political parties. In fact, offloading 49 per cent of shares of financial institutions was held up by public opposition because they suspected that it would result in offloading of shares to cronies of the ruling clique at give-away prices. It is hoped that a national consensus on privatization and on limiting the interventionist role of government has finally removed that constraint.

The most troublesome and persistent constraint in Bangladesh has been the labour situation. All economic units and certainly government offices have surplus personnel. Under unrepresentative military regimes the labour force in public entities came to wield immense political power and they also became adept in playing one political group against another. They have, to a large extent, been spoilt by the last military regime as wage increases were granted by the dictator arbitrarily without even pretending to link it with productivity or price changes. A measure of the political power of the labour force is revealed by the fact that when jute and cotton textile mills were reprivatized, it was stipulated that no labour retrenchment could take place for at least one year. It should be noted that such a concession had to be made by a martial law regime which had forcibly captured power only three months earlier! Privatization or even decentralization of retail distribution of electricity has been held up due to objections of the trade unions. Excessive labour force in virtually all plants and their militancy frighten away investors. The general law-and-order situation is a serious constraint not only for privatization but also for investment growth.

IMPACT OF PRIVATIZATION

The why of privatization is crucial in evaluating its impact. Privatization is undertaken essentially to improve the efficiency of investment in both allocation and return. It is expected ultimately to contribute to the welfare of the consumer in a free competitive market. Privatization has other objectives as well and their importance varies from country to country. One way of looking at the impact of privatization would be to scrutinize the objectives and assess the results in relation to individual objectives. Of course, the general impact on efficiency of resource use and promotion of investment is an issue of fundamental enquiry. One of the objectives in Bangladesh was the usual intention of relieving the public sector of its unmanageable burden. A better public–private sharing of burden was certainly a moot concern. Directly productive activities like agriculture and industry were considered areas from which government should withdraw and provide only support services. In 1982, the government explained that the public sector would not take up activities which can be better performed by the private sector but give precedence to private enterprise whenever the latter is willing to come forward in any sector of economic activities.[18] Presently the policy is even more explicit: except in the six reserved sectors there will be no public enterprise in the industries sector. Statistically the impact is clear: there has been a substantial diminution of the public sector in industry, agriculture and, to some extent, in trade. However, privatization in other areas of economic activities of the public sector has not made significant progress.

In 1982, when the big push for privatization began, there was hardly any revenue objective. In 1986 one of the minor objectives of privatization was stated to be mobilizing additional revenue for the annual development programme. There was always the desire to reduce fiscal and credit pressures which public enterprises were invariably generating. The losses of public enterprises were usually met by government in diverse ways: there would be direct subsidy allocated from the budget; there would be conversion of debt into equity or infusion of fresh equity; there would be deferment or remission of interest recovery on debt; there would be debenture financing for corporations; and there would be provision for short-term loans from nationalized banks. The government did not raise resources for the budget from privatization in a significant degree. Even now, when there are no reprivatization give-aways, the estimate of receipts from privatization in 1992–3 is only Tk. 520 million out of a total receipt of Tk 175.6 billion. Credit to the public sector has come down quite substantially. In 1982, it was 41 per cent of total bank credit; in 1991, it was down to only 19 per cent. The subsidy burden, however, has not declined much because the export of raw jute and jute goods is still heavily subsidized, and this subsidy is paid to both the public and the private sectors.

In the policy statement in 1982, it was stated that one of the chief purposes of privatization was 'to provide greater opportunities to the citizens to participate in the development process and allow private initiative and individual energy and creativity to contribute to national welfare'.[19] In fact, the basic purpose of privatization in all countries is investment promotion and efficiency improvement. Reprivatization in Bangladesh was undertaken also with the additional objective of confidence building among the private sector. It is an anachronism that despite reasonable success of the divestiture programme there is almost complete absence of vitality in the economy. Private investment, and for that matter investment in general, is low; there is hardly any efficiency improvement in any sector. Immediately after denationalization the public sector showed some improvement but as the threat of denationalization disappeared under political and labour pressure the situation worsened.[20]

What can be the reason for such an anachronism? A plausible explanation is provided by the nature of the ruling elite. First, successive military regimes tried to establish an elite which would support them both politically and financially. They sanctioned industries and offered credit to preferred parties who very naturally refused to undertake any obligations associated with industrial investment and debt repayment. This had the contamination effect on the genuine investors as well. This can explain to a large extent most of the unproductive, inefficient and wasteful investments (euphemistically called sick industries), large defaults on bank credit, big loans without collateral, and overall financial indiscipline which is holding up revitalization of the economy. Second, the nature of the arbitrary regime could never inspire confidence in the economy or stability in its political system thus preventing investment in the country. Another oft-quoted complaint is the weakness of policy implementation which really means bureaucratic caprices and political mishandling. The unaccountable despotic regime universalized corruption and every impediment to investment meant illegal gratification, commission and brokerage which went for the enrichment of the ruling class.

BIDS carried out two studies in 1984 and 1986 and found that divestiture had not improved performance of either the public or the private sector. They also cautioned the government to monitor concentration of wealth as a result of divestiture.[21] Based on further studies Klaus Lorch examined the issues of both static and dynamic efficiency of the cotton textile sector pursuant to divestiture.[22] He found that on current production the private sector enjoyed advantage in production, sales and support services while the public sector enjoyed advantage in scale of operations and procurement. Over a five-year period the private sector had an economic gain of 6 per cent and financial gain of 18 per cent. The financial gain was so large simply because, taking advantage of unresolved dispute, they did not pay any interest charge on any long-term debt. But in respect of efficiency over time he noticed no achievement. There was no new investment, no improved technology, nor much of an improvement in management system. The mills were managed as family businesses and the margins of traders and indentors were appropriated by the family members. The mill-owners also gained in income distribution at the expense of managers and workers. In his own words, 'Privatized mills outperformed public ones in static efficiency, albeit by a modest margin, in all but the procurement function'. But 'in terms of dynamic efficiency, the privatized enterprises seemed to enjoy little or no net advantage over those enterprises that remained state owned'. Lorch blames the hasty process of privatization for the lingering dispute on debt liability which he considers as one of the major impediments to the healthy turn-around in the cotton textile industry. But he makes the further point that the overall policy framework was not propitious and there was also the issue of 'confidence of the private sector in a predictable policy environment'. 'All things considered', he rightly concludes, 'privatization did not turn out to be a leapfrogging strategy for industrialization.'

Privatization in Bangladesh has put some life into the stock market. But the security market as functioning now does not permit a vibrant growth. The good thing, however, is that the process of privatization has generated pressures for the reform of the stock and security markets.

Privatization has not made much of an impact on foreign private investment. Again, the all-pervasive regulatory ethos stands in the way. Corruption at high levels also has something to do with the reluctance of direct foreign investment. A further constraint is the deteriorating law and order situation and labour unrest and militancy. As global realignment of production and marketing arrangements by transnational companies is under way, Bangladesh is losing out because of its hesitant steps and poor infrastructure facilities.

Privatization is only a means to better use of resources and promotion of investment and efficiency. Its impact in the short run can be negative: retrenchment of labour may take place, temporary dislocation of production may happen, and restructuring may mean temporary consolidation of investment and hence decline. But it is expected to release creative energies of individuals and contribute to investment and employment growth and upgrading of technology. This cannot, however, be achieved without deregulation and creation of an enabling environment for the private sector. Bangladesh has still a long way to go in dismantling regulations and discarding administrative discretion. A conscious and vigorous policy of contraction of government must be the basis for privatization in the true sense of the term. At the same time the private sector also has to develop social responsibility and learn to stand on its own feet. At the slightest difficulty they rush to the government for help and relief and seek government protection to meet their losses or problems. The culture of bankruptcy is unknown in Bangladesh and there is no concept of salvage cost. This also has to change.

HISTORICAL NOTE

The first phase: Pakistan period

The Government of India prior to the partition of the country in 1947 was one of minimal functions like most governments of the pre-depression period. However, in the post-war period the colonial government started the process of expansion of government by taking up planning of economic development. In the wake of independence both India and Pakistan embarked on a larger role for the government in economic activities.

Prior to partition the only large public corporation (in fact one of the oldest in the world) was the Railway Board. The government was also constructing, maintaining and operating a large irrigation system in northern and western India. Government support services for agriculture, investment in transport network and provision of facilities for education and healthcare were very limited.

With a view to telescoping the development process and overcoming the market imperfections, the national governments of both India and Pakistan undertook expansion of the public sector. In Pakistan, the government did not choose socialism but still expanded the public sector. It set up a commercial bank, started road transport services, took up larger roles in education, health care, housing or social welfare.

Pakistan announced an industrial policy in 1948 giving the pioneering role to the private sector and reserved for government only three sectors of production, namely manufacture of arms and ammunition, generation of hydro-electric power and manufacture of transport and communication equipment like railway wagons, telephones, telegraphic and wireless apparatus. While private enterprise was thus given the vital role in industrial development, the Pakistan Industrial Development Corporation was set up in 1950 primarily to promote enterprises which private parties were unable or unwilling to undertake. The industries which were promoted were jute and cotton textiles, papers, chemicals, fertilizers, cement, sugar, shipbuilding and engineering.[23] To facilitate industrial development, in 1949 the Pakistan Industrial Finance Corporation was set up which was coverted into the Industrial Development Bank of Pakistan in 1961. Later, in 1957, with the support of the World Bank, the Pakistan Industrial and Credit Corporation was established. In the same year, recognizing the importance of small and cottage industry, the East Pakistan Small and Cottage Industry Corporation was set up.

The territory of Bangladesh under Pakistan was an under-administered and neglected area. It remained a predominantly agricultural country with very rudimentary infrastructure facilities. PIDC, and after its bifurcation in 1962 EPIDC, developed some large-scale industries, only a few of which were in the public sector. Fertilizers and chemicals, paper and allied products, cement, engineering and shipbuilding and oil and gas industries were in the public sector;

while jute and cotton textile industries, largely assisted by PIDC and EPIDC, were essentially in the private sector. In 1965 the public sector expanded somewhat as enterprises owned by Indian nationals were taken over by the government under the Enemies Property Act. At the time of liberation the public sector owned 34.8 per cent of industrial assets in Bangladesh. A large part of industrial investment was made by non-local entrepreneurs so that it was estimated that 47 per cent of the industrial sector was owned by them.[24]

A number of public corporations were initiated in the late 1950s and early 1960s mostly under the influence of western donors. Agricultural Development Corporation, Water and Power Development Board, Fisheries Development Corporation, Forest Industries Development Corporation, Inland Water Transport Authority, Road Transport Corporation, Improvement Trust or Development Authorities for cities, Water and Sewerage Authorities for large cities, Trading Corporation, Jute Trading Corporation and a few other autonomous bodies expanded the public sector. But hardly 10 per cent of the GDP emanated from the public sector.

The second phase: emergence of Bangladesh

Bangladesh emerged as a new nation in 1971 in the wake of a bloody liberation war. This left the infrastructure severely damaged, industrial and power plants largely inoperative, agriculture badly stunted, the social fabric rudely disturbed and the entire production process in total disarray. In 1969–70, the normal year before liberation, the structure of the economy was largely agrarian with a small modern sector. Agriculture contributed 60 per cent of the Gross Domestic Product, industry 6.8 per cent, construction power and transport 9.6 per cent, and trade 10.8 per cent.

The ravages of the war warranted a large public sector role in the reconstruction efforts. In industry and commerce, a large number of units were abandoned by non-local owners forcing the government to take them over. In the elections preceding the war of liberation most Bangladesh political parties espoused a limited measure of nationalization. But the liberation war radicalized views and the ruling party, Awami League, became a strong exponent of state socialism. The government in exile immediately upon return to the capital had to take steps to bring under government control and management all abandoned properties. On 2 January 1972 under Presidential Order No. 16, 725 industrial units were taken over by the government.

In March 1972, in a series of sweeping measures, industry, foreign trade and financial institutions were almost completely nationalized. Presidential Order No. 27 nationalized jute textile, cotton textile, sugar, steel, paper, fertilizer, pharmaceuticals, food industries, engineering and shipbuilding, mineral resources and oil and gas industries. Presidential Order No. 29 deployed the abandoned industrial units under public corporations, 10 of which were set up to manage these along with the nationalized industries. The ten-sector corporations owned 313 industrial enterprises whose fixed assets were valued at Tk. 5,120 million or $ 690 million.[25] Public ownership of fixed assets in modern industry went up from 34.8 per cent in the pre-liberation period to 92 per cent in March 1972.[26] This, however, meant that only 10.2 per cent of the indigenous private sector was nationalized as the rest was either already in the public sector or abandoned by the non-locals.

Government monopoly in international shipping was established under Presidential Order No. 10 dated 29 January 1972. Under Presidential Order No. 26, all banking, excluding the branches of foreign banks, was nationalized and six nationalized commercial banks were established. Presidential Order No. 30 did the same for the insurance business and two public corporations absorbed all insurance companies. Presidential Order No. 28 nationalized all mechanized inland water transport vehicles. All these steps were necessary as most units in these sectors were abandoned by the non-local owners and companies.

Nationalization of the import and export trade happened on a limited scale. The two jute trading companies, Jute Marketing Corporation and Jute Trading Company, got the monopoly in jute export trade. The Trading Corporation of Bangladesh started importing cement, milk powder, pharmaceuticals and a number of other items on a near monopoly basis. In addition, large tonnage of foodgrains, edible oils, petroleum, fertilizers, steel scrap and billet, and many other items were all imported by the public sector. In the early days of Bangladesh trade with socialist countries provided the life-line in commerce, scarcities were excessive while the country had no foreign exchange for required import, and trading houses which provided the link with the world were in the other region. Such a situation automatically promoted public sector monopoly by foreign trade.

INDUSTRIES RESERVED FOR THE PUBLIC SECTOR

Industries reserved for the public sector in 1974 were as follows:

1 arms and ammunition and allied defence equipment;
2 atomic energy;
3 jute industry (hessian, sacking, carpet-backing);
4 cotton textiles (excluding handlooms and specialized textiles);
5 sugar;
6 paper and newsprint;
7 iron and steel (excluding rerolling mills);
8 shipbuilding and heavy engineering (including machine tools and assembly/ manufacture of cars, buses, trucks, tractors and power tillers);
9 heavy electrical industry;
10 mineral oils and gas;
11 cement;

12 petro-chemicals (fertilizers, PVC, ethylene and synthetic fibres);
13 heavy and basic chemicals and basic pharmaceuticals;
14 air transport;
15 shipping (including coastal ships and tankers above 1,000 DWT)
16 telephone, telephone cables, telegraph and wireless apparatus (excluding radio receiving sets);
17 generation and distribution of electricity; and
18 forest extraction (mechanized)

In 1975 only 1, 2, 3, 4, 14, 16 and 17, were retained in the reserved list. In 1982 items 3 and 4 were also deleted from the reserved list.

APPENDIX

Public corporations

Productive enterprises

Industry sector:	Bangladesh Textile Corporation
	Bangladesh Jute Mills Corporation
	Bangladesh Ship Building and Engineering Corporation
	Bangladesh Sugar and Food Industries Corporation
	Bangladesh Chemical Industries Corporation
	Bangladesh Forest Development Industry Corporation
Water, gas and electricity, sector	Bangladesh Gas, Oil and Mineral Development Corporation
	Bangladesh Power Development Corporation
	Dhaka Water Supply and Sewerage Authority
	Chittagong WASA
Transport sector:	Bangladesh Shipping Corporation
	Bangladesh Inland Water Transport Corporation
	Bangladesh Biman (Air Services)
	Bangladesh Road Transport Corporation
	Chittagong Port Authority
	Mongla Port Authority
Trade sector:	Bangladesh Petroleum Corporation
	Bangladesh Jute Corporation
	Bangladesh Trading Corporation
Agriculture sector:	Bangladesh Agriculture Development Corporation
	Bangladesh Fisheries Development Corporation
Construction sector:	Chittagong Development Authority
	Rajshahi Development Authority
	Khulna Development Authority
	Capital Development Corporation (RAJUK)

Services enterprises

1 Muktijudhya Kalyan Trust
2 Bangladesh Film Development Corpn

3 Bangladesh Tourism Development Corpn
4 Civil Aviation Authority
5 Bangladesh Handloom Board
6 Bangladesh Inland Water Transport Authority (Regulatory)
7 Export Processing Zone Authority
8 Bangladesh Sericulture Board
9 Rural Electrification Board
10 Bangladesh Tea Board
11 Bangladesh Small and Cottage Industry Corporation
12 Bangladesh Water Development Board
13 Bangladesh Sugarcane Research and Training Institute

Financial institutions

1 Bangladesh Bank
2 Bangladesh Agriculture Bank (BKB)
3 Bangladesh Industrial Bank (BSB)
4 Bangladesh Industrial Credit Bank (BSRS)
5 Bangladesh Investment Corporation
6 Bangladesh House Building Finance Corporation
7 Four Commercial Banks – Sonali, Janata, Agrani, Rupali
8 Bangladesh General Insurance Corporation (BSBC)
9 Bangladesh Life Insurance Corporation (BJBC)

Government departments run as service corporations

Bangladesh Railway Board
Bangladesh Telephone and Telegraph Board
Atomic Energy Commission

NOTES

1 World Bank, *Bangladesh Development of a Rural Economy, Vol I* Washington D.C. 1974: 149–54.
2 Gouri Geeta (ed.) *Privatisation and Public Enterprise: the Asia Pacific Experience*, New Delhi: Oxford and IBH publishing, 1991:5.
3 Government of Bangladesh, Ministry of Industries, *Industrial Policy 1991*, July, Dhaka.
4 Ministry of Industries, Government of Bangladesh, 'The New Industrial Policy', June 1982, reproduced in *Planning Commission Handbook*, Dhaka, November 1983: 199–213.
5 Chowdhury, T.E. *Privatisation of State Enterprises in Bangladesh (1976–84)*, paper presented at KDI/EDI joint seminar in Seoul, November 1987, Mimeo.
6 The principles of valuation are the following: (a) land value is either market price or price fixed by Development or Improvement Trusts or Authorities; (b) moveables like buildings, plants and machineries at 2.85 times the book value or at market price if no book value is available; (c) stocks and stores at book value or in the absence of book value at market price.
7 *Daily Sangbad*, Dhaka 8 Dec 1991.

8 Berg Eliott and Mary M. Shirley, *Divestiture in Developing Countries*, Washington D.C., World Bank, 1987 (discussion paper).

9 Information on GDP and employment has been compiled from three government of Bangladesh publications:

1 Ministry of Planning, *The Fourth Five Year Plan Draft 1990–95*, Dhaka, May 1990: 29–31.

2 *Bangladesh Statistical Bureau, Statistical Yearbook 1991*, Dhaka, 1991: 120–31, 519–25.

3 Ministry of Finance, *Budgets of Autonomous Bodies 1991–92. Vol. I*, Dhaka, 1991: 1–18.

Public sector's share of GDP is estimated as follows: energy and water resource: 1 per cent; public service: 4 per cent; banking and insurance: 2 per cent; construction, transport and trade: 4.2 per cent out of 25.1 per cent; manufacturing industry: 3.4 per cent out of 8.6 per cent.

10 M.S.H. Chisty, 'The Experience of Bangladesh', in Asian Development Bank, *Privatisation: Policies, Methods and Procedures*, Manila, 1985: 265–68.

11 The deficit of railway was as follows in the following years:

1980–1 : Tk. 167 million
1981–2 : Tk. 139 million
1982–3 : Tk. 101 million
1985–6 : Tk. 503 million
1986–7 : Tk. 1,043 million
1987–8 : Tk. 1,490 million
1988–9 : Tk. 1,503 million
1989–90 : Tk. 1,394 million
1990–1 : Tk. 1,021 million
1991–2 : Tk. 1,260 million

Source: Ministry of Finance, *Annual Budget Summaries*, Dhaka, Bangladesh.

12 Richard D. Mallon and Joseph J. Stern, 'The political economy of trade and industrial policy reforms in Bangladesh', in Dwight D. Perkins and Michael Roemer (eds) *Reforming Economic Systems in Developing Countries*, Cambridge, HIID, 1991:210.

13 Ibid.: 190.

14 Chowdhury op. cit.

15 Klaus Lorch, *The Privatisation Transaction and its Long-term Effects, A Case of Textile Industry in Bangladesh*, New York, UNDP, 1988.

16 Perkins and Roemer, op. cit.: 196.

17 A.M.A. Muhith, *Bangladesh Punargatan o Jatiya Aikya* (*Bangladesh Reconstruction and National Consensus*), Dhaka, University Press Limited, 1991: 11–14.

18 Bangladesh Economic Association, *Seminar Report on International Trade and Economic Development*, Dhaka, 1983. Speech on Economic Policy of Bangladesh by Mr A.M.A. Muhith, Finance and Planning Minister, dated 5 Nov. 1982.

19 Ibid.

20 Chisty, op. cit.

21 R. Sobhan and A. Ahsan, *Divestment and Denationalisation: Profile and Performance*, Dhaka, BIDS, 1984. R. Sobhan and S.A. Mahmood, *The Economic Performance of Denationalised Industries in Bangladesh: The Case of the Jute and Cotton Textile Industry*, Dhaka, BIDS, 1986.

22 Klaus Lorch, 'Privatisation through private sale: The Bangladesh textile industry', in Ravi Rammurti and Raymond Vernon (eds), *Privatisation and Control of State-Owned Enterprises*, Washington D.C., World Bank, 1991: 126–52.

23 Ministry of Finance, Government of Pakistan, *The Economy of Pakistan, 1948–68*, Islamabad, 1968: 74–5.

24 R. Sobhan and M. Ahmed, *Public Enterprise in an Intermediate Regime: A Study in Political Economy of Bangladesh*, Dhaka, BIDS, 1980: 101.

25 Planning Commission, Government of Bangladesh, *The First Five Year Plan 1973–98*, Dacca, 1973: 195

The 10 corporations were actually created out of EPIDC. They were Jute Mills Corporation (BJMC); Textile Mills Corporation (BTMC); Sugar Mills Corporation (BSFC); Steel Mills Corporation (BSMC); Engineering & Shipbuilding Corporation (BESC); Paper & Board Corporation (BPBC); Food and Allied Industries Corporation (BFAIC); Fertilizers, Chemicals & Pharmaceutical Corporation (BFCPC); Gas, Oil & Minerals Corporation (BGOMC). In addition there were former pre-liberation corporations which continued, viz. Fisheries Development Corporation (BFDC); Forest Industries Development Corporation (BFIDC); Film Development Corporation (BFDC) and Small Industries Corporation (BSIC). Sena Kalyan Sangstha, a pre-liberation organization, and Mukti Judhya Welfare Foundation, a post-liberation creation, were entrusted with the operation of some industrial units. Later a Tanneries Corporation and a Cottage Industry Corporation were also set up.

26 Chisty op. cit.

15

PRIVATIZATION IN INDIA

S. R. Mohnot

THE HISTORICAL PERSPECTIVE

Given the expanding size of the public sector and the rationale guiding the industrial policy formulations in India, a brief historical perspective is necessary in understanding its privatization model. The public sector was sought to occupy the 'commanding heights'. This was clearly articulated in the industrial policy statements of 1948 and 1956. By 1991, there were 246 central public undertakings (CPUs) with an investment of over Rs 1tn equivalent of over 10 per cent of GDP. The CPUs are engaged primarily in the core sector, in particular infrastructure and the services, for example, steel, minerals and metals; energy, petroleum; chemicals including drugs, pharmaceuticals and fertilizers; heavy engineering; transportation equipment including railway locomotives, aircraft; international trade and marketing; transport and communication, construction, industrial consultancy, financial services, and tourism. Curiously, the CPUs encompass consumer products as well, such as bread and electric lamps, an area not intended for it.

In financial terms, the CPUs do not, on the whole, present an impressive rate card (see Table 15.1). In 1990–1, the aggregate net profit was of the order of Rs 24 billion – 6 per cent of the paid-up capital. And the rate of return including long-term interest was around 4.0 per cent against the market cost of long-term capital at 16 per cent. This is tantamount to a loss of Rs 120 billion annually.

A tally of 843 state-level public undertakings (SPUs) in 1986–7 showed that investments aggregated Rs 112 billion of which equity capital was of the order of Rs 36 billion, with a debt–equity ratio of around 2:1. Table 15.2 indicates their precarious net profit position.

During the Gulf War and its aftermath, India was caught in a critical balance of payments position, along with a downgrading by international credit agencies. There was a fall in dollar value of exports and rise in dollar value of imports. India was forced to approach the International Monetary Fund, the World Bank and other bilateral aid lenders for emergency and standby credits.

Prompted by them, the government resorted to a deep economic introspection. As soon as the new government came to power after the 1991 June

Table 15.1 Basic financial parameters of CPUs

Parameter	1984–5	1989–90	1990–1
A. Manufacturing enterprises			
No. of enterprises	150	160	163
Capital employed	32,918	72,059	69,367
Net investment	24,310	58,522	82,883
Value of output	36,454	74,508	83,380
Cost of production	35,470	71,946	
Profit before tax	1,897	4,416	2,904
a) No. of profit making units	73	84	82
Amount	2,786	4,894	4,445
b) No. of loss incurring units	76	73	79
Amount	889	1,503	2,376
c) No. of other units	1	3	2
Post-tax net profit	847	3,389	2,069
Value-added	12,506	28,208	31,757
Export earnings	3,130	2,004	2,423
Employment*	19	19	19
B. Service Enterprises			
No. of enterprises	57	73	73
Capital employed	7,178	21,032	
Net investment	12,072	25,915	32,336
Value of output	15,860	24,768	28,570
Cost of production	16,152	24,780	28,422
Profit before tax	202	877	915
a) No. of profit making units	41	47	42
Amount	424	856	987
b) No. of loss incurring units	16	25	30
Amount	222	456	688
c) No. of other units	–	1	1
Post-tax net profit	62	399	299
Value-added	–	–	–
Export earnings	2,702	4,362	4,673
Employment*	3	4	4
C. All enterprises			
No. of enterprises	207	233	236
Capital employed	39,304	93,091	
Net investment	36,382	84,759	101,702
Value of output	52,314	99,489	111,452
Cost of production	51,622	96,731	111,802

Table 15.1   *continued*

Parameter	1984–5	1989–90	1990–1
Profit before tax	2,099	5,292	3,820
a) No. of profit making units	114	131	124
Amount	3,209	5,751	5,431
b) No. of loss incurring units	92	98	109
Amount	1,111	1,961	3,064
c) No. of other units	1	4	3
Post-tax net profit	909	3,789	2,368
Value-added	12,505	28,208	31,757
Export earnings	5,831	6,366	1,096
Employment*	22	23	23

Note: All figures in Rs crore (10 million) except those *which are in la khs(100,000 Rs)
Source: Annual Reports: Department of Public Enterprises (Public Enterprises Survey), New Delhi

elections, a bold new policy of liberalization and restructuring was quickly launched. Among the several critical components of the package was the public sector reform and privatization. This is being pursued through the instrument of MoUs (Memorandum of Understanding), restrictions on the budgetary support to existing public enterprises (PEs), both losing and profit making, and opening up areas for private investment which were reserved for the public sector.

PRIVATIZATION IN ACTION

Lack of consensus on privatization

Diametrically opposite sets of opinions have been expressed in the public–private sector debate, and there is no clear consensus. The privatization model as it stands today is geared to four major directions:

1   *Capital divestiture*: Through sale of equity of selected public enterprises. The 1991 July budget provided for Rs 25 billion for the 1991–2 fiscal year. This was followed in the February 1992 budget for the next fiscal year at Rs 35 billion.

2   *Closure of sick and unviable units*: Initially 44 and later 56 such enterprises were identified in the CPU sector.

3   Ad hoc *privatization moves*: Some activities of the public sector are to be disaggregated from the essential or core activity and non-core activities could be privatized.

4   *Incremental privatization*: Several important sectors which were reserved

Table 15.2 State-level PEs and their performance

	Enterprises (no.)	Capital investment (Rs mn)	Cos. with cumulative profits (no.)	Cos. with cumulative losses (no.)	Cos. under liquidation/ construction (no.)	Net profit (Rs mn)
Andhra Pradesh	39	11,360	7	29	3	−1,495
Assam	32	1,829	9	20	3	−256
Bihar	45	4,795	6	24	15	−515
Gujarat	36	5,623	15	15	6	−402
Haryana	19	1,030	4	14	1	−216
Karnataka	57	18,891	14	36	7	−2,249
Kerala	90	7,020	19	65	6	−2,331
Madhya Pradesh	30	2,471	13	15	2	−31
Maharashtra	59	7,035	12	46	1	−1,158
Orissa	70	4,199	13	33	24	−486
Punjab	46	4,655	9	26	11	−371
Rajasthan	19	1,929	5	14	–	−187
Tamil Nadu	46	16,100	21	52	3	−1,789
Uttar Pradesh	97	15,075	33	49	15	−3,857
West Bengal	48	5,993	5	32	11	−2,452
Arunachal Pradesh	3	70	2	1	–	15
Goa, Daman & Diu	8	479	4	4	–	−12
Himachal Pradesh	16	839	4	9	3	−532
Jammu and Kashmir	14	1,390	4	10	–	−221
Manipur	8	117	–	3	5	−2
Meghalaya	9	324	1	6	2	−59
Mizoram	1	94	–	1	–	–
Nagaland	6	234	–	4	2	−87
Pondicherry	7	379	5	1	1	27
Tripura	8	257	1	5	2	−15
Total	843	112,189	206	514	123	−18,683

Source: The Report of the Comptroller and Auditor General of India, 1989

for the public sector have been thrown open to private enterprise. These include powerful segments such as energy, telecommunications, steel.

While privatization by partial divestiture takes place, incremental public investment will be necessary to sustain the unprivatized activity, some of which is critical to the economy and which the government, for one reason or another, will not privatize. Providing for the policy constraints and other overriding factors, the likely phasing of the privatization effort is shown in Table 15.3. If privatization can divert Rs 1,800 billion as envisaged in the extrapolation exercise, the net improvement in GDP could be of the order of Rs 100 billion from the divested resources representing the transfer differential in productivity of capital. Add to this the increased profitability due to the exposure of enterprises to the stock market and the induction of competition to the investment remaining in the PSUs, and the net saving could be further enhanced. If the improvement in profitability is brought up to the modest figure of 12 per cent, in the non-privatized activity, it could add another Rs 200 billion (12 per cent on Rs 1,660 billion minus the existing profit generation). The net gain to the exchequer could be of the order of Rs 200 to 300 billion.

The divestiture programme

India's divestiture programme is seen to demonstrate three basic motivations:

1   as an *ad hoc* fiscal measure, to raise revenues to reduce the budgetary and fiscal deficits;
2   as an exposure, *albeit* only partial, of the PSUs to the market forces, which would lead to greater management transparency and accountability, and hence efficiency;
3   as a part of a series of measures towards total (micro-level) restructuring to be brought about in stages.

Table 15.3 Privatization effort

Year	Base investment (Rs bn)	Incremental investment* (Rs bn)	Divestment[1] (Rs bn)	Cumulative investment[2] (Rs bn)
1991–2	2,000	400	40	2,360
1992–3	2,360	300	150	2,510
1993–4	2,510	250	250	2,510
1994–5	2,510	200	350	2,360
2000	2,360	500	1,200	1,660

*Historical prices
[1]1991 prices
[2]Mix of historical prices

274

If approach 1 is all that is intended, it is not likely to achieve the basic objectives. It is also doubtful if much would be achieved if the programme is limited to approach 2. Considering the frequency with which the changes are made in PSU personnel, the salutory effect of public gaze will be minimal. Should approach 3 form the basis of the divestiture programme, the moves in India would be credited with the political caution which has characterized India's economic policies in the past decades.

The first two instalments of the public sector disinvestment were organized in a hurry to meet the budgetary commitments on which the government did not want to falter. Accordingly, it could not adopt a studied and optimal method. The realization of divestiture proceeds was rather low when compared with the market value of the divested scrips. The auction followed a unique procedure. The 31 companies included in the first round ranged from a large refinery company (Hindustan Petroleum) to a service company (engaged in computer maintenance and software). The shares of good performers were clubbed with those of the middlings and poor performers. The mutual funds and other official investors were to bid for each basket as a whole. They were asked to evaluate each basket and arrive at their own bid against the government's own floor price for each basket. In the first tranche, the floor prices were not disclosed. Only half the lots were sold, involving 28 PSUs. In the second, the number in the baskets was reduced to 16 as there were no takers for the little-known PSUs included in the basket.

Apparently, the government adopted the conventional method to value the shares, which is an average of net asset value and yield value. It was suggested that the assets of the public sector required to be revalued before pricing the scrips; but this called for an intensive effort since the assets of each enterprise were a mix of historical values and technologies, some of which have become obsolete and may in some cases be non-competitive.

The second round of bidding in January 1992 was more fine-tuned. The government set a floor price of Rs 106.20 million for each basket. On an average, the offered prices were 33 per cent higher (Rs 125 million). The divested equity capital of the CPUs was bought by financial institutions at values as set out in Table 15.4. Of the Rs 30 billion, about 70 per cent was paid by Unit Trust of India alone, buying 101 out of 120 lots. The two nationalized insurance corporations paid Rs 3.4 billion – approximately 11 per cent of the total sale.

Eventually, according to present indications, the offers will be made to individual and corporate investors besides mutual and other saving funds and hopefully also to foreign investors. The foreign investors might be limited to institutional saving funds; but once the securities are freely marketable, the stigma on foreign multi-national corporations could disappear.

Table 15.4 Buyers of disinvested stocks of CPUs

Buying institution	First tranche* (Rs mn)	Second tranche* (Rs mn)	Total (Rs mn)
Mutual funds			
Unit Trust of India	7,758	13,315	21,073
Canbank Mutual Fund	1,312	–	1,312
LIC Mutual Fund	274	–	274
PNB Mutual Fund	36	–	36
SBI Mutual Fund	932	130	1,062
Indian Bank Mutual Fund	–	133	133
BOI Mutual Fund	–	410	410
Banks			
Bank of Baroda	–	993	993
Allahabad Bank	–	260	260
Corporation Bank	–	339	339
Insurance companies			
General Insurance Corpn	2,119	–	2,120
Life Insurance Corpn	1,843	–	1,843
Banks' Associated Finance Corpns			
SBI Capital Markets	–	396	396
Canbank Financial Services	–	130	130
Total	14,274	16,106	30,381

* On two dates, 2 Jan and 4 Feb 1992

Future actions on privatization

In February 1992, the government constituted a committee to go into the entire issue of the government divestiture programme from public sector enterprises and recommend on the *modus operandi* of further divestiture and the criteria for valuation of equity shares. The committee is understood to have considerd two modes of sale. The first is direct offer to the open market. It will entail an expenditure of roughly 2 per cent of the value of shares. Under the second proposal – open auction – no such money will have to be spent, and the best bid would be accepted. However, it is feared that open auction might result in some bidders forming consortia and consequential underquoting.

The sale of shares to the financial institutions in the public sector would only mean transfer of funds from one institution to another, which would prevent transfer of management. In the process the main objective of privatization will be missing. The committee appears to be against the sale of equity shares to raise funds for meeting the government's interest and repayment liabilities.

276

Other privatization moves

The Steel Ministry has identified two PSUs, the National Mineral Development Corporation and Metal Scrap Trade Corporation (MSTC), for partial divestiture. (The Steel Authority of India [SAIL] was the first one.) MSTC has a sound financial base and 9.24 per cent of its equity is already in private hands. With paid-up capital of Rs 11 million, MSTC, the canalizing agency for ferrous scrap and ships for breaking, has built up reserves of Rs 320 million.

Responding to the government's present policy, Kandla Port Trust (KPT) has identified some areas of operations for private participation, such as container-handling, construction of warehousing, mechanical loading and unloading and ship-repairing facilities. On the contrary, the Port Trust has submitted programmes costing Rs 4,400 million for implementation during the Eighth Plan.

Among efforts at the state government level, mention may be made of the Rs 2 billion offer by the UP Government for privatization of Uptron Colour Picture Tubes. The large Andhra Pradesh unit, Hyderabad Allwyn, is another example. Many such moves are in the pipeline or on the anvil in several states.

Incremental privatization

Privatization in the sense of divestiture as such has made, on the whole, little progress. It will remain sluggish in the near future because of constraints. With the liberalization policies, however, incremental privatization is anticipated to make heavy inroads in areas hitherto reserved for the public sector. For example, India hopes to attract about $ 2.7 billion of direct foreign investment from the UK and the US in six electric power projects involving a total investment of about $ 4 billion. These will help add about 4,000 MW of additional generating capacity. Of this, the British companies may go in for funding of some 1,600 MW. Rolls Royce-NEI are likely to go in for a 1,000 MW project in Ballagarh in West Bengal. British Gas is discussing with Indian entrepreneurs a 600 MW project in Maharashtra.

The government has given the assurance that:

1 foreign investors will be allowed to hold 100 per cent equity;
2 a 16 per cent rate of return will be built into the tariff; and
3 repatriation of profits of foreign investors can be made without the requirement to match it with export earnings (as required in other sectors).

The government has declined to provide guarantees to foreign loans obtained by private investors in Indian power projects. There will be no guarantees as such for a 16 per cent rate of return on equity, but the two-part tariff formula will be so structured that this return will be built into the rates charged to state electricity boards. These issues are reported to be major bottlenecks in attracting direct financial investments into the Indian power sector.

The telecom sector is another major sector likely to attract foreign investment.

The government proposes to open up value-added telecom services such as cellular telephone, video text and electronic mail to the private sector. There is a growing pressure from GATT to open telecommunication services to the private and foreign investors (in return for a larger entry into labour-intensive products). The local industry is seeking to run parallel telecom services after the privatization of the telecom equipment sector.

It is pointed out that to cater to India's telecom needs, an investment of Rs 1,250 billion equivalent in foreign exchange would be needed for the system and transmission network. None of the private sector units, it is pointed out, has the capacity of making that volume of investment. A number of multi-nationals have shown interest in coming into the equipment manufacturing sector, which it is the government's intention to consider on merits (slowly and selectively).

Finally, the government allowed the private sector to float mutual funds (MFs) thus removing the differences between the two sectors. Elaborate guidelines have been evolved on investments by mutual funds to ensure that they do not participate in takeover bids. The Securities Exchange Board of India (SEBI) has been assigned wide-ranging powers to oversee the constitution as well as the operations of MFs. However, despite the intention shown by several business houses, no private MF has so far been registered.

Privatization in reverse gear

While the moves towards privatization are on, at least some of the state governments are trying to expand even the non-core sector. Illustratively, the Tamil Nadu State government proposes to set up a bagasse-based newsprint project at a cost of Rs 10 billion (over US $ 300 million). It will be the second such unit in the state with an installed capacity of 200,000 tpa. Interestingly, the project is expected to be financed by the World Bank and Indian financial institutions led by the Industrial Development Bank of India (IDBI).

CONSTRAINTS ON PRIVATIZATION

The constraints on privatization may be categorized as:

1 *theoretical* (based on conceptual perceptions);
2 *positive* (the public sector enterprises performing well, no worse then those in the private sector);
3 *negative* (such as inadequacy of private enterprise – in terms of capital or management capability – to take over public sector undertakings or the perception that the public enterprises supply essential goods and services);
4 *alibis* (advanced by vested interests to prevent dismantling of public enterprises);
5 *incidental*, where the public sector continues to exist and calls for fresh doses of investments for expansion, modernization or rehabilitation of obsolete plant and equipment.

A major constraint on privatization emanates from the group psychology leading to irrational behaviour. For the past four decades, it has been imprinted on the minds of development planners and decision makers that there is a direct correlation between public investments and social equity. Public investment is equated with priority investment for supply of essentials at fair prices, and supply of essentials with social justice. The correlation is assumed to be negative in case of private investments since it is believed that the latter are aimed at high profits; high profits are equated, not with productivity, but with profiteering.

As a consequence of the theory of positive association of public investment with social equity, the men in public affairs find it embarrassing to oppose public investment. It is feared that support for private enterprise leads to loss of public support and hence of political power. It was only through the responses of the common people in Eastern Europe and the erstwhile Soviet Union and the outcome in elections in several developed countries in the late 1980s in favour of parties advocating liberalization policies that it was realized that policies and advocacy of market-friendly economic models are not incompatible with political support.

A view repeatedly expressed in India is that reform of the public sector is the only viable, desirable and acceptable policy. Several arguments are put forward to support this theory:

1   In the matter of efficiency it is not ownership but competition which is relevant. If, therefore, competition can be injected, it will not be necessary to take recourse to privatization through divestiture.
2   The PSUs are natural monopolies or are producing public goods or are located in strategic sectors. Privatization may not be feasible in these areas.
3   Many public enterprises are efficiently operated in terms both of internal rate of return or international competitiveness. In many cases enhancement of efficiency is feasible and can be secured by restructuring. Ownership transfer may either not be needed or may in fact be counter-productive.
4   The public sector has pervasive interlocking relationships between growth rates and capital formation.
5   While the public sector has the tendency of overmanning, privatization will generate unemployment.
6   PSUs are instruments for achieving social goals. Dismantling these will call for alternative tools which may be less cost-effective.

Many of these perceptions are fallacies or myths born out of the mindset which has evolved during the four decades of economic strategy in India. Seeds of new ideas have, however, been sown. Full germination will take two to three years.

Successful public enterprises

There are a few successful PSUs. The government might find it politically counterproductive to divest them in the near future, except by way of 'minority' divestiture of equity or induction of fresh capital through the market. Some of these companies are not only doing financially well, they have been growth-oriented; they are absorbers of advanced technologies and they are professionally managed. One of the best examples is the growth-oriented Indian Petrochemicals Corporation Ltd (IPCL) The international journal of the industry, *Chemical Insight*, London, has rated IPCL as the 'World's Best Performing Petrochemical Company'.

Hybrid and successful organizations

Privatization has relevance to the institutional framework of the enterprises. In India, two institutional variations (hybrid structures) have made some inroads: the joint sector and the co-operatives.

The joint sector has been limited mainly to the state government level. The pattern took the form of 26:25:49 sharing in equity capital. The controlling interest of 51 per cent is shared between the state government (26 per cent) and the private promoter (25 per cent). The balance of 49 per cent equity is offered to the public. The titular Chairman of the company is nominated by the government and the Chief Executive Officer (CEO) or Managing Director by the private promoter. A large number of medium and large industrial undertakings have been promoted on this basis. Many of them have succeeded very well; but some have failed miserably.

Similarly, some industrial and agro-based units have been organized as co-operatives. The constitution is hybrid. They are basically sponsored by the government but some part of the capital has been contributed by farmers, cattle owners or by co-operative societies or banks. Most of these are working successfully. Some are quoted on the stock exchanges and have operated mainly as private companies with remote state control through the appointment of the CEO. The normal motivations for privatization are absent or subdued in these cases.

Expansion of the public sector

While the ambience in favour of privatization is building up, the public sector is also going in for substantial expansion: for example, the National Thermal Power Corporation (NTPC), the Indian Oil Corporation (IOC) and the Indian Petrochemicals Corporation (IPCL). Its causes could be viewed as constraints on privatization. The plan capital expenditure of the order of Rs 163 billion has been incurred annually during the last three years and a similar magnitude is anticipated during the current year. In the banking sector, the government had released Rs 7,000 million at the end of March 1992 as its contribution to the equity capital of a select group of nine nationalized banks, as per the recommendation of the Narasimhan Committee on financial reforms, for strengthening the capital base of the public sector banks actuated by the stricter capital adequacy norms now being introduced worldwide. (The Basle Agreement requires that the capital and own funds ratio to the risk weighted assets should be 8 per cent.) At the same time, the World Bank has called for regulation and supervision standards in conformity with those in vogue in the developed countries and has advocated the unimpeded entry of new private institutions, both domestic and foreign, into the financial sector besides permitting the existing banks to expand freely.

The government does not seem to be in favour of denationalization of the banking sector. On the other hand, if the liberalization programme and privatization have to succeed, the banking system and, in fact, the whole financial sector will have to be restructured and reformed. The most critical aspect of all the reforms is the operating efficiency. An expanded private sector and especially the transnationals will not be able or willing to function in the present financial environment.

As of 1992, with the restrictions placed on budgetary financing of the public sector and the rise in cost of long-term funding, the development financial institutions are short of funds and the cost of capital has shot up to extremely high levels. Privatization will make heavy drafts on available capital resources. What was needed by the entire industry a decade ago will not suffice only half a dozen large industrial or infrastructural projects in the private sector. Moreover, the funds will have to be provided at internationally competitive rates.

Constraints on incremental privatization

In the case of large incremental privatization ventures, the two major constraints are:

1 government controls in respect of certain parameters such as pricing and return on investment; and
2 the need for supplementing private sector capital resources through governmental financing routes.

Typical of the problems under 1 is the linkage of the proposed power generating plants with the existing transmission and distribution systems. At what rates will the power generated be supplied to the distribution network which remains, at least for the time being, the monopoly of the State Electricity Boards' supply system? Another major problem is the financial relationship between the two. The public sector generating systems like NTPC and NHPC and equipment supply organization like Bharat Heavy Electricals Ltd have failed to realize the dues from the State Electricity Boards. Being public sector organizations they could somehow manage; but it will be impossible for the private sector to work under such conditions. When these are owned wholly or jointly by foreign investors, the problems will become more complicated – even in legal terms.

Captive units

The World Bank wanted partial privatization of the railway manufacturing units as a pre-condition to approving $300 million credit for the import of rails, special steel, wheels and axles and other components. Discussions with the railways on the proposed loan listed stringent conditionalities which are contrary to the railway policies. The team wanted the railways to float a global tender and even the Chittaranjan and Varanasi units (producing diesel and electrical locos) would have to face international competition. It is understood that it was decided not to pursue the loan. The railways have, nonetheless, proposed privatization of certain services. It includes schemes like 'own your wagon' and 'own your container'.

Structural constraints

Some of the public sector corporations are chartered under Acts of Parliament and have not been converted into companies with share capital, for example, Air India, India's international airline, and Indian Airlines, the domestic carrier. Partial divestiture in such cases can take place only after their conversion into joint stock companies. This will require repeal or amendment of the Act which, when moved in the Parliament, will meet with some opposition.

Pre-divestiture preparation

The government would, no doubt, in larger public interest, like to collect the best divestiture price. The enterprises whose profits are declining will fetch very low prices. An improvement is possible if the operational efficiency of the viable units can be improved. This will call for special management action plans.

Opposition from vested interests

The most effective constraints on privatization emerge from three sources: political interest groups, economists and social analysts, and workers and trade unions. The political opposition has been fairly vocal especially from the leftist parties. The present government, although in minority, is capable of handling the situation with dexterity if the workers' opposition is not so vocal.

The bureaucracy in India generally follows the political leadership. However, it has been noted with a certain amount of concern that the bureaucracy, perhaps owing to vested interests (enjoying the fruits of power and position), has placed impediments to the declared and undeclared policies.

Economic and social analysts leaned in the past on the public sector; but there is a perceptible change. A large section has shifted towards the privatization lobby, although not wholly so.

An attempt was made to measure the effect of reduction in public sector investment on total GDP growth based on a model with some 83 variables. It concluded that a crowding-out effect in public sector investment will cause a negative impact on GDP growth.[1] This is a matter basically of the hypotheses. It is difficult to comprehend that sectoral shift alone would cause such an effect. This would happen only if it is assumed either that the activities which support or stimulate investment will go by default in the absence of PS investment or that the private sector does not or will not have the capacity to make the investment in substitute areas. Now that the government has decided on incremental privatization even in infrastructural areas and is permitting the inflow of DFI at a substantially higher rate, the negative effect should be more than neutralized. The experience of the Asia-Pacific region provides ample evidence to that effect.

The workers have been very vocal and are putting up a hard fight to prevent privatization gaining any momentum. Apparently, they have succeeded so far. They rightly fear loss of jobs, while there already exists a colossal amount of unemployment in the country. Many have become used to receiving wages without doing commensurate work. They find it a great deal more difficult to deal with private employers. They have, therefore, a deep vested interest in the continuation of the public enterprise.

The workers have already gone on two major nation-wide strikes to demonstrate their opposition to the liberalization policies in general and privatization in particular. The first national convention of the representatives of public sector officers' associations resolved in a conference to oppose the policy of divestiture of PSUs. The executives of the PSU General Insurance Corporation (GIC) and its subsidiaries feels that adopting 'the culture of private sector and commercial working can be their best bet against privatization'! But in doing so they find themselves stifled by the 'non-decisive attitude of the higher management'. 'We want', they claim, 'to provide better service to the customers so that the public gets complete satisfaction by dealing with the insurance companies working under the control of GIC.'

The employees of Maruti Udyog threatened to go on a one-day strike when Suzuki Motor Company (the Japanese collaborator) was expected to sign the agreement for raising its stake in the company from 40 to 50 per cent. The increase has, nonetheless, been effected.

The privatization of the UP Cement Corporation, contracted between the UP State Government and the Dalmias, a private business house, had to be reversed by a government decree when it was found by the newly installed government in the state that the workers would not permit the takeover. The agitation by the workers and the subsequent police action had resulted in several deaths. This case was, perhaps, a red signal to the Government of India that it might not be easy to mount a bold programme of privatization in the near future.

Table 15.5 Chronically sick CPUs, end March 1991

	Equity (Rs mn)	Loans (Rs mn)	Accumulated losses (Rs mn)	Coefficient of loss to equity	Coefficient of loss to total investment
Bengal Chemicals & Pharmaceuticals Ltd	128	326	597	4.7	1.3
Bengal Immunity Ltd	157	166	340	2.2	1.1
Bharat Brakes & Valves Ltd	39	119	162	4.2	1.0
Bharat Gold Mines Ltd	378	621	767	2.0	0.8
Bharat Ophthalmic Glass Ltd	67	286	665	9.9	1.9
Bharat Process & Mechanical Engineers Ltd	49	231	419	8.6	1.5
Bharat Pumps & Compressors Ltd	227	364	649	2.9	1.1
Bharat Refractories Ltd	463	597	525	1.1	0.5
Biecco Lawrie Ltd	20	306	460	23.0	1.4
Birds, Jute & Exports Ltd	4	34	59	4.8	1.6
Braithwaite & Co. Ltd	167	482	445	2.7	0.7
British India Corpn Ltd	429	773	775	1.8	0.7
Cawnpore Textiles Ltd	6	162	221	36.8	1.3
Central Electronics Ltd	176	157	195	1.1	0.6
Central Inland Water Transport Corpn	800	746	1,904	2.4	1.2
Cochin Shipyard Ltd	744	968	1,661	2.2	1.0
Cycle Corporation of India Ltd	119	681	1,266	10.6	1.6
Elgin Mills Company Ltd	11	878	1,704	155.0	1.9
Fertilizer Corpn of India Ltd	6,164	6,167	13,854	2.2	1.1
Heavy Engineering Corpn Ltd	2,075	2,550	2,895	1.4	0.6
Hindustan Fertilizer Corpn Ltd	6,692	8,440	11,811	1.8	0.8
Hindustan Shipyard Ltd	674	1,370	3,516	5.2	1.7
Hooghly Dock & Port Engineers Ltd	119	126	214	1.8	0.9
Indian Drugs & Pharmaceuticals Ltd	1,119	1,786	4,341	3.9	1.9
Indian Iron & Steel Company Ltd	3,863	7,230	7,353	1.9	0.7

Enterprise					
Intelligent Communications System Ltd	6	–	6	1.0	1.0
Maharashtra Antibiotics & Pharmaceuticals Ltd	12	26	66	5.5	1.7
Mandya National Paper Mills Ltd	178	306	552	3.1	1.1
Mining & Allied Machinery Co. Ltd	365	500	966	2.6	1.1
Nagaland Pulp & Paper Co. Ltd	484	714	1,806	3.7	1.5
National Bicycle Corpn of India Ltd	57	345	492	8.6	1.2
National Instruments Ltd	57	305	468	8.2	1.3
National Jute Manufacturers Co. Ltd	548	3,688	4,787	8.7	1.1
National Seeds Corpn Ltd	201	136	245	1.2	0.7
North Eastern Regional Agricultural Mktg Corpn Ltd	24	28	40	1.7	0.7
NTC (A.P, Karnataka, Kerala, & Mahe) Ltd	527	1,546	1,524	2.9	0.7
NTC (Gujarat) Ltd	248	1,850	1,975	7.8	0.9
NTC (Madhya Pradesh) Ltd	336	1,827	2,346	7.0	1.1
NTC (Maharashtra North) Ltd	561	2,043	2,364	4.2	0.9
NTC (South Maharashtra) Ltd	452	2,485	1,758	3.9	0.6
NTC (Uttar Pradesh) Ltd	372	2,151	2,321	6.2	0.9
NTC (W.B., Assam, Bihar & Orissa) Ltd	448	2,982	3,257	7.3	0.9
Orissa Drugs & Pharmaceuticals Ltd	5	9	18	3.6	1.3
Rehabilitation Industries Ltd	48	478	1,240	25.8	2.4
Richardson & Cruddas (1972) Ltd	169	434	550	3.3	0.9
Scooters India Ltd	78	1,089	2,607	33.4	2.2
Smith Stanistreet & Pharmaceuticals Ltd	60	85	193	3.2	1.3
Southern Pesticides Corpn Ltd	34	84	79	2.3	0.7
Tannery & Footwear Corpn Ltd	150	509	1,207	8.1	1.8
Triveni Structurals Ltd	95	201	223	2.3	0.7
Tyre Corporation of India Ltd	507	450	702	1.4	0.8
U.P. Drugs & Pharmaceuticals Ltd	9	1	73	8.1	7.3
Vignyan Industries Ltd	5	28	76	15.2	2.4
Weighbird (India) Ltd	3	56	83	27.7	1.4
	30,729	59,922	88,822	2.9	1.0

Source: Annual Report: Department of Public Enterprises 1991–2, *Public Enterprises Survey 1990–1*, Vol. 3

Chronically sick undertakings

Some 58 CPUs and a much larger number of SPUs have been identified as sick and unviable. The government is very keen to sell or liquidate them. The total capital invested in CPUs alone aggregates to some Rs 90 billion, a third of which is in equity (see Table 15.5). They have accumulated losses of Rs 89 billion – wiping out not only the equity but also the loan capital. The coefficient of loss to equity is 2.9. In other words, the equity has been wiped out three times over. (An escape route has been found through a reference of some 30 units to the Board for Industrial and Financial Reconstruction [BIFR].) They employ over 300,000 persons. No one really knows how to deal with them.

The national renewal fund

The answer to the workers' opposition lies first in an intensive education programme, and second in a golden handshake. (The latter is being attempted as a major plank of the privatization programme.)

A National Renewal Fund (NRF) has been created. Among other things, it will finance retraining and redeployment programmes for industrial workers who might lose their jobs due to closure or modernization of sick units. The fund has a total kitty of Rs 22 billion in one year. Apart from the budgetary provision of Rs 2 billion to the corpus of the fund, Rs 10 billion is to be transferred from the divestiture of public sector equity. Another Rs 10 billion will come from recycling of the past World Bank loans amounting to $ 400 million.

The NRF includes an Insurance Fund which would provide a security net to take care of problems arising out of sickness in industries in the future. The government, the industry and the workers would make contributions to the fund and it is expected to replace the NRF over a period of five to seven years.

IMPACTS OF PRIVATIZATION

A number of variables determine the effects of privatization: the size and matrix complexity of the economic structure; the positioning and the penetration of the PSUs; the flexibility (or inflexibility) of the planning system; and the modalities and tools of privatization. Because of the divergent factor compositions, no uniformly applicable model of effects can be developed.

In the current Indian scenario, as perhaps in most developing economies, the impacts could be classified into three major modules:

1   fiscal and financial;
2   economic and technological; and
3   social.

There will be significant political impacts but these are excluded from the present discussion. The fiscal-financial impacts will be related to the size of government expenditures (both investment and current), deficit financing, BoP position, aid disbursals and absorptive capacity and flows of DFI. The economic and technological impacts include overall growth, technology assimilation, productivity, and rates of inflation. The social impacts cover distribution effects, effect on employment, expenditure on social services and consequential changes in Human Development Index (HDI).

International experience shows that the nature of impacts has to be assessed *vis-à-vis* the short term, the medium term and the long term. Each of the phases is significant to a developing economy and, accordingly, it is necessary to evaluate them during different time spans. Based on this analysis, the matrix shown in Table 15.6 is valid for India (and similarly placed economic models).

Effect on fiscal balance

Privatization is anticipated to be a major aid in bringing about the much-needed fiscal balance. The public sector has been a net dissaver in the past. The process of direct and incremental privatization will substantially reduce budgetary flows to the public sector. The fiscal deficit will be reduced in six principal ways:

1 restricted incremental investment in production and marketing activity;
2 greater dependence of the existing PSUs on their own resources (generated internally or raised externally);

Table 15.6 Impacts of privatization

Parameter	Short-term	Medium-term	Long-term
A. *Fiscal/Financial*			
1. State's propensity to invest	L	L	N
2. State's capacity to spend	L	S	H
3. Deficit financing	H	B	N
4. BoP	N	B	P
5. Flow of DFI	L	B	H
B. *Economic/Technological*			
1. Growth	N	H	Hv
2. Technology assimilation and development	L	H	Hv
3. Productivity	L	H	Hv
4. Inflation	H	L	L
C. *Social*			
1. Distributional impacts	S	N	N
2. Employment	L	S	H
3. Social services expenditure	L	H	Hv
4. HDI	L	H	Hv

L: Low   B: Balanced   H: High   S: Same   N: Negative   Hv: Very high   P: Positive

3   raising new capital required by PSUs from the stock market thereby diluting the government share;

4   divestiture programme (unloading of equity);

5   cessation of spoon feeding of sick and closed PSUs; and

6   higher profitability (due to induction of competition or, at any rate, better dividend policy) which will be necessary to satisfy non-governmental investors.

In the first partial divestiture exercise of 1991–2, the total equity of the PSUs involved was of the order of Rs 106.0 billion. The (book) net asset value (NAV) of these undertakings is placed at approximately Rs 190.0 billion. The total amount of equity parted is of the order of Rs 8.7 billion, constituting about 8 per cent of the total equity. The (book) NAV does not take into account the appreciated value of the assets. The assets of the undertakings have been built over a long period. The historical value, therefore, is a gross underestimate of the NAV. Many of these PSUs own vast areas of land, some of which are marketable, though some are not. The plant and equipment has been depreciated in many cases to a very low level.

Considering the price escalation and adjusting for obsolesence of technology and wear and tear of the equipment, a quotient of 3 should be considered a conservative estimate. Based on this, the value of unloaded shares may be computed as follows:

$$
\begin{aligned}
\text{NAV} &= 190.0 \text{ b} \\
\text{GAV} &= 323.2 \text{ b} \\
\text{MAV (GAV} \times 3.0) &= 969.6 \text{ b} \\
\text{NAV}_r &= 836.4 \text{ b} \\
\text{(MAV--GAV} + \text{NAV)} & \\
\text{Total Equity} &= 105.9 \text{ b} \\
\text{Divested Equity} &= 8.7 \text{ b} \\
\text{Nav}_r \text{ of Divested Capital} &= 68.7 \text{ b} \\
\text{(NAV} \times 8.7\ /\ 105.9)
\end{aligned}
$$

Where NAV is net asset value of the PSUs of which a part of the capital stock has been divested; GAV is the gross asset value; MAV is market asset value; and NAV_r is revised net asset value; b = Rs billion (see Table 15.7).

The computed market value of Rs 68.7 billion of the divested capital stock compares with Rs 30.3 billion realized by the government – a possible under-realization of about Rs 40 billion. (Incidentally, it is now revealed that at least one bank had sold two lots of shares at 50 per cent higher prices – even before it was permitted to resell.) If the Steel Authority of India (SAIL) shares are any benchmark, the price differential should be of the order of several times. It is understood that SAIL shares netted an average price of around Rs 11 and are now listed on the Bombay Stock Exchange with a quotation of Rs 180. This price, however, is an obvious exaggeration.

Table 15.7 Financial indicators of disinvested PSUs with partial divestiture

PSU	Equity capital (Rs mn)	Net worth (RS mn)	Gross asset (Rs mn)	Net profit (after tax) (Rs mn)	LT interest (Rs mn)	Disinvestment equity (Rs mn)	NAVd* (Rs mn)	YVd** (Rs mn)
Petroleum								
Hindustan Petroleum Corpn	638	7,816	14,251	1,201	394	20.0	1,568	2,010
Bharat Petroleum Corpn	500	6,640	12,663	1,278	322	20.0	1,328	2,130
Madras Refineries	2,225	2,611	4,071	506	285	20.0	522	846
Bongaigaon Refineries	1,998	3,360	4,053	485	42	20.0	673	800
Cochin Refineries	689	2,518	3,947	608	140	10.0	252	511
Fertilizers								
National Fertilizers	4,906	7,092	12,790	297	444	2.28	162	56
Fertilizers & Chemicals	3,428	3,898	5,893	236	160	1.54	60	32
Rashtriya Chemicals & Fertilizers	5,517	8,786	12,334	408	281	5.64	495	187
Chemicals & pharmaceuticals								
Indian Petrochemicals Corpn	1,860	6,925	14,318	573	1,635	20.0	1,385	967
Hindustan Organic Chemicals	433	1,706	1,982	320	43	20.0	343	539
Engineering								
Bharat Heavy Electricals	2,448	8,368	13,167	369	1,061	20.0	1,675	637
Hindustan Machine Tools	651	2,453	3,674	141	332	5.4	132	63
Andrew Yule	109	425	943	52	57	13.6	58	60
Indian Telephone Industries	880	2,734	4,880	361	860	20.0	547	598
Bharat Electronics	800	2,556	4,143	343	314	20.0	511	576
Hindustan Cables	458	1,226	2,088	23	210	3.6	43	6
Bharat Earthmovers	297	3,497	3,164	461	446	20.0	695	761
Minerals and metals								
Hindustan Zinc	4,037	6,143	5,673	841	35	20.0	1,228	1,372
National Aluminium Corpn	12,886	14,157	30,880	719	1,800	2.7	382	174
Neyveli Lignite Corpn	14,358	19,802	22,360	952	1,553	5.0	990	431

Table 15.7 continued

PSU	Equity capital (Rs mn)	Net worth (RS mn)	Gross asset (Rs mn)	Net profit (after tax) (Rs mn)	LT interest (Rs mn)	Disinvestment equity (Rs mn)	NAVd* (Rs mn)	YVd** (Rs mn)
Trading and marketing								
State Trading Corpn	86	3,288	416	213	9	8.0	268	157
Minerals & Metals Trading Corpn	324	3,500	265	773	771	0.7	32	60
Computer Maintenance Corpn	152	166	452	−68	26	16.7	27	–
Transportation services								
Shipping Corpn	2,612	5,625	21,223	953	734	20.0	1,124	1,566
Dredging Corpn	280	1,056	1,880	148	34	1.4	15	18
Telecommunication								
Mahanagar Telephone Nigam	6,000	10,209	22,352	958	688	20.0	2,041	1,560
Videsh Sanchar Nigam	600	3,452	1,855	786	0	20.0	690	1,308
Steel								
Steel Authority of India	35,457	46,756	96,100	2,447	4,130	5.0	2,338	1,064
Construction								
Indian Rail Construction	50	1,845	980	90	46	0.3	6	2
Consumer goods								
Hindustan Photofilms Ltd	1,195	1,415	383	20	3	16.1	226	19
Total	105,874	190,025	323,180	16,512	16,855		19,816	18,510

*NAVd: Net asset value of disinvested capital.
**YVd: Yield value of disinvested capital.
Source: Annual Report, Department of Public Enterprises, 1990–1

The $p-e$ (price–earning) ratios of companies in India have been rising. Even accepting the recent boom period, several well-known companies with high prospects showed $p-es$ exceeding 20 (e.g. Bombay Dyeing 27, Century Textiles 22, Indian Rayon 40, Tata Steel 36). There are many companies with very low ratios. Providing for low profitability of the package of PSUs divested and the fact that they have intrinsic deficiencies of high capitalization and high manpower deployment, a $p-e$ of 4 to 5 should be considered modest. Taking the lower multiplier we get a value of Rs 72 billion – very close to the one shown by our NAV-based computation. It could be concluded *prima facie*, subject to more detailed computations, that, if the divestiture operation were conducted more effectively, the government could have netted an additional amount of about Rs 40 billion (± 20 per cent).

By the same token, the proposed programme during the current fiscal year (1992–3), placed at Rs 35 billion, could be made to realize somewhere near Rs 70 billion with the same amount of equity unloading as was contemplated under that programme.

The additional amount, if raised, would offer substantial relief to the budgetary position, reducing the budgetary and fiscal deficits further. It would reduce the budgetary deficit by about 30 per cent. This would also help in slashing the fiscal deficit which has become a critical point in the IMF dispensation in meeting the balance of payments crisis. If a part of this is utilized for the revival or closure of sick units, the privatization process could be accelerated.

Productivity of capital

PSU-sponsored projects have to pass through cumbersome and multi-station administrative procedures of planning approval and implementation. Privatization can contribute to higher capital efficiency as a result of the reduction in gestation and lactation periods. This presupposes dismantling of the regulatory system which survives perceptibly even after the announcement of the reforms package. Privatization could also yield better utilization of 'sunk investments'. (The classic example which comes to attention here is the Haldia Fertilizer project in which, over a period of 10 years, an investment of the order of Rs 6 billion has been made but which has not been fully commissioned.) There are many such cases which call for a quick and bold decision in the direction of privatization. Against the original investments, there will no doubt be an accounting loss; but this will yield real gains when idle assets are made productive.

Changed dividend policy

A major benefit which will flow from the divestiture programmes is the altered dividend policy. In the past, the PSUs have been paying paltry dividends on the massive equity investment by the state and central governments. Once the shares are widely dispered among a large number of investors, domestic and foreign, the PSUs will be bound to pursue a reasonable dividend policy. This will benefit the state exchequer.

Competition with private capital market

One of the major effects of the privatization programme – both direct and incremental – will be in the form of draft it makes on the private capital market funds. This will take place in three ways:

1 *Direct divestiture*: Rs 30 billion have already gone from the mutual funds and financial institutions in 1991–2, a part of which will be unloaded to private investors, individual and corporate.
2 *Non-availability of budgetary support*: The new structural adjustment policy has stopped or reduced the support to PSUs for expansion, diversification or modernization and rehabilitation programmes. Several of the PSUs will now issue equity shares or bonds to fill in the gap.
3 *Incremental privatization*: Several activities which were reserved for the public sector have been thrown open for private enterprise, such as the power sector. Large funds which were being made available by the government will need to be fully or partially financed from the common public market.

Except in the first case, the additional load on the private capital market will be in terms of opportunity cost. It is, therefore, not possible to quantify the additional load.

The magnitude of the draft under the three foregoing streams on the private capital market may be of the order of Rs 100 to Rs 150 billion per year over the next five years. The dimensions are quite large considering the generation of funds in the capital market in the past. There will be a considerable amount of competition for the investible funds leading to selectivity by the investors and higher cost of capital.

Economic growth

India has the capacity to push up its growth rate from the 5.6 per cent of the 1980s (and around 3 per cent in the crisis period of 1990 and 1991) steadily to between 8 and 10 per cent in a period of five to seven years. It presupposes, however, the political sustainability of the present reform programme and, in particular, reliance on privatization, direct and incremental, supported by an expanded flow of DFI.

It could create greater income disparities in the short term. Likewise the privatization programme will generate some immediate unemployment, particularly in the affected segments. The overall impact on the employment situation will be positive in the medium term and certainly in the long term with expanded investment and higher GDP generation, which is expected from an increase in economic activity.

Technology flows

The privatization programme is very likely to generate greater induction and lesser development of technology. The behaviour of the public and private sectors in their historical perspective provides such signals; and the recent attitudinal behaviour of the north reinforces this. With an increase in the inflow of DFI, there will also be increased inflow of technology into India. But because of the control of the high technology remaining with the transnational corporations, there will be a tendency on their part to be secretive of the technologies deployed. This, coupled with the low propensity of private enterprises to develop technology – relative to the public enterprises – might not accelerate the process of technology development.

Effects on structural adjustment policies

Privatization has been a common component of the structural reform programmes. The structural adjustment policies have four major components, besides privatization, leading to a shift from the public to the private sector: fiscal reform; improvement in external BoP; deplanning and deregulation; and import liberalization.

The principal manifestation of the economic set-back in the late 1980s, it may be recalled, was in the form of deterioration in the external payments position leading to an erosion of foreign exchange reserves to a critical level. The genesis of this was attributed to the fiscal imbalances visible in the form of budgetary and fiscal deficits. Privatization is an integral part of this reform and reciprocally it will help realization of the goals of the economic reform programme.

Distribution effects

While privatization will accelerate growth, it will, in the short (and medium) term produce adverse distribution effects. The public sector production and disbursement of disposable incomes has had a positive effect, in that profits, howsoever meagre, were not flowing to the high-income brackets. The overmanning of enterprises generated an extra flow of incomes to the wage-earning class. The generation of loss paradoxically benefited the lower-income groups. This, however, was illusory to a large extent; additional generation of value-added would have positive distribution effects in the long run.

CONCLUSION

The public sector in India has attained large dimensions over the last four decades. The dimensions have been disproportionate to an optimal mixed economy model which has been adopted and nurtured by the planners. The privatization programme, if designed rationally and pursued efficiently and effectively, can produce highly salutary macro- and micro-level fiscal, financial, economic and social effects. It will broadbase entrepreneurial and capital resources, generate higher returns and stimulate DFI flows. It will generate unemployment in the short run but larger employment over the long term. It will take some time before positive effects are visible. Patience and perseverance seem to be the prerequisites for the realization of the desired goals. The appendix illustrates the complexity of governmental decision making in respect of privatization.

APPENDIX

The chronology of Indian privatization policies in action since July 1991

1991

July

The government is considering foreign investment proposals even beyond the 51 per cent prescribed limit in the industrial policy. Multi-nationals could have even 100 per cent participation in wholly export-oriented units.

August

The government is planning to appoint a committee for valuation of shares of public sector undertakings, which are to be offered to mutual funds and investment institutions.

The government has decided with immediate effect to give automatic clearance to foreign equity investment proposals up to 51 per cent.

Private sector companies setting up power plants, hitherto not permitted to set up such plants, will be allowed to import power equipment on the condition that such imports are financed through external assistance on concessional terms.

The Finance Minister has stated that the government has no intention to privatize nationalized banks.

September

The Finance Ministry is considering various options for part privatization of banks. These include the offer of equity to employees, partial disinvestment to mutual funds and cross-holding of equity through major public sector organizations.

Perpetually sick public sector fertilizer units will be dismantled and new units allowed to be built up by the private sector using the infrastructure available at the site.

October

Trade unions react strongly to the statement by the Union Finance Minister that sick PS units would be closed down. The World Bank promises assistance for creating a social safety net.

Future expansion of port berthing facilities will be thrown open to the private sector including foreign multi-nationals. Sick indigenous shipyards will be permitted to diversify into ship repairing in collaboration with foreign companies.

Following direction from the Finance Ministry, the Industry Ministry is to undertake an exercise to prune workforce of the public sector enterprises.

November

The Coal Ministry is considering selling ailing coal mines to the private sector. New mines will be allowed to be acquired by the private sector.

The AP State Government decides to sell four sick sugar units in the co-operative sector to private entrepreneurs.

The government withholds its decision to privatize six mills of the National Jute Manufacturers Corporation.

The Indian Railways is considering private sector participation in the manufacture of coaches, wheels and axle sets as well as ownership of wagons by user industries.

The World Bank asks for postponement of new public investment involving unsourced foreign exchange.

Private participation in the power sector is put off until a special task force in the Power Ministry submits findings on a two-part tariff structure.

The government identifies eight chronically sick units for reference to BIFR (Board of Industrial and Financial Reconstruction).

The Prime Minister indicates that no additional outlay for the public sector during the Eighth Plan will be permitted.

The government's divestiture in select public sector units is likely to begin next month. About 150 packets with a minimum floor price of Rs 100 million each will be put on auction to garner about Rs 15 billion.

The government identifies 58 chronically sick public sector enterprises with a total capital investment of Rs 30 billion and negative net worth of over Rs 26 billion.

The railways starts leasing its surplus land to private parties to raise resources for infrastructural development.

The government introduces a new bill to empower BIFR to deal with sick public sector units with a view to winding up or rehabilitating them.

The World Bank offers $ 500 million for the proposed National Renewal Fund to help evolve an exit policy for preventing industrial sickness.

The Union Cabinet approves the divestiture of government equity in 31 PSUs.

December

The Finance Ministry directs the mutual funds to submit their bids for acquiring shares of public sector units by 20 December.

A tripartite MoU is signed between the Orissa Government, the State Electricity Board and the US-based Southern Electric International Company for setting up of a 1,940 MW capacity thermal plant in Orissa at an expected cost of Rs 60 billion.

The National Textile Corporation mills are allowed to sell surplus assets to augment resources for revival.

1992

January

The government issues procedures for approval of foreign equity holding up to 51 per cent primarily in industries engaged in export activities.

The 58 public sector sick units identified as sick and in need of immediate restructuring are likely to receive priority when the proposed National Renewal Fund is set up.

The government is formulating a scheme to allow foreign companies to increase their equity stake to 51 per cent at a price lower than that prevailing in the market.

March

The Finance Minister has agreed to provide to the public sector National Textile Corporation a sum of Rs 5.5 billion for a voluntary retirement scheme.

The government is weighing the option of pumping in Rs 25 billion to rehabilitate 58 chronically sick PSUs as against investing the same amount in new units to generate 1.5 million new employment opportunities.

April

In order to professionalize the PSUs and reduce bureaucratic interference, the Boards of Directors of several PSUs are being restructured.

The government has made it mandatory that all sick PSUs be referred to the BIFR if they fall into the criteria laid down in the Sick Industrial Companies Act.

The government has decided to allow up to 49 per cent foreign equity in the PSUs to finance technology upgradation and expansion programmes where considered necessary.

May

The National Renewal Fund is set up with an initial corpus of Rs 2 billion to provide security to the labour force in both public and private sectors.

The proposal to disinvest 50 per cent of the government's stake in term lending institutions over a period of three years is cleared by the Finance Ministry.

The government allowed listing of shares of PSUs so that mutual funds could unload them in the open market. About 78 public sector units have approached the Bombay Stock Exchange for listing.

The government will encourage private sector participation in coal washeries and coal mines for power generation. The Coal Mines (Nationalization) Act is being amended to facilitate private sector entry.

The ailing National Textile Corporation with Rs 2.2 billion of loss in 1991–2 is attempting to privatize the more profitable subsidiaries.

The government takes a policy decision against expansion of public sector units, exceptions notwithstanding, to reduce the size of its bureaucracy and PSU operations.

The government will close down unviable public sector enterprises and will disinvest up to 49 per cent equity of select blue chip PSUs.

The West Bengal Committee of Centre of Indian Trade Unions submits a detailed study on 17 sick central PSUs in the state along with proposals to revive them.

Unilateral action in regard to closure of 58 chronically sick PSUs is ruled out. BIFR might be involved to explore revival.

UP Government has decided to seek private participation to set up hydel units to augment power generation.

June

The Indian power sector gets proposals from foreign companies worth $ 6.7 billion.

The government proposes to open mineral exploration and exploitation (non-fuel and non-atomic) to foreign companies.

Tamil Nadu Government receives offers for 1,800 MW power project valued at Rs 35 billion in the private sector from NRIs in the United States, Singapore and Malaysia, apart from some other foreign parties.

Inspite of trade union opposition to the privatization of the public sector, the government goes ahead with its decision to sell shares of profitable public sector undertakings to raise budgetary resources.

The government is working out a compensation package for retrenchment of surplus workers of unviable sick units.

Assistance to Heavy Engineering Corporation, a continuously loss-making but prestigious PSU, is slashed from Rs 140 million to Rs 30 million.

The National Textile Corporation may have to close at least 15 of its 100 or so mills due to mounting losses since the government is not keen to give any further financial assistance.

The government has recently approved a Letter of Intent to set up a 9 million-ton capacity refinery in the west coast by Reliance Industries Limited with equity participation of a consortium of C-Itoh of Japan.

July

The government is considering allowing private companies, Indian and foreign, to own pipelines for crude oil and petroleum products.

The All India Industrial Finance Corporation Employees Association has threatened a country-wide agitation if the government goes ahead with its 'ill-advised path of privatization'.

The government decides to use a part of the proceeds from public sector disinvestment to provide equity to entrepreneurs who have set up enterprises in backward areas.

The 'own your own wagon' scheme of the railways, its first attempt at privatization, has evoked a none-too-encouraging response.

The nationalized commercial banks order an immediate suspension of credit facilities to sick PSUs.

The government has allowed private and foreign investment in three refineries and in the development of a few discovered oilfields. Foreign or private equity to the tune of 26 per cent will be allowed in the case of refineries.

August

The government has hinted at the possibility of allowing public sector banks to tap equity capital from the market without, however, giving up control over them.

The Indian Petrochemicals Corporation Limited (IPCL) is slated to be the first PSU to invite direct equity participation from the public.

The Government of Karnataka has signed MoUs for setting up seven power projects in the state (five thermal and two hydel) envisaging cumulative generating capacity of 2,838 MW at an estimated cost of about Rs 60 billion.

The government approves a turnaround programme of two ailing NTC undertakings with an investment of Rs 5.3 billion. A significant feature is the creation of a rehabilitation fund of Rs 500 million for retraining and redeploying employees by setting up small units of powerlooms.

The Prime Minister assures the Parliament that the opposition would be consulted on any further sale of shares of public sector units.

The Cabinet Committee on Foreign Investment (CCFI) has approved two power projects costing over Rs 30 billion with majority foreign participation. This is the first time foreign companies will be participating in the power projects in the country.

The government will open up the highly sensitive nuclear power sector to private participation. Both nuclear power generation and industries based on spin-off nuclear technologies will be open for private investment to ward off the resource crunch plaguing the core sector.

The government may allow public sector banks to raise fresh equity from the market without diluting its control over their functioning.

NOTES

1   Kalyan Raipuria and Rajesh Mehta (1991) 'Public and Private Sectors: Macro-Economic Model Simulation', in S.R. Mohnot (ed.) *Privatisation: Options and Challenges*, New Delhi: Centre for Industrial and Economic Research.

16

PUBLIC ENTERPRISE POLICY AND THE MOUs IN INDIA

Suresh Kumar

INTRODUCTION

The important role played by the public sector in many developing and even developed countries cannot be doubted. It is certainly true of India, where it has indeed attained commanding heights in many crucial areas and has been in the vanguard of the country's variegated development since independence in the late 1940s. The central public enterprise sector, which accounts for almost 10 per cent of the GNP, accounts for 100 per cent of the national production in coal, lignite, petroleum, copper, lead and about 60 per cent of steel. It employs about 2.3 million people. While it plays a key role in the infrastructural sector of the nation's economy, it has also entered many other areas over the past 40 years. With an investment of more than Rs 1 lakh crores (US$ 50 billion) in about 250 central public enterprises, the nation has a right to expect a reasonable performance from it. The judgement on performance is generally based on aggregate return on aggregate investment, which is not necessarily the best way in the case of public enterprises.

Results in terms of aggregates inevitably fail to project the effects of public ownership which may be different in each case.

It may be remembered that public enterprises are instruments of public policy. Their operations should enhance social welfare. Since an increase in financial profitability is neither a necessary nor a sufficient condition for the enhancement of society's well-being, any system of evaluation primarily and solely based on that would be unjust.

A public enterprise has two dimensions, the 'public' dimension, which refers to public purpose or social returns (or social obligations such as generation and protection of employment, which has remained a very important requirement in India) and the 'enterprise' dimension, which refers to the commercial functions of the enterprise, the purely financial returns (i.e. profits). In contrast, a private enterprise has only one dimension, i.e. to maximize financial returns for the enterprise, whose ownership and operation lies largely in a few private hands. Thus the methodology for the evaluation of a public enterprise must necessarily differ from that used for a private enterprise and has to keep in view the

299

comparative importance of the different roles assigned to each.

The evaluation process (or methodology) for a public enterprise cannot be a static one-off affair. It must change with changes in the market position of the enterprise, changes in public expectations from the enterprise and changes in the needs of the country as a whole.

Many committees, commissions and eminent academics who have reviewed the policy of management of public enterprises have emphasized the need for modification and strengthening of the prevailing systems of evaluation through which accountability of public enterprises is enforced. However, not much worthwhile progress has been made in recent decades in the search for a single methodology to evaluate the performance of a public enterprise keeping in view both its 'public' and 'enterprise' dimensions and also considering the 'static' and 'dynamic' effects. This strongly felt need was tackled by the performance contracting system developed in France, refined in countries like South Korea and adopted in India as MOUs (Memoranda of Understanding). This system amounts to a performance evaluation as well as improvement system which can render justice to the enterprises and their management.

PROFIT PERFORMANCE

Let us now look at the performance of public enterprises in India on the basis of conventional data in order to see how we can go wrong. As of 31 March 1990, there were 244 central public sector enterprises (PSEs) owned by the Government of India with a total investment of Rs 993.15 billion (see Table 16.1), 60 per cent of the investment is in the core sector industries. Total profits of these enterprises increased from Rs 11.72 billion in 1985–6 to Rs 37.82 billion in 1989–90 and the percentage of net profit (i.e. profit after depreciation, interest and tax) to capital employed increased from 2.73 per cent to 4.48 per cent, despite an

Table 16.1 Indian central PSEs – overall scenario

	1987–8	1988–9	1989–90
Total no. of PSEs	235	238	244
Total investment (Rs million)	711,230	856,280	993,150
Total net profit (Rs million)	20,300	29,940	37,820
Profit making PSEs	114	118	131
Profit of profit making PSEs (Rs million)	37,750	49,170	57,410
Loss making PSEs	103	106	98
Losses of loss making PSEs (Rs million)	17,450	19,230	19,590
No-profit-no-loss making PSEs (PSEs under construction/PSEs newly formed)	18	14	15

increase of nearly 100 per cent in the quantum of capital employed during this period. While the oil group of enterprises increased their net profits from Rs 16.51 billion in 1985–6 to Rs 29.00 billion in 1989–90, the non-oil group of enterprises showed marked improvement by changing over from net loss of Rs 4.79 billion in 1985–6 to net profit of Rs 8.82 billion in 1989–90.

The disaggregated analysis indicates that during 1989–90, a total of 131 enterprises earned an overall net profit of Rs 57.41 billion and 98 suffered loss of Rs 19.59 billion (see Table 16.1). Further analysis of the 131 profit making public sector enterprises (PSEs) indicates that 84 of them earned a net return of less than 8 per cent (of these 60 earned even less than 5 per cent – see Table 16.2). Analysis of the 98 loss-making PSEs indicates that as many as 77 PSEs fall into the category of competitive market structures with very low social obligations (except protection of employment – see Table 16.3). Of these 77, 40

Table 16.2 Taxonomy of profit making PSEs (131)

Ratio of net profit to capital employed	No. of PSEs 1989–90	Net profit 1989–90 (Rs million)
Above 20%	16	13,160
Between 12% to 20%	15	20,150
Between 8% to 12%	16	4,500
Between 5% to 8%	24	12,560
Below 5%	60	7,040
Total	131	57,410

Table 16.3 Taxonomy of all central PSEs in India

Market structure	Efficiency	Social obligations and externalities	No. of PSEs
Monopoly	High	High	50
Monopoly	High	Low	5
Competitive	High	High	15
Competitive	High	Low	61
Total			131
Monopoly	Low	High	13
Monopoly	Low	Low	2
Competitive	Low	High	6
Competitive	Low	Low	77
Total			98

Note: In the first four categories of profit makers there are implicit loss makers; the last four categories are explicit loss makers.

enterprises have been showing cash loss continuously for the last five years and have a negative net worth and can be thus categorized as chronically sick PSEs (see Table 16.4).

The above analysis shows very poor returns on the aggregate levels, shows some improvement at slightly disaggregated levels, but does not give any 'warning' or 'guidance' to the government (i.e. the owner) or to the manager as to what the strong or weak points of the performance of public enterprises in India are, because the objectives of the enterprises are not a part of evaluation.

For want of a proper evaluation system and methodology there is a uniform mind set about the objectives of all public enterprises. Any evaluation methodology must constantly ask, enterprisewise, whether there is a change in objectives, whether the social obligations have been fully met so as not to be pursued any further and whether there is now a need to vary the focus of the objective of investment in favour of commercial profits.

Instead of tackling the problem in this way the general prescription the world over has been privatization. It is considered best and easy to change the multiple objective situation to a single objective situation rather than tackling the problem of evaluation. In the Indian case, however, the slightly changed method of taxonomic analysis showed that, in order for central public sector enterprises to do well and benefit society, what is needed in the majority of cases is to improve their performance rather than privatize them because in many cases, social objectives could not be washed away and hence the profitability criteria would not judge the level of the performance adequately. It was also found that this could give better returns to the nation immediately, since a mere 5 per cent improvement in costs could double the profits achieved in the fiscal year 1989–90.

NEW INDUSTRIAL POLICY

As a part of restructuring the Indian economy undertaken by the government from July 1991, a New Industrial Policy (NIP) is in process of being implemented. A new policy for public sector is also a part of the NIP 1991. It was felt that, while MOUs have succeeded quite well in changing public sector management culture and hence in improving performance, they would not deal with structural deficiencies like persistent sickness of some enterprises, which could not be tackled due to inadequate budgetary resources. Therefore, India is now following not only the path of performance contracts – the Memoranda of Understanding – but also other strategies of improving performance, dealing with sickness, creating competition and disinvestment in appropriate cases. The current policy options are given in Tables 16.5 and 16.6.

The Memorandum of Understanding is rooted in an evaluation system which not only looks at performance comprehensively, i.e. at both commercial and non-commercial criteria of performance in their static and dynamic aspects, but also induces improved performance by making managerial autonomy and account-

Table 16.4 Taxonomy of loss making PSEs (98)

Market structure	Social obligations	Total no. of PSEs	No. of chronically sick PSEs[1]	Capital employed (Rs million)	net loss (Rs million)	Net worth (Rs million)	No. of regular employees
Monopoly	High	13	3	98,050	4,660	25,250	402,631
Monopoly	Low	2	1	440	660	−770	12,493
Competitive	High	6	3	1,660	960	−5,100	42,555
Competitive	Low	77	40	24,210	13,310	−35,490	334,880
Total		98	47	124,360	19,590	−16,110	792,559

[1]Norms for chronic sickness:
– continuous cash loss for five years
– equity fully eroded
Observations:
(a) highest losses in competitive sector with low social obligations – hence uncompetitive
(b) of the 40 enterprises in this category 27 are sick taken-over PSEs

Table 16.5 Options in regard to profit-making central PSEs

Market structure	No. of PSEs	Efficiency	Social obligations and externalities	Portfolio of options
Monopoly	50	High	High	MOU Encourage workers' participation in – management – ownership Create competition
Monopoly	5	High	Low	MOU Encourage workers' participation in – management – ownership Create competition Sale of equity to public
Competitive	15	High	High	MOU Encourage workers' participation in – management – ownership
Competitive	61	High	Low	MOU Encourage workers' participation in – management – ownership Sale of equity to public

Table 16.6 Options in regard to loss-making central PSEs

Market structure	No. of PSEs	Efficiency	Social obligations and externalities	Portfolio of options
Monopoly	13	Low	High	Improve efficiency Steps proposed Restructuring of: – financial base – managerial base – technological base if required

				Create competition through – splitting into different units – allowing private-sector units – exposure to international competition Encourage workers' participation in – management – ownership Sign MOU for improving efficiency
Monopoly	2	Low	Low	Divest through – sale to workers – sale to private parties – closure
Competitive	6	Low	High	A) Improve efficiency Steps proposed Restructuring of – financial base – managerial base – technological base if required Diversification Encourage workers' participation in – management – ownership Sign MOU for improving efficiency B) If still not improving then divest through – sale to workers – sale to private parties – closure
Competitive	77	Low	Low	Divest through – sale to workers/private parties If divestment not possible – partial closure – merger in a holding company – merger of units with other PSEs

ability more transparent. It is an annual document which is an intrinsic part of a long-term corporate plan, in which the government (represented by the line ministry) and the public enterprise lay down their mutual obligations and responsibilities. The idea is to choose appropriate criteria, assign mutually acceptable priorities to them and decide at the beginning of the year how the achievement of targets (and deviations therefrom) will be evaluated.

As on date the MOU system has firmly taken root as 102 PSEs along with 38 subsidiaries (making a total of 138 PSEs) have been vetted and approved for signing MOUs for 1992–3. These 140 PSEs account for 93 per cent of the total turnover of the central public enterprise. During the current year itself, more or less, the entire public enterprise for the chronically sick PSEs and some units of relatively insignificant size, would get covered under the MOU system. Concerned administrative ministries/departments are required to place the MOU in Parliament in order to facilitate a fuller discussion on PSE performance.

THE MOU SYSTEM

Let us have a look at how the MOU system operates. It has the following components.

Corporate mission

Every enterprise has a corporate mission which is a succinct statement of its reason for existence and addresses the question regarding what business the enterprise is engaged in and, in effect, is the superordinate objective of that enterprise.

Corporate objectives

The corporate objectives stem from the corporate mission and are interlinked with one another. They relate to 'what' an enterprise is expected to do. The 'how' relates to the strategy for achievement of the objectives and the two are often confused in the MOUs. Objectives are required to be quantified and given a time horizon.

Further:

1 Objectives covering the key performance area of an enterprise should be few in number and preferably not exceed 12.
2 Areas which are not in the main line of business of an enterprise are to be excluded.
3 Objectives should preferably relate to outcomes rather than processes.
4 Objectives are to be listed as per the priority attached to their attainment by the owner.
5 The Memorandum of Association (MOA) is to be used in culling out the

306

objectives. In case the MOA does not refer to any social obligations the same are not to figure in the objectives.

Performance criteria

The corporate objectives must have performance indicators which are called performance criteria in the MOU system. These reflect the key performance areas of an enterprise as well. By implication performance criteria and key performance areas are interrelated. A performance criterion must have a specific measure which is both objective and growth oriented. The selection of a proper performance criterion is as important as the selection of an appropriate measure.
Further:

1   Performance criteria, like corporate objectives, should not be more than 12.
2   There should be congruence between objectives and performance criteria.
3   There should not be any duplication in the selection of performance criteria.
4   Selected performance criteria should be measurable and their evaluation method predetermined and laid down in the MOU.

Criteria targets

A performance criterion has five levels of targetting, ranging from 'excellent' to 'poor' with 'very good', 'good', and 'average' as the three intermediate levels. The Performance Budget and/or Plan Targets are required to be placed under the 'very good' column.

Criteria weights

A performance criterion is assigned a weight (on scale ranging from 0 to 1) in such a manner that the sum of the weights of all criteria add up to 1. The weight attached to a particular criterion depends on the subjective assessment of its relative importance by the owner.

Composite score

A composite score ranging from 1 (excellent) to 5 (poor) is computed by evaluating the actual achievement with reference to the targets set on a 5-point scale and determining their weighted average on the basis of weights assigned to each criterion.

Thus the MOU composite score is a summary measure of the performance of an enterprise in terms of attainment of its stated mission; or, putting it differently, the score measures the extent of accomplishment of the mission of an enterprise. It is somewhat more advanced than a balance sheet. The accomplishment level is graded as per the composite score. When one says that the MOU composite score of an enterprise is in the 'excellent range' it only means that the level of accomplishment of its stated mission can be graded excellent. The two issues, though not separate, are not to be confused, as profitability is only a part of the whole, i.e. the mission. It is quite possible that there may not be much congruence between profits/profitability and the MOU composite score, depending on how the mission has been stated.

The issue that emerges from the above then is what constitutes enterprise performance. Is it profits or an MOU score? Is it not possible to combine the two so that an upward trend in one leads to a similar trend in the other? It can be done in several ways and the simplest is to attach a higher weight to profits. This approach is not totally desirable as what is required is a redefinition of the mission and also ensuring that the objectives and performance criteria flow from it. The process of redefinition, therefore, becomes iterative and self-correcting whereby each year the mission, objectives, criteria, criteria measures, targets and weights are redefined until the MOU system for a particular enterprise gets stabilized and MOU scores genuinely reflect total enterprise performance.

MOUs in their present form have now entered the fourth year of their existence though the first set of 11 MOUs using the French methodology was signed in 1988–9. The experience gained during this period shows that enterprises and their administrative ministries/departments in some cases are not clear as to the enterprise mission and objectives. As a consequence the remaining exercise of defining performance criteria and their measures, targets and criteria weights is not carried out in the expected fashion. Though the Ad-hoc Task Force attempts to improve upon the work done by the administrative ministries/departments and PSEs, the very nature of its role of acting as quality controller limits its functions to making only marginal changes; and as such some shortcomings do remain in the revised MOUs.

On an analysis of the performance of PSEs for the two years for which data are available, we notice from the contents of Table 16.7, that 15 out of 23 enterprises have attained scores in the excellent range during 1990–1 as against 8 out of 17 during 1989–90, and that 11 out of the 15 have exceeded the profit targets set for them in their annual plan and/or budget as compared to 5 out of 8 during the previous year. Though the sample size is small and figures available are for only two years, it can still be deduced that enterprises which have earned excellent scores have by and large exceeded the profit targets as set for them in their annual plan and/or budget despite the fact that only 11 per cent weight was attached to profit or profit related criteria during 1990–91 as compared to 18 per cent in the previous year. Hence, it can be said that there is a fair amount of correlation between MOU scores and profits. This fact needs to be re-established in the coming years in order to reach any definite conclusion on the subject.

Further refinements are not only required but are being pursued vigorously. Some of the steps taken to improve the MOU system are as follows:

1   Performance budget and MOU targets are required to synchronize and

MOU targets must reflect an improvement over the previous year's plan/budget target in order to be categorized as 'very good'. Otherwise they shall be categorized as 'good/average'.

2   The weight for profit and profit related criteria in the MOUs for 1992–3 would be around 50 per cent in order to improve the congruence between MOU score and financial performance.

3   The Ad-hoc Task Force (ATF) would henceforth (i.e. from MOUs for 1993–4 onwards) be doing the vetting of MOUs in two stages. In Stage I, to coincide with the final evaluation of the previous year's MOUs during October–December every year, the performance criteria selection and other framework of the MOU would be firmed up; whereas in Stage II, when performance budget targets of administrative ministries/departments are available, target setting for the performance criteria earlier selected in Stage I would be done. It is expected that by introducing a two-stage vetting process the charge that PSEs are going in for 'soft' performance criteria selection would in some manner be taken care of, since more time would be spent on that aspect.

4   To provide a level playing field, swings between the five levels of targetting have to be rationalized. On a random sample analysis of 34 PSEs which have signed MOUs during 1992–3 it has been observed that swings with respect to budgeted figures (taken as 100) are the following:

Excellent	Very good	Good	Average	Poor
107	100	90.86	82.23	74.06

The following range of scores emerge for each category of targetting:

Excellent = 103.51 and above.
V. Good = 95.43–103.50
Good = 86.34–95.42
Average = 78.14–86.33
Poor = 78.13 and below
(when budget target value = 100)

The above analysis reveals that excellence is achieved when performance budget targets are exceeded on an average by 3.51 per cent.

One of the most important features of an MOU is that it attempts to make the objectives of the public enterprise clear and transparent. The objectives are agreed between the owner and the manager in negotiations, with the owner indicating *inter se* priorities among multiple objectives. This permits the owner to vary the emphasis on different objectives from time to time, depending on their full or partial fulfilment. Consequently, decisions with regard to partial or full divestment could flow out of such negotiations, since they provide clarity in regard to the objectives of public investment and their fulfilment. For example, investment in a steel mill could have various objectives: development of a backward area, employment generation, ancillary development, infrastructure development, help to tribal or deprived classes, etc. But, after all the objectives are met, say, in a period of 10 to 15 years, the priority would then be to produce steel at the lowest cost and competitively. These variations in objectives would be clearly encompassed in the MOU negotiations over a period of time.

A performance incentive system is an integral part of any performance improvement system. In India, initially a non-monetary award is being given to the CEO and the PSE. Further, a financial incentive scheme has been approved in principle under which the quantum of incentive will be related to the composite score. Since it is linked to the composite score, the incentive will vary from year to year according to the variance in the composite score of the company. For the year 1989–90 the prime minister gave non-monetary awards to companies which had composite scores between 1.5 and 1. It is expected that in due course this incentive scheme will have a favourable impact on wage policy for the public sector enterprises, where increasing thought is being given to linking wages with productivity.

CONCLUSION

It is expected that with the signing of 102 MOUs (140 enterprises) covering 93 per cent of the turnover of the central public sector the public enterprise performance would not only be measured comprehensively but be improved both quantitatively as well as qualitatively. In this connection the budgeted profit before tax for the entire public sector for 1992–3 has been estimated at around Rs 6,300 crores, and, based on past achievement levels in terms of MOU scores, it should be possible for the public enterprise sector to earn a profit before tax of around Rs 6,000 crores during the current year, provided chronically sick enterprises which are not signatories to the MOU do not incur losses higher than those estimated at the commencement of the year.

Another important feature of the Indian MOU system is that it enables the government to compare the performance of essentially dissimilar enterprises. While the commitments for each public enterprise are different and the list does not permit comparisons, the enterprises' ability to meet their individual commitments is certainly comparable, especially when such commitments have been negotiated on the basis that there must be an improvement on current levels of performance in the following year. This comparison of so-called incomparables will bring a sense of competition to the public enterprises, some of which are functioning under monopolistic conditions. And competition means improved performance.

The simulation of a competitive environment between PSEs is thus one of the important possibilities inherent in the MOU mechanism and this aspect gives it tremendous strength. Such a mechanism is ideal for developing countries in general.

In the Indian situation today the public enterprise sector policy is

Table 16.7 Performance of MOU signing enterprises

Class	Range of scores	No. of PSEs		Net profit in excess of plan/budget target		Weightage assigned to profit and profit related indicators	
		1989–90	1990–1	1989–90	1990–1	1989–90	1990–1
Excellent	1.00–1.50	8	15	5	11	18	11
Very good	1.51–2.50	4	7	2	2	20	13
Good	2.51–3.50	5	–	2	–	15	–
Average	3.51–4.50	–	–	–	–	–	–
Poor	4.51 and above	–	1	–	–	–	12
Total		17	23	9	13	18	12

comprehensive in the sense that it is looking at all possibilities in the spectrum of policy options available to it for improving the performance of the enterprise portfolio. The MOUs will not only continue to play an important role but would be crucial in producing the correct policy options in each case and would facilitate the case-by-case approach advocated by many in public enterprises policy making.

17

PRIVATIZATION OF STATE-OWNED ENTERPRISES: A FRAMEWORK FOR IMPACT ANALYSIS

Andrew D. Cao

INTRODUCTION

The increased acceptance of privatization initiatives in recent years throughout the developing world, Eastern Europe and the former Soviet Union, reflects a recognition of the failure of state-owned enterprises (SOEs) to produce net positive economic effects. However, many decision makers do not know precisely what impacts should be expected because systematic assessments are not conducted prior to implementation, nor are results measured after privatization. It is therefore essential to have a system of impact evaluation to give decision-makers defensible justifications for programme implementation and to maximize the efficiency of programme management.

The purpose of this study is to explore a systematic and practical analytical framework to assess the impacts of privatization. The first section of the report provides a brief review of the key studies on impact analysis. The second section proposes an analytical framework for practitioners. Finally, the third section applies the proposed framework to a sample of case studies in order to develop lessons learned from the experiences of the sample set.

LITERATURE REVIEW

The body of knowledge on the impact of privatization is rather limited. One study performed by V.V. Ramanadham identifies the micro and macro variables which are most likely to be affected by privatization, such as profit, cost, price, technology, government subsidies, employment, tax and social benefits.[1]

Another study, sponsored by the World Bank, proposes a methodology which relies on factual versus counterfactual approaches. The factual approach compares performance over the five year periods immediately prior and subsequent to the privatization activity. The counterfactual approach moves from correlation to causation to determine how much of any change is attributable to privatization. The authors attempt to describe what the performance of the SOE would have been if had it not been privatized. Projections are then made and welfare valuation and distribution among the buyers, government, consumers, employees and competitors are measured.[2] The World Bank study is based on work conducted by Borcherding, Pommerehne and Schneider[3] and compares the efficiency between private and public production in five countries. It also relies on studies of the welfare effects of privatization done by Bos[4], Culyer[5], Le Grand, and Robinson[6] and on market structure studies done by Peters[7], Kay and Silberston.[8]

Various other studies which address the issues of performance assessment and impact management of public firms rather than privatized ones provide useful insight for this study in terms of the practicality and applicability of certain methods. Leroy Jones suggests evaluating the performance of public firms by starting with private profit and making a series of adjustments, such as converting market prices to shadow prices. He recognizes the differences between private and public valuations and focuses on performance trends rather than on the absolute level of performance.[9]

Jack Diamond measures performance in terms of efficiency. He makes the distinction between technical efficiency defined as the maximum possible output produced for a given amount of inputs, and allocative efficiency which focuses on the costs of inputs rather than of output. His study is based on Harvey Leibenstein's work[10] which indicates that the cost of any output is minimized by combining inputs in such a way that one input cannot be substituted for another without raising costs.[11]

A special feature of Diamond's study is that it is one of the few studies to propose a quantitative methodology using regression analysis, a statistical technique which attempts to establish cause and effect. Diamond also proposes using data envelope analysis (DEA), a non-statistical technique first introduced by M.J. Farrell. The data envelope technique does not rely on the average relationship between variables like regression analysis does. Instead it examines them from the standpoint of best possible performance as represented by the outlying observations against the actual performance.[12] Using linear programming, DEA weighs input and output variables to produce a single summary measure of their relationship for each decision-making unit. Similar techniques of measuring efficiency were applied by Banker and Charnes in dealing with multiple outputs.[13]

Although these studies are useful, they tend to be too complex for decision makers to apply on a country-by-country, or enterprise-by-enterprise basis in the planning, execution and evaluation of privatization projects. Therefore, it appears useful to explore an analytical framework which is practical enough to allow decision makers to manage privatization efforts in a more practical and systematic fashion. The framework identifies indicators relevant to privatization impact assessment and management, proposes a practical measurement method, and suggests realistic standards for comparison.

FRAMEWORK FOR IMPACT ANALYSIS

The foundation

The proposed framework emphasises practicality. Although advanced methods such as shadow pricing have their merit, they are not feasible in practice because it is impossible to identify and measure social welfare impacts accurately. Due to this general complexity of measurement methodologies, many countries have neglected to assess the impact of their privatization efforts. The methodology proposed in this study recognizes the limitations of certain advanced measurement techniques, and is targeted towards practitioners involved with the monitoring of privatization activity.

The basic premise of privatization is that enterprise efficiency will be enhanced as a result of ownership transfer. This premise is based on the relative success of the free competitive market system with private ownership versus the planned economic system with SOEs. It is hoped that improved efficiency will make the SOEs more self-sustaining and hence less reliant on government subsidies. As a result, the limited resources can then be made available for other purposes. This premise is based on the fundamental belief that profitable private sector firms contribute to a healthy economy and have positive spill-over effects on society.

The framework

The framework proposed in this study focuses initially on the balance sheet and the income statement of the privatised SOEs. It uses two types of analysis: first order of impact analysis, which identifies how improved efficiency in each area of the firm might have a direct impact on the firm, and second order of impact analysis, which relates each account to other entities within and outside the firm.

The indicators of micro impacts

The most aggregate indicator to measure the performance of the firm is the return on asset ratio (ROA), also known as the Dupont model as shown by Figure 17.1. It is the ratio of net income (NI) divided by the total assets (TA) of the firm, as shown in Tables 17.1 and 17.2. The Dupont model is useful in impact analysis because it permits the analysis of performance within different departments of the firm as represented by the various accounts of the balance sheet and income statement.

It is expected that, after being privatized, the firm will be better managed in all areas such as marketing, finance, production, personnel and general administration. The combination of the right marketing strategy, the right financing strategy, the right production strategy and the right personnel and general administration strategy would improve the ROA of the firm in all kinds of environments. The formulation and application of the *right* strategy in all areas

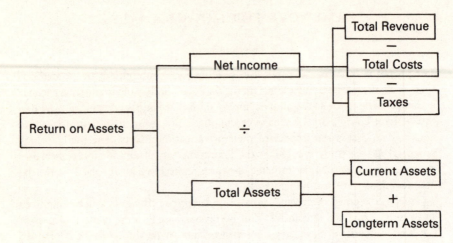

Figure 17.1 Dupont model of impact analysis

Table 17.1 Analytical matrix of departmental efficiency and impact indicator

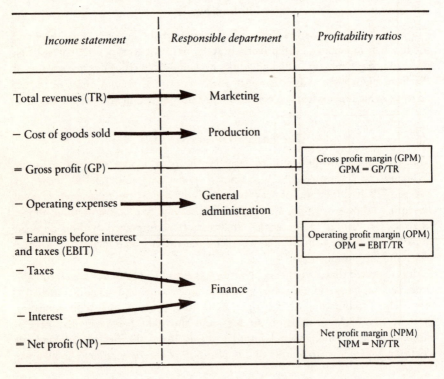

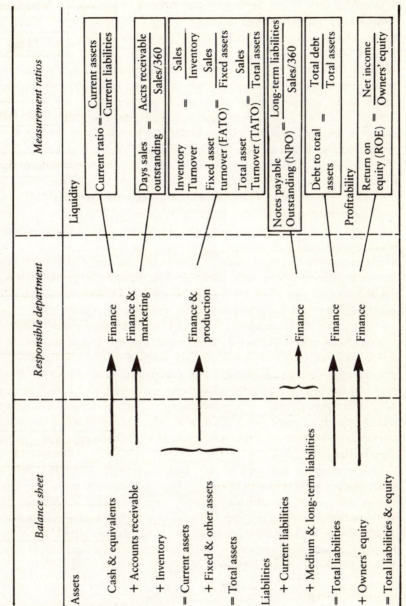

Table 17.2 Analytical matrix of departmental efficiency and impact indicator

Balance sheet

Assets

Cash & equivalents

+ Accounts receivable

+ Inventory

= Current assets

+ Fixed & other assets

= Total assets

Liabilities

+ Current liabilities

+ Medium & long-term liabilities

= Total liabilities

+ Owners' equity

= Total liabilities & equity

Responsible department

Finance

Finance & marketing

Finance & production

Finance

Finance

Finance

Measurement ratios

Liquidity

$$\text{Current ratio} = \frac{\text{Current assets}}{\text{Current liabilities}}$$

$$\text{Days sales outstanding} = \frac{\text{Accts receivable}}{\text{Sales}/360}$$

$$\text{Inventory Turnover} = \frac{\text{Sales}}{\text{Inventory}}$$

$$\text{Fixed asset turnover (FATO)} = \frac{\text{Sales}}{\text{Fixed assets}}$$

$$\text{Total asset Turnover (TATO)} = \frac{\text{Sales}}{\text{Total assets}}$$

$$\text{Notes payable Outstanding (NPO)} = \frac{\text{Long-term liabilities}}{\text{Sales}/360}$$

Profitability

$$\text{Debt to total assets} = \frac{\text{Total debt}}{\text{Total assets}}$$

$$\text{Return on equity (ROE)} = \frac{\text{Net income}}{\text{Owners' equity}}$$

of enterprise management implies knowing how to cope with good as well as bad situations.

One can argue that privatization might not be responsible for improving the ROA of the firm. It may in fact be due to other factors such as an improved economy. On the other hand, it could be argued that ROA had deteriorated because of a poor economy, not because of poor management. To overcome this problem of cause and effect, some measurement yardsticks and standards are proposed to control these variables. Instead of using one year's results as a reference standard, which may represent an exceptionally good or bad year, a trend measure is used covering a three- to five-year period.

Besides the ROA, which is an aggregate indicator of impact analysis, other indicators are proposed in order to check the vital signs of the firm's post-privatization such as: its liquidity, measured by the current ratio (CR); its efficiency, measured by the turnover ratios (TO); its leverage, measured by the debt ratio (DR); and its profitability measured by the various functions of the firm such as the return on equity (ROE), the gross profit margin (GPM) and the operating profit margin (OPM) (see Tables 17.1 and 17.2.)

Impacts can also be measured from ratio indicators using accounts of both the balance sheet and the income statement. One example is efficient cash management which is the holding of sufficient cash in order to meet current payments without leaving cash idle. Idle cash earns no return since it is not invested in some type of money market instrument. Efficient cash management requires efficient cash budgeting and marketable security management.

Other single micro indicators which relate to the production function are incremental capacity utilization, level of production, unit cost of production, and productivity. In terms of personnel, indicators used for impact assessment examine incremental wage levels, funds allocated for human resource development and for benefits, labour displacement, new hiring within each privatized SOE, absenteeism, and employee-turnover ratio. In terms of marketing, indicators used examine incremental funds allocated for product research and development, for promotion and for distribution development as well as the level of price change.

The proposition advanced in this study is that it is not the change in *ownership* per se that improves performance, but rather it is the focusing on *accountability* used by efficient private firms discussed as follows which promotes better *management* that has a positive impact on the efficiency of the privatized firm. Although the impact of exogenous factors plays a lesser role in this practical analytical framework, it is considered in the second order of impact analysis, i.e. the residuals or spill-over effects.

The indicators of macro impacts

The indirect impacts are traced from the direct impacts on each of the accounts of the balance sheet and income statement of the firm. Basically, the attempt is to link the firm to its environment. The indicators proposed here are based on the Keynsian model which provides measurable indicators such as government subsidies (G), personal and business income taxes (T), business investments (I), personal consumption (C), exports (X) and imports (M). The framework also includes the measurable impacts on the institutional setting such as on the financial markets.

Subsidies, which include direct as well as indirect transfers such as subsidized loan rates, are also included as indicators. Personal income taxes include net incremental personal income taxes received from employees of the privatized SOEs whose income changes between pre- and post-privatization periods and income received from new hires, minus the income of laid-off employees. Business income taxes include the net incremental income taxes which result from increases or decreases in the taxable income of the privatized SOEs. Impacts on investments include the net realized change in business investment committed by new private investors who acquired the SOEs. For personal consumption, the indicator used is the net incremental income received by the employees of the privatized SOEs, net of the average national saving rate and amount. Exports and imports are measured by the net incremental exports and imports realised by the privatized SOEs.

The measurement yardsticks and standards

Micro impacts

For ratios such as the return on total asset ratio or the current ratio, the proposed yardstick is five-year and three-year averages. These are used as standards and compared to a moving average of the post-privatization ratios for a three- to five-year period in order to overcome the problem of cyclical variations from exogenous factors. Hence the standard of performance evaluation is based on historical performance of a given SOE when there is no comparative industry standard. Alternatively, when an industry standard exists, it is employed as the measurement against which post-privatization performance is compared. Standard deviations are used to allow ranges of comparison for ranges of asset sizes.

As example, the impact on capacity utilization is measured by the difference in capacity utilized during each year following privatization compared to the three- and five-year average capacity utilized before privatization. Starting the second year after privatization, moving averages are used to compare to pre-privatization averages, with allowances given using standard deviations as discussed above. The same methodology can be applied to all single indicators discussed earlier.

Macro impacts

For the government subsidies indicator G, the measurement yardstick is the reduction in subsidies to the privatized SOEs. The standard used to evaluate the impact on G is a function of the government's objective, as determined during the planning phase. The results of the impact analysis might indicate the need for alternative ownership transfer methods, or alternative methods of selecting buyers which better meet programme objectives.

Impact on employment is equal to the sum of the number of employees who are displaced by privatization in different SOEs during the first year of privatization. The number of increases in employment by the privatized SOEs is included as a measurement yardstick during the first five years after privatization to incorporate the spill-over effect of privatization on employment using moving average.

The yardstick for impacts of privatization on the financial markets is the number of new shares floated publicly by the privatized SOEs and the incremental capitalization value created from these new shares.

For the other macro indicators, the yardstick is straightforward, using incremental analysis as well. For example, for the reduction of debt, the yardstick used is the amount of funds allocated from the proceeds of privatization used to pay off debt.

Quantitative framework

The impact of privatization can also be measured by the change in the bankruptcy risk of the privatized SOE which results in the improvement in efficiency of the firm. This measurement can be done with a statistical technique called multiple discriminant analysis (MDA) discussed as follows.[14]

MDA can be applied to determine how a privatized SOE moves away from a high bankruptcy risk zone to a lower bankruptcy risk zone, as shown in Figure 17.2. This graphical representation can be done by many computer softwares. The MDA function which allows such analysis is as follows:

$$Z = a + bX_1 + cX_2 + dX_3 \ldots nX_a$$

Each SOE is given a Z score which determines where it is situated on the graph. The parameter a is a constant while $b, c \ldots n$ indicate the weight or effect of the variable $X_1 \ldots X_a$ has on the likelihood of bankruptcy of a given SOE. This method has been widely used for bond rating based on the Altman model which uses five ratios: the ratio of net working capital to total assets, retained earnings to total assets, earnings before tax to total assets, market value of equity to book value of debt and sales to total assets.

As there are many possible explanatory variables, a special statistical technique called factor analysis can be used to reduce the number of variables to be included in the MDA function.[15] This technique graphically shows that

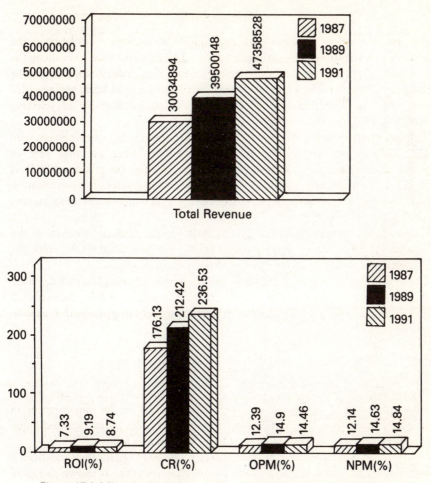

Figure 17.2 Micro-impact indicators for non-financial SOEs in Indonesia

variables which do have some common but not observable construct tend to be clustered together in a factor extraction. The ones which have the highest weights, or factor loadings, are selected. The maximum number of factors can be determined by the scree plot, as shown on Figure 17.3. In this instance, only five or six variables need to be used because, after the sixth one, the marginal explanatory value becomes negligible, as shown by the scree where the Eigenvalue starts to level off.

To overcome the uncertainty of whether post-privatization performance is significantly different from pre-privatization, the *t test* of hypothesis can also be used to determine the significance of the difference between mean performance before privatization versus mean performance post-privatization.

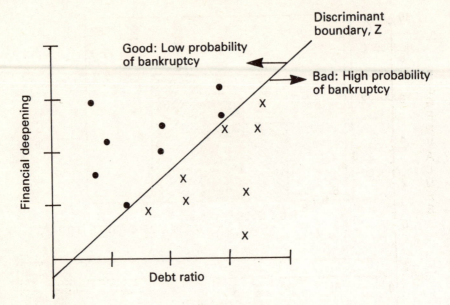

Figure 17.3 Impact on bankruptcy risk: a multiple discriminant analysis

CASE STUDIES

In order to show the importance of impact analysis, three case studies are presented as examples. The first case deals with Indonesia to show the importance of objective setting in impact analysis. The second case deals with the United Kingdom to point out the importance of impact measurement. The third case deals with Egypt to show the necessity of impact analysis before privatization.

The case of Indonesia in objective setting

As discussed earlier in this study, impacts need to be evaluated against the objectives set out by governments when they privatize their SOEs. Objective setting needs to be appropriate to the private business practice of maximising the value of the firm rather than to the public practice of meeting other non-commercial objectives, which the SOEs were set to do.

In Indonesia, the SOEs are not only supposed to meet non-commercial objectives but they are also supposed to remain solvent. The objective is to minimize the requirement for subsidies from the government for insolvency due to lack of liquidity. For this reason, the SOEs are judged by their 'solvency'. This signals to the SOEs that their 'efficiency' evaluation is based on the level of their liquidity. The impact of such an objective is shown in Figure 17.2 by a tremendous current ratio of between 176 and 236 times for the period 1987 to

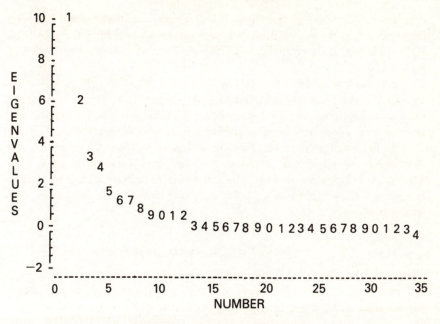

Figure 17.4 Scree plot of Eigenvalues

1991. This extreme conservatism in financial management leads to significant waste in non-interest bearing cash holdings and minimal reliance on short-term sources of financing.

The lesson learned from this example is that impact analysis needs an efficient objective setting which lends better to the private sector practice so that there is less confusion due to conflicting signals to the management of the privatized SOEs which in turn would impact on their performance. Privatization cannot be done half way and the objectives of the firm need to be based on standard private business practice.

The case of the UK in impact measurement method

Kay and Bishop measured the impacts of privatization using point-to-point data to compare the performance of the privatized SOEs with those which remained public.[16] The indicators used are total revenue ('turnover'), profit before interest and tax, return on equity, return on sales, employment and productivity between 1979 and 1988. Their findings are mixed among the indicators. In terms of sales, they conclude that most privatized industries have grown since privatization took place compared to the ones which remained public between 1979 and 1988. In terms of profit, their point-to-point comparison indicates that most public and privatized firms have grown, but those which have been privatized have had a higher rate of growth. The most notable are Telecom and Gas. Employment has

323

dropped considerably for the public firms. In terms of productivity, however, improvement in the public firms has been greater than that of the privatized SOEs. This has been seen in the case of British Telecom, which is the flagship of privatization.

The lesson learned from the UK case is that although the indicators used are appropriate, the point-to-point methodology is misleading. This is because the years used for comparing the before versus the after performance might cover unusual years which may not be representative of typical performance. This use of point data might explain why Kay and Bishop, as well as many others, are not sure about the impact of privatization. Their conclusion could have been different had they relied on more refined data points such as average-to-average and the *t test* of hypothesis in order to systematically make inferences with greater confidence.

The case of Egypt in impact projection

Like many other countries, Egypt started discussions on privatization many years ago. However, not much has happened because of the common fear of labour displacement which might be caused by privatization. Unemployment in Egypt has been a major problem because the government provides guaranteed employment for university graduates. According to the Central Agency for Public Mobilization and Statistics, the latest data available shows an increase in unemployment rate from 5.3 per cent to 12.4 pe cent between 1976–86.

As shown in Table 17.3, impact projection can be done prior to actually implementing the privatization programme. The projection is based on different scenarios and strategies from which the government can decide which one should be used. Before the results of this exercise on impact projection the media, labour unions and management of the SOEs had great concern about labour displacement. Based on the results of the impact analysis, these fears have subsided and more informed and rational decisions can now be made. There were talks about millions of displaced labour prior to the impact estimation. As shown in Table 17.3, the total number of employees in non-strategic SOEs which are candidates for privatization totals only around 368,000. Depending on the strategy the government chooses to use, the level of displacement could be as small as 15,000 to 30,000.

The lesson learned from the case of Egypt is that impact analysis should not only be done at the end of privatization but should be conducted right at the beginning as well. The projected impacts help the decision makers to foresee the potential consequences of their actions more clearly. Hence their decisions tend to be based on better information and actual impacts can be compared to the projections for better monitoring and adjustments of post-privatization.

Table 17.3 Impacts on labour displacement in Egypt: a scenario analysis

Scenarios Total non-strategic base of 368,000	Redundancy scenarios		
	Optimistic (1/4)	Average (1/3)	Pessimistic (1/2)
○ Number of displaced workers	92,010	122,680	184,020
○ Remaining balance net of retirement			
– scenario 1–65 and older (a)	79,129	105,505	158,257
– scenario 2–60 and older (b)	73,608	98,144	147,218
○ Remaining balance net of 'Ghost Workers' and illness (c)			
– scenario 1–65 and older	75,172	100,230	150,344
– scenario 2–60 and older	69,928	93,237	139,855
○ Remaining balance with training (d)			
– scenario 1–65 and older	37,586	50,115	75,172
– scenario 2–60 and older	34,964	46,618	69,928
○ Remaining balance with increase in SOE's efficiency and labour demand (e)			
– scenario 1–65 and older	33,827	45,103	67,655
– scenario 2–60 and older	31,467	41,957	62,935
○ Remaining balance with phasing			
– scenario 1–65 and older. −25% per year	8,467	11,276	18,914
−50% per year	16,914	22,552	33,827
– scenario 2–60 and older. −25% per year	7,867	10,489	15,734
−50% per year	15,734	20,978	31,467

Notes:
(a). Estimated at 13.8% (rounded to 14%)
(b). Estimated at 20%
(c). Estimated at 5%
(d). Estimated at 50% relocation due to effective training
(e). Estimated at 10% per year

CONCLUSION

Because impact analysis is rather tedious, it has rarely been done in privatization. Yet without impact analysis, it is impossible to determine whether privatization is effective in improving the efficiency of SOEs and in bringing about other intended objectives such as subsidy reduction or increased employment. It has been found that complex methods of economic analysis of impacts are not being used in the management of privatization because, although they are theoretically complete, they are inaccurate and impractical.

This study proposes an alternative framework for analysis which utilizes practical indicators, realistic yardsticks of measurement, and standards for comparison. Based on the findings of the case studies discussed in this study, it is necessary to conduct impact analysis prior to actually undertaking the privatization. This impact projection will allow decision makers to achieve results which tend to be closer to the intended objectives by defining goals at the outset of the privatization programme. Impact assessment requires a realistic set of quantifiable objectives, an appropriate signalling system of accountability, a reward-punish system and an appropriate management information system to carry out the measurement and reporting process. Thus it is the goal of this analytical framework to fill the requirements of impact analysis in a simple and useful way in the hope that it will contribute to the rationalisation and improved effectiveness of privatization programme management.

NOTES

1. Ramanadham, V. V. (1992) *Privatization: Constraints and Impacts.* Basic Working Paper, Expert Group Meeting on Privatization, United Nations Development Programs, Geneva, August 17–21.
2. Galal, Ahmed, Jones, Leroy, Tandom, Pankaj and Vogelsang, Ingo (1992) *Questions and Approaches to Answers, Welfare Consequences of Selling Public Enterprises- Case Studies from Chile, Malaysia, Mexico and the UK*, World Bank Conference, Washington D.C., June 11–12.
3. Borcherding, T.E., Pommerehne, W.W. and Schneider, F. (1982), 'Comparing the efficiency of private and public production: the evidence of five countries', in D. Bös, R.A. Musgrave and J. Wiseman (eds) 'Public Production', *Journal of Economics*: 127–56.
4. Bös, Dieter (1986) 'Welfare effects of privatizing public enterprises', in *Sonderforschungsbereich 303. Information für die Koordination wirtschaftlicher Aktivitaten*, Bonn, November.
5. Culyer, A.J. (1985) 'Privatization and the welfare state', *Economica* (52): 533–4.
6. Le Grand, Julian and Robinson, Ray (1984) 'Privatization and the welfare state: an introduction in Julian Le Grand and Ray Robinson (eds) *Privatization and the Welfare State*, London: Allen & Unwin.
7. Bös, Dieter and Wolfgand, Peters (1986) 'Privatization, efficiency and market structure', in *Sondersorschungsbereich 303. Information für die Koordination wirtschaftlicher Aktivitaten*, Bonn, October.
8. Kay, J.A. and Silberston, Z.A. (1984) 'The new industrial policy – privatization and competition', *Midland Bank Review*, Spring: 8–16.
9. Jones, Leroy, P. (1991) *Performance Evaluation for Public Enterprises*, Discussion Papers no. 122, World Bank, Washington D.C.
10. Leibenstein, Harvey (1966) 'Allocative efficiency versus x-efficiency', *American Economic Review 56*: 392–415.
11. Diamond, Jack (1990) 'Measuring efficiency in government: techniques and experience', in A. Premchand (ed.) *Government Financial Management – Issues and Country Studies*, International Monetary Fund.
12. Farrell, M.J. (1957) 'The measurement of productive efficiency', *Journal of the Royal Statistical Society, Series A. 120* (III): 253–90.
13. Banker, R.D., Cooper, W.W. and Charne, A. (1984) 'Some models for estimating technical and scale inefficiencies in data envelope analysis', *Management Science 30* (9): 1078–92.
14. Andrews, D.F., Gnanadesikan, R. and Warner, J.L. (1973) 'Methods of assessing

multivariate normality', in P.R. Krishnaiah (ed.) *Multivariate Analysis 111*, New York: Academic Press.

15. Alwin, D.F. (1973) 'The use of factor analysis in the construction of linear composites in social research', *Sociological Methods and Research*, February: 191–214.

16. Kay, J.A. and Bishop, M.R. (1989) 'Privatization and the performance of public firms', in *Role and Extent of Competition in Improving the Performance of Public Enterprises*, Proceedings of the Interregional Seminar on Performance Improvement of Public Enterprises, United Nations, New Delhi, 12–19 April: 33–52.

17. Cao, Andrew, D. (1991) *Privatization and Labour Displacement Issues in Egypt*, Price Waterhouse.

18

ACCOUNTING ASPECTS OF PRIVATIZATION IMPACTS

Tony Bennett

PURPOSE AND SCOPE

The purpose of this chapter is to review the role of accounting in identifying and measuring the impacts of privatization and to discuss how accounting might better fulfil this role.

The study covers the privatization of public enterprises (PEs) only, with emphasis on privatization by divestment, and on developing countries and economies in transition from socialism.

Section two narrates the goals of privatization. Sections three and four set out a general methodology for the measurement of two commonly assumed goals – economic efficiency gains and fiscal gains, and the appropriate sources of data including accounting data. There are, of course, other impacts of privatization, notably the impact on employment and labour costs, but these do not raise any accounting issues. Section five considers the accounting aspects of post-privatization regulation. Sections six and seven describe the general limitations of accounting and the particular limitations applying to PE accounting which affect the privatization process.

THE OBJECTIVES OF PRIVATIZATION

The objectives of a privatization programme or any individual privatization are stated in different ways (or not formally stated at all) but commonly include variations of one or more of the following:

1 economic efficiency gains;
2 fiscal gains; and
3 distributional changes, such as the spreading of ownership.

Much of the criticism of privatization has been based not on the declared objectives but on its side effects such as the increase in joblessness, and the greater concentration of wealth in the hands of a few families or an ethnic group. Evaluation should therefore be made against not only the declared objectives, such as the above, but also other national objectives, such as equitable distribution of income and wealth, reduction in unemployment and internal and external monetary stability.

GENERAL METHODOLOGY OF MEASUREMENT OF IMPACT OF PRIVATIZATION ON ECONOMIC EFFICIENCY

A clear distinction should be made between financial profitability and economic efficiency. An enterprise may increase its profits in a number of ways which are not based on increases in efficiency and may in fact mask a decline in efficiency. In an imperfect market it can increase its prices and profits at the expense of consumers, i.e. higher revenue is not matched by higher economic benefit, and vice versa on domestic inputs. It can lay off workers who have no alternative employment and no economic cost. It can lobby for increased tariff or non-tariff protection, or lower prices of inputs such as state-supplied energy. It may reduce its interest burden by getting low-cost finance from the state or state-guaranteed sources, or arrange a debt for equity swap. If an evaluation is to have any credibility it must be based on economic analysis, and, since economic analysis is unfamiliar to most people, whereas financial statements are rather more familiar and trusted, the evaluation must reconcile with the financial statements by listing the differences, and showing who (such as consumers or the government) gains or loses from these differences.

The change of ownership does not change the criteria of economic or social merit. For the measurement of economic efficiency at the micro level there is a well established methodology of cost–benefit analysis. The same technique and criteria which are used to test the *ex ante* economic viability of a project may be used to test the *ex post* performance of an enterprise. Essentially a cost–benefit exercise compares inputs and outputs of the enterprise, valuing them at their border prices (import and export prices on world markets). This technique corrects for monopoly pricing, protection from import competition, and distorted domestic prices of inputs. A similar comparison of inputs and outputs *before* the privatization may show (hopefully) that output/input ratio has improved. Inputs and outputs are valued at constant prices (the border prices in a base year) so as to remove the effects of price changes which have nothing to do with the change of ownership. To reduce the effect of random variation from year to year, a period of years should be examined.[1]

An apparent improvement in performance is open to the objection that it was not due to the change of ownership but to other factors, such as changes in the business environment. One way to standardize for environmental factors is to compare the change in the privatized enterprise with the change in other enterprises in the same sector and environment. To illustrate, if the benefit/cost ratio of an enterprise improves from (say) 0.8 before privatization to 1.2 after privatization, it is still necessary to measure the improvement of a control group of similar enterprises over the same period. If these rise from (say) 1.0 to 1.25, the interpretation is that privatization has raised the relative efficiency of the enterprises from 0.8 of the control group to 0.96 of the control group (1.2/1.25). This is a 20 per cent improvement. It can be valued in money terms.

In many cases, however, public enterprises are unique, and no valid comparisons can be made. If there are no other enterprises subject to the same influences, the analyst is forced to identify possible causes of performance change (other than ownership change and consequential management change) and cost their effects. This is not so difficult as it may appear, as most of the environmental changes are already excluded by the use of constant border prices in the cost–benefit analysis. Changes in the level of protection or monopoly, for instance, would not affect this analysis.[2] This method was used in a recent evaluation of privatization in developing countries.[3]

The data and sources for efficiency impact measurement are as follows:

1   The enterprise is the only source of data on the quantities of inputs consumed and outputs produced during the period evaluated.[4] This data and the market prices at which purchases and sales have been made should be checked with the audited financial statements.[5]

2   The enterprise may also be the best source of world prices since the enterprise is able to specify its inputs and outputs very precisely and obtain appropriate world prices of tradeables from suppliers and trade journals. The evaluation agency may try checking their figures with official trade statistics from customs data, but the classification may be insufficiently detailed, or show nil imports or exports in the period.

3   Shadow prices of labour, capital, land and non-tradable inputs such as electric power are in many countries calculated and made available by the central project planning office.

Access to reliable enterprise data may be difficult where the privatized enterprise resists government 'interference', unless the data is required from *all enterprises*, e.g. by a statistical office having statutory powers.

The position is different in an enterprise which expects to be regulated, either because it has monopoly power and its pricing is controlled, or because of its social importance, such as transport and communications utilities, and financial institutions. In these sectors, the data for efficiency measurement may be included in regular reports custom-designed for these purposes. Where the new owners have given undertakings in the privatization agreement, e.g. to introduce new technology, train indigenous managers, or clean up the environment, there should be agreement also on the manner of verification. This access to the firm may be extended by mutual agreement to include data for privatization impact measurement.

GENERAL METHODOLOGY OF MEASUREMENT OF FISCAL IMPACT OF PRIVATIZATION

The direct fiscal effects of an enterprise consist of the following government receipts and payments[6] in a given period.

Receipts

1 Taxes collected from the enterprise.
2 Interest, dividends, rents and royalties on government investment in the enterprise.
3 Redemption of capital, i.e. amortization of government loans, and sale of equity (privatization proceeds net of related costs).
4 Borrowing from the enterprise, e.g. by take up of Treasury bills or government bonds.

Three *imputed* receipts should be added:

5 Expenses and revenue losses arising from pursuit of any non-commercial objectives insofar as these are not reimbursed by the government.[7]
6 Transfers from the enterprise to other government agencies or to the PE sector, which substitute for transfers from the government.[8]
7 Goods and services provided by an enterprise to the government or the PE sector which are not paid for.[9]

Payments

1 Subsidies and other unrequited non-repayable transfers to the enterprise.
2 Interest and discount charges on government borrowings from the enterprise.
3 Loans to the enterprise and purchase of equity.
4 Repayment of borrowings from the enterprise.
5 Costs of pre- and post-privatization monitoring and regulation.
6 Costs of safety nets such as severance payments, unemployment benefit, re-training, job-finding and re-location costs, net of any donor aid.

Two imputed payments should be added:

7 Services provided by government at no cost or below cost, such as low-cost finance,[10] research, export facilities, legal and management services, computer services, etc.
8 Transfers to the enterprise from other government agencies or the PE sector in substitution for the government, e.g. energy at below market rates.

The net balance of all the above, positive or negative, benefit or burden, is a broad measure of the overall fiscal impact of an enterprise in a given period. It excludes payments for goods and services supplied at fair market value by the enterprise to government, or vice versa, which are often significant but for which a quid pro quo is given. These do not count toward the fiscal impact. On the other hand, PEs are sometimes not paid on time by the government, or by other PEs, to whom goods or services have been supplied. Any increase in such arrears during a period should be included as imputed receipts in category 7.

No general norm or standard can be applied to evaluate this overall balance, nor even to its decomposition into capital and current account balances. Net capital flows may be positive or negative in a given period, depending on the respective capital needs of the PE and the government, on debt service obligations and on the liquidity of each party. Current account flows include property income from and to the PE (receipt category 2 and payment category 2 above), which depend on the size of the respective investments. Property income *from* the PE depends of course on continuing public ownership, so privatization will eliminate all or most of this flow. Tax collections (receipt category 1) depend indirectly on investment, since investment generates the flows on which taxes are levied. If these investment-dependent items are excluded, the remaining current account items (receipt categories 5, 6, 7 and payment categories 1, 6, 7, 8) might be expected to cancel out, i.e. that the standard is fiscal neutrality in any given period. However, even these remaining flows are dependent on a multitude of factors which require case-by-case analysis. One complication, for instance, is that capital transfers to PEs substitute for current subsidies irrespective of their stated purposes.[11] Another complication is the treatment of severance payments, which could be interpreted as a capital subsidy to compensate the PE for its non-commercial role as an employment agency in former years.

The 'budgetary burden' of a PE is commonly defined[12] to include the excess of explicit payments 1 through 4 over the explicit receipts except for tax revenue, that is recepts 2, 3 and 4 above. The reason for excluding tax revenue is that this is equally collectible from a private enterprise, i.e. it is not specific to public enterprise.[13] However, for our purpose taxes should be included, as a public enterprise may benefit from a different tax status. Conversely, the purchaser of the enterprise may have obtained tax incentives as a part of the deal or may have reduced its tax payments by setting off past PE losses, as Fiat did on the purchase of Alfa Romeo from IRI. There may be differences also in the level of tax compliance. PEs in liquidity difficulties frequently delay payment of their tax dues, both direct taxes and taxes such as excise duties collected from customers. In effect they force loans from the government.[14] If privatization improves profitability and liquidity, tax revenues should increase and be paid sooner. All these potential effects are consequences of privatization.

Therefore an evaluation of the fiscal impact of a privatization should, it is suggested, include all the above flows, both before privatization and after privatization, for as long a period as data are available. The analysis of this impact should separate out capital flows. Privatization proceeds, net of costs, should be related to the estimated future dividends foregone.

In principle all explicit fiscal flows between the PE and government treasury can be measured equally in the enterprise accounts or in the government accounts. In practice there are timing differences even on cash transactions. Furthermore, accounts may not be suitably classified or detailed. Government accounting systems rarely distinguish tax revenues from public and private enterprises, and even current subsidies to PEs may not be distinguished from other current transfers.[15] In PE accounts, all explicit fiscal flows are likely to be included in the ledger classification of accounts with the exception of import duty (which is commonly merged in the cost of the item imported), and some minor taxes such as stamp duty. It is probably easier for an evaluation agency to obtain fiscal data from the PE than from the revenue accounts of the levels of government involved. Exceptions are the privatization proceeds, cost of free/subsidized services, cost of regulation and cost of safety nets, which do not normally pass through the enterprise accounts. Privatization receipts are sometimes classified as capital receipts and sometimes as current revenue. In Poland and France they go into special funds for capital uses.

ACCOUNTING AND REGULATORY CONTROL

Many developing countries are considering privatizing PEs which have monopoly power in some or all of the markets in which they operate. It is generally agreed that monopolies tend to be inefficient, even in the private sector, because they can pass on the higher costs of inefficiency to their customers, and there are no competing firms for customers to turn to. If privatization is intended to increase efficiency, either competition must be created, or it must be simulated by government regulation.[16]

The role of accounting in promoting competition is to provide quantitative data on costs, prices and profit for policy making and the negotiation of specific privatizations. Economies of scale and economies of scope in the incumbent PE may be measured empirically by distinguishing the direct and indirect costs, variable and fixed, associated with each strategy. The welfare losses (reduction in joint producer surplus and consumer surplus) caused by monopoly, and the efficiency gains that may be expected by privatization of ownership and management, are not empirically determinable as they rest on comparison with hypothetical alternatives, but accountants may contribute data on relevant variables such as marginal cost at different levels of production.

Marginal cost is itself a shadowy concept, resting as it does on the attributability of each of a multiplicity of cost items to a unit increment of production. Attributability is divided and cross-divided, direct and indirect, short term and long term. Moreover, marginal cost is highly variable over time, over capacity ranges, and over changing production conditions and opportunities, especially in developing countries where standardized production methods are the exception rather than the norm. In the real world of, say, a bus service, the incremental passenger-kilometer may require only a drop more fuel, or a new bus, or even an extra depot, depending on which of a succession of capacity constraints has to be broken. Where more than one service is produced from the same process (e.g. passenger transport and goods transport using the same locomotive, track, etc.), either in proportions fixed by the technology in use or in variable proportions but with no consistent corresponding variations in process cost, then there is no such thing as individual product cost, whether marginal or full. The product and its market price may be defined, but its 'cost' depends on arbitrary apportionments of common costs. Accountants in regulated firms have an endless supply of arguments in favour of bases of apportionment which work out to the firm's advantage!

These natural limitations to cost accounting apply equally to the attempt to regulate monopolies by fixing maximum prices/tariffs (without losses of quality or service availability). These are based either on cost (as in US privately-owned utilities) or on the Littlechild (RPI-x) formula (as in British Telecom, British Gas and the British Airports Authority).

GENERAL LIMITATIONS OF ACCOUNTING

General-purpose financial statements produced for external consumption, that is, the income statement, balance sheet and statement of changes in financial condition,[17] are intended to provide information which will assist in economic decision-making by present and potential investors, employees, lenders, suppliers and other trade creditors, customers, governments and their agencies and the public (IASC 1989).[18]

Past and future data

Since all economic decisions are choices between alternative options for the future, past financial data is useful only insofar as it has predictive value and can be used for forward projections or forecasts of profits or cash flows – their size, timing and certainty. In the context of privatization, public enterprise financial data is used to assess the future viability of the enterprise, its suitability for privatization in terms of government criteria, the method of privatization, the price at which the business will be offered, and the need for any post-privatization monitoring or regulation.

In countries undergoing cataclysmic change such as war, hyperinflation or transition to market pricing, past financial data has very little predictive value. Even in a stable economy, data needs to be carefully reviewed to allow for future differences due to changes in technology and markets, acquisitions and disposals, start-up of new lines of business and close-down of old lines, and a wide assortment of transactions which are not expected to recur regularly in the future (unusual and exceptional items, prior period correction items, etc.).

A number of national and international accounting standards attempt to improve the predictive value of financial statements by requiring specific disclosure of: non-recurring transactions,[19] judgemental items such as depreciation and loss provisions,[20] some discretionary expenditures such as most research and development expenditures,[21] and any changes in accounting policies and their financial effects.[22] All these items and their effects on period results should be disclosed so that analysts can assess the probability of their recurrence separately from ongoing operations.

Non-financial data

Accounting standards require very little non-financial information. National and international accounting standards (IAS) deal almost exclusively with financial information needed by investors and creditors (actual and potential). Non-financial data is required only where it clarifies or supplements disclosures of financial data.[23] The scope of audit is similarly defined. Other groups of users are identified, such as employees, customers, the community and general public, and government agencies,[24] but IAS do not meet the information needs of these groups except where they coincide with the needs of investors and creditors.

Accountability is nowadays defined to include *all* the groups which are affected by business operations or otherwise have a legitimate interest in their activities.

Externalities

A fundamental concept in all accounting is the entity or boundary of measurement. Business accounts measure all transfers across the boundary of the business, which may be defined to include subsidiaries, associated companies, joint venture shares, etc. as appropriate, and to exclude shareholders, employees, etc.

Externalities are defined as costs or benefits arising out of the actions of the accounting entity which are not paid for or received by the entity, i.e. they are paid or received, willingly or unwillingly, by other entities. Thus, business accounts do not include credit for civic beautification projects, nor do the national accounts of one country include the costs to other countries imposed by (say) acid rain caused by its power plants.

Environmental accounting at the enterprise level should develop by way of legal requirements for a special report[25] linked to the basic financial statements, rather than by confusing the boundary of business accounting. Environmental reporting by PEs would facilitate the privatization process by revealing the potential environmental liabilities, and the need for investment in new environmentally friendly technology.

Changing unit of measurement

All accrual-based business financial statements add and subtract currency units of different values. Alone among the professions, accountants and economists work with a fluctuating measuring unit. Economists routinely adjust their figures for inflation: accountants do not. The effects, after 50 years of continuous inflation in every market economy and more recently in transitional economies also, are that financial statements cannot be interpreted or validly compared as presented, whether between years, companies, industries or countries, with rare exceptions.[26] In some countries and in some companies, partial corrections are made in the accounts, eg. by fixed asset revaluations, or LIFO inventory accounting. Analysts make various corrections of their own according to the data and indices available to them.

The effect of mixed-unit statements is that resource allocation decisions are misguided, unless users make appropriate adjustments to the data themselves.[27]

At the enterprise level, failure to adjust accounts for inflation results in an overstatement of profit[28] and an understatement of assets and equity capital.

Non-comparability

Financial statements may not be comparable from year to year, firm to firm, or country to country, for reasons other than inflationary distortions.

The intercountry harmonization of accounting and auditing standards has become a principal issue in the globalization of capital markets,[29] in the control of multi-national corporations,[30] in regional integration such as the European Community,[31] the promotion of foreign investment, and, in particular, foreign investment in privatized PEs.

In the transitional economies, the former accounting methods and practices were based on the needs of centralized planning. These are inappropriate to the needs of a market economy in which capital is allocated according to the expectations of investors, based partly on reliable and uniform financial statements. These countries are introducing new accounting laws which amend their existing laws to meet the needs of foreign investors as well as local investors.

Weak accounting infrastructure

A survey of the state of accounting in 37 African countries in late 1989 found that there are too few indigenous fully qualified accountants, particularly in the public sector. The position in other regions is only slightly better overall with considerable variation from country to country[32]. This is probably at present the highest priority area for accounting reform.

Accounting infrastructure is similarly undeveloped in some transitional economies such as Mongolia, Laos and Cambodia. In Central and Eastern Europe, however, the problem is different. These countries have well trained cadres of book-keepers, who have kept enterprise books and rendered reports to central planning authorities in former years. The need now is to train these cadres to implement the adapted accounting systems being legislated in their countries and to take on new roles in the interpretation of financial statements and solving of management problems in a market directed environment. There is also a need to create a large number of auditors.

LIMITATIONS OF PUBLIC ENTERPRISE ACCOUNTING DATA

Public enterprises have been controlled in most cases by similar accounting, reporting and auditing legislation and regulations as apply to private businesses.[33] However, there are major differences in practice. The actual record of PE accountability has been poor.

Privatization sets up a need for past profitability data of a higher quality than may have been required or provided before. For instance, profits may need to be segmented by division or location to provide information for the break-up of the PE. Commonly all accrual adjustments need to be reviewed, such as depreciation,[34] loss provisions, and pension liabilities (see below). Prior year adjustments due to mistakes and omissions in former year accounts have to be analysed and apportioned back to the respective years.[35]

Public share offerings require further preparation and the use of past data for future projections requires a further set of adjustments for factors which will change, such as past subsidies, monopoly privileges, protection, special inter-PE prices, guaranteed loans at low interest rates, tax exemptions, etc., which were enjoyed by the PE, as well as non-commercial obligations on the PE which will not apply to its new owners. Second, profits have to be analysed into one-time windfalls, continuing activities and discontinued activities.

Privatization decisions are made according to various criteria, not all of which require accounting data.

On a change of ownership, all assets and liabilities taken over need to be fully listed and valued.

A major liability arises in the case of retrenchment of employees.

A contingent liability may arise where the enterprise was inconclusively appropriated from a former owner.

Another possible liability is the liability to make good former damage to the environment, if environmental legislation has created this liability.

Contingent liabilities of uncertain incidence such as environmental clean-up costs and claims by former owners, and in fact any liabilities of uncertain amount, should be absorbed by the government where it values them at less than the private purchaser. This maximizes the net fiscal gain.

SUMMARY

This study has discussed the role of accounting in identifying and measuring certain financial and economic impacts of privatization against its stated objectives and national objectives in general. It has been shown that these measurements depend on data from various sources, including sources outside the jurisdiction or competence of the enterprise itself. While enterprise-produced data is an essential input to the evaluation of privatization, it is incomplete, whether to measure changes in efficiency or changes in the impact of the enterprise on the public purse. Any agency, such as a supreme audit institution or commission of enquiry set up for this purpose, should have powers to call for data from any source within the country. Having regard to possible abuse or leakage of confidential commercial data, such powers should be strictly confined and controlled. This type of evaluation is a limited purpose socio-economic study, requiring expertise in economics, finance, accounting, and special knowledge of the respective industries and markets. It is not a substitute for the normal process of documenting and making transparent each privatization and allowing it to be subject to public scrutiny.

The study has also described a number of ways in which accounting, in its present state in developing and transitional economies, limits and constrains the privatization process. Decisions on which PEs to privatize, what method to use, and sale price rest partly on accounting data, which may be out-of-date, inappropriately formatted, distorted by inflation, insufficiently detailed, or just plain wrong. The enormous quantity of technical assistance currently being poured into preparing PEs for privatization is an indicator of the inadequacy of past PE accounts, and of accounting generally, as a guide to decision making. Valuations of PEs, for instance, vary over a scale of 10 or more to one, particularly in economies in transition, in which past prices and accounts have little relationship to a future market environment.

A number of general limitations to the prevailing accounting model were outlined and their effects on the privatization process mentioned. Some effects, such as those resulting from the failure to report in units of constant value, cannot be quantified, though they are believed to be significant. However, this is a problem which has been recognised since the 1920s and it is not likely to be solved in time to assist medium-term privatization programmes. The same applies to the generally poor accounting infrastructure in developing countries, and the state of public enterprise accounting. This is probably today the highest priority accounting area for technical assistance; this kind of human resources development also takes time.

The role of accounting in the regulation of privatized monopolies is a large one, turning on calculations of product costs and productivity. A major theoretical limit is imposed by the existence of joint costs and the consequent indeterminacy of individual product costs. The remaining problems of determining marginal cost are purely practical, though often complex.

NOTES

1 In practice this will be constrained by the number of post-privatization years for which audited accounts are available. As a rule of thumb at least three years after privatization should be compared with three years before.

2   Except indirectly in that a higher share of the market may allow greater economies of scale. This may be adjusted for.

3   Galal *et al.* (forthcoming).

4   Even a centrally planned economy which allocates raw materials to enterprises cannot tell what quantities are consumed in any period. This is always an internal accounting function.

5   An early evaluation of the Bangladeshi privatizations showed that production was up and employment down but somehow the privatized enterprises did not have the cash flow to repay their loans to the government on schedule. In fact the firms kept separate accounts for the government (Sobhan and Ahsan 1984).

6   These are measured on a cash basis, not an accrual basis as used for the national accounts, as it is actual receipts which increase government's ability to make payments and activate demand for goods and services in the rest of the economy. 'Monetary policy, fiscal policy and balance of payments policy are all formulated basically in financial terms and draw primarily upon statistics measuring payments and financial balances' (IMF 1986: 32).

7   The enterprise subsidizes the government insofar as it pursues non-commercial objectives (NCOs) which cause additional costs or losses which are not reimbursed. Some of these implicit subsidies can in principle be estimated, but unless the government requires the information and pays accordingly, which is rare in developing countries, the estimation is not made. NCOs which involve joint costs with commercial objectives cannot be estimated, even in principle. There is also a grey area in the definition of 'commercial'. If the privatized enterprise continues the NCO, as British Telecom did by retaining uneconomic callboxes as a condition of its licence, it need not be costed as it washes out in the comparison. For an analysis of NCOs see Gray 1984: Appendix 1.

8   It is a common practice for government to allow profitable PEs to make loans and advances (which may be disguised subsidies) to PEs in difficulties. After privatization this is unlikely. The reference to other government agencies assumes that these agencies are not consolidated with the central government accounts (the usual case).

9   Governments which are strapped for cash often fall into arrears in paying their bills, e.g. for electricity and telephone services provided by PEs.

10 Gray 1984: 63

11 Since funds are tangible, sources cannot be objectively identified with particular uses. Classification resting on subjective intentions have no relevance for economic analysis.

12 For example by R.P. Short (1984: 78).

13 This distinction could equally be made for net lending to the government and perhaps other items.

14 The same applies to private enterprises. In fact tax evasion and default are notoriously high in small private enterprises. Large enterprises tend to be too prominent and politically vulnerable to default on their tax dues. The same may be expected of large privatized enterprises.

15 Out of 120 governments reporting their financial statistics to the IMF in 1991, only 26 (22 per cent) reported their subsidies to non-financial PEs in the latest year for which data were available. (IMF 1991: Table C, line 3.1.1).

16 However, Bradburd (1992: 24) has argued that even modest efficiency improvements arising out of privatization of utilities outweigh the welfare losses of monopoly. Governments are more worried about the distributional effects of privatization (specifically, higher prices to poor electors) than the efficiency effects.

17 Presently being replaced by the cash flow statement by some accounting standard setters.

18 This refers only to enterprises in the public and private sector, not to government agencies.

19 IAS 8 requires separate disclosure of unusual items, viz. gains and losses that derive from events or transactions that are distinct from the ordinary activities of the business and therefore are not expected to recur frequently or regularly.

20 IAS 2 requires disclosure of provisions for loss on current inventories and IAS 4 and 5 require the disclosure of depreciation charges, but there is no requirement for disclosure of provisions for losses on receivables, except in banks under IAS 30.

21 IAS 9 requires disclosure of total R&D costs, including amortization of past development costs carried on the balance sheet. However, R&D is interpreted narrowly to include only R&D expenditure on new products or processes. The standard does not cover personnel R&D, such as human resource development which is not product/process-related, nor administrative development, such as software development and introduction of new management systems.

22 IAS 8 allows changes in accounting policies within limits but requires disclosure of changes, the reasons they are made and their effects on the financial statements.

23 See IAS 5 – Information to be Disclosed in Financial Statements (1977). In the USA, listed companies are required to provide a 'management discussion and analysis'. This also is directed towards the needs of investors.

24 One might add non-government organizations and international organizations to the list of users.

25 Such as was recommended by ISAR (1992: 97–8).

26 Full inflation adjustments are made in the hyperinflationary economies of Argentina, Brazil and Chile, and by 60–70 per cent of enterprises in Iceland (UNCTC 1990: 50).

27 Portfolio investment is likely to be worse affected than direct investment, insofar as the latter uses discounted cash flow criteria rather than reported earnings criteria. Portfolio investment relies heavily on reported earnings data, which cannot be corrected for inflation without further data such as the composition and age structure of assets, which are not normally available.

28 Profit is overstated (in real terms) insofar as depreciation and cost of sales are calculated on a historic basis, offset by the gain to the firm on its net monetary non-indexed liabilities.

29 IASC cite the case of Telefonica de Espana, the Spanish telephone company, which made a profit in 1987 of 53 billion pesetas, calculated according to Spanish accounting standards. As the company is listed on the International Stock Exchange (London), it has to restate its accounts according to IAS. This showed a profit of 64 billion pesetas. Restatement for the US stock markets according to US generally accepted accounting principles gave a profit of 130 billion pesetas! (IASC News, December 1989).

30 Since 1982 the main objective of the Intergovernmental Working Group on International Standards of Accounting and Reporting (ISAR) sponsored by UNCTC has been the promotion of international accounting/reporting harmonization in order to make the activities of transnational corporations (TNCs) more transparent to host countries and to reduce the volume of reports the TNCs must file.

31 The Fourth and Seventh Directives of the Council prescribe a uniform format and content of annual financial statements of companies in the 12 members of the EC. These directives allow considerable discretion to member-states, e.g. inventories can be valued on LIFO, FIFO or other bases.

32 Fifteen developing countries in Asia and the Pacific in 1984 had an average of 57 fully qualified accountants per million of population, or 113 accountants per US$ billion of GDP. 34 developing countries in Africa in 1990 had only 40 accountants

per million of population, or 76 per US$ billion of GDP. (Sources: IFAC/ADB/IBRD 1984 and CTC 1991).

33 The IFAC Public Sector Committee has issued a guideline, 'Financial Reporting by Government Business Enterprises', which says that such financial statements should be presented in accordance with accounting principles, accounting standards and other requirements that are generally accepted for other business enterprises, ie. IAS and the appropriate national accounting standards. Note that some PEs are run as departmental enterprises and keep their accounts on the governmental cash accounting basis. Even if a departmental enterprise is reconstituted as a corporation before it is privatized, it is necessary to recast earlier years' accounts on an accrual basis so as to provide five years' comparative data, as in the case of British Telecom. A few PEs set up as companies or corporations also retain cash accounting. The great majority of PEs, however, keep accounts on an accrual basis.

34 In the UK, British Gas had over-depreciated their fixed assets by £500 million over a three-year period (UNCTC 1992).

35 Developing country PE accounts are notoriously inaccurate. Even if auditors find major errors, they are not always disclosed in the published audit report, and may be corrected only in the following year's statements.

REFERENCES

Bradburd, Ralph (1992) 'Privatization of regulatory monopoly: the regulation issue', *Policy Research Working Paper*, WPS 864, Washington: World Bank.

Galal, Ahmed *et al.* (forthcoming) *Welfare Consequences of Selling Public Enterprises*, World Bank (reviewed in *The Economist* 13 June 1992).

Gray, Clive (1984) 'Toward a conceptual framework for macroeconomic evaluation of public enterprise performance in mixed economies', in Robert H. Floyd, Clive S. Gray and R.P. Short, *Public Enterprise in Mixed Economies – Some Macroeconomic Aspects*, Washington: IMF.

IASC (1990) *International Accounting Standards 1990*, London: International Accounting Standards Committee.

IFAC/ADB IBRD (1984) *Asia and Pacific Conference on Accounting Education for Development*, Manila.

IMF (1986) *Government Financial Statistics Manual*, Washington: IMF.

IMF (1991) *Government Finance Statistics Yearbook*, Washington: IMF.

Intergovernmental Working Group of Experts on International Standards of Accounting and Reporting (ISAR) (1992) *International Accounting and Reporting Issues 1991 Review*, New York: United Nations.

Sobhan, R. and Ahsan, A. (1984) *Disinvestment and Denationalisation: Profile and Performance*, Research Report New Series No. 38, Dhaka: Bangladesh Institute of Development Studies.

Short, R.P. (1984) 'Public Enterprises: A statistical comparison', in R.H. Floyd, Clive S. Gray and R.P. Short *Public Enterprise in Mixed Economies – Some Macroeconomic Aspects*, Washington: IMF.

UNCTC (1990) *International Accounting and Reporting Issues 1989 Review*, New York: Commission on Transnational Corporations.

UNCTC (1992) Intergovernmental Working Group of Experts on International Standards of Accounting and Reporting, *Identification of Accounting Problems arising during Privatization and their Solution* plus case studies of Czechoslovakia, France, Germany, Hungary, Mexico, Poland and U.K. Tenth Session 5–13 March 1992, New York: Commission on Transnational Corporations, United Nations.

19

CONCLUDING REVIEW

V.V. Ramanadham

This chapter aims at focusing on some of the major points that emerge from the different papers. It also draws on the discussions which took place at the Expert Group Meeting held in Geneva in August 1992, at which the papers were presented. The review is broadly in three parts. It commences with a country-oriented analysis of the highlights of privatization experiences. Parts two and three are issue oriented, respectively, on constraints on privatization and impacts of privatization.

COUNTRY-ORIENTED ANALYSIS

The UK

The UK experience, as presented by George Yarrow, has several points of interest to developing countries. To start with, there is repeated emphasis in his paper on competition as a factor in realizing the good results expected of privatization. Where it is absent or weak, the benefits tend to be a function of regulatory effectiveness concerning the operations of the privatized enterprise. In the UK the monopolies that persist post-privatization are broadly in the nature of natural monopolies. In developing countries, monopolies will continue to exist for yet another reason, namely, small-sized markets. (Many small-sized countries automatically come under this description.) There would be little scope for more than one or two economically sized units to operate in several sectors of activity – e.g. steel, drugs, fertilizers, machinery and airlines. It is, therefore, of primary importance that governments in developing countries clearly address the constraints on the benefits of privatization stemming from the ubiquitous elements of monopoly likely to persist in many sectors of business activity. Where serious fear prevails as regards successful regulation, the very decision to privatize might be under constraint.

The point has relevance even to the major non-divestiture option being pursued in many developing countries today, namely, performance contracts. A basic question, which does not seem to be sufficiently addressed through the contracts, relates to the degree of price-raising opportunities resting with

342

monopoly-prone public enterprises. Even in the UK, as George Yarrow suggests, the impact of strict financial targets on productivity performance has been 'much weaker' for state monopolies than for competitive enterprises. We may suggest that the technique of performance contracts should either contain or be suitably supplemented by regulatory restrictions on easy price enhancements for the sake of making a show of accomplishment *vis-à-vis* financial targets.

Another point, whose weight is not fully realized in discussions on privatization, concerns the 'agency costs' which arise in the context of the non-commercial outputs expected of privatized enterprises. These have not been a major problem in the UK, though they seem to have affected 'the attractiveness of the privatization option' where they assumed importance. The problem would be infinitely more complex in developing countries, considering the substantial externalities associated with many enterprises in their circumstances. Further, one should not ignore the possibility of unfair or irregular practices developing in the implementation of the compensations deemed necessary in a large multitude of such cases. It is, therefore, possible that governments in many developing countries might be inclined to sequence privatization in such a way that full divestitures on a large scale take place gradually, consistent with the pronounced evolution of market forces which would render the problem of 'agency costs' relatively tractable.

Considering the emphasis which, in some quarters, is placed on ownership change as a condition for performance improvements, George Yarrow's view against such an easy hypothesis is worth underlining. Whether competition prevails is a basic determinant of improved efficiency. Whether managerial and technological capability is available with the privatized enterprise is another. Besides, there is a fundamental issue: whether micro efficiency is all that we should look for, rather than micro-cum-macro efficiency, especially in developing countries. This comes in for some comment in the third part of this chapter.

George Yarow's comment that the 'golden share' technique adopted in the UK, whatever its merits, tends, with its bias against take-overs, to protect 'incumbent managers' from the full sway of market disciplines, is worth serious consideration. It is, of course, up to the government to exercise the prerogative of the golden share. If, on the ground that the incumbent management deserves protection from take-over bids until the enterprise consolidates its viability and stability, the prerogative is over-protectively exercised, the efficiency objective of privatization might be correspondingly constrained.

East Germany

Dieter Bös's paper on Germany proposes a definition of 'viability' which takes into account the costs (and therefore the benefits) of restructuring an enterprise. This is of more than theoretical interest. Applied to a majority of public enterprises in the developing world, it contains elements of justification for restructuring an enterprise prior to divestiture, if – and only if – the restructuring is genuinely calculated to place it on the road to viability. (The incidental benefits in the sequencing of privatization come out in most papers. In fact Jersy Cieslik's paper on Poland underscores the importance of restructuring as a highly desirable first step in the divestiture process. On the other hand, Olivier Bouin argues, with reference to Czechoslovakia, that the 'systemic vacuum' resulting from the dismantling of central planning is not an appropriate environment for enterprise restructuring.) The point may be broadened to cover the case of reform strategies widely applied to the public enterprise sector – even under World Bank projects, e.g. in Uganda. Assuming that the reforms, which should include restructuring at some stage, lift an enterprise into a state of viability from its current state of inefficiency and loss making, calculations of the comparative advantage of its remaining in the public sector or of its transfer to the private sector ought to be based on the post-reform potential of its viability.

While producing an excellent case for restructuring, Dieter Bös terms it 'second-best' and rejects it, concluding that neither the government nor a large state-owned holding company is a good instrument for expediting restructuring. One has to make a distinction, however, between the intrinsic worth of a restructuring proposition and the instrument of implementation. The latter could be a non-centralized, non-departmental organization, including a contractee for a given purpose, capable of improving the viability of an enterprise through a well-conceived programme of restructuring. Of course we should agree with Bös that restructuring must not be a 'disguise' for the subsidization of non-viable firms.

Hungary

Gusztáv Báger's reference to 'a socially responsible market economy' as an aim of the Hungarian economic transformation is pregnant with meaning. There are traces of it in the other papers as well, which reiterate social efficiency as an important test of the success of privatization. The recent legislative action, taken in Hungary, on creating a distinctive holding company for looking after the many enterprises that will long stay in the public sector is a development which several other countries might study with interest. For many of their public enterprises are likely to stay under public ownership; and it would be preferable to separate responsibility for them from the agency entrusted with divestiture *per se*. This, no doubt, begs the problem of co-ordination between the two agencies; but the problem is there in substance even in the absence of such a distinctive arrangement, perhaps in a fuzzy manner.

Another point of interest made by Bager concerns the acceleration of privatization through the 'investor-initiated privatization' route. If we analyse the issue, the hypothesis here seems to be that a given enterprise is attractive enough to a potential investor. Assuming that it is one of the enterprises chosen by the government for divestiture, there is no special reason why the divestiture (of an attractive enterprise) should await a buying initiative on the part of a potential investor. It is where the enterprise in which he expresses interest is either one that the government is not willing to divest or a loss-making one which he might snatch away at a bargain price that problems arise. There can be yet another complication: is the private party that expresses interest in buying an enterprise the best available, not only offering the highest divestiture price but capable of efficient continuance of operations? Is the sale likely to be effected without the benefit, to the exchequer, of the most competitive price, or under a cloud of suspicion concerning the divestiture negotiations?

Poland

One of the difficulties that plague privatization in most countries is what Cieslik terms, with reference to Poland, as 'lack of clarity as to the ultimate goals and objectives of privatization'. Governments are learning the hard way that the absence of a clear policy statement on privatization creates problems of misunderstanding and misapprehension in different quarters on several crucial issues implicit in its implementation, e.g. on the role of foreign capital and on the treatment of labour lay-offs. There is something in the practical argument that governments might prefer to keep away from clear statements on issues which they are not quite certain of how to resolve. This might be a matter of momentary comfort; but the problems will stare them in the face as times goes by and solutions begins to be introduced on an *ad hoc* basis. This process does not erase the fundamental need for a clear position on crucial issues; in fact it complicates it.

Cieslik's description of the incentives for foreign investors not to participate in Poland's privatization programmes suggests a broader comment relating to the investor's options. The investor might prefer a joint venture to buying a public enterprise; or he might simply prefer to invest in a new project rather than expose himself to the complexities of taking over a public enterprise, what with its labour, managerial and financial (in particular, debt) problems. There would be ample scope for such options as long as there is scope for investment opportunities other than in buying divested enterprises. Most developing countries are replete with such opportunities, the more so when it is assumed that governments simultaneously liberalize investor entry into any line of business at his choice.

The technique of 'sectoral privatization' in Poland is, in fact, another term for overall industrial policy in some significant senses and underscores the role of the government in effectuating policies considered good from an overall standpoint while undertaking or permitting individual pieces of privatization. To interpret the technique in this way might be unpalatable to the centrally planned economies in transition. But the fact remains that individual privatizations have interrelationships in process and effect; and that someone has to take care of optimizing these as far as possible, though not through a re-introduction of the command-type governance of the era that is dumped into oblivion. To cite a major example, enterprise restructuring calls not only for restructuring decisions appropriate to a given enterprise but for the most economical expending of the limited resources available for the purpose through some mechanism of prioritizing among the client enterprises.

Czechoslovakia

Olivier Bouin's intensive discussion of the voucher system adopted in Czechoslovakia raises some serious issues. Basically it owes to three factors: the absence of capital markets, political limits to the influx of foreign capital, and the government's undoubted commitment to speed up the transformation of the economy. Novel as it is, it is not the most important route of privatization in that country, however. On the whole, it appears that the cross-section of enterprises which opted for the voucher technique represent the less prosperous segment of the public enterprise sector. The way the coupons are held does not permit us to draw any definite conclusions in favour of management efficiency and prospects of enterprise restructuring. The funds which seem to be the king pin of the exercise might legitimately be tempted to take a short-termish attitude to enterprise operations. Several of the enterprises might fail – not because of the voucher system; and some funds might also face financial difficulties. Whether the government will (and can) bail them out is an open question. It would, however, be too simplistic to assume that such matters would be left exclusively to the private investors and market forces.

It seems necessary to separate the issue of ownership transfer from the government, which the voucher system rapidly brings about, from the basic issue of enterprise efficiency through managerial and technological excellence. There is also the problem of many voucher holders being disappointed through capital losses and of vouchers sliding into concentrations of ownership. Investor confidence at the level of the small investor might be seriously affected. While it is too early to predict the precise trend of events in all these respects, analytically these problems merit the government's attention; and well-devised monitoring would be of value.

Central and Eastern Europe

John Howell's paper brings out the primacy of political objectives underlying privatization in Central and Eastern Europe. This explains the emphasis on speed. In an extreme sense one can think in terms of a trade-off between political compulsions and the deficiencies in the implementation of privatization. It is of interest to note his views on the blame that the advisers to the governments in this region have to share and on 'more than a little absence of intellectual integrity in much of the advice being given'. The impacts of political conditions in countries like Poland, Russia and Ukraine on the pace and techniques of privatization are clearly delineated in his paper.

Guyana and Argentina

Carl Greenidge's paper brings out the difficulties in the path of privatization undertaken during a period of acute recession – 'one of the worst economic recessions since the 1939–45 war' in Guyana. Unfortunately, several countries are currently in a similar plight; yet they have determined, partly under expert advice from outside, that privatization is a high-priority item in their economic strategy. An interesting feature of Guyanese privatization, by no means special to Guyana, is that it has been fiscally driven; and 'efficiency' has not attracted the importance it deserved in the privatization debates. Alejandro Rausch takes a similar view on Argentinian privatization – it is 'mainly fiscally driven' – and expresses serious doubts about the 'short term narrow view' concerning the consequent benefits. Enrique Saravia's statement of Brazil's objectives of privatization cites reducing the public sector debt, promoting wider share ownership and increasing competition; 'efficiency' is not specifically mentioned, though, with qualifications, this could be construed as subsumed by the competition objective.

The phenomenon of weak regulatory structures is another significant point that comes out of Carl Greenidge's comments. That this is not exceptional to Guyana is at once borne out by Rausch's conclusion that the rapid privatization in Argentina proceeded with 'insufficient consideration of the regulatory framework'. The basic issue is this: where conditions of competition are not effective to produce the good results of the free market, how justified is the transfer of ownership from the public to the private sector in the absence of an effective framework of regulation governing the operations and investment policies of the enterprise owners?

Carl Greenidge's detailed survey of many aspects of privatization processes and impacts offers excellent support to our suggestion that there ought to be appropriate monitoring of privatization as it proceeds, to understand, at the minimum: whether it is unfolding itself as per the publicized objectives; whether, in particular, the major objective of efficiency is being realized; how ownership is shaping itself; whether pockets of monopoly are emerging; and whether divestiture pricing and other negotiations are taking place, as per the written word of law and, in any case, untarnished by irregular, if not corrupt, practices. Further well-designed monitoring can play the role of an early warning system where changes seem to be necessary and useful. In particular, where a privatization is followed by conditions on the rate of growth in enterprise activity – investment, capacity, output, employment etc., monitoring is obviously imperative.

The last point seems to be of particular relevance to Argentina where, for example, ENTEL (Telephone Company) is subject to an investment schedule over a five-year period. Similar conditions are likely to be contemplated in certain basic sectors in many developing countries, on grounds of national economic development. Whether they are met is one important issue for monitoring; and how they are met is another – for example, through an exercise of monopoly power and/or deteriorating service standards? Alejandro Rausch provides a kalaedoscopic account of the micro results of several privatizations in Argentina, including ENTEL, which lend support to our comments.

Among the difficult circumstances in which privatizations are undertaken in developing countries and in the centrally planned economies in transition, one that merits special attention but, for various reasons, is little publicized, consists of the 'deadlines' set for privatizing. Alejandro Rausch mentions this with reference to Argentina. Enrique Saravia cites a 240-day time table in the case of a privatization transaction in Brazil. Hungary, Poland, and so many other countries have been facing this problem in some form, with the result that privatizations are effected under conditions of relative unpreparedness, or they are rushed through, often provoking criticism on grounds of transparency and fairness, or they are just not completed within the programmed time-frame. The last circumstance raises the eyebrows of some international agencies. Basic to this difficult situation is the urgent need to improve the capability of the top echelons in policy making and implementation, so that, within whatever limits of capital markets and saleability of enterprises prevail, implementation does not suffer from lack of capability in managing the privatization process. It is worth noting that a serious component of this lack is the hindrances that certain government departments themselves create to the action of a privatizing agency, as mentioned in Enrique Saravia's paper on Brazil.

Brazil

Brazil's 'privatization certificates' are an interesting device which directs the use of investible funds by one who has them for purposes dictated by the government. The result might be in favour of making a non-government party buy a share which the government owned; but the means is incompatible with the free market concept as applied to investment decision and use of resources. If nationalization meant a dictated and compulsory share sale by a private party to the government, privatization through the use of privatization certificates connotes a dictated and compulsory purchase of a government share by a private party. There might be some option as to what, among available shares, to purchase; but the option not to buy is not there.

Morocco

Alfred Saulniers' review of privatization in Morocco suggests that it has been taking place in a relatively easy environment. To start with, most public enterprises have been profit making. Those that make rather low profits or sustain losses are those which have a 'social role' or features of publicness; and many of these are 'heavily regulated monopolies'. What is important to note is that their low viability is a function not of managerial inefficiency but of public policy objectives. In the absence of a change in the latter, privatization *per se* will not relieve the exchequer of the burdens of some subsidization of the outputs of such enterprises. These will go as compensations to privatized enterprises or transfer payments, in some other way, direct to the consumers concerned. We find a similar point in Muhith's account of subsidies to jute and jute products in the case of Bangladesh, offered as a sequel to national policy to both public and private enterprises. We may recall, at this point, the 'agency costs' mentioned by George Yarrow.

The six criteria adopted in the selection of privatizable firms in Morocco reflect the ease of decision. They are profitable and already operate in competitive markets; they have no overstaffing problems; they do not have important elements of publicness or a social role; there is already a significant private shareholding participation in them; and they are regionally diversified too. And none of the 75 enterprises listed for divestiture needs corporatization; they already work as commercial companies.

Further privatization – in its several options – has been in progress for 30 years in Morocco, 'devoid of ideological content'; and portfolio sales of shares, which privatization yet largely connotes, has been no new practice here. There is the added point of convenience: unlike in many other countries the motivation here is 'strictly local', in the words of Saulniers.

Tanzania

The basic objective of privatization, as described by George Mbowe, is to locate an enterprise in the sector where its comparative advantage is superior, rather than effect a mere ownership change. Several non-divestiture options have been tried in Tanzania with a view to ensuring the turn-around of enterprises and preparing the base for their easy divestiture.

Tanzania provides an example of how difficult it is to balance between the pros and cons of transparency in privatization. Several bureacratic systems have been created and the screening process for transactions lengthened with a view to enriching transparency. But prospective investors feel frustrated by delays and indecision in finalizing the deals – particularly interested foreigners. True, establishing the right degree of transparency is a difficult and delicate task and has to vary with the socio-political circumstances of the country in question. Broadly, however, it would be undesirable to compromise on it in respect of basic policy formulation and objective specific, divestiture pricing and choice of buyers, admission of foreign capital, treatment of labour, and the sequencing of privatization transactions, because the wrong degree of transparency can lead to uninformed criticism and gossip, to the embarrassment of policy makers and implementors of privatization.

Israel

Privatization in Israel has not been triggered by a pressure to sell public enterprises on the ground that they are loss making. Most of them have been doing well, under the law that requires them to work on business principles, except under governmental direction to the contrary. And corporatization itself, implying the removal of an enterprise from the departmental status, has helped improve the micro efficiency of the enterprises concerned, Bezek (the telecommunication enterprise) being the best example; and this has in fact enriched the prospect of a good divestiture price in the course of time.

Shlomo Eckstein *et al.* suggest that the main, 'if not the dominant, goal' of privatization in Israel is the expected fiscal contribution, but not in a situation of fiscal burden on the exchequer from public enterprises. This they dismiss as 'only a short-run effect'. Here is a faint echo of Alejandro Rausch's view on the subject.

The composition and size structure of the public enterprise sector in Israel seems to make for relative ease in implementing privatization. Ten enterprises account for 87 per cent of the aggregate employment in the sector and, with perhaps one exception – a retail store – belong to the fairly 'core' category. (There is some similarity with the UK situation.) The government can, therefore, have the advantage of concentrating on the most appropriate privatization techniques, taking full note of each enterprise's characteristics – its market conditions, technological status, size economies, and implicit externalities, and endeavouring to create the broadest possible scope for competition and, to the extent it is absent, to set up a tailor-made regulatory framework for each of those enterprises. Not that privatization techniques in the other (small) cases can be determined or implemented in a casual manner, but the costs of poor judgement would be drastic in the ten cases; hence the need for especial caution.

Bangladesh

Abdul Maali Muhith's description of privatization in Bangladesh highlights, among the unfortunate features, lack of clear policy and of comprehensive attention to the terms of a divestiture agreement. Public enterprises have been a serious drain on the exchequer; hence the government's anxiety, initially, to sell away the losing units. This naturally proved difficult. He highlights 'the unaccountable despotic regime' in the country, which 'universalized corruption', as one serious cause of defective privatization and of dampened private investment initiative.

India

S.R. Mohnot brings out the outlines of the new economic thinking in India, of which divestiture is a spectacular, if overdue, element. In a sense it demonstrates that privatization would not have had a chance of initiation in the absence of a conducive change in 40-year-old national thinking on economic development. The limited divestitures contemplated yet have two features of analytical and practical significance: they seem to be grossly underpriced; and they related to the most profitable enterprises in the central government sector. The incremental privatization, which Mohnot discusses, is an option which has relevance to countries where substantial needs exist of expanding outputs in sectors now occupied predominantly by public enterprises. Given an overall scarcity of resources, governments might find it convenient to take the route of letting private investments in rather than inducing them to buy into public enterprises. The private entry might even be into existing public enterprises.

Another interesting point Mohnot makes is that conflicting signals emerge from the central government's policies of some kind of privatization and some state governments' expansion of investments even in non-core sectors. If it is safe to assume that there is no dearth of private capital for entering the latter areas of operations, the state governments' actions deserve being brought into consistency with the approach of the central government.

The MOUs in India

Suresh Kumar's presentation focuses on one basic idea and on one operational technique. The idea is that the 'mission' of a public enterprise should be re-defined, as warranted by changing socio-economic circumstances, instead of simply harping on the goal of an increased profit. Instead of tackling the problem in this way, he argues disapprovingly, a change of the multiple objective situation into a single-objective situation and privatization are considered 'best and easy'. It is true that the weight attached to profit (among the performance criteria in a given case) can be increased over time, as in fact has been happening in the generality of cases in India; but the fundamental *raison d'être* lies in reflecting the current public perception of the mission of the enterprise (i.e. its composite public-and-enterprise role) in the outcomes of its operations. It is interesting to find from his recital of experience that profit and MOU score have generally gone together. In other words, those which have satisfied the totality of the score criteria have presented a good record of profit as well. To a large extent this is natural; for successful performance by many non-profit criteria is often paralleled by profit-earning capability on the part of the management. It is not clear, however, whether the MOUs in every case in India (and similar performance contracts in several other countries) have given sufficient attention to defining the non-commercial segments of activity on the part of a given enterprise – for example, surplus employment, employment reservations, investments in difficult areas, and product mix which is not the most commercially beneficial. It is also doubtful if the criteria, weights and evaluation sufficiently take cognizance of the elements of monopoly power enjoyed by the enterprise.

The technique which the paper addresses is the Memorandum of Under-standing (MOU), by which the government and an enterprise agree, subject to the above comments, on the enterprise mission. It operates, through the score element, as an evaluation technique too; and has the inherent force of inducing the management into improved performance. Suresh Kumar attributes to it the virtue of simulating a competitive environment. If this does happen, the objective of efficiency gains can be achieved. It is in this sense that the MOU offers itself as an important non-divestiture option.

The matrices that Suresh Kumar provides, bringing together market structures, current efficiency conditions, and social obligations and externalities, and using them for the delineation of options of privatization (in its broadest sense), are well worth deep attention. Some obvious lessons are that constant attempt should be made to reduce the elements of monopoly, raise the efficiency of operations, and rationalize the social-obligations perception. Answers in the last column concerning options of privatization policy automatically change as the substantive content of the first three columns improves.

CONSTRAINTS ON PRIVATIZATION

This part seeks to focus on the issue of constraints on privatization, of which many details are found in the individual papers. Many of them are common to a majority of the countries covered in this volume and amply vindicate the analytical framework contained in my basic working paper. The following comments provide an annotation by way of an overview.

First, the low profitability (or the unprofitability) of an enterprise has generally figured as a practical constraint on divestiture – even in the UK (e.g. coal, rail and nuclear energy). No wonder, in countries where a majority of public enterprises have been poor profit-wise, the difficulty has been enormous, as evidenced by Tanzania and the centrally planned economies in transition, but not by Morocco or Israel. Here is a hopeful lesson for those who emphasize non-divestiture options capable of raising profitability, while improving performance on whatever 'score criteria' are adopted in the process.

Second, constraints experienced in undertaking rapid and large-scale divestitures have, in many countries, prompted governments to take seriously measures of improving performance through non-divestiture options. Tanzania and India are typical examples. Many of the least developed African countries appear to fall into this category, even as the large-scale reform projects on public enterprises in Uganda and Kenya (with World Bank loans) suggest. The argument that reforms do not work and that ownership change is a necessary condition for performance improvement warrants rigorous circumspection today, thanks to the inviolable pressures of the International Monetary Fund on the public exchequers of developing countries.

Third, non-divestiture options are not a bed of roses. They themselves are under constraints of various kinds. Tanzania unfolds problems of experience. The concern of lessees in the case of a lease arrangement is found often to be linked with maximizing short-term gains irrespective of the proper maintenance of assets and a long-term perspective on the business plan. The record of management contracts has been uneven. Performance contracts are still considered experimental and reveal certain basic constraints on success: the enterprise's heavily debt-ridden condition remains; the massive restructuring needed is not accomplished; enterprise operations are under several external constraints over which the managers have no control – e.g. lack of foreign exchange or excessive labour force; and 'targets' have limited significance, since neither fixing them nor adjudging them is technically sound yet. As performance contracts are bound to be widely practised in respect of enterprises not divested – e.g. in Hungary and other centrally planned economies in transition – it would be purposeful to identify precisely, and deal with, the factors that restrict their success. In particular emphasis should be placed on organization and financial restructuring, so as to provide clarity of objectives and simulate competition to the maximum extent possible. Besides, the contracts have the best chance of fulfilling their role as a non-divestiture option if conditions are provided for the technological restructuring which is basic to the success of the enterprise.

Fourth, unchanging public policy objectives are a serious constraint on the pace and success of privatization. This is a common phenomenon in many developing countries and in the centrally planned economies in transition. The Guyana paper refers to 'widely accepted principles of social equity and justice' with which privatization actions have to be consistent. Wherever such objectives imply the provision of outputs, offer of prices, location of investments, intake of labour, and choice of technology, which the conditions of a free market do not countenance, there is an inherent constraint on what to privatize – through divestiture or otherwise – how fast to privatize, and how free the privatized enterprises will be in charting their operational and entrepreneurial decisions. Some of the papers – Guyana in particular – mention this problem; and Morocco has assigned high priority to three 'social objectives': to permit share sales combatting increased concentration of wealth, to develop regional economies, and to safeguard employment. To broaden the point, privatization is a means to development and not an end in itself; and where a country has plans of development or a development strategy (avoiding the words 'plans' and 'planning') the full force of a free market would be difficult to manifest itself *vis-à-vis* privatized enterprises. Thus privatization is likely to remain either a slow process or a truncated phenomenon, under swings of the pendulum of regulation or public policy measures. Another version of the constraint is implicit in Rausch's view that, for Argentina, it would be a 'long-term mistake' to sell out all participation in the oil enterprise which represents the nation's 'greatest wealth and potential'. (Chile's non-divestiture of the copper enterprise is another case in point.)

Fifth, the state of efficiency of the domestic private sector, to which the enterprises get transferred through divestiture, seems to be very much in the minds of policy makers and implementors. Often this operates as a constraint, even if in the subconscious. The Guyana description of 'six characteristics' of private enterprise applies to several other countries, while in the centrally planned economies in transition, the very absence of meaningful private enterprise is a starting problem. Add to these the unwelcome potential of privatized enterprises with foreign ownership (exclusively or in a joint venture) to syphon off foreign exchange resources through irregular devices. Once again Guyana itself offers excellent evidence through the activities of the G T & T, explained in my basic working paper. To express the point differently, reservations on the potential of private enterprise happen to be a reflection of the continuing segments of market failure, to deal with which public enterprise was conceived in many countries. Of a secondary, but by no means unimportant, order in this connection is the government's covert resentment of transferring privatized ownership into the hands of certain ethnic groups. Several African countries illustrate this constraint.

Sixth, considerations of labour have been one of the heaviest and most obvious constraints in many countries where unemployment is already high and public enterprises carry excessive numbers on rolls. If efficiency were to be attained at the micro level, some lay-off would be inevitable; and this is the most knotty problem defying resolution, except in a few countries like Guyana and Israel. No wonder divestitures have been accompanied in several countries like Bangladesh by conditions against retrenchment for at least a year. This inherently conditions the efficiency gains which are supposed to be the aim and rationale of privatization. Germany, Poland, Czechoslovakia and Bangladesh illustrate how the employment issue constitutes a major hindrance in privatization, even through non-divestiture options. The UK's chronology in the treatment of this problem has been one of planned manpower adjustments over a long period prior to the date of divestiture itself – e.g. in British Airways and in British Steel.

Seventh, the country experiences recorded in this volume indicate systemic incompatibilities of several kinds. There is a painful absence of what I termed, in my basic working paper, the 'parallel requisites' for the success of privatization, both in pace and in results. There are elements of lack of co-ordination within the government at various levels – among ministers, departments, civil servants and privatization agencies, as indicated in the papers on Argentina, Brazil, Bangladesh and Israel. To reiterate a point mentioned earlier, there is hardly an attempt to monitor the processes of privatization. If monitoring were in place, several hindrances to privatization and its success have a chance, certainly, of being identified and, hopefully, of being rectified.

Without repeating the many details of constraints presented in the papers and outlined analytically in my basic working paper, we may conclude this part with the following consolidated table on the major categories of constraints experienced in different countries, the difficulties faced in tackling them, public perception of the efficiency of the private sector, transparency of privatization actions, and the importance of non-divestiture options, country by country. The table is constructed from the material specifically supplied by the authors (who participated in the Geneva Meeting).

Table 19.1 Constraints on privatization in fifteen countries

Country (1)	Major category of constraints (2)	Difficulties in tackling constraints (3)	Perception of private sector efficiency (4)	Transparency of privatization actions (5)	Importance of non-divestiture options (6)
UK	Non-viability of operations (e.g, coal, rail, nuclear power)	Social costs of restructuring	High	High, with minor exceptions	Important at local government level
Germany (west)	Trade unions' opposition	Not to damage trade unions' autonomy	High	Medium (sufficient coverage in the media)	Very important (e.g, PTT, Rail)
(East)	High wages Restitution-in-kind Lack of infrastructure Lack of entrepreneurial spirit Inflexible public administration	Trade unions' strength Missing land registers Bureaucratic complications	High, after new operations start	Not much, either in practice or in public perception	Important only in respect of public utilities
Hungary	Situation of the economy Infrastructure Lack of restructuring	High inflation and rate of interest Low investment propensity	Potentially high, by historical experience	Fairly transparent	Importance now realized. Mainly performance contracts and leases

Table 19.1 continued

Country (1)	Major category of constraints (2)	Difficulties in tackling constraints (3)	Perception of private sector efficiency (4)	Transparency of privatisation actions (5)	Importance of non-divestiture options (6)
Poland	Negative attitudes at company level Lack of political determination Lack of efficient implementation machinery	Lengthy political debates	Not high	Relatively high, but not in public perception	Leasing important in the liquidation route – management contracts under discussion
Czechoslovakia	Poor financial situation of companies Absence of stock markets Under-developed banking sector	Lack of expertise in public administration, especially at the ministerial level Lack of clear regulations because of time time constraint	Marginal Developing gradually in services with a high profit margin	Not high in private sales	Only in 'small' privatizations; Leasing contracts
Russia	Political opposition Enterprise valuation problems Role of foreigners in divestitures		Mostly very small enterprises in trade & productions	Constant allegations of 'nomenklatura' and 'mafia' privatization	
Brazil	Legal impediments Trade unions	Parliament	Medium to high (depends on sector)	High at the Federal level Could be better at the States level	Contracting-out joint ventures performance contracts

Argentina	Economic problems Labour Institutional and legal problems	Inadequacies in policy making, technical skills, and political capability	Varies	Improving gradually	'Sell-first' attitude – only some restructuring
Morocco	Timing	Inadequate preparation	High	High, by laws; low in public perception	Not much – management contracts in long use
Ivory Coast	Political environment Economic crisis Institutional factors Social environment		High in agro-industries and commerce	Little	Performance contracts Management and technical agreements; leases
Tanzania	Attitudinal problems Macro-economic situation	Gradual introduction of reforms	Efficient in comparison with public enterprise	Not high in public perception	Not yet successful Leasing, management contracts, performance agreements
Kenya	Law and order situation deterring foreign capital		Not high	Not high	Few yet: performance contracts, leasing, management contracts

Table 19.1 continued

Country (1)	Major category of constraints (2)	Difficulties in tackling constraints (3)	Perception of private sector efficiency (4)	Transparency of privatisation actions (5)	Importance of non-divestiture options (6)
Israel	Political Lack of adequate planning	Political constraint less acute now	High	High State Controller's Reports and very vigilant press	Corporatisation
India	Trade unions with political support Inadequacy of capital	Political Large sizes of many PEs	Mixed: partly efficient and partly very inefficient	Need for higher transparency	Memorandum-of-Understanding widely used
Bangladesh	Macro attitudinal and policy-related problems No articulated policy Breaucratic opposition Labour militancy Low saving potential	Political weakness State of development of the economy	Not high, though better than in public enterprise	Now high	Very limited

IMPACTS OF PRIVATIZATION

The country papers show that enough thought has not yet been given in most countries to the issue of impacts of privatization. Andrew Cao states so in the opening paragraph of his paper. One reason mentioned in some of the papers is that it is too early to make an impact study, as privatization is still 'of recent vintage', in the words of Carl Greenidge. Gusztáv Báger refers to the short span of privatization and Jersy Cieslik terms as 'short-term effects' the few conclusions he deduces from his questionnaire. As many qualifications to the study of impacts mentioned in my basic working paper suggest, it is not easy – it might even be 'tedious' as Andrew Cao concludes towards the end of his paper; and conclusions cannot yet be definitive. However, considering that privatization is a means to an end, one has to watch the way results are evolving themselves. Bager's conclusion in favour of 'intensive future activities in estimating likely impacts' is commendable.

There are two reasons which particularly justify efforts at estimating the likely impacts, conceding that all impacts cannot yet be measured conclusively. First, a great lack of clarity surrounds privatization policies and practices; and the desired degree of transparency is absent in many situations. Second, privatization conjures up political undertones in many countries yet. It would, therefore, be to the good of society if the impacts are dispassionately identified and estimated as the process proceeds. It would not be necessary to pass definitive and final judgements at every point in the exercise; in fact it is implicit in the exercise, if conducted with technical competence, that areas where conclusions cannot yet be drawn get highlighted. That would prevent uninformed and methodologically questionable conclusions being underscored by biased interests. If we constantly keep in mind that privatization is not an end in itself and that it is intended to produce certain results which may be encapsulated in the term 'efficiency', it follows at once that not to identify the impacts amounts to a negation of our starting position.

Three basic qualifications need attention in the interest of unbiased conclusions. First, the connotation of the term 'efficiency' has to be visualized on a comprehensive scale, for – as mentioned at several points in the papers as well as in this review chapter – the 'end' of privatization is development or an improvement in the national well-being. This has its micro and macro components – a point we shall develop as we go. Second, all impacts are not likely to be uniform in direction. Some may be considered favourable in themselves and some otherwise. What is necessary is a composite evaluation of the trade-offs. From this point of view S.R. Mohnot's Table 15.6, showing the varying nature of a short-term, medium-term and long-term impact and the diverse direction of different impacts, is of immense interest. An exercise in estimating numerical values, even if approximate, in different countries is certain to bring out diverse conclusions on the nature and intensity of impacts. It would be futile to assume that they will all be similar everywhere. Third, where the net favourable potential of privatization is not obvious or substantial, one has to examine whether the systemic circumstances conducive to its success are fully in place. This is of particular importance in the least developed countries and the centrally planned economies in transition. Once again, Mohnot's comment is valid that for private investments to come into certain sectors the government's willingness and ability to bring in the requisite dose of public investments – e.g. in related infrastructure, as well as withdrawal of price controls (which operate as a disincentive to private investment – is a necessary condition. Jersy Cieslik's reference to the seriously constraining force of macro-economic factors – 'poor and deteriorating macro-economic environment' – and John Howell's mention of 'the lack of infrastructure and institutions' also show how the impacts of privatization are not necessarily traceable wholly to the operating efficiency of the enterprise(s) concerned. The impact-estimating exercise will really do justice to the case for privatization as it helps isolate the factors exogenous to privatization, which have been limiting its favourable impacts or aggravating its unfavourable impacts. By the same token it should show up the outside factors – other than internal efficiency of the enterprises concerned – to which the credit for certain favourable results recorded really belongs. A sudden increase in demand for their outputs and an extraordinary foreign-exchange crunch are examples, respectively, of helpful and unhelpful factors in the performance of privatized enterprises.

To reiterate the point: the impact analysis is not an easy one; that is no reason, however, not to undertake it. Efforts at estimating the likely impacts, at the minimum, provide policy makers and implementors with ideas on how to reshape privatization programmes with an eye on maximizing their net favourable impacts. Instituting an appropriate regulatory framework would be an important part of the lessons of the impact analysis. The Argentine paper shows how privatization proceeded at a rapid pace 'with insufficient consideration of the regulatory framework'. The unfavourable results cited in the case of ENTEL, airlines and gas enterprises are probably a function of the poor regulatory system that accompanied privatization.

George Yarrow and Carl Greenidge covered several of the impacts, particularly of the macro variety, analysed in the basic working paper. In most of the other papers limited references have been made, mainly to micro efficiency, labour and public exchequer impacts. And Andrew Cao's issue paper focused on micro-efficiency aspects – on 'return on assets' in particular, while brief mention was made of some secondary effects, followed by an interesting numerical exercise on the likely impacts of privatization on employment in Egypt. From the latter he rightly deduces a lesson, namely, that impact analysis should be initiated 'right at the beginning' of the privatization exercise.

The empirical accounts on micro efficiency contained in the papers are in the nature of a mixed bag. The UK experience on the operating results of privatized enterprises suggests the need for great caution in attributing all favourable results to the event of privatization. And George Yarrow emphasizes the strengthening of competitive forces as a guarantee of good results. Gusztáv Báger says that efficiency indicators are in favour of 'transformed companies' in Hungary, only where the share of foreign ownership is high. In Poland, Jersy Cieslik argues, there are 'clear signs of disillusionment' concerning 'immediate positive results', nearly as many of the privatized and transformed companies reported an improvement in financial status as they did a deterioration. (The moral is not that privatization is bad but that the basic conditions for the success of enterprises are not adequately in place.) Guyana's experience is uneven – some privatized enterprises are in financial straits, some have been seeking 'exceptional fiscal concessions', and some have spectacular profit increases. The enterprise-wise data provided by Alejandro Rausch present a disturbing picture of price enhancements and quality deteriorations post-privatization in Argentina. The Moroccan situation appears to be unique in that the privatized enterprises already operate as if in the private sector and are price takers; Alfred Saulniers does not foresee any immediate change in their management practices or prices, thanks partly to the kind of regulations already in force. Abdul Mall Muhith's remarks on privatized enterprises in Bangladesh do not convey a clear and uniform picture of efficiency improvement. He cites Klaus Lorch's conclusion of 'no achievement' in respect of 'dynamic efficiency' on the part of the divested cotton mills. Once again a close reading of his comments suggests that the economic conditions in Bangladesh have been such that there is 'hardly any efficiency improvement in any sector'.

Analytically two issues may be highlighted at this point. There is no fundamental reason why a privatized enterprise should not make good profits. Within the limitations of the economic conditions encountered every investor aims at making the highest profit possible, that is, every investor in the private sector. It should, therefore, be no matter for surprise that a privatized enterprise is found to be making higher profits than in the pre-privatized era. However, several questions arise concerning the anatomy of the profit: is it too high; is it the result of technical efficiency; is it a product of the exercise of monopoly power including cross-subsidizations; is the quality of the output satisfactory; is technology the best possible; and does the enterprise present a reasonable growth rate? Conclusions drawn on the profit record or even bare output (increase) statistics have to be vetted for these questions in order to provide useful answers on the efficiency gains expected of privatization. Where the answers tend to be negative, doubts are justified concerning the overall efficiency results of privatization in respect of a given enterprise, or a number of them in one or more sectors.

This line of thinking leads us to the next step in impact analysis. What an economy should aim at is, not just the profitability of privatized enterprises, but a contribution to the well-being of the community. The latter represents the macro aspect of the analysis on which, as authors such as Carl Greenidge opine, we need more facts than are available to reach conclusions. It is essential, however, that we do not push this aspect under the carpet in our keenness to privatize and at a fast pace, and that we build up a sound analytical framework of analysis for estimating the likely impacts in the immediate run and in the long run.

One area of impacts to which most papers referred is the public exchequer. This is not surprising; for privatization is fiscally driven in several countries, as shown in part one of this chapter. George Yarrow mentions the high divestiture incomes to the exchequer, as well as increased corporation tax revenues from the rising profits of privatized enterprises. Privatization operations in Germany are resulting in a big deficit for Treuhandanstalt. The chance of some public debt reduction is offered by divestitures in Guyana and (to a limited extent) in Hungary. Current transfers from the exchequer to the public enterprise sector have substantially contracted in Guyana. Bangladesh features the impact of heavy assumption of public sector debts by the government, together with continuing subsidies in some cases, e.g. jute. And the disadvantage of low divestiture prices surfaces in some papers, e.g. in the case of the steelworks sold to a French group in Argentina.

Three broad comments are in order at this point. First, distinction is not commonly upheld between the capital and revenue aspects of the impacts on the public exchequer. Divestiture incomes flowing in are a one-off affair. To rejoice that the annual budget deficit is removed by such incomes is highly questionable. It will not be long before the budget deficit re-enters the picture, other things being equal. (The Indian situation, as analysed by S. R. Mohnot, provides an apt illustration in this context.) Second, by not using the divestiture incomes towards public debt reductions, the government continues to sustain debt-servicing charges on the continuing public debt attributable to the investments divested. Third, enough notice is not taken of the fact that the divestiture of profitable enterprises will entail a recurring loss of profit incomes for the exchequer. (In the case of losing enterprises, this argument does not apply.)

These analytical aspects of the issue are not adequately appreciated yet, probably because the importance of undertaking a systematic estimate of impacts of privatization on the public exchequer is not fully realized, or because it is a somewhat complex and, in general, unpleasant exercise to initiate, given the pressures on quick privatization.

Another area of impacts commonly mentioned in the papers concerns labour. There have been serious reductions in employment in East Germany. Jersy Cieslik's observation that unemployment, 'unknown three years ago', is growing rapidly, applies not only to Poland but to the entire region of Central and Eastern Europe in transition. The theoretical argument we come across in this area is that, as privatization improves the efficiency of enterprises in general, the demand for labour expands and the displaced workers will be re-absorbed. Andrew Cao's illustration from Egypt is interesting in this connection. However, the hopes contained therein need to be tested in practice in the environment of a country already suffering from high levels of unemployment as well as relatively poor circumstances of growth. One has to attach special weight to the employment effects of privatization, since, whatever the micro-efficiency results, society incurs a cost in maintaining a growing army of unemployed people in several ways. Transfer payments through the budget are an obvious way. This illustrates the need for taking a comprehensive view on the impacts of privatization at the micro and the macro levels.

As regards the distributional impacts analysed at length in my basic working paper, there have been relatively few empirical references in the other papers. An interesting point made by George Yarrow and Shlomo Eckstein *et al.* is that a wide distribution of privatized shares minimizes distributional inequity by spreading the benefits of divestiture under-pricing among a large number of people. One may add, the profit benefits foregone by the tax payer on divestiture will also get widely distributed. While this view is valid, experience already shows that privatizations have nowhere been accompanied by the width of share spread requisite to the view. In fact there are many instances of private sales and concentrated (or block) ownerships, which invalidate the hopes contained in the argument. As a policy prescription, however, wide share ownership must be upheld, without overlooking the need to reckon with its possible impacts on managerial efficiency.

As governments begin to look seriously into the issue of impacts of privatization, problems of measurement assume prominence. Not only does one need to identify the impacts sought to be reviewed, but the changes in the identified areas have to be measured and techniques of adjudicating the trade-offs among dissimilar results have to be designed. By and large, these issues have only been touched in the present volume, though Andrew Cao goes into the rate-on-assets index and Tony Bennett examines the methodology in connection with one major impact, namely, the impact on the public exchequer. One question which inevitably arises in all exercises of estimating the impacts concerns the role of accounts in facilitating the exercise, their reliability as presented under prevailing legal requirements, the adjustments to be made for exploring the micro and macro impacts we have in mind, and the precise agency – enterprise men and outsiders – that may be associated with the exercise at the fact-establishing levels. Tony Bennett looks at some of these aspects and brings out the limitations of accounting in this whole process.

The contributions compiled in this volume clearly suggest that attention to impacts has high priority in all exercises on privatization at the level of policy making as well as implementation. The distributional implications, in particular, are certain to warrant serious concern in the less developed countries.

INDEX

Accor of France (Novehotel) 227
accountability 318, 337
accounts/accounting 9, 328–41;
changing unit of measurement
335–7; control 333–4; failure to
adjust for inflation 336; general
limitations 334–7; inadequate,
foreign exchange earnings 34; LIFO
inventory 336, 340n; past and future
data 334–5; reform 336
ad hoc measures 19, 272, 274, 308,
309
Adam, Christopher 56n
Adda, W.A. 56n, 57n, 58n, 59n, 61n
Africa 8, 340–1nn; *see also* Egypt;
Ethiopia; Gambia; Ghana; Kenya;
Morocco; Namibia; Nigeria; South
Africa; Tanzania; Uganda; Zanzibar
Aftab Ahmad Khan 59n
aggregate demand/supply 99
Ahmed, M. 269n
Ahsan, A. 268n, 339n
airlines 147, 168, 173, 208, 282
Akerlof, G.A. 81–2, 88n, 89n
Albania 6–7, 59n
Alfa Romeo 332
Al Houari, Abderaffie 224n
Altman model 320
Amor, Muncef Bal Hadj 59n
Amrani, Hassan 224n
ancillary industries 52
Andhra Pradesh 277
Andonov, Anton 57n, 59n
antagonists 235
apathy 144
apparatchiks 121
Argentina 166–96, 340n, 347–8, 358;
constraints 170–2, 353, 354; GDP
166, 167, 188, 189, 193, 194, 195,
196; impacts 172–6; *see also* ENTEL
assets 76, 100, 105, 133, 160, 169,
204, 206, 320; absence of title deeds
to 234; areas not necessarily reflected
in valuation 159; book value or
earning capacity 232; bought from
foreign investors 166; concentration
of 233; decent return for 155;
deteriorating values 171; difficult
evaluation of 122; fear of foreign
ownership 232–3; fixed 45, 336;
idle, made productive 291; important
176; industrial 264; maintained in
good order 158; major 234; major
sales 71, 72; mobile 44;
non-performing 230; normal business
222; portfolio restructuring through
sale of 218; revaluations 336; risk
weighted 281; sale to foreigners 142,
172, 229; sold at a loss 46; sold off
too cheaply 141; valuations 10, 41,
45, 118, 124, 159, 233; *see also*
GAV; MAV; NAV; ROA
Associated British Ports 79
Atanor S.A. 168
attitudinal factors 16
auctions 128, 130–1, 133, 134, 135,
206, 275; Dutch 121–2; small 120,
121, 122; Walrasian type 137n; *see*
also bidders
Awami League 259, 264

Baez, Manfred 57n
Báger, Gusztáv 61n, 344, 356, 358
balance of payments 95, 287; deficits
167; external 293; surplus 93
Banco Bozano 206